THE LAST
EMPTY PLACES

THE LAST EMPTY PLACES

A PAST AND PRESENT

JOURNEY THROUGH THE BLANK SPOTS

ON THE AMERICAN MAP

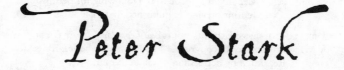

BALLANTINE BOOKS
NEW YORK

Published in the United States by Ballantine Books,
an imprint of The Random House Publishing Group,
a division of Random House, Inc., New York.

BALLANTINE and colophon are registered
trademarks of Random House, Inc.

LIBRARY OF CONGRESS CATALOGING-IN-PUBLICATION DATA
Stark, Peter
The last empty places: a past and present journey through the
blank spots on the American map / Peter Stark.
p.   cm.
Includes bibliographical references.
ISBN 978-0-345-49537-2
eBook ISBN 978-0-345-52190-3
1. United States—Description and travel.   2. Stark, Peter—Travel—United States.
3. United States—History, Local.   4. United States—Geography.   5. Wilderness
areas—United States.   6. Wilderness areas—Social aspects—United States—History.
I. Title.
E169.Z83S685 2010   973—dc22   2010009942

Grateful acknowledgment is made to the following for permission
to reprint previously published material:

GLOBE PEQUOT PRESS: Excerpts from *Aldo Leopold: A Fierce Green Fire*
by Marybeth Lorbiecki, copyright © 2005 by Marybeth Lorbiecki.
Reprinted by permission of Globe Pequot Press.

OREGON HISTORICAL QUARTERLY: Excerpts from emigrant journals that appeared in
"Cut-Off Fever: Part IV and Part V" in the September 1977 and December 1977 issues.
Reprinted by permission of *Oregon Historical Quarterly*.

OXFORD UNIVERSITY PRESS: Excerpts from *A Sand County Almanac with Essays on
Conservation from Round River* by Aldo Leopold, copyright © 1949, 1953, 1966 by
Oxford University Press, Inc. Reprinted by permission of Oxford University Press.

UNIVERSITY OF ARIZONA PRESS: Excerpts from *The Discovery of New Mexico by the
Franciscan Monk Friar Marcos de Niza in 1539* by Adolf Bandelier, translated by
Madeleine Turrell Rodack, copyright © 1981 Arizona Board of Regents. Reprinted by
permission of the University of Arizona Press.

Printed in the United States of America on acid-free paper

www.ballantinebooks.com

2   4   6   8   9   7   5   3   1

FIRST EDITION

Book design by Mary A. Wirth

CONTENTS

PROLOGUE

On cold January mornings, we four children would sit down to corn-bread and bacon on the warmed plates my mother handed out while a frigid draft—a thin wafer of stiff breeze—sliced at my chest. From my bench at the kitchen table, I would lean back against the thick, bare logs of the house—roughly squared, still showing the chip marks of the hand adze that shaped them 110 years earlier. Between the logs pro-truded globs of chinking—a tacky slew of horsehair and putty—packed not quite tight enough, in my corner of the kitchen, to block Wisconsin's bitter winter winds.

This rough-hewn cabin was my romantic father's idea of the perfect home for his young family, one my mother had warmly retrofitted with rag rugs, blue print curtains, a big stone fireplace. He loved the stories of the Scandinavian pioneers who penetrated the great forests of the Upper Midwest to build a new life from the wilderness, and told us of the Potawatomi Indians for whom this "wilderness" was home. A man named John Rudberg, one of the first Swedes to immigrate to Wiscon-sin Territory, had hewn these logs with his own hands in 1849 near the shores of a beautiful lake known to the Indians as Chenequa, or Pine Lake.

My parents had discovered the old cabin inside an abandoned re-sort hotel on the shore of the lake. A house had eventually been built using Rudberg's original cabin as its core, and then the resort hotel around the house. As the hotel was torn down, revealing the cabin, my parents marked each log, extracted them, and reassembled them on a nearby piece of land they had purchased. This is where I grew up—in Rudberg's rebuilt old pioneer cabin surrounded by oak forest, with our nearest neighbor an old dairy farmer, who, still running a team of workhorses, lived a quarter mile away through forest and pasture.

As a boy, I spent hours searching for arrowheads buried in our log walls. I loved to think of our cabin as a lonely bastion in the vast Wisconsin wilderness of the 1840s, the young Swedish pioneers spending their days swinging axes to finish their dwellings or clear their fields, chased indoors by the occasional Indian attack. I roamed the oak forests, the hills and valleys around our cabin, searching out the wildest spot, loving it best in a howling blizzard when the wind moaned through the bare oak branches and the deep, soft snow muted my bundled movements.

In some subconscious nine-year-old's way, I understood that as an American, I had inherited this legacy of wilderness, that it shaped my forebears, and me, and all those who immigrated to this country, as the continent had shaped those Native Americans who were already here. I sensed, too, that it didn't lie so very far away. Only three generations, more or less, had passed since John Rudberg lived out his elemental drama within these same log walls.

Every day, along with my two sisters and my brother, I attended the country grade school two miles away. Many of my classmates, with their Scandinavian or German last names, had young hands tough as cowhide from their daily chores on dairy farms that their great-grandparents had cleared like Rudberg. I doubt that any of the farm boys read the copy of *The Story of My Boyhood and Youth* by John Muir that sat on our classroom bookshelf, but I did—several times.

I felt a deep boyhood bond with young John Muir. In 1849, just when Rudberg was finishing his cabin, the ten-year-old Muir emigrated with his family from Scotland to Wisconsin and purchased a piece of wilderness forest at Fountain Lake, about fifty miles from where I grew up. Young John had loved to explore the Wisconsin woods and rivers and lakes, as I loved to do, too. But when he grew old enough to help with the crushingly heavy work of clearing the farm from the wilderness, his idyll ended.

He finally escaped when a talent for mechanical inventions gained him entrance to the University of Wisconsin. Here he was exposed not only to botany and geology but to the era's great American thinkers on wilderness and Nature—Emerson and Thoreau. They changed his life, propelling him toward a passionate advocacy of the great, empty places—a Prophet of the Wilderness.

Thoreau, likewise, figured in my own youth. I started high school in the late 1960s, at the height of the countercultural "back-to-the-land" movement that embraced Thoreau and his *Walden* as its gospel. During the first Earth Day ever held—1970—I was a sixteen-year-old sophomore helping to plant trees on our school grounds. I distinctly recall—in a kind of embarrassingly un-Thoreauvian irony—reading *Walden* that year while sitting in the orthodontist's waiting room about to get my braces removed.

"If you're reading Thoreau," said my mother, who had trained at the University of Wisconsin as a landscape architect, "you should also read Aldo Leopold. He was an environmentalist far ahead of his time, and lived in Wisconsin, too."

It would be years later that I read all the thinkers I address in this book, writers who, over the last three centuries, have transformed our ideas about wild nature—starting with Rousseau and William Bartram in the eighteenth century, then Coleridge and Wordsworth, Emerson and Thoreau, John Muir and Aldo Leopold. I've detected a common thread not only in the influence of Wisconsin's landscapes, but also in the countryside around Concord, Massachusetts, where Thoreau pondered nature, and outside Philadelphia, where William Bartram came of age, and even in Rousseau's home city of Geneva, Switzerland, sitting on its long lake at the foot of the Alps.

It's this: all these thinkers grew up in landscapes that were half cultivated, half wild.

Wisconsin, to me, is the perfect example—its green, rolling farm fields, its knoblike glacial hills crowned with wild oak forests, its windy little streams leading through blackbird-trilling marshes, its blue pothole lakes spilling into gentle rivers. This patchwork of small-scale civilization and "Wild Nature" (as the Romantics came to call it) offers a fecund landscape for the imagination. I understand perfectly what John Muir or Henry Thoreau felt in their youthful ramblings through woods and fields. It's exactly what I felt—the urge to explore, to travel to the next little valley hidden in the woods, see what's back there, check it out. What's going on today? A new pondful of snowmelt. A knee-high patch of mayapples, with their umbrella leaves and green fruit. A thick-limbed white oak to climb. A marsh of croaking frogs. A good, roaring storm.

"For many years," wrote Thoreau, "I was self-appointed inspector of rainstorms and snowstorms . . ."

What's *in* there? What's *out* there? I sought the secret, hidden *feel* of the place. Something always pulled me farther, something hidden, something precious, something back in there. I always wanted *more* of it. These patches of wild intermixed with the cultivated landscape were never quite large—or wild—enough.

Virtually every one of these writers shared another emotional bond, as I do. Ruin threatened their precious landscapes. In certain eras, the threats converged powerfully, undeniably. From the mid-1700s onward, the Industrial Revolution gathered momentum in Europe and its cities swelled and factories clanked into existence. It's no coincidence that this is exactly when Rousseau first started to write lovingly of the emotional benefits to be gained in Wild Nature. The sentiment was soon embraced by the British Romantic poets in the 1790s and early 1800s, who watched their green isle's patchwork of wild places chopped down and dug up to fire the steam engines that powered the Industrial Revolution.

When the industrial onslaught landed in America in the New England of the 1840s, Henry David Thoreau watched as railroad tracks were laid through his precious Concord woods and fields, and along nearby Walden Pond. Emerson, his friend and mentor, bought forty acres along the pond to save it from being logged, and it was here on Emerson's land that Henry Thoreau built his cabin. The tide of development surged all around him. Timber fellers cut the forest nearby, and work crews arrived at Walden in winter to saw out blocks of ice for Boston's summer refrigeration. This sense of imminent threat and destruction made what remained of Wild Nature all the more precious for Thoreau.

While Thoreau scribbled away on his *Walden* manuscript (it took him many drafts and several years to write), John Muir and his family arrived at Fountain Lake in Wisconsin, in 1849. There wasn't even a wagon track through the wilderness forest where they settled. A few years later, when Muir left the Fountain Lake farm to go off to the university, farms and wagon roads covered the landscape. That decade—the 1840s—was a pivotal period in how wilderness was perceived in America, mostly because it was disappearing so fast.

I know how they felt—Thoreau, and Muir, and the others—because, in my teens, I watched subdivisions move out from the city and pave over my fields with cul-de-sacs and self-consciously curving roads. Bulldozers advanced into those precious valleys of mine hidden in the woods, and sprawling houses with three-car garages and rolled-out sod lawns replaced the mysterious patches of mayapples and my climbing oaks and my snowmelt ponds. For a time, it made me almost physically nauseated to see another new subdivision plowed into my landscapes. Finally I moved away—to Montana, where I didn't have to watch it happen so fast, although it still goes on nevertheless. My soul mate in this escape, John Muir, fled to the Sierras almost exactly a century before.

That compulsion to seek out the wild, secret places—the blank spots—never left me but has only grown stronger, and, with time and age and resources, extended over a greater geographical range, as it did for Muir, and Thoreau, and Bartram, and Leopold, too. The search has taken me over the decades to wild, empty regions of Africa and the hidden valleys of Tibet, to the ice fields of Greenland and forests of Manchuria, and many places between.

The geographical search, however, accounts for only one part of the overall endeavor. Just as compelling—perhaps more so—is the quest to discover why places like this are important. Reading these wilderness philosophers, Thoreau, Muir, Leopold, I'm left with a deep sense that this is what drove them, too. From the time they were young, they felt an urge to seek out these wild places, to explore them, to ramble through them, to love them. In some ways, it was a search—as it's been for me—for a childhood paradise lost, to recapture those exciting jaunts through woods and fields and streams. As they grew older, however, these writers each tried to understand *why* these wild places were important—to each of them, and to all of us.

Thus, in this book, in the course of these journeys, I want to explore not only the blank spots themselves, but also to write about those who spent their lives thinking about these wild places and exploring them and what they had to say about why these blank spots, these wild areas, were important.

There is no one answer. The various answers put forth by these thinkers all build on one another, however, and each has a common theme. It has to do with understanding our own place, as a species on this planet. It has to do with understanding our insignificance, as individuals. Although he found writing excruciatingly difficult, John Muir was nonetheless a catchy phrasemaker who pointed the direction: "The clearest way into the Universe is through a forest wilderness."

WHILE I'VE TRAVELED all over the world in the last forty years seeking out the empty, wild places—first as a lone traveler, then as a writer, finally as the husband of a ready-to-go-at-any-moment vagabond—I've largely ignored my own country. Too settled, I've thought. Too civilized. Too *developed*.

But is it really?

Has wilderness been wiped off the face of America? Have all the empty places been blanketed with roads, with farmers' fields, with subdivisions, shopping malls, and the sprawling cities themselves? In my eagerness to find the truly remote spots of the world, had I too hastily dismissed my own country?

You could pick up any *Rand McNally Road Atlas* and see the vast highway system thrown like a giant fishnet over the entire United States. Thick ribbons of red and blue, black and yellow, wrapped nearly every corner of every state. What empty places could survive this onslaught of asphalt?

Yet I'd flown over a good deal of the country since I'd left Wisconsin, two and a half decades ago, and, lured by the emptier spaces of the Northern Rockies, moved to the small university town of Missoula, Montana. Especially in the West—but in certain parts of the East, also—you could look down from an airplane window at thirty thousand feet and spot what appeared to be vast, roadless stretches—miles upon miles of mountains or forests or badlands that, as far as I could tell, were largely untracked.

What were these?

I SET UP A lunch date with my friend Alex Philp. A specialist in both historical geography and geographic information systems, Philp works, among other things, with images of Earth from outer space. He quickly became my guru of blank spots.

"What you want to do is find the nighttime image of the U.S. taken from NASA's satellites," he told me over the phone. "Look where the lights are. Then look at the places where they are not—the black holes. I think you'll be surprised at how many you'll find even near the large urban centers in the East."

When we met a few days later, I unfurled what's known as the "Nighttime Map of the United States" on the café table between us. Scruffily bearded, fortyish, Jesuit-educated, and the father of two young girls, Philp half closed his eyes behind his glasses, almost as if meditating over the satellite image on the table.

He swept his hand across it. Like an image of the starry sky, the page was mostly black except for a pattern of dots and swirls and clustered nodes of lights.

"See how this image is not rectilinear—not Cartesian. It's not based on grids and lines—the kind of map a land surveyor would make. It's much more of a viral pattern, a biological expression. Now, I don't mean to compare humans to viruses, but viruses need certain things to survive and so do humans. For instance, water."

Philp gestured to the image's left half—the West. Here the dots and clusters of light lay much more sparsely scattered. You could almost draw a line down the center of the map, dividing the thick lights of the East from the sparse lights of the West.

"This is roughly where the hundredth meridian runs," said Philp. He was referring to one of the lines of longitude inscribed on the globe from pole to pole. The hundredth meridian runs down the center of North and South Dakota, Nebraska, through Kansas and Texas, and on south into Mexico. "West of the hundredth meridian it becomes too dry to grow crops easily," Philp said. "Very few people live there."

A great galaxy of light exploded at the image's right side—New York City at its center, morphing into Boston and Washington. It looked a bit like a giant crab with legs radiating outward—millions upon millions of house lights, streetlights, headlights, apartment lights, fast-food joints, toll plazas, parking lots, sports stadiums, shopping malls, factory compounds. But between these radiant Eastern Seaboard crab legs lay a few patches of utter blackness. Some appeared surprisingly large.

OVER THE NEXT SEVERAL WEEKS, I spent hours staring at the Nighttime Map of the United States, comparing it with my Rand

McNally and my *Times Atlas*. I discovered that some of the biggest black holes on the photo did, in fact, show on the map that they had a road or two running through them. The nighttime photo made it abundantly clear, however, that almost no one lived there.

To add more layers to my understanding of what I was seeing, I made trips to the university library and scoured through the "exploration and discovery" shelves, digging out the journals of early explorers of North America such as Henry Hudson, Jacques Cartier, and Samuel de Champlain. I cared less about the places they visited than the "Unknown Lands" they alluded to but never reached. I studied the brittle, sketchy maps folded among the leaves of the crumbling old accounts, tracing my finger over them for the empty spaces where there were no lines, no trails, no rivers, only phrases like "terra incognita" or "unmapped."

I went through my own shelves for my frayed and marked-up copies of wilderness and nature philosophers such as Thoreau, Emerson, and Rousseau, and refreshed my reading of the classics in the field of wilderness studies, Roderick Nash's *Wilderness and the American Mind* and *The Idea of Wilderness* by Max Oelschlaeger. These provide wide-ranging and incisive understanding of how our notion of "wilderness" has evolved over the centuries.

And yes, I surfed the Internet, although I found it less helpful than one might think in actually identifying blank spots, but very useful in digging out odd items of history. Generally, I avoided zooming in on places using Google Earth. It's very difficult to identify from those aerial photos how truly "blank" an area is—there can be dozens of houses hidden under tree canopies that you simply can't see from the aerial image—and I also didn't want to detract from the excitement of seeing these places for the first time with my own eyes.

In narrowing my choices to five or six "blank spots" to explore, I followed some basic criteria:

1. I avoided U.S. National Parks and designated federal Wilderness Areas (although I eventually made one exception to the latter). I wanted wild, empty places that were also relatively unknown and obscure.

2. While the West has more and larger empty spaces, I wanted to

explore some blank spots in the East also. I excluded Alaska, as it's so well known for its wild areas.

3. I looked for compelling stories about the first European encounters with the American wilds and Native Americans.

4. Aware of the criticism that "once you write about these places they won't be blank anymore," I sought out wild areas that could use some help and attention to keep them wild.

5. Finally, I sought out places that have shaped America's greatest thinkers and their ideas about wilderness. I wanted the places to help tell how, over the centuries, our American idea of "wilderness" has evolved from a kind of satanic hell to a place of spiritual inspiration.

And so off I went. Sometimes with family in tow, sometimes alone, over the course of two and a half years, I explored my chosen blank spots.

Photograph of lights of the United States at night from a satellite orbiting 800 kilometers (480 miles) above the Earth's surface.

PART I

WHERE
THE ACADIANS
DISAPPEARED IN
NORTHERN
MAINE

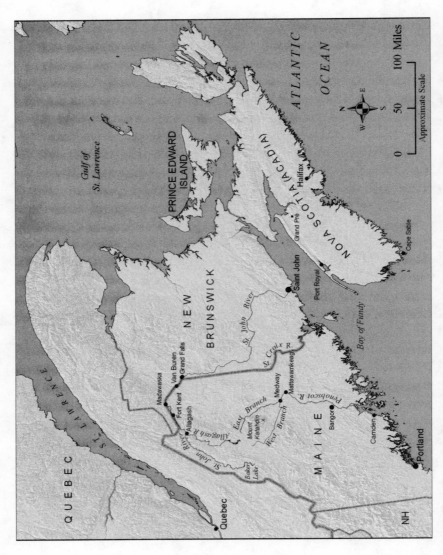

Regional map of Maine and Nova Scotia (formerly Acadia) showing St. John River headwaters at upper left and Port Royal, lower center.

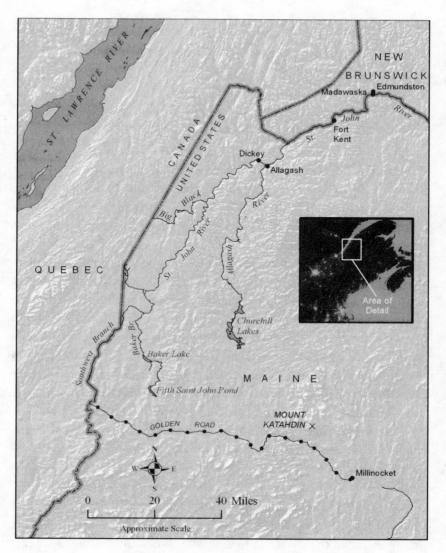

Route of canoe trip on upper St. John from Baker Lake to Allagash village. Inset shows region at night, with lights of Boston at bottom and Montreal at left.

*F*rom far off, it was said, you could hear the women and children screaming. If you'd been there, in Nova Scotia—they called it Acadia then—in September of 1755, you would have seen the women down on their knees along the dirt lane, pleading, praying, wailing, reaching up with extended arms as their men and boys were marched from the church at Grand Pré down to the British ships that waited with the high tide.

All men and "lads" over the age of ten had been summoned to meet at the church at this Nova Scotian port town at exactly 3:00 p.m. on September 5. When 418 of the Acadians were gathered within the church, British soldiers barred the doors and windows. Colonel Winslow, the British commander, in a powdered wig, sat at a table surrounded by soldiers and read aloud from a document containing orders that supposedly originated with the king. It detailed the fate of these French-descended inhabitants of Nova Scotia—the Acadians—as the British soldiers went from port to port to round them up.

"His instructions and commands, to wit, That your lands and tenements, cattle and live-stock of all kinds are forfeited to the Crown, together with all your other effects, except money and household goods, and that you yourselves are to be removed from this his province."

The decree was translated into French. The Acadians, most of them, didn't read or write. No one recorded their precise reaction at that moment in the church at Grand Pré more than two hundred years ago except as it lives on today in stories and songs among Acadian descendants in the bayous of Louisiana, deep in the North Woods of Maine, and still in parts of Nova Scotia. We have instead the words of Colonel Winslow himself, who wrote that the Acadians were "greatly struck." He couldn't understand the imprecations hurled his way in their ancient dialect of French.

Inside the church at Grand Pré, the British pointed their muskets at the outraged Acadian men and boys. The Acadian ancestors had migrated from France and settled here, on this great peninsula of land they called Acadia and we know as Nova Scotia that hovers out in the Atlantic east of Maine. By the time the British read their decree at Grand Pré in September 1755, the Acadians had lived on the peninsula for a century and a half. They'd been among the very first permanent northern European migrants to the New World, arriving in 1606—even before the first British colonists founded Jamestown far south in Virginia. The Acadians had hunted the forests for furs and for meat, fished the bays and coastlines, diked the tidal salt marshes into fields. Unlike many of the British settlers to the south, they'd lived harmoniously with the Indians, learned to craft birch-bark canoes and snowshoes, traded with them, intermarried with them, raised *métis* families. They "trucked with the savages," as the British put it disgustedly. They were an independent, self-sufficient people, a people of the forests and the marshes and the rivers—not quite French, not quite Indian, but both; or, rather, a unique people that blended both.

And now the end had come for Acadia. The British had won the great peninsula from France in 1710 in a military victory, and for more than forty years, during a time of peace between the two great empires, had let the Acadians be. But now war was again afoot between Britain and France. The Acadians, way out here on the remote fringes—on the vague borderlands between the two clashing worlds—were caught between.

T HE HEAVY RAINS STARTED as we drove our rental car up the New England coast toward northern Maine—toward the lands where fleeing Acadians had disappeared. After flying east from home in Montana, we'd spent the night outside Boston, in Concord, close by Thoreau's Walden Pond. That morning, in the motel's breakfast room, where the children gleefully made waffles on the do-it-yourself iron, the television had predicted rain for the next four to five days. As I paid the bill in the lobby, a fine, warm Gulf Stream drizzle was falling on the electric-green motel lawn. A few hours later on I-95, when our economy rental car reached L.L.Bean at Freeport, Maine, a blurry deluge crashed on the windshield and streamed up from the tires. At Bean's, I bought a tarp, poles to suspend it, extra tent stakes, and a new rain jacket to replace my old one, as it suddenly seemed woefully inadequate. As a kind of treat to myself, I also bought a new fly rod. For the children, already well outfitted with rain jackets and pants, Amy picked up a couple of extra insect headnets—the kind with brims. The previous night, over an expensive bistro dinner in Concord, she'd been much bemused by conjuring the image of me taking notes while wearing a headnet propped up on sticks.

"*That's* why it's blank where we're going," she'd choked through tears of laughter over her soup, to the children's bewilderment. "No one wants to *live* there! Because of the *bugs!*"

But it was the prospect of rain that bothered me more than the threat of bugs. I was slightly cheered after we left the coast past Bean's, heading inland, almost due north, on I-95, and the rain tapered off. By the time we reached Medway—the gateway to the Maine Woods, a couple of hours inland—the rain had stopped altogether. Stuffed to the ceiling with our camping gear, our little white car bumped off the dry highway and into the graveled parking lot of Nicatou Outfitters, a wood-sided building scattered with a few others beside the road. The late afternoon gloom and heavy gray skies held low over the pointy tips of the dense fir and spruce forest behind the shop. I was thinking, *Five days. That's a whole lot of rain on an eight-day canoe trip. Especially on a wilderness river. With children. And no way out of the forest. Except paddling onward into the cold downpour.*

"Are you Betsy?" I asked the wiry, blondish, thirty-something woman who emerged from the shop to greet us, followed by a bouncy young black Lab.

"I am," she said.

I later would learn that her mother's family, the Faloons, had settled here in the mid-1800s when Medway was still known as Nicatou—located at the forks of the East and West Branches of the Penobscot River. Her husband, Galen Hale, held a regular job with the Maine environmental inspection branch while she ran their outfitting shop. Inside, fishing lures and billed hats and paddling gear lined the walls, and a wide assortment of mosquito repellent. I inspected the varieties while she gamely showed our children, Molly, eleven, and Skyler, eight, how the black Lab, Nicky, could roll over.

"It's been so wet lately. I was out in my garden today and the bugs were pretty bad. You'll want to bring plenty of bug dope," she said, in an accent full of dropped "r"s and open "a"s.

I'd heard the same mantra—"bring plenty of bug dope"—from at least three other Mainers, including her husband, Galen. From Montana, I'd spoken to him by phone several times, telling him I was looking for the emptiest, blankest spots on the map, as well as an outfitter to help us.

"Do you know the Saint John River?" I'd asked him.

"Ayup," he replied, with that famous Mainer laconic brevity.

Could he rent us canoes for it?

Ayup.

Could he guide us down it if we wanted?

Ayup.

Did he know the other rivers of northern Maine?

Ayup.

Then, in a burst of loquaciousness, he volunteered his qualifications.

"I been living here in Medway all my life. My family started guiding here in 1833. When Henry Thoreau came to the Maine Woods in 1846, his guide was Thomas Fowler. That's my great-great-great-granduncle by marriage, on my mother's side. I can show you pretty much exactly where Thoreau went, if you want. I can even show you where he spent the night here in Medway. Supposedly at Mom Howard's."

I knew I'd found my man. You could say that in a strange, roundabout way it was Galen Hale's great-great-great-granduncle by marriage (on his mother's side) who inspired me—and other like-minded Americans—to have a passion for wild places to begin with, to yearn for the blank spots remaining on the map. Until Thoreau and company came along in the early 1800s, most of what European people strove for during their first three hundred years on the American continent was to stamp out every spot of blankness that they could reach. They sought out these blank places, this largely uncultivated continent thinly peopled by Indians, as cheap land to homestead. They saw nothing good—but rather evil—in the "wildness" of it. The value of blank spots, of wild places, lay only in their cultivation—in "civilizing" these spots and "taming" the natives. It was in good part Thoreau—and his trips to the Maine Woods—who changed all that.

"YOU'RE A BRAVE WOMAN, Amy," remarked David Skipper as another gust of rain lashed the windshield of his van.

A burly, friendly man, Skipper drove shuttles to the Maine rivers for Galen and Betsy Hale's clients who wished to canoe. He now steered the big blue van—our rented canoes lashed on top, our mound of gear loaded in back—down a gloomy mud-and-gravel forest road. The wipers whipped back and forth. The rains had begun that morning, reaching from the coast up into the Maine Woods, when we woke up in the little motel across from the Hales' shop in Medway. For nearly three hours since Medway, we'd been driving on these graveled roads through the soaking wet fir and spruce woods, through this great green sponge of evergreen trees, woody brush, dripping moss.

"How much longer?" Skyler finally asked.

"Five minutes," Skipper said.

Fifteen minutes later the gravel road curved right, and we barreled off it down into a low, grassy clearing with a small campground that opened onto the shore of a large gray lake.

Gauzy gusts of rain blew across its surface, veiling and unveiling the low, darker gray bands of pointed spruce and fir that ringed the far shore. I spotted one other human presence in the campground, the first we'd seen for the last hour or so of driving—a pickup truck and camping trailer at the clearing's far end, buttoned up tight against the weather. It was early June, but the gloom made it feel like late November.

This was Baker Lake, and we were at its foot. Its outlet stream ran past the campground, about fifty or sixty feet wide, sliding past us before disappearing between the walls of forest. Here lay the headwaters of the St. John River. The village of Allagash, the first settlement downstream from this spot, sat a hundred miles away. Those hundred miles we'd paddle by canoe.

We climbed out of the van into the downpour. Amy scrambled to help Skyler and Molly pull on rain pants, rain jackets, and rain hoods while David and I unstrapped the canoes and laid them on the wet gravel landing at the river's edge. As quickly as I could, I nestled our ten or twelve waterproof dry sacks containing sleeping bags, clothes, tent, and two large coolers crammed with food into the canoe hulls. It was already three o'clock, and I was eager to make some distance before dark.

Back in the Nicatou Outfitters shop at Medway that morning,

Galen and David had mentioned that, along the right riverbank a few hours downstream from Baker Lake, sat an old trapper's cabin.

"Remember that cabin," David now reminded us. "That would be a mighty nice place to spend the night in weather like this. It's there for anybody who wants to use it."

Skyler abandoned his hunt for arrowheads along the shore and we climbed in—Skyler in the bow of one canoe and I in the stern, Molly in the bow of the other and Amy in the stern. David helped shove us out into the river.

We four raised our paddles, swiveled the canoes to point downstream, and began stroking into the gusts of a stiff headwind, waving goodbye to David as we slipped into the rainy, gray-green forest.

ACADIA, ONE MIGHT SAY, was born of indifference by rival empires, and was finally killed off by the same imperial rivalries.

In 1541, Spanish spies, skulking around French ports, got wind of a French expedition, under Jacques Cartier, headed to North America to establish France's claims to regions around the St. Lawrence, which Cartier had explored a few years earlier. Spain, of course, decades before in the wake of Columbus, had established American colonies farther south—in Mexico and then South America. After catching wind of Cartier's expedition for French settlements in the New World, the Spaniards consulted with the Portuguese, who also had their own American colonies, in Brazil. Should they should take action against the French plans for settlement near the St. Lawrence?

"They can do no harm at Baccalaos," the Portuguese diplomats soothed the upset Spaniards.

Baccalaos was the Spanish and Portuguese name for the northern region. It meant "Codland"—the rich shoals of fish on the Grand Banks, the continental shelf off today's Newfoundland. Since the early 1500s, the Grand Banks had drawn an annual fishing fleet of Basque, Portuguese, and Breton vessels that stuffed their holds with salted codfish and sold them in Europe (Portuguese recipes today still call for the salted cod known as *bacalhau*). But, thick as these cold, foggy regions were with schools of offshore cod, the Spanish and Portuguese apparently didn't think it worth fighting the French over settlement claims to them. The wealth of cod lay offshore, for one thing, and, besides, the Spanish and Portuguese claimed far greater empires—rich with gold and silver—in the lands to the south.

Initially, they proved to be right. It wasn't worth fighting for. After suffering a terrible winter from scurvy and cold along the St. Lawrence, Cartier returned to France the next summer commanding what turned out to be a boatload of quartz "diamonds" and fool's gold. As an explorer, Cartier was put out to pasture in a crude manor house near St.-Malo, while for the next fifty years, throughout the late 1500s, the French mostly ignored their claims to North America as they fought decades of civil war between the Catholics and the Protestant Huguenots. When the religious wars ended, however, eyes again turned to the New World.

In 1604—this was three years before the British Jamestown settlers arrived down in Virginia—a French ship navigated by Samuel de Champlain anchored off northeastern America in the region known to the French as "L'Acadie," or "La Cadie" and, eventually, "Acadia." Delineated simply by lines of latitude on the map, L'Acadie or La Cadie took in everything from 40 to 46 degrees north—roughly from today's Pennsylvania and New York up through New England to the Maritime Provinces and Quebec. Leading the new settlement enterprise was a French nobleman with the weighty name of Pierre du Gua, sieur de Monts. King Henri IV had granted to de Monts the concession to settle La Cadie. The king specified that de Monts's mission on behalf of France was to look for wealth (which included gold or beaver skins), create a settlement, and spread Christianity among the heathens. King Henri also granted de Monts the power to press into service any of France's idlers, vagabonds, and criminals they might find useful. De Monts recruited his friend and fellow aristocrat, Jean de Biencourt de Poutrincourt, the baron of Saint-Just, to help lead the expedition. A distinguished soldier and enthusiastic adventurer, Poutrincourt's commitment ultimately established the French colony in Acadia.

De Monts and Poutrincourt landed their expedition in the New World and then Poutrincourt returned to France for more supplies and men. Those who stayed built a small settlement on an island at the mouth of the St. Croix River (today's Maine–New Brunswick border). They found it a lonely, windswept, hard-luck outpost.

"From the Spanish settlements northward to the pole," wrote the historian Francis Parkman a century and a half ago in *Pioneers of France in the New World,* "there was no domestic hearth, no lodgements of civilized men, save one weak band of Frenchmen, clinging, as it were for life, to the fringe of the vast and savage continent."

The northern winds blasted down the frozen river and through their crude dwellings. Thirty-five of the seventy-nine members of the "weak band" perished of scurvy that first winter. While de Monts sailed back to France that spring, the remaining survivors decamped from their exposed island and sailed across the Bay of Fundy, to that great protrusion of land that would soon become known as the Acadian Peninsula and, later, Nova Scotia. There they built a fort on a beautiful harbor, sheltered on virtually all sides from the winds and heavy seas and rich in marine life and pasturelands. They named this idyllic harbor Port-Royal.

The following spring, in May of 1606, the expedition's other aristocratic leader, Poutrincourt, departed France with a fresh contingent of forty men and supplies aboard a ship named *Jonas* to restock his and de Monts's enterprise in La Cadie, or Acadia. On board were not only the senior Poutrincourt, but also his adolescent son, Charles Biencourt, aged fifteen, and his fourteen-year-old nephew, Charles de La Tour. One wonders how the two cousins' aristocratic mothers greeted the proposal that they should leave home on a colonizing expedition to the New World. It's not difficult, however, to imagine a teenaged boy's excitement at joining this great enterprise of men in a largely unknown continent.

After a rough crossing of two months, the joy of arrival was captured by the passenger Marc Lescarbot, the forty-year-old Parisian lawyer of M. de Poutrincourt. Lescarbot had recently lost a major lawsuit and decided that the New World offered the chance to "fly from a corrupt world" and the opportunity to exercise his flair for poetry.

Fogs kept the *Jonas* tacking off the Acadian coast for a week. Then, on July 15, after a thunderstorm, the skies cleared and the sun came out, the coastline appeared, and they spied the sails of two longboats approaching from shore. The Frenchmen and young Biencourt and La Tour were crowded at the rail and, at this moment, Lescarbot writes, " . . . there came from the land odors incomparable for sweetness, brought with a warm wind so abundantly that all the Orient parts could not produce greater abundance. We did stretch out our hands as it were to take them, so palpable were they, which I have admired a thousand times since."

From that first visceral taste, the new land captivated the two boys. Uninterested in clearing farms and building rigorous Christian communities, unlike their British counterparts to the south, they would range these wilds in their quest for furs and enthusiastically embrace the Indian life. They would become what Henry David Thoreau, growing up two centuries later in the green-manicured, white-clapboard, God-fearing town of Concord, Massachusetts, wanted to be. They were children of the wilderness.

The two young Charleses represented a new environmental consciousness for Europeans, whether the boys were aware of it or not. They understood the wilds as a place benign rather than hostile, uplifting rather than evil, generous rather than depriving. Two centuries or more would pass, however, before this wilderness consciousness gained broader currency among most other Europeans who had come to America. That wilderness consciousness had to be mightily helped along by writers and thinkers such as Jean-Jacques Rousseau and William Bartram, Emerson and Thoreau, John Muir and Aldo Leopold, by the women who shaped their ideas, and by others whose names will never be known.

I WONDERED HOW MANY TIMES young Charles Biencourt and Charles de La Tour had paddled this same stretch of the St. John River, which from Baker Lake flowed four hundred miles down to the Atlantic's Bay of Fundy. It was a well-known route through the forest, then, in the early 1600s. Many of my "blank spots," I would discover, had been far less "blank" in centuries past than now, like northern Maine.

In the gusty downpour, we waved goodbye to David at the Baker Lake campground and, digging our paddle blades rhythmically into the rain-pocked river, we twisted into the spongy forest. Shallow and rocky and maybe three or four canoe lengths wide, the river gurgled swiftly through bends, slacked in flat, marshy sections, dropped gently, bubbling over boulders. Clear but slightly tea-colored, the water had been stained by vegetation. It was a nice-sized little river, a kind of cozy river.

We saw neither person nor dwelling, but within a half hour of leaving Baker Lake encountered our first moose. A yearling, it stood in shallow water along the brushy left bank on stilty legs, dipping its head to pull up mouthfuls of vegetation with its big dripping lips. Paddling side by side, we all shouted excitedly to one another—"Look! There's a moose!"—and of course the moose swung its head toward us in alarm, turned, trotted up the bank, and disappeared into the forest.

I'd been surprised by Molly's and Skyler's cheeriness from the start, despite the steady rain. After that first encounter, they eagerly looked for more moose. Around a few woody bends we encountered more— a mother and calf. We shushed one another and, paddles stilled, drifted quietly toward them on the smooth, rainy surface. The mother was enormous, her shoulders looming taller than my head, and probably weighing close to a ton. Where squirrels and songbirds speak to the daintiness of lawns and parks, a moose is a *presence*. She stood in the river, silently staring at us drifting closer, little eddies of current gently spinning around her legs, unyielding and vast and mysterious as the forest itself.

Eventually she, too, turned and lumbered up the bank with her calf in tow.

Around seven, as the wet daylight began to fade, we spotted the cabin's grayed logs. It sat in a grassy clearing against a backdrop of dark spires of spruce trees—like a classic woodcut engraving of a cabin in the forest. We beached the canoes and clambered up the steep cut bank. With a swaybacked roof and low to the ground, it looked like it could have been built by young Biencourt or La Tour themselves in 1606. Unlike the horizontally laid logs of the pioneer cabins I knew, the logs of its walls were planted vertically to the earth in a style that appeared Abenaki Indian in origin.

The elaborately carved latch testified to long winter nights spent in front of a fire while the snow piled up deep outside, passing the time with a whittling knife.

Amy pushed open the heavy door. Low windows admitted a dusky light to reveal a table sprouting drip-waxed candles, a cast-iron wood-stove, a crude counter holding an enameled washbasin, log roof beams varnished with a patina of woodsmoke. A partitioned nook at the rear enclosed a few old bedsprings padded with slabs of ragged cardboard and thin foam.

"This is great!" she said.

The children poked around, exploring. Amy found a note hanging on a nail near the door.

"It's in French," she said, studying it. "It's the score of a whist game."

I was checking the kindling box near the stove. The old newspapers inside it were in French, too, papers from small towns somewhere across the border. It felt as if we'd suddenly slipped beyond the United States, and had entered a vast, ambiguous swath of territory—the North—and slid hundreds of years back in time. Since the arrival of the first few Europeans four centuries ago, this region had been neither really French nor really British but a borderlands whose contours shifted with the waxing and waning of the two great empires an ocean away.

Rough, rocky, and forested, it was nearly useless as farmland. European settlers didn't stampede in to stake land claims and grow crops, as they did in many parts of America. Rather it served as wildlands, a buffer between empires. Biencourt and, especially, La Tour lived their lives almost entirely within this enormous region, within this blank spot. This is the life they chose, not seeking to create the careful settlements of farmers, but living instead on the wild, ragged edge of the known. What was it about this region that attracted them so, I wondered, and attracted Thoreau much later?

Amy and I watched, shivering, as the children swam contentedly in a clear pool of the river, just in front of the cabin. Soon they were bundled up and sitting before the popping woodstove, sipping hot chocolate. Candles guttered on the table. Glowing headlamps shone cheerily from the dark-smoked roof beams where Molly had decorously hung them from nails amid our drying clothes.

"Can we sleep in tomorrow?" she asked, liking the look of the place.

Amy tended to a makeshift pizza baking under a foil tent on our camp stove. I sat beside the woodstove with a camping cup full of wine. Scribbling the occasional note by candlelight, I read from Thoreau's essay about these same wild regions, titled "Ktaadn" and written in the 1840s—more than two centuries after the French arrival.

WHEN THOREAU FIRST MET HIM, as he recounts in "Ktaadn," Young Tom Fowler—Galen Hale's great-great-great-granduncle by marriage—was in the act of sawing through the two-foot-thick log walls of the cabin he'd just built on a pond beyond Nicatou. These openings would be the holes for the cabin's windows. Thoreau closely observed Fowler's construction, for he'd recently completed his own cabin on the shore of Walden Pond. On the spot, Thoreau reports, Young Tom agreed to serve as boatman for Thoreau's party for its expedition deeper into the Maine Woods. Tom dropped his tools and went to throw a few items in a pack, serving the waiting party drafts of his homemade spruce beer. This, Thoreau wrote with typical ardor, tasted as strong and stringent as cedar sap, and drinking it was "as if we sucked at the very teats of Nature's pine-clad bosom . . ."

Thoreau was a true oddball, a rebel against his time. He took to the woods so passionately because he'd been roundly rejected by conventional society generally, and by two young women in particular.

Thoreau had come of age at a moment of intellectual rebelliousness in the United States, when major change wafted in the air. I think of him breathing it in with the concentrated, lung-pumping vigor that marks his writing. Born in Concord, Massachusetts, and always loving its gentle woods and fields, he entered college at nearby Harvard—with considerable economic sacrifice from his family—just as the Romantic movement spread from Europe's youth to the United States. Gone was the great faith in rationalism and classicism. Rather, passions and the senses ruled. Youth rejected the ossified authority of the musty old guard, nowhere more brazenly than among Thoreau's schoolmates in the Harvard class of 1837—instigators in what became known as the Dunkin Rebellion, a1960s-style revolt that erupted in the 1830s.

It started the spring of Thoreau's freshman year, on May 19, 1834, presumably one of those warm, sunny days when ebullience and revolution float in the air. A student who was reciting in Instructor Christopher Dunkin's freshman Greek class abruptly stopped. When commanded by Instructor Dunkin to proceed, the student replied, "I do not recognize your authority," and shut his book.

That was all the spark it took. By nightfall students were destroying classrooms, smashing furniture, breaking out windows, and ripping the shutters off buildings and burning them in bonfires on the steps. The college set guards on a watch to quell the violence. Students attacked by pummeling the guards with stones. Fights broke out. One of the most shocking acts, in a college founded by Puritans two centuries before, was the disruption of the mandatory morning prayers by groans, whistles, scrapings, and, according to the official report, various other "offensive noises" emitting from the chapel's pews and by contemptuous latecomers bursting through the doors.

The immediate target of the rebellion was Harvard's new president, Josiah Quincy, a politician who'd recently served as a get-the-garbage-collected-on-time mayor of Boston. He had instituted an unpopular point system that rewarded the students for rote memorization and good attendance in classes and chapel and discouraged original thinking and discussion. Students petitioned the faculty—Thoreau being a signatory—and burned President Quincy in effigy. But still the point system had gone forward.

In the years preceding the Harvard uprising, starting about 1800, Europe's intellectual youth had been set aflame with the Romantic cult of the individual, embracing the power of emotion, embarking on grand Byronic adventures, celebrating what came to be called Wild Nature. Rather than the stern Old Testament deity that prevailed at Harvard, imported by Puritans from a medieval Europe two hundred years before, God had become a creative and divine force embodied in both Art and in Nature. God had become a Bohemian.

The Romantic spirit was channeled directly to Harvard by the preacher-turned-philosopher Ralph Waldo Emerson. Heir to a long line of those same stern New England Puritans and preachers dating back to *Mayflower* days, Emerson, in 1832, after his young wife died, had fled both the pulpit and Boston for Europe. He encountered Romantic writers and thinkers such as Coleridge who caused him to question his traditional religious beliefs. Adapting much from these Romantics, he began to formulate his own philosophy of the self and nature—what became known eventually as "Transcendentalism."

Returning to Boston in 1833—the same year Thoreau started at Harvard—Emerson soon gained a wide following among youthful intelligentsia and was reviled by their conservative elders. He shocked Harvard with his "Address at Divinity College," in which he spoke out against Jesus as the foundation of the Church's divinity, advocating that man needs to look inward to find it instead. Thus man could "transcend" the material world—the concrete world defined by facts and the senses, which included the historical Jesus—by instead experiencing the divine that infused all parts of the universe, including the self and nature. He laid out his fundamental ideas in the essay "Nature," which

Thoreau twice checked out from the Harvard library. At Thoreau's graduation in 1837, Emerson gave his famous "American Scholar" address, in which he rallied the graduates to create a literature and way of thinking that was American. In a way, the address could be viewed as a compass course that Thoreau followed the rest of his life:

> We will walk on our own feet; we will work with our own hands; we will speak our own minds. The study of letters shall be no longer a name for pity, for doubt, and for sensual indulgence. The dread of man and the love of man shall be a wall of defence and a wreath of joy around all. A nation of men will for the first time exist, because each believes himself inspired by the Divine Soul which also inspires all men.

My head nodded as I read Thoreau that first evening before the whispering orange embers of the woodstove. We went to bed, and rose late in our trapper's cabin on the banks of the St. John, lulled by morning rain pattering on the shake roof. We were exhausted by the several days of travel simply to reach this spot, still at the start of our wilderness journey. We'd driven a frantic eight hours from our home in Missoula across two states to catch our flight in Seattle, flown through the night across the entire country, and landed in Boston at dawn. Jamming gear bags into the rental car, we'd driven into Cambridge, where Amy wanted to show the children her old house at Harvard. Silvery-haired alums in their blue reunion blazers tottered to breakfast across the shady green lawns of Harvard Yard. I had thought of Thoreau, cutting down these very footpaths with, as one classmate later described it, "his grave Indian stride."

Then we'd headed north to Medway and the St. John.

No one was in a hurry to leave the dim, calm hush of the cabin. I recorded yesterday's events in a notebook, lying in my bag on the sagging bedsprings, while Amy and the children flipped pancakes. It was a pleasant, lazy morning—a sleep-in morning. It took several hours to repack our gear, which we'd hastily stuffed in the canoes in the gusty rain at Baker Lake.

We finally got back on the river in mid-afternoon. As we pushed out from the bank, the rain touched the surface with a tinkling sound.

"Can leeches kill you?" Skyler asked thoughtfully.

He and Molly had spotted them crawling in the muddy shallows. He'd seen giant leeches in the movie *King Kong*. I'd noticed before how he constantly assessed threats to himself—the distances of falls out of trees, the possible attacks of wild animals, the power of a tornado—and wondered if this were an instinctive male trait, especially when in unfamiliar territory, with all his senses attuned, as I knew mine were.

Molly's was a more scientific curiosity about the leeches.

I made the children practice their draw strokes again. I was surprised how easily they could both pull the bows of their canoes to one side or the other, a crucial maneuver for the rapids that lay ahead, and one that I'd taught them before leaving Montana. The map showed the first rapids four miles downstream from our campsite, and both Molly and Skyler were eager for them to arrive. I was more anxious, wondering how powerful they'd be for our little party.

A young male moose with antlers held his ground—or his patch of water—in the middle of the river. As the distance closed between us from three hundred feet, to two hundred, to one hundred and fifty, he still didn't move, staring us down.

"I'm getting scared," Molly said.

"Let's paddle gently to the right bank," I ordered quietly.

I knew moose could make lethal charges when challenged, and I didn't want to test this one. I'd been on a kayak expedition to an African river—Rio Lugenda in remote northern Mozambique—where we faced highly territorial male hippos in similar circumstances. Our guide gave them a very wide berth.

With the river running low, rocks protruded in shallow sections. The St. John headwaters drain a relatively small area of rocky terrain, and so the water levels of the upper river fluctuate dramatically—running very high during spring's heavy snowmelt and after big rains, but dropping rapidly after that. We'd arrived just as the Upper St. John fell toward its low summer levels. It offered just enough depth to float the canoes through the rocky sections, although if the rains continued the level surely would rise. It wasn't a total surprise, then, that when we reached the first rapids marked on the map, they amounted to little more than riffles trickling between a shallow scattering of boulders.

We careened from one rock to another, the plastic-hulled whitewater canoes easily ricocheting off them. Skyler stood in the bow of our canoe to scout the way ahead, like George Washington crossing the Delaware, as Amy remarked. He shouted out directions to me.

"Go right! Now left!"

The rapids emptied into a flat, quiet section of river and we drifted along, hanging on to the gunnels of each other's canoe, eating a river lunch of crackers and a French cheese spread, apples, and granola bars. Everyone seemed happy enough, drifting down the river in the rain.

It wasn't until seven o'clock and the light was beginning to fade again that we stopped to camp, where the Southwest Branch tumbled out of the forest on the left and joined our stem of the river, known as the Baker Branch. A beautiful campsite at the confluence centered on a big white pine, with a grove of spruces behind it providing a kind of canopy for a tent site. As Amy and Molly pitched our big tent, Skyler and I collected dry wood from under sheltered trees and built a fire using birch bark as tinder, to cook a steak dinner over the coals.

Put to the match, our birch bark flared up like it was soaked in kerosene. Skyler watched with fascination.

"That burns better than paper," he remarked.

There was something inherently very satisfying in passing on to him these woods techniques that I'd learned over many years, something qualitatively different from, for instance, helping him learn to read, although that had its own satisfactions. Here, literally, was a skill for survival. How could a human be complete without understanding how to create and wield fire? I began to see that here was one reason Thoreau took to the woods.

As the Industrial Revolution in the early 1800s gathered steam and spun people off the land and into the cities, Thoreau viscerally understood that these basic skills for survival—to use one's own hands to acquire food, fire, shelter—define what it is to be human, to have a higher consciousness and be an animal among animals.

As he expressed it in his famous explanation at the outset of *Walden,* "I went to the woods because I wished to live deliberately, to front only the essential facts of life . . ."

This theme appears again and again in the writings of those seeking out the wilds. Marc Lescarbot, the French lawyer with a flair for poetry who'd just lost a big case, was disgusted with life in French society, with its aristocratic hierarchies and rigged courts. Joining that 1606 expedition to Acadia allowed him to "fly from a corrupt world" to the purity of the New World, to life in the woods, where he, as Thoreau did much later, would front only the essentials. Rousseau, one hundred and fifty years after Lescarbot and nearly a century before Thoreau, likewise rejected the "artifice" of Parisian society, the gilded intellectual salons with their beautiful ladies and clever repartee among *philosophes,* the social posing, the currying for favor, the corruptness of it all. In solitude, in Nature, he could find his true self.

"Strip off the artificial habits of civilized man," wrote Rousseau in his novel *Émile,* in 1761, "return to your own heart . . . permit yourself to be guided by the light of instinct and conscience; and you will rediscover that primitive Adam . . . long buried under a crust of mold and slime . . ."

In the wilderness—in Wild Nature—humans wearied by corrupt society, disillusioned men such as Lescarbot, Rousseau, and Thoreau, could find redemption and purity. It shimmered out there, beckoning them. It was a fantasy, a mirage, a promise hovering beyond the ocean or just over the woodsy horizon.

I know this mirage very well, for I've chased after it my whole life. The promise of something indefinable, ineffable, waits in those blank spots on the map—those wild places—as it did for these disillusioned men. What? What *is* it? I don't know the answer. I don't think they knew the answer. It's less an answer than an expectation, a hope, or rather the hope of an answer. But an answer to *what*? To the ills of a corrupt society. To ennui. To disillusionment. To a sense of spiritual emptiness. It's the answer to purposelessness. To rejection. To sadness. It somehow contains the answer to all these things. In the wild places, in the blank spots, what exists, we hope, is meaning.

MARC LESCARBOT WAS JOYOUS when the *Jonas* at last sailed into the huge natural harbor at Port-Royal in July 1606, after escaping the corrupt life in Paris and arriving in the pristine New World. Its sheer wildness and uncultivated aspect struck him forcefully: " . . . it was a wondrous sight for us to see its fair extent and the mountains and hills which shut it in, and I wondered that so fair a spot remained desert, and all wooded, seeing that so many folk are ill-off in this world who could make their profit of this land if they only had a leader to bring them thither."

The *Jonas* approached a promontory deep within the harbor where the French had built a small wooden fortress the preceding year. The ship's crew expected a party to rush out joyously to salute and greet their arrival. Nothing stirred. You imagine consternation rippling across the deck—what had gone so suddenly wrong with this shining adventure that was to be New France? You imagine the boys thinking not of the danger, but of the excitement. I could imagine Skyler there, fascinated by the quiet fort in the distance and the tension on the *Jonas*'s deck beneath the ship's creaking rigging, by the swords now strapped on and cannons at the ready, by the armor quickly donned, to meet this first encounter with the unknown. Had the Frenchmen frozen during the winter? Had they perished of scurvy? Had the Indians killed them all?

In fact, it was the Indian leader, Membertou, who at that moment was rushing into the French fort and shouting "like a madman" to rouse the two French guards nodding off over their midday meal in the otherwise deserted structure.

" 'Wake up, there. You are dawdling over your dinner . . . and do not see a great ship which is arriving, and we know not who they are!' "

Thus reports Lescarbot. The others of the French party at Port-Royal had temporarily deserted the fort. After waiting for the *Jonas* and its supplies until this late in the season, they thought they'd been abandoned and finally set off in their longboat to look for French fishing vessels off the Grand Banks to hitch a ride back to France.

But the two sleepy guards were now roused, spotted the white ensign on the *Jonas*'s mast, jammed the cannons with charges, and let loose with a four-gun salute, which rolled and echoed among the low wooded hills, while the *Jonas* responded with cannon shots and trumpet blasts.

It was emblematic that the guards had been roused by Membertou. From the beginning, this Micmac chief, or "Sagamore," kept careful watch over the French in Acadia—these innocents to the ways of the forests, to the hills and the rivers. Membertou and his people essentially taught the French how to survive in the New World.

After a happy reunion with the guards, the *Jonas* crew and passengers spent the day visiting the small, dark French "manor house."

Membertou then led them to the temporary Indian summer village nearby, much larger than the tiny French outpost, and centered around large meeting halls made of carefully woven bark.

The party began a few days later, after the return of the group that had gone off in the longboat, which included the navigator Champlain. For the next month the French at Port-Royal, reports Lescarbot, "made very merry." The openhanded M. de Poutrincourt, young Charles Biencourt's father and the expedition leader who had gone back to France to fetch supplies and brought them to Port-Royal aboard the *Jonas*, set up a barrel of wine that was free to drink for all comers, "some of whom made gay dogs of themselves."

Lescarbot rhapsodized about the beauty and richness of the new land. Exploring up the Dauphin River (now the Annapolis), which emptied into the big harbor, they found lush meadows bordering the banks where moose grazed, countless clear brooks flowing into it, and dense forests covering the hills. A waterfall cast rainbows of spray at the harbor's mouth and young whales frolicked in the waters. The carpenters and stonecutters and other workmen labored only three hours each day constructing the settlement, and spent the rest of the time collecting mussels on the tidal flats, as well as crabs, cockles, and other delicacies. There was abundance and generosity everywhere. The Indians gave them salmon, sturgeon, beaver, moose meat and other game, or traded the hunted meats for the bread baked by the French.

That autumn unfolded in a kind of pleasant idyll at Port-Royal, but by November the situation grew tense. At the end of August, the *Jonas* had sailed back to France with the plan to resupply Port-Royal the following spring. At the same time, Champlain and Poutrincourt headed south in the longboat toward Cape Cod, seeking a still warmer spot than Port-Royal for France's ultimate settlement in the New World. With them was Poutrincourt's son, Charles Biencourt, and no doubt his cousin, Charles de La Tour, as well as another boy, Robert Gravé, son of Du Pont, the leader of the whole enterprise.

At first, on this journey south, the encounters with the Indians were friendly. Eager to trade for French knives, pots, and glass beads, flotillas of Indian canoes paddled out to greet them. Indians ran joyously along the shore to keep pace with the sailing longboat, carrying bows in hand, arrow quivers on their backs, and singing. Lescarbot wrote: "Oh, happy race! yea, a thousand-fold more happy than those who here [in France] make us bow down to them, had [the Indians] but the knowledge of God and their salvation."

The French liked the land's fertility and abundant grapevines as they sailed south, but hostility from the Indians grew. Near present-day Chatham on Cape Cod, a party went ashore for several days to bake bread. When Indians stole a hatchet from them, a few of the younger, cockier French apparently fired at the thieves with muskets. Poutrincourt then noticed bands of Indians sneaking through the woods, and ordered the obstreperous young bakers into the longboat before nightfall, but they refused, insisting on remaining ashore to eat the bread they had baked.

Sometimes I wonder, if only those five bakers had returned to the longboat when ordered, whether France would have managed to establish its New World colony farther south—in the warmer climate and better growing season of present-day coastal New England instead of Canada. Boston, and maybe much of North America, would be French-speaking today. But, as the sweep of history sometimes turns on the flukes of personality, the five cocky bakers stayed on shore that night on Cape Cod. At dawn, a thick volley of arrows awakened the young Frenchmen, killing two of them instantly. The others leaped into the shallows, where the longboat rescued them, although two more of the bakers would soon die of their wounds. The French kept up a volley at the Indians on shore. Young Robert Gravé, in his enthusiasm to shoot at the Indians from the longboat, overloaded his musket and its barrel exploded, accidentally blowing off three of his fingers. On the beach, the Indians mocked the French by standing with their backs toward the boat and throwing handfuls of sand between their buttocks while howling like wolves, then quickly ducking out of the way whenever they saw the French lighting another cannon fuse.

For the two aristocratic young Charleses this was surely far more interesting than sitting in a musty library back in France and reciting their Latin declensions to some disapproving tutor.

Those who remained back in Port-Royal, meanwhile, had begun to wonder what had happened to the longboat group that had gone south. September turned to October. Lescarbot, who had stayed behind to oversee the contingent of men at Port-Royal, began to hear grumbling as winter approached without word from the expedition's leaders, who'd sailed south. The tension built as the weather chilled. A mutiny appeared to be in the making. What to do to stave it off? The lawyer-poet had an idea: *Let's put on a show!* Maybe some slapstick, farcical playacting would occupy their mutinous minds.

In mid-November, the longboat under Pourtincourt and Champlain finally sailed into Port-Royal's beautiful but chilly harbor, after the two leaders, due to the hostilities between bakers and Indians on Cape Cod, had abandoned the idea of a more southern colony. The returning expedition was greeted by a humorous play written by Lescarbot, titled *Neptune's Theater*. This reunion was yet another excuse for a wild celebration. At Port-Royal, *every* day was an excuse for a party. It was Champlain who first proposed L'Ordre de Bon Temps—"The Order of Good Times"—on the observation that it was *melancholy* that caused scurvy, and the saddest and loneliest of men died first. The best preventative to the disease, he reasoned, was to make merry. Under his scheme, each day a different member of the fifteen who made up the order was designated to assemble a feast for the others. The day's "Ruler of the Feast" actually started preparing two days in advance by going off and, with the help of the local Micmac Indians under Membertou, fishing and hunting for the choicest game. The feast's ruler oversaw the preparation of the meats by the cook, and delivery of the dishes to the table in a grand parade of the members, each bearing a dish, which the ruler headed with a napkin draped over his shoulder, a staff in his hand, and a chain or medallion draped around his neck that "was worth more than four crowns."

Wine flowed abundantly during this winter of 1606–07 and the fare rivaled the restaurants in the Rue aux Ours back in Paris—especially the tender moose meat, the delicate beaver tail, and the sturgeon that the Micmac caught. While twenty or thirty other Micmac looked on, Membertou and other chiefs, when they weren't away on their frequent hunting expeditions, ate and drank at table with the order.

"And we were glad to see them," writes Lescarbot, "while, on the contrary, their absence saddened us."

WE HAD OUR OWN FEAST that second night on the St. John River around the campfire Skyler and I had ignited with birch bark. The rain had stopped, for now. Over the glowing embers we grilled steaks, and the children made s'mores, and afterward, in the calm evening, with the backdrop chorus of the soft ululating rush of the Southwest Branch whispering in the darkness from the opposite bank, where it spilled into our main river, Amy, Molly, and Skyler played their recorder flutes together, to the lilting shush of the water. Then we climbed into our bags inside the big tent, read a story aloud, and fell asleep.

It was raining again in the morning—our third day on the river. With the addition of the Southwest Branch swishing out of the dripping forest on the left bank and swirling its dark waters into the St. John, the river had swelled to fifty or sixty yards in width. The morning's rain blew in hard gusts up the river's straight sections, spraying across the ruffled gray surface, plastering our faces. It seemed pointless to stop. For what? Along the right bank, we spotted a pair of geese with a line of fuzzy goslings trailing behind. As we paddled, they chased downstream ahead of us, the goslings falling farther back.

"Hurry up! Hurry up!" Molly called out to them.

A bald eagle perched in a treetop, scanning the river for fish to pluck in its talons. A pair of loons bobbed lightly on the current midstream, the fine white speckles on their black backs looking like flurries of snow against dark firs. Loons, with their haunting cry, were the emblematic bird of the north.

We'd seen no other people since waving goodbye to David two days before, nor any other signs of human activity except for the old trapper's cabin where we'd spent the first night and a few small campground openings in the forested shore.

Amy and Molly sang rounds in their canoe. In ours, paddling forward into the spraying gusts of rain, Skyler wanted to hear stories. I told about canoeing as a child.

"One time my father—your grandfather Poppy—was paddling in the canoe ahead of my cousin and me on a little twisty river and he disappeared around a bend. We came around the bend and he ambushed us by suddenly swinging out over the river on a rope, like Tarzan, and giving a war whoop, but all of a sudden the rope broke and he crashed down into the middle of the river with a huge splash."

Skyler laughed heartily at that one, to think of his grandfather plunging into the middle of the river.

I told him about the time my uncle attempted a backflip off a cliff above the Wisconsin River and bellyflopped, almost knocking himself unconscious.

On another trip, also on the Wisconsin with my father, we were setting up camp deep in the woody bottomlands along the shore, and two boys wandered into our camp, true Huck Finn characters—ragged, barefoot, grubby, smiling with gap teeth, and each toting a big bowie knife strapped to his waist, foraging for river clams.

"Those were river rats," my father told me after they'd left, with a kind of wonder and admiration, as if this were a rare, throwback breed of human to two hundred years ago, like fur-trapping mountain men and French-Canadian voyageurs.

"Poppy really liked fireworks," I told Skyler, "and on these canoe trips he always brought along a few huge ones. He'd light them off at night on the end of a big sandbar where we were camping, and they went way up and exploded in big flower shapes. Then my friend Stephen and I would take glowing sticks from the fire and throw them up into the air, and watch them spin into the black sky against the stars, and come crashing back down on the sandbar in a shower of sparks. Those were our own fireworks. That was really fun."

"Tell me another story," Skyler said, dragging his paddle blade aimlessly through the water.

"Let's paddle to warm up," I replied.

I was getting chilled. The headwind drove the rain up the surface of my rain pants and under my rain jacket. I felt my chest soaked underneath.

"I think we should stop for lunch and get out and walk around," I called out to Amy.

Dense forest lined the banks. A rocky bar in mid-river offered the only open spot. We beached our canoes, opened the lunch cooler, and took out crackers, cheese, apples, chocolate. Wind swept the rain through the willow bushes, making them twitch and sway, across the rock bar. I stumbled around over the glistening stones, but I couldn't get warm. The children and Amy sat on the gunnel of a beached canoe, quite happily nibbling chocolate and cookies in the blowing rain. I began to shiver.

It felt bleak enough here in midsummer, on the Upper St. John. What would it be like, say, during a cold sleet storm in autumn? I thought of young Charles Biencourt and Charles de La Tour, paddling on this river in the early 1600s, dressed in furs. The two fascinated me. I wanted to understand them, know what motivated them to take to the life of the woods rather than, when the chance arose, return to France. What was it they saw in these blank spots? To them, these regions were not really blank. They lived in them and learned them well. What we call "blank spots" are only blank insofar as there is little or no recorded history—written memories—in these places. But for thousands of years they served as hunting grounds and waterways to the Indians. Their landforms, their lakes, their streams all had names, legends, memories, and knowledge attached—weather and currents, animal migration patterns, medicinal plants. Part of this region along the St. John was called Madawaska by the Indians—"Land of the Porcupine"—while the Maliseet Indians knew the St. John itself as Wolastoq—"the Beautiful River"—and themselves as Wolastoqiyik, "People of the Beautiful River."

These "blank spots," in other words, were very much "known" centuries before the Europeans arrived. What the Europeans brought to these places, initially, was ignorance.

I could imagine the excitement for the young Charleses in simply learning—learning the secrets of these places that were utter mysteries for the European arrivals. Privy to the esoteric knowledge of the woods, the boys resembled, in a fashion, those two Huck Finn characters whom we met along the Wisconsin River when I was a boy canoeing with my father. They suddenly appeared in our camp, carrying the secrets of the thick, tangled bottomlands—the animal paths through the forest, the clamming spots, the fishing holes, the fox dens, the sloughs to swim across to reach an island. I'd felt that same excitement myself. As a boy, I knew the few hundred acres of forest, meadow, and swamp surrounding our log cabin better than anyone alive. A special power comes with that knowledge, a sense of privilege. You are the possessor of secrets. The young Charleses felt it in Acadia in the early 1600s. I'm certain Thoreau did also, two centuries later in his woods and fields of Concord, and so did John Muir, in the 1870s, in his beloved High Sierra.

In this New World, the two French boys learned to survive from the Micmac, under the careful paternal guidance of Membertou. During that first winter of the boys' residence at Port-Royal, l'Ordre de Bon

Temps signified much more than an ongoing party that saved a few dozen Frenchmen's lives from scurvy. Their continual hunting and feasting together bonded the French and the Indians. To keep the feast supplied, the French learned the Indian methods of hunting and the Indian ways of understanding the rivers and forests. One man spent six weeks that winter hunting in the forest with the Micmac, reports Lescarbot, "in their fashion, without salt, bread, or wine, sleeping on the ground on skins, and that too in time of snow. Moreover they took greater care of him, as also of others who often went with them, than of themselves, saying that if any of these died, his death would be laid at their door . . . for this tribe loves the French."

And the affection was mutual. The French admired the Micmac— a handsome people bearing themselves with pride, as the French saw them. Poutrincourt insisted to his men that the Micmac be treated with equality and fairness. Membertou himself—to the surprise of the French—considered himself to be an equal of King Henri IV. This closeness of Indian and French from the start was captured by Champlain, who in one of his early speeches to the Indians remarked, "Our sons will marry your daughters and we will be a single people."

"No Puritan," as the historian John Mack Faragher notes, "ever said anything vaguely similar."

AFTER OUR WINDBLOWN, RAINY LUNCH on the rock bar, we passed the Northwest Branch, another obscure stream emptying in from the forest on the river's left. It occurred to me that this very confluence was far better known four hundred years ago than it is now. Hardly a blank spot, it served as a major thoroughfare—a huge shortcut—between the Atlantic Ocean and the Indian settlements on the St. Lawrence. They paddled their birch-bark canoes up the main stem of the St. John and, using long wood poles to gain traction against the rocky bottoms, poled them upstream through these St. John tributaries such as the Northwest Branch. Reaching the tiny headwater streams, they portaged their canoes overland a few miles to the headwaters of the streams that drained northward into the St. Lawrence River. This saved the Indians a detour of hundred of miles and many days far to the north to reach the St. Lawrence mouth before having to paddle hundreds of miles up that river to the same settlements.

The Micmac could make the shortcut journey in ten or twelve days. I imagined the satisfaction a young Micmac felt on paddling his canoe into the Indian villages on the St. Lawrence after this rapid journey, bearing news and goods from the coast. Maybe, today, in this era of instant communication, we've utterly lost a sense of what that meant—news of relatives just born or just dying. News of war, or news of peace. News of strange craft off the coast. News of mysterious diseases, powerful new weapons, trade goods. There was heroism in the act itself—and a celebration with the arrival of a messenger from far away. In a nomadic society, it occurred to me, a high value was placed on simple movement itself.

WE CAME TO A BROAD, shallow, rocky stretch of river—all swirls of water, shiny dark rocks, and little cresting waves, a kind of mosaic of movement. We had to jam our paddles against the river bottom and lean on them hard, like the poles the Micmac used, to slide the canoes over the shallow rocks. Even after three days of rain, the water remained low. Skyler and I, winding through the maze of rocks toward the left bank, inadvertently jammed our canoe into a semisubmerged rock bar. Across the river, I could see Amy and Molly easily gliding down a narrow channel against the right bank. I had to get out and push, tripping on a rocky hole in the bottom and falling down into the shallow water.

I swore.

"It'll be okay, Dad," Skyler said. "Just be patient."

Where had I heard that before?

After fifteen minutes of dragging and pushing, paddle blades crunching against rocky bottom, we shoved our way past a rock ledge protruding from the left bank. Only a trickle of water spilled over it. I checked the river map.

"Hey, this must be Ledge Rapids," I said.

"You mean this is a Class Two rapid?" asked Skyler in dismay. He thought for a moment. "Will the rapids get bigger than this?"

"Probably. A lot depends on how much rain we have and how much water is in the river. Do you want them to get bigger?"

"A lot bigger."

We swung around a bend and came to a rickety bridge sagging across the river on spindly, fractured concrete pilings, like some drooping Jacob's ladder. One piling had toppled into a heap in the river, no doubt knocked down by an ice jam. These occur on the St. John and similar rivers in early spring when the frozen river suddenly thaws and a huge pile of ice sweeps down like an avalanche rumbling down a mountain slope. I could see "scour lines" along the riverbank where ice jams had scraped away all vegetation for about ten feet up the steep banks, like the mown strip on the shoulder of a highway. Later I would learn that certain plant species unique to the St. John grow only on this scour line.

We raced under the bridge on a fast current, and swung the canoe hard toward the left bank where we spotted a grassy campsite. Two picnic tables sat under a mossy log-and-shingle shelter roof. Any reservations I felt about a sheltered picnic table marring my "wilderness" experience disappeared as the rain intensified into a downpour, blurring the river into a fuzzy, pebbled gray sheet. It was already beginning to rise. Amy and Molly quickly fitted together poles to erect our big tent—the "family tent," we called it, as opposed to the small ones we used in the mountains—while Skyler and I set off down a two-track dirt road for firewood. It led back to the bridge. A sign in bold letters posted at the entrance to the sagging span warned of a load limit of 6,000 pounds, a speed limit of 5 mph, and a maximum of one vehicle at a time. It was easy to see why.

"Pass At Your Own Risk," it cautioned.

Surprisingly, next to it was another sign, "The Nature Conservancy." I would eventually hear the story of how the Nature Conservancy, the quiet, far-reaching nonprofit that preserves land from development, had several years earlier acquired land along eighty miles of the Upper St. John from huge paper companies. At the time, it was the largest project the group had ever undertaken. They'd targeted the St. John because it was one of the wildest remaining rivers in the Lower 48 states and they wanted it to stay that way. The sign on the bridge indicated we'd now entered the stretch protected by the organization.

Skyler and I plunged into the forest, climbing over fallen trees, trying to find dry wood beneath the dripping evergreen canopy on the mossy forest floor. We dragged a few downed limbs back to the campsite but it was now raining so hard I didn't even try to kindle a fire, even with the dry birch bark I'd stashed in my bags. Molly and Skyler pulled off their wet clothes and retired into the tent and its warm nest of sleeping bags. Amy and I hunkered under the picnic shelter and opened cans of corned-beef hash—the fastest dinner we had—frying them in skillets on our two-burner camping stove. We could hear Molly's and Skyler's soft voices as they happily played cat's cradle. String games were an ancient pastime of Inuit children, too. It made perfect sense—something engrossing that keeps the hands and mind moving, something totally portable to occupy children during long, long waits for the weather to change. In a nomadic society, movement depended on weather.

Frying hash and sipping sherry with Amy under the picnic shelter while the rain poured around us, listening to the children playing in the warm tent, it seemed as if our little band of humans had struck some primordial note of harmony in the wilds.

SOMETIMES I WONDER if I would have any interest in wilderness at all—and if the Nature Conservancy, and groups like it, would even exist—if Henry David Thoreau hadn't been so ardently rejected by conventional society back in the late 1830s and early 1840s, or if he had not so ardently rejected it.

By the spring of 1845, Thoreau, at twenty-seven, was beset by frustrations. Upon graduating from Harvard seven years earlier, Thoreau had been hired in the prestigious post of teacher at the Concord School, but quit abruptly after only two weeks. Deacon Ball, of the school committee, looked in on his classroom, judged it too noisy, pulled Thoreau out into the hallway, and told him he had to whip the students occasionally or "the school would be spoilt." Thoreau thereupon arbitrarily pulled several students from class, beat them with a ruler, and resigned his teaching post that night. It was Thoreau's first principled stand against convention. He may have absorbed that antiauthoritarian spirit he'd witnessed at Harvard during the Dunkin Rebellion.

On October 22, 1837, a month after the caning incident, Thoreau, unemployed, living with his parents, and hanging around Concord after offending much of the town by resigning his teaching post, wrote the first entry in his later famous *Journal* after a chance encounter with Ralph Waldo Emerson on the street:

" 'What are you doing now?' he asked. 'Do you keep a journal?' So I make my first entry today."

Searching widely in New England but unable to find another teaching job, Henry, along with his brother John, founded an "alternative" school in Concord that, besides basic subjects, emphasized hands-on learning through field trips and boating expeditions on local rivers in the Thoreaus' homemade craft. When, after three years, John fell ill and the school closed, Henry worked as a live-in handyman and gardener for the Emerson household. He also started to write seriously. He fell in love twice, once with a young woman he met through the Emersons. He wrote a poem about her, "To the Maiden in the East":

> *Low in the eastern sky*
> *Is set thy glancing eye . . .*

Both young women rebuffed him. Rather, Ellen Sewall apparently accepted his marriage proposal but quickly reversed course after her father demanded that she write in a "*short, explicit* and *cold* manner" to turn down Thoreau. Then Thoreau's beloved brother John cut his finger while stropping his razor and died a few days later of lockjaw. Thoreau sunk into despondency, even displaying the paralyzing symptoms of lockjaw himself. After recovering and casting about again for teaching work, he took a job tutoring for Emerson's brother's family on Staten Island. He didn't go with great enthusiasm, but with the hope to break into the New York City literary scene.

"It will be something to hate; —that's the advantage [New York City] will be to me . . . the pigs in the street are the most respectable part of the population. When will the world learn that a million men are of no importance compared to *one* man."

Thoreau made no headway selling his essays to New York magazine publishers. He even failed at door-to-door selling magazine *subscriptions.* Desperately homesick for Concord and his family's back porch looking out on the poplar tree, he returned home and went to work in his father's small pencil-making factory, where he invented a new type of pencil that became popular with professional draftsmen, and spent his spare time writing and walking the woods and fields of Concord. The short-lived Transcendentalist magazine *The Dial* published some of his poems and a few of his natural history essays, which caught the attention of other intellectuals.

Like Rousseau nearly a century before in the Parisian salons,

Thoreau began fashioning himself as a kind of natural man among the Concord literati. The novelist Nathaniel Hawthorne, a new resident of the growing literary community at Concord, described Thoreau as "a wild, irregular, Indian-like sort of character [who writes] very well indeed."

Thoreau had tasted truly wild country—far wilder than Concord—during brief excursions to New Hampshire and looking for teaching jobs in southern Maine, where he met an old Indian who engrossed him with stories of the ways of the North Woods. As he was casting around for a purpose in his twenties, you sense that Thoreau's inherent unconventionality and his love of nature were reinforced by the praise of older intellectuals like Emerson and Hawthorne—*here's an Indian sort of character who can write very well indeed*—until he wholeheartedly embraced the role, his identity of nature-philosopher-wildman. He then began his pursuit of wilderness in earnest, first in the woods at Walden Pond and then in northern Maine.

Thoreau, for several years, had been talking about going off to live by himself—both to write a book about his and his late brother's week-long boating expedition on the Concord and Merrimack rivers that they'd taken back in 1839, and to come "face to face" with his own person. In the fall of 1844, Emerson purchased forty acres of woodlot on Walden Pond, to preserve it from being felled by loggers or as possible homesites for his extended family. Thoreau's friend Ellery Channing urged him to build a cabin at Walden and find the solitude and writing life he'd been talking about for so long. The following spring, 1845, at age twenty-seven, and still struggling to really start "living" his life, Thoreau borrowed an axe from Bronson Alcott, Louisa May's father and a fellow Concord Transcendentalist, or, depending on the story, from Emerson, walked the two miles out to Walden Pond, and began to chop down pine trees for his cabin.

On Independence Day that summer of 1845, he hauled his belongings out of his parents' Concord house, loaded them into a wheelbarrow, and carted them out to the cabin he had built on the shore of Walden Pond. Henry David Thoreau then settled in to write, read, observe nature, and tend his bean field.

At last his life would begin—deliberately, or so he hoped. He sought many things: the essence of wildness that he believed lies within us all, a life stripped down to its barest essentials, and something he called "Indian wisdom." It was this latter wisdom in particular that, a year after moving into his cabin at Walden, he set off to find on a monthlong excursion to the Maine Woods.

In many ways Thoreau hungered for the life young Charles Biencourt and Charles de La Tour lived in Acadia two hundred years before. A Scottish Presbyterian visiting Acadia in 1629 pungently captured the lifestyle of La Tour, who "live[s] in the country a savage kind of life traveling, trucking, and marrying with the savages."

Insofar as someone born in Europe could learn to think like a Micmac, La Tour and Biencourt embodied Thoreau's "Indian wisdom." When the French venture in Acadia collapsed, they stayed, taking up the life of the Micmac.

The colony at Port-Royal had struggled for support from France for several years, starting about 1610. Its original leader, de Monts, quit the whole enterprise after King Henri IV pulled de Monts's monopoly on the fur trade to give others a chance at it, too. In de Monts's absence, young Charles Biencourt's father, Poutrincourt, took over the venture. He sank deep into debt trying to keep supplies flowing from France. When an assassin killed King Henri, his widow, Marie de Médicis, complicated life for the Acadian colonists by demanding they bring along Jesuit priests to make devout Catholic converts among those known as the *sauvages*.

Upon the Jesuits' arrival, they and Poutrincourt butted heads, with the Jesuits demanding half the fur-trading profits and a managing hand in the business.

"I pray to you leave me to do my duty, which I know very well," Poutrincourt told off the arrogant Father Biard, as related by Lescarbot. "Show me the path to heaven—I will give you guidance on earth."

When Poutrincourt returned to France to hustle up more funding, his son Charles Biencourt, now turning twenty, temporarily took over the Acadian colony's leadership, and relations between Jesuits and colonists finally snapped. The Jesuits removed themselves to start a separate colony on Mount Desert Island (on today's Maine coast), taking much of Port-Royal's remaining supplies and tools. Lacking supplies, Charles Biencourt and his group of colonists took to the woods to live with the Micmac in their hunting camps that winter of 1612–13. Back in France, Marie de Médicis, hearing the Jesuits' version of the dispute at Port-Royal, threw Charles Biencourt's father into debtors' prison.

The death blow to the early French Acadian colony arrived in November 1613, when a Welsh privateer dropped anchor by moonlight off the fort—or "manor house"—at Port-Royal. The privateer, Samuel Argall, had been sent by the governor of the new British colony down at Jamestown in Virginia to wipe the French out of what Britain considered its New World holdings. Argall had first attacked the Jesuit outpost at Mount Desert Island and captured Father Biard, who now guided the enemy privateer—willingly or unwillingly is not clear—into the harbor at Port-Royal and to the fortified manor house, which stood on a promontory.

It was deserted. Charles Biencourt and his men were out hunting with the Micmac and working their crop fields in natural meadows two leagues off from the manor. The British raiders stripped the manor of everything of value, including its iron hinges and the pigs that roamed about, bashed into oblivion the fleur-de-lis the French had carved into a rock at the entrance, and burned it to the ground. Argall then sailed upriver to the meadows, hailed the French from his deck, and offered them a deal—one year's servitude helping to start Jamestown, followed by free passage back to France.

"Get thee behind me, Satan!" shouted back a Frenchman, according to one French version of the incident.

The British sailed off. When Poutrincourt, released from prison and leaving France early the following spring with a supply ship, arrived at his colony in Acadia, he was shocked to discover only rubble remaining. The colonists, with little else to eat but lichen and seaweed, had spent another winter living with the Micmac. Most of them boarded the ship and, with the shattered Pountrincourt, returned to France for good.

"Poutrincourt," writes the historian Faragher, "was a broken man. The project had cost him his reputation, his fortune, his marriage, and perhaps his mental balance."

Soon after his return, civil wars erupted again in France and the queen summoned Poutrincourt to retake a town near his former feudal holdings in Champagne. Leading a confused charge against a town that apparently had already surrendered, hoping to regain his lost glory, he took a cannon shot straight to the chest, dying on the spot at age fifty-eight.

His death left the two young men, Charles Biencourt, with Charles de La Tour as his right-hand man, in charge of whatever remained of the Acadian enterprise—now consisting of the two of them, the ruins of the manor house at Port-Royal, and a handful of Frenchmen.

They would receive almost no support from France for nearly two decades. Biencourt and La Tour abandoned Poutrincourt's dream of an agricultural settlement—a kind of Eden in the New World—and fashioned their own life in the woods. Using the dilapidated remains of Port-Royal as their base, they mostly lived and traveled with the Micmac, trapping and trading for furs, to supply European aristocrats' taste for beaver-skin hats and soft, luxurious coats of marten and otter. Each year a single ship delivered Biencourt and La Tour supplies from France—mainly wine, gunpowder, flour, and trade goods for the Indians—and sailed back across the Atlantic to the Old World laden with some 25,000 of the valuable pelts.

"With great toil," La Tour later wrote, they learned the region's Indian languages. They lived, he said, as "people of the country."

Unlike the Indians to the south, where the British had started to settle, the Micmac were nomadic hunters and fishers and did not clear land around villages to cultivate corn, beans, and squash. They moved frequently to follow seasonal migrations of game and fish. The young Frenchmen learned how to move constantly, too, honoring the nomadic life. They learned how to fashion *raquets*—snowshoes—of bent wood and animal-gut strings to navigate the deep forest snows of winter, and how to bend ribs of cedar and stitch together sheets of birch bark with root fibers to make a canoe, sealing the seams with fir pitch. The Micmac traveled in these strong, lightweight canoes with everything they possessed—"wives, children, dogs, kettles, hatchets, matachias, bows, arrows, quivers, skins, and the [skin] coverings of their houses," wrote Lescarbot.

The young French wore capes made of beaver or otter, leggings of moose or bearskin in winter, and shod their feet with moccasins of tough moose hide, which grips easily on ice and snow. When traveling, they learned to subsist on the rich Micmac food known as *cacamo*—or "moose butter"—marrow extracted from boiled moose bones. The

Micmac taught them, when they were tired and thirsty in the woods without water at hand, how they could suck the sap of the sugar maple for refreshment. They learned to paddle the streams and rivers through the forests, and how to portage their canoes on their backs over the low divides separating one drainage from the next, thus able to traverse broad swaths of forest by moving from river to river. They didn't think anything about traveling one hundred or two hundred miles alone through the woods like the Micmac, who, Lescarbot marveled, went these vast distances without "path or inn" such as you'd find in France. Instead, they carried only tinderbox, tobacco, a bow in their hand, and a quiver on their backs.

"And we in France," Lescarbot writes, "are much troubled when we have lost our way ever so little in some great forest."

Perhaps the "Indian wisdom" absorbed by Biencourt and La Tour even extended to the Micmac belief in the spirits of nature. All things in their world were made by a creator in which every creature, every object, had a spirit and the supreme spirit was Manitou. Medicine men communicated with these spirits and could foretell the future and heal the sick. The Europeans who came later—the Jesuit priests, the Puritans down in New England—would call it "devil worship." But Charles de La Tour was known to be tolerant of the Micmac beliefs, and perhaps even accepted them himself. Samuel de Champlain, then trying to establish his own colony on the St. Lawrence River, reported how his men came to believe, like the Indians, in giant cannibals who made "strange hissings."

And there was more to keep a young French male engaged in the Indian way of life. Young unmarried Micmac women were free to have sexual relations with men at their choosing, which included the young French, although they learned the hard way that forcing themselves on the Micmac women would result in death.

" . . . [V]igorous and tough," wrote a later French colonial administrator of this little culture of transplanted Frenchmen in the New World, "well built and firmly planted on their legs, accustomed to live on little, robust and vigorous, very self-willed and inclined to dissoluteness; but they are witty and vivacious . . . they imitate the Indians, whom, with reason, they hold in high regard . . . strive to hold their regard and please them."

So this small band of Frenchmen living isolated from Europe

learned the Micmac way—learned, as Thoreau would say, "Indian wisdom." What a profound difference in attitude toward the native peoples and the North American wilds when one compares these fur-hunting young Frenchmen in Acadia to the crop-raising British down in Jamestown and the Puritans at Plymouth. From the outset—that first winter of celebration in 1606–07 and l'Ordre de Bon Temps—the French forged a bond with the Micmac. Down in Jamestown and Plymouth, the soon-to-arrive British colonists, in contrast, kept themselves separate from the native populations. While the French in Acadia *embraced* the wilds of North America, the British framed their lot in the New World as an epic *struggle* against a wilderness of vast, biblical proportions, and one infested with deviltry. Both the wilderness and the satanic heathens who lived there had to be eradicated to bring forth the light of Christianity and civilization.

FROM THE MOMENT he set foot on Cape Cod in autumn of 1620, William Bradford, the leader of the religiously inspired "Pilgrims" aboard the *Mayflower* anchored offshore, cast the colony's fate in opposition to the American wilds:

"[W]hat could they see but a hideous and desolate wilderness, full of wild beasts and wild men . . ."

The early New England preacher and poet Michael Wigglesworth wrote of the same evil desolation:

> *[A] waste and howling wilderness,*
> *Where none inhabited*
> *But hellish fiends, and brutish men*
> *That Devils worshiped.*

To the Puritans it was a simple fact that Satan had long ago seized the New World wilderness and its Indian inhabitants for his own purposes, and it was their God-given role to counter him. While to the French Acadians, the Indian chiefs, or sagamores, like Membertou were held in high respect for their wisdom, generosity, and knowledge of the woods, to the New England Puritans the greater the sagamore, the greater his evil. The "chief Sagamores" of the Indians, wrote the preacher Cotton Mather, are "horrid Sorcerers, and hellish Conjurers and such as Conversed with Daemons."

By the time of Thoreau's birth, in 1817, that old Puritan New England fear of wilderness and its deviltry still resonated. The wilderness and its Indian inhabitants were still something to be eradicated, although both now lay far from his placid Concord, where the Indians long ago had been run off or killed and the forests mostly cultivated into farms. When Thoreau went to live on Walden Pond and then headed to the Maine Woods in search of "Indian wisdom," he attempted a radical leap from the New England past—away from two centuries of that old Puritan fear of the evil and desolate wilderness, and toward the embrace of it as once absorbed by young Charles Biencourt and Charles de La Tour and the other French who had lived with the Micmac in Acadia.

I WONDERED HOW OFTEN Charles Biencourt or Charles de La Tour encountered other humans while paddling the Upper St. John—Micmac or Maliseet Indians in birch-bark canoes, most likely, or perhaps their own French colleagues. We saw no one, until the fourth night. Again it had poured all day, causing the river to rise noticeably. During the day's paddling, it had broadened to one hundred yards, swishing fast between dark, forested banks—undulating walls of green. The forest looked impenetrable. I sensed why it might have repelled the Puritans, and why Biencourt and La Tour, taught by the Micmac, traveled by canoe along the open streams instead of through the tangled, dark woods.

In late afternoon, a grassy opening with a campsite appeared on the left bank, at a place known as Nine-Mile Bridge. Once serving an old logging road, the bridge itself was long gone, washed out in a decades-ago ice jam. Now only a cable stretched over the river with a pulley system to haul supplies across.

From our campsite, through a gap in the woods, we could see a cabin a few hundred yards off. On the map a spot was marked "Warden Camp." A shiny white pickup truck parked next to the cabin glowed eerily in the gloomy woods, like a bit of pearly shell on a black sand beach. We didn't approach it.

After dinner, we were sprawled on our bags, reading aloud to one another as dusk and steady rain fell outside, when there was a sudden, startling voice.

"I have two yellow Labs, but don't be afraid of them," it said, just outside the tent.

I pulled on my pants and rain jacket and climbed out.

A gray-bearded man stood there, the droplets streaming off his baseball cap and past his glasses. He looked like he'd been in the woods a long time. His khakis were soaked, and he had left his heavy flannel shirt unbuttoned, over a T-shirt. Red, angry splotches of blackfly welts banded his neck and wrists. He carried a large, insulated coffee mug, from which he sipped. It made me feel itchy just to look at him.

"I saw the children down here, and I didn't want them to be afraid of the dogs," he said.

"Are you the warden?" I asked.

"No, no," he replied. "The warden camp hasn't been here for years and years."

He said people called him "Nine-Mile Mike." A professor from up-state New York, where he was married and lived most of the year, Nine-Mile Mike had long ago bought the cabin as a vacation spot. He'd come up here for a few weeks to make repairs. Nine-Mile Mike was very eager to talk. In fact, it seemed as if he hadn't talked for days, and hungered for it.

"Do you know anything about the local history?" I asked.

The words came pouring out of Nine-Mile Mike, in the dusky rain, as I stood and nodded and dripped water from my hair and he dashed from subject to subject and the cascade of words rushed over me, and the children and Amy remained hunkered in the tent.

"Have you heard of Seven Islands?" he asked.

I knew it only as a group of islands on the map a short way down-stream. I knew Nine-Mile Bridge was so named because it lay nine miles above these Seven Islands.

Nothing there now, Mike said, it's all overgrown, but it was a booming logging camp in its day. It had a hotel, a school. There were farms along the river, too, to supply the camps. There was a camp here, too, at Nine-Mile. You can still see the old cellar holes out in the forest.

I'd seen them earlier, while searching for dry firewood—dank, mossy depressions in thick groves of fir, with an old corroded iron bedstead poking out from the moss, and ancient scatterings of rusted buckets and cans.

"Do you know who Helen Hamlin is?" he asked.

I didn't.

"She lived here in the thirties with her husband, who was a warden. She wrote a book called *Nine Mile Bridge*."

It struck me as odd that out here—in the middle of what I called a "blank spot"—some seventy years before had lived a woman who wrote a book about this very place where I expected to find a kind of historical nothingness. But, later, as I thought about it, I realized that it was my concept of "historical nothingness" that didn't really exist.

So much had happened here, along the St. John, over the centuries—to use one conventional marker of time—or over the millennia, or over the geologic ages since the Appalachian Mountains uplifted and eroded and Ice Age glaciers scraped and sculpted the rock and melted, and the St. John River took its current form. Through the great cycles of time and geology animals lived and died in forests along its banks, fish swam and spawned in its waters, and, starting perhaps 12,000 to 14,000 years ago, humans traveled along this river—on foot and in canoes. They loved and they warred, they married and they died, they hunted and they fished, they built alliances and they chose leaders, they danced and they feasted, they worshipped spirits and they healed the ill, they told stories and they had dreams, they cradled children in their arms and sang them to sleep.

It *existed*, all of this, along the St. John. Our notion of "blankness" reflects whether an unbroken chain of *people* has passed down the events—either in stories told or accounts written. Big gaps yawned. In my own mind, these wild, uppermost reaches of the St. John had largely remained a "blank spot" from the early 1600s, when Marc Lescarbot recorded stories of the first Acadians, until today. Rather, it remained a blank spot to me until Nine-Mile Mike, dripping wet and blackfly-bitten, popped out of the rainy woods that fourth evening and told me about Helen Hamlin.

HELEN HAMLIN'S BOOK, *Nine Mile Bridge: Three Years in the Maine Woods,* had, in fact, been a bestseller in its day.

Helen Leidy was the eldest of six children growing up in the 1920s and 1930s in Fort Kent, Maine, a bilingual town along the middle reaches of the St. John River, where it forms the Canadian border. With both English and French at her command, she attended teacher's college in nearby Madawaska. The principal at the school told her riveting stories about his adventures in the Upper St. John area hunting and fishing, and about the life in the lumber camps. Leidy was not entirely new to the woods—her grandfather and uncle were game wardens, and she had spent her summers canoeing Maine's rivers and lakes. Upon graduating from Madawaska, she jumped at the chance to take a teacher's post at a remote lumber camp at Churchill Lake. Surrounded by French-Canadian lumberjacks and teaching children in the small log school, she met a young game warden named "Curly" Hamlin—"a tall, broad-shouldered woodsman, with a square jaw and clear blue eyes." They soon married, and, after the winter of 1938–39 together in a warden's camp on Umsaskis Lake, they transferred to the "Warden's Camp"—as it was marked on my map—at Nine-Mile Bridge.

They spent two years here in the isolation of Nine-Mile Bridge on the Upper St. John, where Helen learned to drive a dog team, hunt for deer, snowshoe, and live snowbound for months, eagerly awaiting winter to lift and the river to thaw.

On April 27, Helen and Curly were sitting lazily on the front porch of their cabin as the snow dripped from the roof in the warm spring sun when they heard a sound like a distant but large motor that brought them to their feet. In her book, she describes the scene as it unfolded.

"It's the river!" she shouted to Curly.

Curly started for the bridge. "The ice is going out!"

I raced after him . . . soon the faint roar became thunderous and angry. A ten-foot wall of tumbling, crackling, fast-moving ice rolled around the upper bend of the river, sweeping everything before it, gathering momentum and throwing two-ton ice floes on the high banks. It uprooted trees and crumbled the fettered ice sheet in its path. The dammed water behind pushed relentlessly, increasing in force and power and coming closer and closer . . . We stepped off the bridge just as the ice struck. The iron girders quivered and the ground around us was shaken. From the knoll I stopped to look back, thinking it had surely carried away the bridge. But with a muffled rumbling it ground its way slowly between the piers . . . had it gone out, so would the camp.

Hamlin captured the old way of logging just as it was ending, with the big lumber camps, the French Canadians with their axes, the horse-drawn sleds hauling the logs over the frozen roads, and the spring river drives to send the logs downstream to the mills. With the end of the river drives, motor-powered logging arrived, and logging roads and large trucks began to crisscross the Maine Woods.

Hamlin left the woods with the birth of their daughter and Curly's illness, and wrote *Nine Mile Bridge,* which fascinated readers with the exploits of a woman in the wilderness. After the book spent several weeks on the *New York Times* bestseller list in 1945, Helen used the proceeds from its publisher, W. W. Norton, to help buy an outfitter's camp on a Maine lake, soon divorced Curly, and married a young grad-uate student in ichthyology who worked for a summer at a timber com-pany in the Maine Woods. Curly died two years later at age forty. Thus began a second life for Helen Hamlin—and three more children—far from the Nine-Mile Bridge as she accompanied her husband, Robert Lennon, in his work as a fisheries researcher in various posts through-out the United States and the world, as if she were making up for the isolation of her early life.

When Lennon worked in the Midwest, she returned to school, now at the University of Wisconsin, to reaccredit herself as a teacher of French. She taught on and off throughout the rest of her life, at both high school and college level. When Lennon's job took them to West Africa for six years on a UN mission to prevent river blindness, Helen worked as a French translator for the State Department. Through the years, she also developed a love of painting, and took commissions to paint portraits. While she took her children on regular visits to north-ern Maine to make sure they understood their heritage, Helen and Robert Lennon finally retired to Minnesota.

Now the Nine-Mile Bridge, where she had once lived, was no more—not even pilings in the river. The ice had taken it all away. Helen had died in Minnesota in 2004. In the course of two years, she had managed to preserve an entire bookful of stories that happened right here—in this spot in northern Maine I called "blank." How many thousands of other stories had occurred here that I would never know?

HENRY DAVID THOREAU ILLUMINATED another corner of this blank spot. If Thoreau hadn't tried to climb Mount Katahdin, Maine's highest peak, in 1846 and described his attempt in intimate psychic detail, we might think of wilderness in an entirely different way today. Our idea of "wilderness" might include people, for it was on that climb up Mount Katahdin that Thoreau tossed out humans from his vision of "wild."

He temporarily closed up his cabin at Walden Pond in the last days of August 1846, having lived there just over a year, tending to his bean field and filling his journals with nature observations. A combination of factors probably beckoned him to the north. During this first part of his two-year stint at Walden, he'd immersed himself ever deeper in the notion of "wild." The woodlots and farmers' fields around Concord might have been wearing a little thin in their tameness, despite his ardent proclamations of love for them. Northern Maine represented a very large chunk of wilderness, not far away. Conveniently, Thoreau had a relative who lived in Bangor, then the hub of Maine's lumber mills. This unnamed relative was making a trip up to northern Maine, scouting lands for lumbering, and invited Thoreau along.

Leaving Walden, Thoreau traveled by steamship up the New England coast and Penobscot River to Bangor. Met by his relative, the two rode by buggy up the Penobscot riverbank until Mattawamkeag, where they stayed at a public house and where two other acquaintances from Bangor joined the Thoreau party. Here the buggy road ended. Jumping a settler's fence, the foursome tramped along a dim footpath that led upriver. In thirty miles, they passed only a half dozen cabins.

"Marm Howard's," which the outfitter Galen Hale had mentioned to me as the place Thoreau stayed, was a public house near the confluence of the Penobscot's East and West Branches—what the Indians called Nicatou and today is Medway. Here Thoreau detected the beginnings of a village. He imagined that in a thousand years some poet would come here and write his version of the eighteenth-century English poet Thomas Gray's "Elegy Written in a Country Churchyard," proclaiming all the unsung local heroes who had lived and died in this spot. But here at Nicatou, the seed of what would become Galen and Betsy Hale's hometown, the unsung heroes were "yet unborn."

A short way past Nicatou, the party stopped at the farm homestead of "Uncle George" McCauslin—a veteran logger and boatman on the Penobscot. Living off Uncle George's generous hospitality and farm-raised hams, eggs, and butter for two days, the foursome finally gave up waiting for the Abenaki Indian guides who were supposed to meet them here. Thoreau's party then persuaded Uncle George—"a man of dry wit and shrewdness"—to carry them in his *batteau* up the West Branch to Mount Katahdin, which Thoreau aimed to climb. For their second boatman they engaged Young Tom Fowler—son of the oldest settler in these parts, Old Thomas Fowler—while he sawed the window openings in his cabin.

Using twelve-foot-long spruce poles tipped with iron with which they pushed against the river's bottom, Young Tom in the bow and Uncle George in the stern poled the *batteau*—a kind of large, flat-bottomed canoe—so deftly into the current that they "shot up the rapids like a salmon." The party of six soon reached the last human habitation along the river—a crude logging camp with a simple cabin. Beds of cedar boughs lay under its low eaves, and its cook fed them pancakes and tea. The crew was out in the forest cutting the giant white pines that were the choice timber trees of northern New England; in places, they had once been marked with the king's sign to reserve as tall, straight masts for the British Royal Navy. After their repast, the Thoreau party pushed upriver and into a lake just as a nearly full moon rose. Crossing the lake four miles by moonlight, they took turns at the paddles while singing the Canadian voyageurs' boat songs:

> *Row, brothers, row, the stream runs fast,*
> *The Rapids are near and the daylight's past!*

They paused paddling at moments to listen for the howling of wolves. In his prose Thoreau's joyful exuberance at being truly in the wilds is palpable. He seems eager to *embrace* the wilds, to wrap his arms around this green forested world he had entered, to, as he would say, "suck the essence out of it." Concord's gentle woodlots and meadows and ponds were a tame paramour by comparison to the passions promised by *this.*

The party slept restlessly on the shore of a lake under their propped-up *batteau*—sparks from their overenthusiastic bonfire having torched their cotton tent—and the next day worked their way farther upstream and through more lakes. Bald eagles and fish hawks screamed. Though loggers had culled out the white pines from the forested lakeshore, notes Thoreau, the traveler couldn't detect the difference. From one lake, they caught a good view of several lesser peaks and the great, mesalike mass of Katahdin itself, standing above the surrounding landscape.

"The summit," Thoreau enthused, "had a singularly flat tableland appearance, like a short highway, where a demigod might be let down to take a turn or two in an afternoon, to settle his dinner."

Katahdin is a great knob of granite. Over the last 350 million years, geologists believe, streams and rivers eroded away a layer of softer surrounding rock that was thousands of feet thick. This left Katahdin projecting above all else, its summit one mile above sea level. The more recent sculpting of Katahdin started about 1 million years ago, when the great glacial sheets of the Ice Age flowed over its crest, carving its ridges and cirques, and finally melting away to leave the shape that Thoreau described, which, viewed from the west as he saw it, looks flat on top.

That day the party made fifteen miles before camping at the mouth of Murch Brook and the Aboljacknagesic, both streams which drained off Mount Katahdin into the Penobscot's West Branch. The foot of the mountain lay several miles away through dense forest. That evening, using birch poles and pork-baited hooks, they caught a mess of trout for supper from the creeks, tossing the wriggling, rainbow-colored fish up onto shore. Thoreau stood over them in starry-eyed wonder "that these jewels should have swum away in that Aboljacknagesic water for so long, so many dark ages; —these bright fluviatile flowers, seen of Indians only, made beautiful, the Lord only knows why, to swim there!"

The rainbow fish reminded him of Proteus, the shape-shifting, future-telling Greek god who rules over certain beautiful sea creatures. History, writes Thoreau—and by history he appears to be referring to "actual" facts and events, like the fish wriggling at his feet—"put to a terrestrial use, is mere history; but put to a celestial use is mythology always."

Call it an act of genius, or, as Henry James, Sr. (father of the novelist and the philosopher), did after meeting Thoreau, an act emanating from a personality that was "literally the most childlike, unconscious and unblushing egotist it has ever been my fortune to encounter in the ranks of mankind." Here's Henry David come along to take history— those wriggling rainbow fish at his feet—and make *mythology* out of it. Here's Henry David come along to take the historical fact of *himself* and make mythology out of it. He aims to climb to the high, wild summit of Mount Katahdin, and there—almost as an equal, his tone implies, or at least an honored guest—consort with the gods themselves. On that high, wild summit would climax, like on some great altar, his passionate embrace of Nature.

Mount Katahdin lay about sixty miles south of us. Thoreau had never made it as far north—as deep into the wilds—as the St. John. As we packed up that morning at Nine-Mile Bridge after the previous evening's rainy encounter with Nine-Mile Mike, the heavy gray sky finally dissolved into fleecy clouds and patches of blue. It was the first we'd seen of the sun in five days on the St. John. It blinded us. We paddled down through quick water and bouncy little rapids in a perfect combination of cool breeze and warm patches of sun. We drifted along talking, then broke into canoe races. Molly and Skyler loved to steer the canoe bows so they would plow through the biggest waves they could find in these minor rapids. Drifting along midstream, we nibbled a lunch of goat cheese and smoked oysters on crackers. I'd gotten over my high pique from the previous day's river lunch when I'd left a whole unopened salami—our only one—on a cooler lid while waiting to slice it. Skyler, amusing himself by making one of his pirate boardings, leaped from one canoe to the next. The canoe rocked, my precious salami rolled from the lid, dropped into the river, and sank from sight with me groping madly after it. My curses echoed from shore to shore.

Now Molly and Skyler decided they loved smoked oysters. I thought of the first French people in Acadia and how they picked shellfish off the mudflats at Port-Royal.

The river braided at Seven Islands downstream from Nine-Mile Bridge. The forest briefly opened here to the sky, leaving the islands beautiful and serene and airy. We paddled past grassy banks and wove through narrow channels. Birdsong drifted from the meadowy shores. I heard the throaty melodious trill of a redwing blackbird, reminding me of my Wisconsin childhood and the little pothole swamps I loved to explore in the woods. More geese and their goslings paddled busily along shore, and ducks—mergansers, we thought—swam in the river. An occasional seagull swooped in the distance. Seven Islands projected a sense of fertility and peace.

What it didn't give any sense of was human habitation, yet Seven Islands, a century ago, had been the center of logging on the St. John. We could see nothing left of the bunkhouses and hotel, or the skid roads where horse teams and sleds pulled the logs from the frozen forest to the river, waiting for the thunderous ice breakup of spring to carry the logs downstream.

We made twenty-five river miles by day's end—by far our best mileage. The broadening river and the surge of rainwater sloshing down it had swept us along, over the rocky sections, through sunshine and bunching afternoon clouds, through an iridescent, sunlit cloudburst, and into blue sky again. Two helicopters flew in formation in the distance and disappeared. Homeland Security on the Canadian border? I wondered. We heard a distant motor briefly—probably a logging operation back from the river. We spun our canoes around in eddies, sang. At last, the rains seemed to have moved on. But by the time we camped in late afternoon, on a high bank in a dark patch of forest at Basford Rips, the many days of drenching rain followed by the sun's warmth had hatched ferocious swarms of insects. Molly's eyes were nearly swollen shut from countless blackfly bites. Swollen red mosquito welts pocked all over Skyler's tender skin. Powerful mosquito lotion gave only a slight lull in the attacks. Even the headnets the children wore around camp didn't entirely stop them until the bugs retreated at darkness and we had a pleasant evening sitting on the ground before the sparking campfire under the stars.

I understood why the Indians moved to the breezier coastline for their summer camps, and why Thoreau wrote that during the summer months, the Maine Woods, or so he must have been told, were nearly uninhabitable due to insects. He visited in the fall.

Waking the next morning, Molly sat bolt upright and studied the outside of the tent door's netting for danger signs.

"There are *tons* of mosquitoes on the door!" she exclaimed to her younger brother. "You better hide in your sleeping bag when we open it."

Amy was rubbing my lower back, sore from paddling and hauling gear and shoving canoes over rocks. Suddenly she started laughing.

"What's so funny?" I asked.

"What we got ourselves into."

Molly picked up the map, studying it as she did every morning to mark our progress. We'd paddled nearly two thirds of the way from Baker Lake to the tiny dot that marked the village of Allagash, sitting where the Allagash River joins the St. John.

"Is there a five-star hotel in Allagash?" she asked, peering at it intently. "Do you think it will have room service?"

I laughed.

"I don't think so."

In 1627, Charles de La Tour sent a desperate plea for help to King Louis XIII of France. For nearly twenty years, he and his band had wandered in the wilderness of Acadia, developing the fur trade and using the St. John River as one of its main arteries. Little written history remains from this period. Lescarbot, the Parisian lawyer who had documented the early doings of Acadia, had returned to France, and, after the English torched the manor at Port-Royal in 1613, the handful of remaining French lived mostly with the Micmac.

De La Tour had become the de facto head of French Acadia in 1623 after Charles Biencourt, then in his early thirties, died. (The cause of his death is not clear.) There is no record of whether Biencourt had married, but La Tour had taken a Micmac wife, with whom he had several daughters; his men likewise intermarried with the Micmac and lived easily among them. La Tour's band faced a constant battle, however, to stave off European poachers—the British, the Dutch—and rival French outfits on the St. Lawrence, or "Great River," who would pull into the hundreds of remote, hidden coves of the Acadian coastline and trade with the Indians for furs.

Acadia was a "beautiful and good country," he wrote to King Louis XIII and Cardinal Richelieu, but one that France was in danger of losing. "In the four years since [Biencourt's] death I have had no help or relief from anyone. On the contrary, I have been, and am now pursued to death by the French who come from the Great River . . ." What was worse, he'd learned from his intelligence sources that the British would soon push north from their New England outposts and seize New France, this after hostilities in Europe had recently erupted between the two countries over the ongoing Protestant-Catholic divide.

He was prepared to defend New France from the English, La Tour wrote, having at his disposal his "little band of resolute Frenchmen," as well as one hundred Micmac families whom he had trained with firearms, plus the three small ships he possessed. He also could, if necessary, muster a potent guerrilla force of Indians—"a large number of people who do not like [the British] and can take them by surprise." But better than taking to the woods and harassing the British with guerrilla attacks would be for His Majesty to send adequate supplies and men to Acadia so La Tour could deal with the British in "another way."

La Tour also wrote to his father, Claude, for help, and asked him to deliver the letters to the king and Cardinal Richelieu. The senior La Tour had returned from Acadia to France years earlier, after accompanying Poutrincourt—and both their sons—on the original expeditions of the Order of Good Times. Known for his irresistibly charming manners, thirst for adventure, and dire financial straits, Claude had risen from modest beginnings as one of seven children of a master mason, and charmed his way into marriage to a landed noblewoman. Her estates near Saint-Just had conferred on him the aristocratic title "de La Tour" and she had given birth to their son, Charles, before dying at a young age.

As Charles dispatched his plea for help from the Acadian wilds, the senior La Tour was enjoying a brief stay in the ancient confines of St. Eloi prison for his unpaid debts, having already sold off most of his late wife's properties to fund various grand schemes, including the Acadian colonization. Sprung from prison by a friend in close contact with Cardinal Richelieu, Claude de La Tour heeded his son's plea and helped muster a flotilla that launched from France the next spring to rescue his son and New France. Unfortunately for Claude de La Tour, however, Britain and France were back in a state of war. Lying in wait for the flotilla was an ambitious Scottish poet by the name of Sir William Alexander who sought a convenient means to fund *his* attempts to settle what the French called Acadia.

Alexander had served as one of the favorite tutors to the young, poetry-loving James VI, king of Scotland, who became James I, king of England, after Queen Elizabeth died in 1603. At that time, England's Puritans were clamoring for changes in the Church of England. While King James ignored most of them, he did grant one demand— appointing a group of scholars, among them his ex-tutor William Alexander, to translate a new version of the Bible. This, of course, is what's known as the "King James Version," first published in 1611.

A new Bible translation didn't placate the radical Puritan Separatists, and they fled England, eventually—as we well know—wading ashore at Plymouth in 1620. Back in Britain, King James, generous to a fault, wanted to recompense the poet Alexander for his loyalties and labor. So he awarded him exclusive trading rights to a huge, and very controversial, chunk of the New World—everything between New England and Newfoundland, which he called "Nova Scotia," or New Scotland. Of course, this same swath had also been long claimed by the French, who called it Acadia.

It turned out that Sir William, like the French, couldn't come up with enough money to actually colonize his enormous grant called Nova Scotia. So, as the Acadia historian John Mack Faragher aptly explained, this Scottish poet and Bible translator reverted to "more tried and true methods of accumulation—plunder and conquest."

Alexander got wind of the large French flotilla heading to the New World to succor Charles de La Tour in Acadia and resupply Champlain's fledgling French outpost at Quebec. He hired the three notorious Kirke brothers, privateers, whose preferred tools of the trade ran to heavily manned frigates bristling with cannons. Lying in wait off the Acadian coast, the Kirke brothers managed to ensnare the entire French flotilla, including Claude de La Tour.

It also happened that the never-saw-an-opportunity-he-didn't-like Claude de La Tour was quietly a French Huguenot—a Protestant, like the British. Taken as captive back to London, the senior La Tour very quickly charmed his way into the Royal Court, married an English noblewoman—a maid of honor to the queen of England, this after having been married to a French noblewoman—renounced his loyalty to the king of France, and swore allegiance to the king of Britain. A year after his capture during his would-be rescue mission for son Charles, Claude de La Tour sailed triumphantly back to Acadia as a newly knighted baronet of Nova Scotia, sworn vassal of Britain, and part of a Scottish colonization expedition headed by the son of the poet and Bible translator Sir William Alexander.

They landed at the site of Port-Royal. They found it abandoned. Charles de La Tour and his roving band of French had left some years earlier, and established a fort at the very lower tip of the Acadian Peninsula in the vicinity of Cape Sable.

The Scottish settlers disembarked and started a small colony at the ruins of old Port-Royal. Claude de La Tour then sailed with two Scottish ships to the stronghold at Cape Sable to have a face-to-face meeting with his son.

It must have come as quite a surprise to Charles. Or perhaps he knew his cagey, charming father all too well. Three years had passed since Charles had written to his father and the king of France with pleas for help in the Acadian venture. Now, instead of French ships offering help, two Scottish ships suddenly anchored in the cove near his Cape Sable fort. From one of them his father, Claude, was rowed ashore while Claude's highborn English bride waited aboard ship.

Meeting face-to-face with Charles on shore, father offered son a deal. He could have help, and plenty of it. He could have settlers. He could have a royal title and a barony (father would have one, too) that took in much of the southern Acadian Peninsula. To receive all this the son had only to switch sides and pledge loyalty to Britain instead of France.

The son, very politely, the accounts say, declined. He thanked the king of Britain for the high honor he had shown him. But his allegiance remained to the king of France.

"This answer," writes Nicolas Denys, who personally knew both father and son La Tour, "obliged his father and all the commanders of the vessels to use the very finest language on earth to persuade him. But it was in vain, for he remained firm in his resolution, and boldly told his father that neither he nor his wife should ever enter the fort."

Claude returned to his ship in the cove and his British bride and the British commanders. The next day he sent a letter ashore, telling Charles that if he wasn't going to switch sides by good words of persuasion, Claude would make him switch by force.

Charles sent the messenger back to the ships with his verbal reply to this threat.

"[T]he commanders and his father could act as they thought best," writes Denys. "He and his garrison were entirely ready to receive them."

The two ships landed an attacking force. During a two-day battle, Charles and his garrison staved them off, killing and wounding several, until the British sailors who had been recruited to attack the fort simply gave up the fight, having been promised by Claude that Charles would flip loyalties easily—without all this fighting—once offered a barony. The British withdrawal put the senior La Tour and his bride in desperate straits. If he returned to Britain, he feared he'd be beheaded, and fare not much better in his native France. Homeless, he and his wife retreated to the struggling new British colony at Port Royal. It was not an easy life. Scurvy had wiped out thirty of seventy during the first winter, and the Micmac, their loyalties with Charles and the French, refused to help.

Soon after Charles repelled his father's and the British attack, two French supply ships finally arrived heavily loaded with building materials and workmen to help Charles de La Tour. After France had neglected Acadia for nearly two decades, the ships bore a letter from the Company of New France promising Charles, for reasons that would become clear in letters to follow, all the support he needed to start a colony at any place of his choosing.

Of all possible places, he choose the mouth of the St. John River. By now Charles had traveled by birch-bark canoe into the wilderness of Acadia long enough to know that the St. John and its tributaries—the Upper St. John, the Northwest Branch, the Allagash—were by far the richest source of furs in this entire region of eastern Canada, except for the vast St. Lawrence itself, where Champlain had his own outpost and fur territory. As the small fort on the St. John—Fort Sainte-Marie, he named it—was being built in the spring of 1631, another ship sailed across the Atlantic bearing more good news for Charles, after his years of isolation in the wilderness. This came in the form of a letter from none other than Louis, the king of France, and Cardinal Richelieu. It anointed Charles de La Tour as lieutenant-general for Acadia due, as Louis himself wrote in the commission, to his "good sense, discretion, fidelity, experience and great industry."

The French court had suddenly started to pay attention to Acadia, in great part due to its concerns that the British colonies to the south were developing so quickly since the *Mayflower* landing in 1620. Their remarkable growth was powered by the many new arrivals coming from England, their own well-organized governments, and their densely clustered agricultural settlements, unlike the fur-trading livelihood of the French, which sprawled over vast expanses of wilderness. Cardinal Richelieu, thinking strategically, believed that a strong French Acadia would serve as a kind of blockade to stop any further spread of the British to the north.

La Tour ecstatically accepted the commission with a bold, flourishing signature and pledge of loyalty to the king of France. He was now, in essence, the official ruler of all Acadia. Britain—at least for a while—gave up its formal claims on Acadia after the two countries made a peace pact in their religious wars back in Europe. Sir William Alexander, his failed colony now booted from the New World, died in poverty. La Tour soon forgave his father—for the most part. Charles invited his father to live at Cape Sable, although he still refused to admit Claude inside the fort. Instead, he built a nice house near the fort for his father and his father's noblewoman wife, who had remained at Claude's side through his multiple changes of loyalty. There the couple took to a life of ease, tended to by four French servants, thoughtfully provided by Charles before he went off to his new fortress on the St. John.

"They were very amply provided," Denys remarked after dining with Claude and his wife, who delighted in having a visitor to dinner.

For Charles, however, the real fight for Acadia had only begun. It would be a battle against the most unexpected kind of rival—not against the wilderness, nor against the Indians, nor against the British. Rather, his bitterest enemy would be a fellow Frenchman.

As WE PACKED UP on the sixth morning on the St. John—hauling coolers and dry bags on another sunny day down the steep, rocky bank to the canoes—I hoped Skyler's swimming skills would be enough for the rapids ahead. The river map placed Big Black Rapids only a few bends downstream from our camp, rating it a Class III—substantial waves and rocks, strong currents, and requiring deft maneuvering. I hoped Skyler had the strength, and our canoe the maneuverability, to make quick turns. If we broadsided a rock and tipped, I would probably be wrestling the canoe to shore and he'd have to swim by himself through the rapids to a quiet eddy. He had a strong dog paddle, and, in calm water, could perform a freestyle stroke, but, at age eight, weighed only sixty pounds.

One of the most profound qualities of the wilderness—to me, at least—is that it constantly forces you to assess your strengths and your weaknesses. What are the dangers? What are the risks? What are the chances? These decisions greet you at every bend. The Pilgrims, the Puritans, and the New Englanders detested this calculation. They wanted certainty, predictability, they wanted to exert *control* over the forces of nature. They framed their world in absolute terms—there was God's way, and there was Satan's way. You chose one or the other. They strove to abolish gray areas. The forest, in effect, represented a giant gray area, a realm of uncertainty and unpredictability. It had to be eradicated, the evil rooted out. They busily cleared the forests and planted their farms, settled into the predictability of the seasons, the rain and sun, the warmth and cold, the sprouting and harvesting of the crops.

In sharp contrast, the French in Acadia, by adopting Micmac ways, also learned to adapt to this constant calculation of risk in the wilds. The predictability lay in its very unpredictability. Were there animals to contend with? Were there rapids? Was the river high or low? They moved through an uncontrolled landscape, improvising as they went. Along with the techniques of crafting snowshoes and birch-bark canoes, they also adopted Indian legends associated with the forest and the wilds. Like the Indians, the French learned to imagine the forces of nature in animal or spirit form. They learned to accommodate this spirit world of nature, to live with it. Unlike the New Englanders, they learned to thrive on ambiguity.

It was that sort of ambiguity I had to contend with as we approached Big Black Rapids with eight-year-old Skyler in the bow. The current picked up. We heard the rushing of tumbling water ahead and detected the river's downhill slant, the trees lining the bank a few hundred yards ahead appearing a good deal lower down than the trees on the bank nearby. Paddling to the left bank, we swung our bows upstream and nosed them into the woody shore to scout. Clambering out, we traced a faint path into dense groves of fir and spruce until the path faded. We climbed over fallen logs, through sun-dappled carpets of fern and moss, blooming patches of a five-petaled trillium-like flower that I couldn't identify. It was quite beautiful, and, right here, in this mossy, ferny, flowering patch, I could see how the very earliest French and then Jamestown colonists had been tempted to write home to Europe, at the height of the springtime bloom, about the giant Eden they had discovered in the form of the New World. Of course, when winter arrived, they would suffer greatly from famine and scurvy. Eden vanished.

We climbed out on a large log cantilevered over the river to get a good view of the rapids. They looked manageable, if we stuck to the right side of the river and maneuvered between a few big, foaming boulders. I mentally marked some low cliffs on the opposite bank to know where to begin our moves between the boulders, and explained to Amy, who would be following, what to look for.

"Okay, does everyone know what to do if one of us tips over?" I asked.

We rehearsed the safety drill. Molly and Skyler had rafted on Montana whitewater rivers and knew the basic techniques of swimming in rapids in the event of a flip. The difference was that our open canoes, heavily loaded with gear, couldn't absorb nearly the size waves that a buoyant rubber raft could. And we were a long, long way from any help here. We were totally on our own.

Our route chosen, we hiked back through the forest to the canoes. Skyler and Molly took turns leading the way, searching excitedly for faint traces of path. I showed them how to retrace our footsteps, pointing out the crushed leaves of a plant. We lived in a small city—a very controlled environment—and although it *was* in Montana and we had mountains rising up at the end of our street, it wasn't quite the same as a log cabin in the woods, where I'd grown up, or the wild Acadia of the young Charles Biencourt and Charles de La Tour.

I wondered how the Micmac fathers and mothers, the grandparents and elders, taught their children about the forest, showing them how it is a place of sustenance and familiarity. We associate darkness with lack of learning—as in the Dark Ages—and knowledge with light, as in the Enlightenment. The New England woods were "dark" and "gloomy" to the Puritans in part because they knew so little about the forest.

Henry Thoreau possessed a vast body of knowledge about the natural world. Like the Indians, he could identify many of the plants and trees and animals of this and other forests. But Thoreau, for all his time spent strolling through the woods and fields of Concord, for all his time studying botany, entered the Maine Woods largely ignorant of the profound unpredictability of the wilds. The "Nature" he and Emerson knew had been settled by the Puritan farmers two hundred years before—since September 12, 1635, to be exact, as I'd read on a marker on the Concord village green. On that day Major Simon Willard bought "6 myles of land square" from the Indians in a deal transacted under an ancient oak known as "Jethro's Tree" for the future site of Concord "plantation."

For two centuries that "plantation" land had been worked by the Bible-toting New England farmers, its animal spirits eradicated, its "evil" exterminated, the Devil and his heathen minions banished. Sculpted into a gentle landscape of woodlots, fields, and streams, it had been cleared of its ambiguity and unpredictability. When Thoreau headed north to Maine in search of "Indian wisdom," he sought what Concord lacked—the untrammeled wilds, with all its ambiguity and unpredictability still intact. But nature's pure, passionate embrace in the Maine Woods ended up being too much even for Henry Thoreau.

After leaving his cabin at Walden Pond, taking the steamer up to Bangor, traveling by buggy north along the Penobscot River until the road ended, and hiking to Uncle George's homestead in the woods, Thoreau and his party rode in the *batteau* poled up the Penobscot's West Branch by Uncle George and Young Tom Fowler. Nearing the flanks of Mount Katahdin, they camped where Aboljacknagesic Brook flowed into the West Branch. That evening, Thoreau marveled at the metaphorical mess of rainbow-colored trout they had hooked from the brook and, reminded of the shape-shifting god Proteus, thought how facts, by putting them to "celestial" instead of "terrestrial" use, can be forged into mythology. That high, anvil-flat summit of Mount Katahdin hovering a few miles off was exactly where Thoreau planned to do the forging of fact into myth.

On the morning of September 7, 1846, roughly a week since leaving Walden, Thoreau and his party departed their camp at the Aboljacknagesic and West Branch and struck out through the forest toward Katahdin. Neither of their guides, Uncle George nor Young Tom, had traveled beyond this point before. For them it was a blank spot, too. Though well known to the Penobscot Indians, Katahdin's first recorded climb had occurred only forty years earlier, in 1804, by Charles Turner, Jr. Few whites had climbed it since, partly due to its remoteness and partly to the fact that mountaineering was still in its infancy as a sport, not really existing in America, but being pioneered in Switzerland and France as the Romantic era brought emotional cachet to hands-on encounters with the fearsome Alps. Its great mass standing alone in this great expanse of wilds—its Penobscot name meant "the greatest mountain"—Katahdin, on this Maine sojourn, was a natural destination for Henry David Thoreau.

After following one of the streams away from their camp on the riverbank, the party cut through dense spruce and fir stands by compass bearing, occasionally tracing faint paths made by browsing moose. They paused to eat wild blueberries on ground that ascended gently to the mountain's base, then sloped up more steeply. At 4 o'clock, partway up the mountain's flank and still in forest, they chose a campsite along a brook rushing down from the summit. While the others set up camp, Thoreau took an exploratory jaunt higher up the mountainside, eventually finding himself climbing along a torrent at an angle of forty-five degrees, grasping roots and branches to pull himself up a "giant's stairway" of great slabs of rock, and finally crawling on all fours over a dense, springy mat of black spruce trees that had been dwarfed by cold. He climbed until he reached a cloud layer that he couldn't see beyond. Then he turned back to camp, planning to make his final ascent in the morning.

THE MAINE WOODS was presenting us with our own challenges in the shape of the Big Black Rapids of the St. John River. After scouting from the big log, we climbed into the canoes, secured any loose ropes so they wouldn't tangle us in the event of a capsize, tightened our life jackets, and pushed off. Skyler and I paddled out into the river until we were lined up near the right bank, Amy and Molly maneuvering their canoe behind us.

"Okay? Are you ready?" I called out.

"Okay," he said.

We dug in our blades and paddled forward, downstream. The sky shone a deep blue that darkened the water to an almost black-blue between the high, forested banks. Boulders scattered across the river foamed bright white, like bleached bones hissing on the dark water. We could see the whole river dropping visibly downward and swinging to the right around a bend, in a rambunctious slide of water that roared all around us, as the canoe suddenly accelerated and tilted forward over the smooth bulge of the first drop.

"Draw left!" I called out.

Skyler pulled hard on his paddle and we swiveled left, threading between two boulders and the surging wakes of foam cascading off them.

"Now right!"

He swung his paddle across the bow and drew on the right while I paddled and steered us between another set of foaming boulders. Waves slapped at the sides of the canoe, jolting us sideways. Spray broke over the bow, soaking Skyler. I could feel the breeze caused simply by our forward motion down the quickening river.

"Now straight ahead!" I called out.

We slid downward toward a set of large waves near the bottom of the rapids. The canoe was swinging toward the right. I straightened it out as much as I could.

Wham! we hit the first wave. The canoe lurched, the wave breaking over the left side, water pouring over the gunnel. The upsurge held us in place, the craft trembling with the pressure of the current.

"Paddle!" I called out.

We both dug in hard, and the canoe popped out forward, straightened out, sliced through the next wave. We'd passed through the roughest stretch.

We paddled into a quiet eddy along the right shore, water sloshing in the canoe's bottom among our bags, and turned upstream to watch Amy and Molly. The wave twisted their canoe the same way, dumping in water over the sides, but they managed to pop out, too, and paddle to the calm riverbank beside us. Canoe bottoms sloshing with water, we cheered and all high-fived one another.

THE THOREAU PARTY'S ATTEMPT on Katahdin was not quite so harmonious. That night they camped on the mountain's flanks, a strong wind roared through the trees and blew about the sparks of their campfire. In the morning, the party breakfasted on raw pork and hard bread and headed upward, on a slightly different route than Thoreau had chosen the evening before. Now, in the morning, the enthusiastic Thoreau soon had charged upward far ahead of the other five. You sense their reluctance—these practical-minded boatmen and business-men who had no Transcendentalist or Romantic agendas—to take part in Thoreau's maniacal mountain-climbing scheme. He clambered upward for a mile or so over massive boulders toward the summit, which was still capped in cloud despite the blue skies around it. The mountain struck him as a huge pile of loose rock that had rained down from somewhere above—"the raw materials of a planet dropped from an unseen quarry, which the vast chemistry of nature would anon work up, or work down, into the smiling and verdant plains and valleys of the earth."

Henry David—he who sought to make *mythology* out of natural history—was now approaching the source of creation itself.

Pulling himself up the boulders, he ascended into the mountain's blowing cloud cap. He soon topped out on the high rocky ridgetop—the tabletop—from which protrudes Katahdin's topmost peak. There he stood "deep within the hostile ranks of clouds" with the wind blowing fleeting patches of sunlight across the jumbled rock. He tried to spot the summit through the spinning mists but instead glimpsed only the dark, damp crags to his right and left. He thinks of Atlas, of Vulcan, of Prometheus, of the great figures of myth. But now, instead of leaping forth to take part in the scene, to frolic with the gods who inhabit these high, wild places, Thoreau starts to have doubts—doubts whether he should *be there at all*. He begins to get very nervous up there among the dark, mist-driven crags, with good reason.

"It was vast, Titanic, and such as man never inhabits. . . . He is more alone than you can imagine."

Thoreau looks about to find comfort—*any* comfort—in the warm, forgiving embrace of the Nature that he knows so well from gentle Concord. Here on Katahdin it's not forthcoming. The transcendent moment he long anticipated becomes fright as he finds himself a mere speck of life clinging to the mountainside, thousands of feet up among clouds and freezing wind, boulders and dark cliffs. Rather than welcoming him, Nature rebukes him, rebuffs him, almost *abuses* him. Later, in his Katahdin essay, he wrote:

> . . . inhuman Nature has got him at a disadvantage, caught him alone, and pilfers him of some of his divine faculty. She does not smile on him as in the plains. She seems to say sternly, why came ye

here before your time? I have never made this soil for thy feet, this air for thy breathing, these rocks for thy neighbors. I cannot pity nor fondle thee here, but forever relentlessly drive thee hence to where I am kind. Why seek me where I have not called thee, and then complain because you find me but a stepmother? Should thou freeze or starve, or shudder thy life away, here is no shrine, nor altar, nor any access to my ear.

He *should* have been scared. The spot where he stood on the edge of Katahdin's rocky tabletop lies quite a distance from the actual summit, which rises a few hundred feet above the table. Thoreau realized, if he were to seek the summit itself, how easily he could become disoriented in the thick, blowing mist sweeping the tableland. With such poor visibility, he could have stumbled off the cliffs that drop nearly two thousand feet from the table's eastern edge. Even if he'd managed to find the summit, it would have been very difficult to retrace the same route back across the tableland in the blowing fog to the exact spot where he ascended from camp, unless he'd carefully marked his way, as modern-day mountaineers do with wands in white-out blizzards. He could have mistakenly descended the mountain on its wrong flank, encountered cliffs or an impassable route, and spent days wandering through the dense Maine Woods trying to find his companions or his way back to civilization. He writes that he was carrying a pack for this eventuality. But the idea of wandering off the wrong side of Katahdin is clearly too much even for Thoreau. If he continues toward the summit, he understands there is the distinct possibility that Nature will callously let him "freeze, or starve, or shudder thy life away."

Thoreau—to our everlasting benefit—possessed a unique strength for turning rejection into literary advantage. When the two young women with whom he fell in love in Concord spurned him, he went to the woods and, quite literally, embraced its plants and animals. "All nature is my bride," he wrote. Now when Nature herself spurns him— "why came ye here before your time?"—on the wild top of Katahdin and he retreats, perhaps frightened, descending out of the cloud layer and down the steep, rocky mountainside with the unbroken forest and rivers and lakes spreading out below, shimmering distantly in the sun, Thoreau draws a much larger lesson from it.

Eventually finding his companions where he had left them, picking blueberries and mountain cranberries, Thoreau and party headed down the mountain through thick forest toward the Penobscot River. They soon emerged into a large, meadowy strip of "burnt land," which Thoreau assumed was created by lightning fires. It's here on the "burnt lands" that he underwent some of his most powerful revelations about nature. Who, he wondered, is the "proprietor" of this meadowy place?

> It is difficult to conceive of a region uninhabited by man. We habitually presume his presence and influence everywhere. And yet we have not seen pure Nature, unless we have seen her thus vast, drear and inhuman . . . Nature was here something savage and awful, though beautiful. I looked with awe at the ground I trod on, to see what the Powers had made there, the form and fashion and material of their work. This was that Earth of which we have heard, made out of Chaos and Old Night. Here was no man's garden, but the unhandselled globe. Man was not to be associated with it.

Right *here,* from this very spot, we get so much of our modern idea of "wilderness." *Man was not to be associated with it.* The Henry David who so comfortably embraced Nature in the woods and fields of Concord, where man is "at home" in Nature, had just been spooked by the craggy, misty upper reaches of Mount Katahdin. Coming into this large barren clearing in the forest, Thoreau lays out a definition of wilderness that has endured for 150 years. We wrestle today with the legacy of this moment. Though Thoreau virtually eliminates man's presence from the wilderness, Abenaki hunters may well have burned that particular strip of forest to allow meadow grasses to sprout, which would attract deer and moose and other game. This intentional burning of forest and prairie was a widespread practice by Native Americans. While these "burnt lands" at which Thoreau marvels may have been fertile and well-known Abenaki hunting grounds, humans don't appear anywhere in Thoreau's concept of it. This, in some ways, is a loss. By banning the humans who have traditionally used these "wild" landscapes, you ban the deep understanding of them.

But there is something to be gained, too. Thoreau dwells on the *alien-ness* of humans to this landscape. And it is because the landscape is so alien to humans that Thoreau finds the divine there. Yes, he can find the divine in his cozy woods and fields of Concord, too, but not like *this*—not with this profound power. Here on Katahdin and the burnt lands it is the hard fact of matter itself—including his own body—that moves Thoreau to some of his most soaring spiritual reveries.

> We walked over it with a certain awe . . . [It was like] being shown some star's surface, some hard matter in its home! I stand in awe of my body, this matter to which I am bound has become so strange to me. . . . What is this Titan that has possession of me? Talk of mysteries!—Think of our life in nature, —daily to be shown matter, to come in contact with it, —rocks, trees, wind on our cheeks! the *solid* earth! the *actual* world! the *common* sense! *Contact! Contact! Who* are we? *where* are we?

We'd had plenty of contact, that sixth day on the St. John, with Thoreau's *matter*. Rocks, trees, wind on our cheeks—and *moving water*. Running wilderness rapids like the Big Black, as we did that day in open canoes laden with our survival gear and with our children in the bows, makes one as alive as one can possibly be to the actual world—aware, tuned in, taking in every nuance in the sound of rushing, in the curl of a wave, in the flash of spruce trees on the bank, the low soar of a bird, the sun glistening off the wet, flexing arm muscles of a child.

The sun lowered over the St. John at the end of that sixth day and we scouted the banks for a good campsite. We passed a marked campsite called Ferry Crossing and one called Seminary Brook, walked around, and kept going. Too buggy, too closed in, too open, too far from the river—always something. We finally chose a spot called Boom Chain, tucked in among a thick stand of birches on the right bank. It looked unused. Ferns poked up around the rock fire ring. The rich light of the lowering sun skittered across the river, reflected upward, and illuminated the arched underside of our campsite's bower of birches in a dappled fresco of green and gold.

"Don't look, Dad," Skyler said to me.

He was crouching down at the fire ring near the pile of wood we had collected. He wouldn't let me approach as I brought in one more armload and dumped it.

"Okay," he finally said, "you can look now."

He stepped back. Inside the fire ring stood a perfect teepee of small, dry sticks that he'd constructed and within the teepee he'd crumpled sheets of birch bark.

"That's really good, Skyler," I said with a glow of pride. "That's a really good fire you made."

I helped him set a match to it. The birch bark flared with bright yellow flames, quickly igniting the sticks. We placed on larger logs. Soon I was reclining beside the fire, propped on one elbow, while Skyler and Molly roasted hot dogs on sticks. I was so pleased that he'd taken the lesson. While for an outsider the forest is unknown—a great blank spot—to those who paddled its rivers and treaded through its groves in hide moccasins over the many centuries, knowledge of it was codified into names, stories, songs, useful tips, and little phrases passed from grandparent to grandchild. In these many ways the knowledge carried through hundreds of generations. What may be a "blank spot"—that state of ignorance about a place—at one time may not be at another time, while long and unseen connections link the two.

I'd learned that birch bark makes excellent tinder years before, from horse-mounted hunters in the birch forests of Manchuria, members of a small, seminomadic tribe called the Orochen. As it started to spit rain one afternoon, I noticed the lead hunter, Mung, sidle his horse against the trunk of a birch and peel off several large sheets of bark, rolling them up like scrolls and stuffing them into the inner pocket of his coat. We rode on into the rain and swamps, and, that evening, he produced the dry bark. Despite the soggy woods, the fire flared to life. Now, in Maine, we sat in the same birch forest—part of the great post–Ice Age boreal forest that encircles the earth. The Orochen tribe from whom I learned in Manchuria was probably an ancient, distant ancestor of the Abenaki and Micmac hunters whose forebears had crossed the Bering Strait and eventually roamed these banks of the St. John. And so the knowledge traveled in an arc of time and space.

This boreal forest contained thousands upon thousands of bits of useful knowledge like the birch-bark tinder, most of them now lost. I knew of some myself that had disappeared. The earliest French explorers—Jacques Cartier's expedition, in particular—chronicled how they learned from the Indians to make tea from the bark and needles of the "annedda" tree, which finally saved them from scurvy after 25 of their party of 110 had died. The tree was probably the white cedar, which, its seedlings taken back to France, received the name *arborvitae*, or "tree of life." Many of the later European explorers were nevertheless ignorant of its antiscorbutic properties and died all the same. Knowledge of the arborvitae tea nevertheless was passed down in the New World from the Indians to the Acadians and on to their mixed or *métis* descendants. Thoreau quotes a French-Canadian loggers' ditty about the cedar tea his party brews one night en route to Katahdin:

> *A quart of* arbor-*vitae*
> *To make him strong and mighty . . .*

Unfortunately, the swirls of smoke from Skyler's campfire barely kept the mosquitoes at bay in our bowered camp at Boom Chain. Through the smudge, I spotted a short length of extremely heavy, rusted chain hanging from a nail driven into a birch tree, each link the size of a saucer. Here, I realized, was a bit of the actual "boom chain" that lent its name to the little campsite. Right here, loggers annually stretched this chain, or rather a huge length of it, out into the river to corral the logs driven down the St. John on the spring flood of snowmelt.

Now this scene of frenetic human activity had passed simply to a name marking a campsite. That afternoon, at "Seminary Brook," I'd wandered over the little meadow with a pretty brook running alongside it, wondering if this were in fact the site of an old seminary. The previous day we'd passed an old homestead, now overgrown, called Simmons Farm, and before that the long-abandoned logging center at Seven Islands. It had a post office once. These had become marks on the map, or the name of a campsite, or a few aging memories, or a chunk of rusting iron, or recollections in a book.

Slowly, the region had slipped back into a state of "blankness." To modern eyes like mine, unfamiliar with the logging life that had unfolded here before, this was an "untracked wilderness." Likewise, so many early Europeans saw North America as an "untracked wilderness" when in fact to the Micmac and Abenaki and the other tribes it was as well mapped as the pages of a *Rand McNally Road Atlas*. In the early exploration literature, you constantly read how the Indians would squat down and with a stick or a finger trace in the earth a map to show the ignorant European how to travel through the rivers, lakes, and mountain chains that lay ahead. The Inuit, among whom this talent has been scientifically studied, are able to sketch a remarkably accurate map—detailing mile upon mile of coastal headlands, inlets, rivers—from their geographic memory.

I've watched, with rising alarm, subdivisions and culs-de-sac flatten those woods and fields that I loved around the Wisconsin cabin of my childhood and firmly believe all the momentum of human life on earth seems to move toward eradicating the blank spots on the map—these places which I so hankered to visit. But here along the St. John was a blank spot almost literally forming before my eyes.

It is a kind of paradox. Blank spots on the map, in my mind, cease to exist when the map shows the straight and curving lines—black or blue or yellow—of roads running through them. "Blank spots," as I define them, are technically just that—patches of the map showing no human features. A good part of the Maine Woods, starting especially in the 1950s, had been crisscrossed by small log-hauling roads, along which trucks hauled out the logs instead of floating them downriver. Paradoxically, these roads meant the end to the need for big logging camps like Seven Islands, and places to feed them like Simmons Farm. Because of the construction of these roads into them, the Maine Woods, while more deforested, actually became "blanker"—they had less human presence, and humans had less hands-on knowledge of them.

Skyler's fire flamed in the rock ring. I sipped my camping cup of wine. Here was a bit of firsthand knowledge of the forest's intricacies—the use of birch bark as a superior tinder, as well as a remarkably versatile building material for canoes, wigwams, containers—that would be lost without a human presence. I found it distressing that Thoreau had banned humans, and their knowledge, from his wilderness. I realized that, in this way, a "blank spot" represented a *tragedy*.

ACADIA MAY WELL HAVE STAYED FRENCH, and kept far more of its original "Indian wisdom," if not for a magnificently nasty feud among the French who gained control of it.

With the Scottish gone—at least for now—Charles de La Tour essentially split Acadia and its fur-trading profits with the French vice admiral Isaac de Razilly. In 1632, Vice Admiral de Razilly had helped to rescue La Tour from his years of abandonment by leading an expedition of three hundred colonists to reestablish France in Acadia. While the king named La Tour the governor of Acadia, Razilly was put in charge of the larger entity of New France, which included Champlain's settlements on the St. Lawrence River as well as La Tour's in Acadia. When Razilly chose to settle in Acadia, La Tour agreed, in 1633, to split the fur-trade profits in half, with each man having a key to the other's warehouse for inspections.

The arrangement worked well for two years until Razilly, known for his fair-handedness, suddenly died at age forty-eight. (La Tour's father, Claude, in his house at Cape Sable, died about the same time, in the mid-1630s.) On Razilly's death, his half of the Acadian fur trade went to a highborn nobleman who had served loyally with Razilly's fleet, Charles de Menou d'Aulnay—soon to be known in the New World for his hauteur and ambition. D'Aulnay reestablished a French colony on the site of Port Royal, after its forty-six remaining Scottish colonists had sent been back to the British Isles. He married the daughter of a shareholder in the Company of New France whom he met when she visited Acadia—twenty-one-year-old Jeanne Motin. Her dowry no doubt included some of her father's company stock, further consolidating d'Aulnay's position in Acadia and further threatening La Tour's. In a letter, d'Aulnay described his bride-to-be as "a modest little servant of God."

The forty-six-year-old La Tour, whether in retaliation or out of a yearning for companionship after three decades in the woods of the New World, sent an agent to France to arrange a marriage contract of his own. The document still exists, signed on New Year's Eve 1639 in the fashionable Paris district around Rue de Honoré, signed by La Tour's agent and by the family of Françoise Jacquelin, daughter of a well-respected doctor in the town of Nogent, some seventy miles from Paris. It is not clear whether Charles de La Tour had met Françoise Jacquelin during a society function on an earlier trip to Paris, or if they first met in person when she stepped off the ship in Acadia.

Nor is her background entirely clear. Some stories—without any factual basis—place her in Paris as an aspiring actress. Some historians speculate that, based on her fluent writing, she was well educated, and thus presumably versed in property laws, as in her era, property management was considered a proper part of a young woman's education. An old Celtic tradition then codified in parts of France—but later to disappear—stipulated equal property rights for married women. Whatever her exact background, Françoise Jacquelin was no "modest little servant of God," as d'Aulnay had condescendingly described his own French bride. She would soon cut a dashing and formidable figure in the New World.

Awaiting the arrival of his bride-to-be, Charles de La Tour spruced up his fort at the mouth of the St. John River by enlarging and strengthening it. Surrounded by a log stockade on a grassy promontory over the St. John's harbor, the quadrangle of buildings measured about 120 feet in length and could house ninety people. La Tour ordered his men to build a courtyard paved in stone, and two massive stone fireplaces, each eleven feet long, which heated the living quarters, one for the men's dormitory and the other for the officers' living and dining areas. For himself and his bride, La Tour had the men construct in the same wing a private sitting room, fireplace, and bedroom.

In late March 1640, Françoise Jacquelin traveled aboard the *Amity* and arrived a few weeks later at Cape Sable. The elegant Françoise-Marie stepped off the ship from France—one thinks of her in petticoats and a velvet cape—to a crude fortress in the wilderness and a husband who had spent his entire adolescence and manhood engaged in "a savage kind of life, traveling, trucking, and marrying with the savages." One hopes he shed his buckskins and beaver pelts for something more Parisian. It is not clear what happened to La Tour's Micmac wife. She may have died some years earlier, because on his journey to Paris in 1632 he'd brought the youngest two of his three *métis* daughters to be educated in France. The third and eldest daughter, Jeanne, stayed behind in Acadia. She would have been fourteen when her new French stepmother stepped off the *Amity*, along with the two maids La Tour provided for her in the marriage contract.

After the formal marriage ceremony, the newlywed couple sailed on the *Amity* to La Tour's remodeled fortress on the St. John with its honeymoon quarters. They spent only a few weeks in residence before La Tour and Françoise Jacquelin sailed north to d'Aulnay's settlement at Port Royal. One theory holds that La Tour wanted his bride to meet d'Aulnay's young French wife, "the modest little" Jeanne Motin, while another says that he went solely for the purpose of examining d'Aulnay's warehouse, convinced d'Aulnay was cheating him in furs. There had also been disputes between the two over control of fur-trading territory along the St. John.

D'Aulnay wasn't in his fort, away resupplying his fur outposts along the Penoboscot River, and his men, on instruction, refused La

Tour permission to land. The insult clearly stung La Tour in front of his bride. He brooded all night in the harbor, and in the morning, with his two small ships, began to sail back to the St. John. Leaving the entrance of Port Royal's large sheltered basin, La Tour's men spotted the two approaching sails of d'Aulnay's returning ships. No one knows for certain who fired the first shot, but La Tour's cannons unleashed a broadside that toppled one of d'Aulnay's mainmasts and killed several men.

D'Aulnay, an experienced mariner, returned heavy fire, killing several, and managed to force La Tour's ships into the shallows, where they foundered. He then captured the survivors, among them La Tour and Françoise Jacquelin, and imprisoned them all in his fort, which contained a heavy dungeon. With two Capuchin friars (part of the Franciscan order) working as intermediaries, it was finally agreed to let the king of France decide the matter, whereupon d'Aulnay released the captives. Surely, it was an incident that did not endear d'Aulnay to Françoise. D'Aulnay dismissed her as not worthy of his respect, describing her in his accounts as the daughter of *un barbier*—a barber. She was not a woman, it turned out, to take such insults lightly.

With d'Aulnay using his powerful influence at the royal court, the king's and Richelieu's judgment went against La Tour. That winter, 1641, they stripped him of his Acadian governorship, which was granted to d'Aulnay instead, and ordered La Tour back to France. Letters arriving late that spring of 1641 via ship from his allies in Paris, however, warned La Tour that he should not return to France or he would be "doomed." Instead, his allies said they would covertly try their best to resupply him in Acadia.

La Tour and Françoise withdrew to their fortress on the St. John, abandoning his Fort Saint-Louis at Cape Sable to d'Aulnay, who, defying the king's orders, promptly torched it along with its Récollet monastery and church, to the deep dismay of its vow-of-poverty Récollet monks. In response to d'Aulnay's aggressions, La Tour looked to the most powerful source of help he could find nearby—the British colonies down in New England. Having grown tremendously in the twenty years since the *Mayflower* landings, they now numbered some thirteen thousand colonists in their dense agricultural villages, compared to a paltry four hundred or so in New France's far-flung fur-trading outposts. They possessed their own manufactories, water mills, and a thriving transatlantic commerce, due to few trade restrictions on the part of the mother country, which was distracted with its internal wars.

There followed a wooing of Governor John Winthrop and the English colonists down in Boston by both La Tour, his wife, Françoise Jacquelin, their archenemy, d'Aulnay, and envoys for all parties, to which the Bostonians extended cordial hospitality. Madame La Tour, according to the early New England chronicles, was a favorite in Boston, her status helped by her Protestant leanings. She was called "a wise and valiant woman and a discreet manager" and "justly esteemed for her sound Protestant sentiments and excellent virtues." By contrast, d'Aulnay's envoys portrayed Françoise to the Bostonians as a kind of dragon lady— "known to be the cause of [La Tour's] contempt and rebellion."

She sailed back to France twice to enlist aid for her husband, as letters of arrest had been issued there for him, due to d'Aulnay's influence at court, and it was too dangerous for him to go himself. In one instance she had to slip past d'Aulnay's ship blockade around the St. John harbor and the La Tour fort. Back in France, she, too, was ordered to be detained. She managed to slip the authorities again, by making her way from a French port to England, where she located a British ship bound for Acadian waters. D'Aulnay himself, on patrol with one of his ships, intercepted her British ship as it approached Acadia but Françoise and her maidservants managed to escape detection by hiding deep in the hold.

The winter of 1644–45 found Charles de La Tour back in Boston trying to convince the Council of Magistrates not to side with d'Aulnay—an *homme d'artifice.* The Bostonians now regretted that they ever got involved in this infighting among the French that so distracted them from establishing Winthrop's vision of a "City upon a Hill" in the wilderness. While he pleaded his case in Boston, La Tour left Françoise Jacquelin and their young son at the fort on the St. John River. She and the Récollet friars attached to the fort apparently quarreled because the friars were convinced that she'd become possessed by the devil's ideas down in Boston. The friars fled in a small boat to the more Catholic shelter of d'Aulnay's fortress at Port Royal. Upon learning that Madame La Tour was in charge of the fort, d'Aulnay seized the moment, sailed into the St. John's mouth with his three-hundred-ton, sixteen-cannon warship *Grand Cardinal,* along with many scores of men, and demanded immediate surrender.

They were greeted from the ramparts by jeers, insults, and the red flag of defiance. The roar of battle began. Fierce bombardments from both sides—from the fort, the ship, and from the cannons d'Aulnay had moved into place behind the fort under the cover of night—echoed throughout Easter Day 1645. With the fort's wooden palisades shattered, d'Aulnay started a final foot charge. The few remaining defenders rallied behind Françoise Jacquelin, who had led throughout the battle. It was then, realizing the hopelessness of the situation, that she finally surrendered on the condition that her men be granted amnesty. D'Aulnay agreed to the terms. He then went back on his word and hanged all the survivors but two collaborating men plus Françoise, her young son, her maidservant, and the one other woman in the fort. D'Aulnay forced Françoise to stand with a rope around her neck and watch as each of her men was in his turn strung up and strangled by the tightening noose.

She remained d'Aulnay's captive for three weeks, at first granted a measure of freedom to move. When she tried to send a message via the Micmac to her husband down in Boston, d'Aulnay either locked her up or put her in irons or both. As a captive of the La Tour archenemy, Françoise Jacquelin fell ill and died—either from sadness and resentment (according to her servants) or from rage (according to d'Aulnay's people) or from poisoning (so the Acadians believed).

D'Aulnay had finally wrested from Charles de La Tour the whole of Acadia and its rich fur trade—but only briefly. La Tour, his fort lost and wife dead and now fifty-two years old, seized a ship of the Bostonians, who had hosted and helped him. (Governor Winthrop, stung by La Tour's betrayal, quoted the Bible, "there is no confidence in an unfaithful or carnal man.") With his stolen ship, La Tour repaired to the safety of Quebec, where he was out of reach of both d'Aulnay and the Bostonians, and remained there for the next several years, a respected and solid citizen of the settlement.

D'Aulnay sat atop his Acadian fur empire for five years, although it apparently never made enough of a profit, and it came to a sudden and ignoble end. In May 1650, a season when the water was still frigid from winter's cold, d'Aulnay and one of his staff members were paddling a canoe in the Dauphin River near Port Royal. Somehow the canoe capsized. The servant was able to swim to shore but the forty-five-year-old d'Aulnay became hypothermic and weakened in the icy water, and was later found dead, sprawled over the hull of the overturned canoe. In the aftermath, a Capuchin father at the colony testified that, in the six months before his death, a new d'Aulnay had emerged—one who had repented to the church for his aggressive behavior of the past and in his will, begging forgiveness, asked to be buried underneath the Port Royal church steps, pleading "for all who pass by to have pity for a person who merits only the thunderbolts and chastisement of a justly angry God."

Neither La Tour nor d'Aulnay's creditors respected his last wish, showing him as little pity in his death as he showed them in life. D'Aulnay left behind his widow, Jeanne Motin—the "very humble and modest little servant of God," then aged thirty-five or so—their four daughters and four sons, as well as a staggering debt to creditors back in France who had funded the prolonged war he had waged against the La Tours. Soon after d'Aulnay's death, his major creditor, Leborgne, showed up at Port Royal, threw Jeanne Motin and her children out of the governor's quarters, and proclaimed himself the ruler of Acadia.

Charles de La Tour now saw his opportunity, too. From his refuge in Quebec, he hurried back to France and persuaded the royal court to give him back the governorship of Acadia. He then sailed back across the Atlantic to Port Royal and convinced creditor-hounded Jeanne Motin to marry him, as a way to secure Acadia for both of them and to deal with their debts. On his third wife, Charles de La Tour became stepfather to Jeanne's eight young children, and, starting at age sixty, fathered another five children with her.

By now, however, two decades of strife among the French had so torn Acadia that the New Englanders jumped at the chance to exploit its weakness. In 1654, four years after d'Aulnay perished on an overturned canoe, a fleet commanded by Boston's Major Robert Sedgwick attacked the Acadian ports held by La Tour and Leborgne. After short but bloody battles he took them. Down in Boston, the citizens, by court order, celebrated "a publick and solemn Thanksgiving to the Lord for his gracious working."

La Tour, no doubt drawing on the adaptability he had learned while living so many decades in the forests, *still* didn't give up his dreams of a fur empire in Acadia. Sedgwick hauled La Tour as a prisoner back to England. Like his old man, Claude, Charles de La Tour charmed his way back into his father's old title of baronet of Nova Scotia. He then sold off all his claims to Acadia, or Nova Scotia, to wealthy English investors in order to pay off his debts. Charles de La Tour reserved Acadian estates for his wife and their many children at Port

Royal and Cape Sable. He died, probably at Port Royal, in 1663, presumably happy and certainly after a very full life, at seventy years of age.

THE NEXT MORNING, our seventh day on the St. John, we couldn't flee our campsite at Boom Chain fast enough. As the sun rose higher, the blackflies, mosquitoes, and no-see-ums ferociously descended on us. Molly and Skyler took refuge in their headnets. Amy rolled the tent and I tried to pack the canoes. We just wanted out of there. Molly's eyes were rimmed with little scabs of dried blood, and the glands of her neck had swollen. Skyler had counted seventy-three welts on his soft skin, and he seemed hot and listless. We shoved off from the bank, pushed out into the river. Already the day shone warm and sunny, with a slight breeze blowing, and no bugs on the water.

A giddy sense of relief overcame us at simply escaping the bugs. I'd read that in June, the height of the season for bugs, an average of 450 moose are killed per month by cars on Maine's roads. The moose emerge from the forest to escape the insects and to lounge on the relatively bug-free road openings. That statistic now made perfect sense. Likewise, it made perfect sense that the Micmac set up their camps along the bug-free coasts during the summer, and, when the bugs had died off, returned to the forests to hunt in fall and winter.

As we paddled along, Skyler made up a song:

> *Oh dear, oh dear, oh dear*
> *I fear I have a fly in my ear*

We laughed and sang, steering easily through a few sets of small but lively rapids. We heard motors in the distance on the sunny, still air. We now could see clear-cuts on the hills back from the river where logging companies had sawed whole tracts from the forest's thick nap. I sensed that the end of the trip drew near. Soon we were pushing each other out of the canoes into the warm river, splashing wildly, laughing. Simply to have warm sun, and no rain, and no bugs, and a beautiful river with the bluish-green hills, even logged-off ones, rising around—suddenly it all seemed so plentiful.

We'd planned to camp that night, our seventh, on the river, but by mid-afternoon, we had covered far more miles on the swift current than we'd anticipated. We were in striking distance of Allagash. Molly asked again if it had nice motels. I tried to quiet her expectations, but I was ready for a nice motel myself.

"Let's see how it goes," I said.

"Please, let's not camp out again," Skyler pleaded from within his galaxy of bug bites.

I sensed our family beginning to lose its determination, exhausted from paddling for a week straight, battered by bugs. The four or five days of rain hadn't bothered them; but they couldn't take the bugs much longer.

We saw a house on the left bank—a strange occurrence, after so many days without spotting any dwellings except a few cabins. So square and solid-looking, a neat piece of geometry and bright paint in a land of tall, dark trees and twisting, dark water. Past the house we approached the largest rapid on the river, Big Rapid, a long fallaway that swept around a broad bend to the right. The canoeing guidebook recommended unloading your gear, running it in empty canoes, and portaging the gear around on a road that now came close to the river.

But Big Rapid tumbled at least a mile in length and, without a vehicle of some sort to carry the gear, portaging it presented a major problem. Instead, we stopped, scouted it as best we could from the top—it looked straightforward enough—and battened down our canoes. We then ran the rapids in our loaded canoes, our bows splashing through the big waves without mishap, though shipping water.

Spinning out into the sunlit eddies at the bottom, we gave a whoop. I was proud of our little family.

Now the St. John opened wide, the hills pulling back. It felt as if we were exiting the North Woods into a broader agricultural valley. A hamlet of a few houses appeared on the left bank. Then a bridge suddenly spanned the river, and we paddled beneath it.

The river had become almost a lake now. Cottages lined the high right bank—vacation cabins and small homes of local residents. The Allagash River—designated one of America's Wild and Scenic Rivers—flowed in from the right. We steered our canoes up the Allagash, paddling and pushing for several hundred yards, until we reached a bridge at Allagash village, which was really just a few houses.

To Molly's dismay—to all of ours—there were no nice motels in Allagash. There were a few cabins, and a kind of bunkhouse where we ended up staying, after being recruited by eighty-eight-year-old Evelyn McBrearity, who, moments after our canoes crunched to a stop in the gravel of the landing, showed up with a cane in her hand and a small cloud of flies swarming around her head ("After a while you get used to them."). She pointed out her big old frame house, just up the hill from the landing. She was a Pelletier, she told us proudly, who married a McBrearity. Her father had run the ferry across the river—she owned the landing itself where our canoes sat—for thirty-six years before the highway bridge was built in the 1940s. He was also a boatbuilder and crafted the towboats that horses hauled up the Allagash and St. John to supply the logging camps.

"Do you speak French?" Amy asked.

"Oh yes, of course. That's what I miss, is the French."

"Is your father's family Acadian?" I asked.

"No, not Acadian," she replied, saying her father's family had come from other parts of Canada.

After a burger at a roadside café and a night in the bunkhouse, we were met the next morning by David Skipper, sent by our outfitters, Galen and Betsy Hale, who arrived with the big van and hauled us and our gear back down to Medway. I succumbed to the pressure from within our family to escape for a few days down to the Maine coast, like the Indians making their summer camps, away from the insects. And so we decamped for a couple nights to the chic little port of Camden on beautiful Penobscot Bay, once heavily contested by British and French. After this interlude of lobster and seascapes, I delivered Amy, Molly, and Skyler to the airport at Bangor and they flew back to the West while I took our little rental car and headed back to the Maine Woods for a few more days.

I spent a Sunday morning riding beside Galen Hale in his big pickup truck, bouncing deep into the woods until we reached the cellar hole of Old Thomas Fowler's first cabin. We saw the family graveyard, with Old Thomas's grave, and nearby the grave of Aurora, daughter of Uncle George McCauslin, head boatman to Thoreau. She married Young Tom Fowler, explained Galen. Apparently Aurora died young and Tom remarried, because nearby, among this section of Fowlers, lay the grave of the infant Anna, who was the daughter of Young Tom Fowler and his second wife, Olive. In another row rested Galen's immediate ancestors, the Hales—Albert, Tily, and Elmer. The latter was a famous guide, explained Galen. And so the wheel slowly turns through the generations in northern Maine.

Galen pointed out to me the stones of Mom Howard's chimney barely poking above the backed-up waters of the Penobscot River, where, decades ago, it had been dammed into a small reservoir for power and paper mills. We then laid out a map of Mount Katahdin and Baxter State Park on the hood of his pickup. With his finger he traced the Thoreau party's route up the Penobscot West Branch and Thoreau's ascent of Katahdin. I said goodbye to Galen and drove an hour to the park that hot, sunny, Sunday afternoon. Starting in mid-afternoon, I hiked hard and fast, jogging its gentler lower reaches, on Thoreau's route up the mountain, following what today is called the Abol Trail. I panted and sweated as the mountainside tilted ever steeper, scrambling over the massive boulders that looked like they had rained from the sky, from some "unseen quarry." As I climbed higher, the sun dropped lower to the hazy, blue-green horizon. About two thirds of the way up Katahdin, I stopped—tired, out of water, not wishing to be caught in darkness near the top. Thoreau, too, had turned back, but in the blowing clouds, the cold wind, among the dark crags.

Here occurred some of his most profound realizations about Nature, that not all Nature offered humans her warm embrace, that places existed on this earth where humans didn't belong. High on the barren, boulder-strewn face of Katahdin, this was one such place.

I sat on a big, rounded, whitish boulder catching my breath, draining the last drops of water from my plastic bottle, and gazing off over the great northern forest extending toward the horizon in all directions. To the west, toward the lowering sun, it glinted silver with sunlight reflecting on jeweled lakes and sinewy rivers—a view that hadn't changed all that much since Thoreau climbed over this same boulder slide 150 years ago. I waited for my own profound realization about Nature. Nothing happened. Sweat dripped off my chin and splashed in rough, grit-flecked droplets on the broad face of the boulder, the only evidence of human life in view. I waited. Still no epiphany. The boulder felt warm from the day's sun, its low, golden ball casting its rich, summer-evening light—an almost buttery warmth—on my cheeks. Rather than overcome with thoughts about the inhospitality of Nature in this spot, as Thoreau had been in the cold and clouds, I wanted to lie down and take a nap.

After twenty minutes or so, I started down Mount Katahdin, lowering myself through the steep clog of boulders. I realized that my most profound moments in the wilds of northern Maine had occurred not on the side of Katahdin but in the rapids of the St. John. There all my senses had been utterly attuned to nature in its minute and vivid detail—the curl of a wave, the undulating rush of the current, the boiling reflection of light, the swoop of a bird, the ripple of muscle on a child's glistening arm. These were moments when I was most vulnerable to the unpredictability of nature, just as Thoreau's greatest moments of vulnerability to nature's unpredictability occurred not at Walden Pond or in the gentle woods and fields of his Concord, but alone in the cold wind and blowing clouds on rocky Katahdin, where he had some of his greatest insights. Likewise, the two young Charleses, Biencourt and La Tour. In the wilds of Acadia, traveling through the endless forest, living like the Micmac, they discovered for themselves this profound sense of Nature's unpredictability. To live this way, they had to be utterly attuned to the natural world, far from the musty, worn, manorial life that awaited them should they return to Old France.

A blank spot was not simply an unpopulated area on the map, as I'd started out believing, nor was it only a reflection of our own ignorance, as I'd later come to see it. Rather, what is compelling about blank spots—these wild places—is their unpredictability, and the uncertainty that it engenders, so unlike the safe, well-trodden paths most of us travel in our daily lives. The unpredictability provokes our awareness of the natural world, otherwise we won't survive. Our awareness, if we're open to it, pushes us toward insights that don't occur in our routine lives.

From Katahdin, I drove the next day northeastward to the middle reaches of the St. John Valley along the Maine–New Brunswick border, where small farming towns appear regularly on its broad banks. I crossed the border into Canada and stopped for a look at the thundering, misty Grand Falls of the St. John. The story that I had heard, from a Maine lobsterman down on the coast who had married a woman of Acadian descent, was that when the British finally expelled the Acadians a small group fled up the St. John River past the Grand Falls. They knew that British warships could never chase them above its drop.

Back on the Maine side, I drove a two-lane highway above the Grand Falls and through more small towns along the St. John for another forty miles or so, each with a large church out of proportion to the size of the town, like a cathedral in a French village. We hadn't canoed this stretch of the St. John, as we'd taken out at Allagash, another sixty or seventy miles upriver. Driving along, I spotted a massive white cross, known as the Cross of St. David, planted in a pasture beside the pastoral riverbanks. I drove down a lane to reach it. Beneath it lay a row of stone markers commemorating families that had staged reunions here—Thibodeau, Ouellette, Chasse, and on and on.

The original wooden cross had been erected on this spot by Joseph Daigle in June 1785 after a party of Acadians, fleeing the British, landed here.

After Charles de La Tour's death in 1663, Acadia went on bouncing back and forth between the two empires, French and British, for the next forty years, until it was captured for good by the British in 1710. The Acadian population had soared, meanwhile, as each family had six to eight children, and more immigrants arrived from France. The old Poutrincourt and La Tour dream of an Acadian fur empire headed by an aristocratic leader was supplanted by small but very fertile farms the Acadians established in the tidal marshlands of the Acadian Peninsula that could support the large families, along with hunting and fishing.

Through the first half of the 1700s, the British merely tolerated the Acadian presence in the peninsula they called Nova Scotia, forcing the Acadians to take loyalty oaths to the British. They viewed the Acadian farmers as strategically necessary to raise food to supply the British forts, while disparaging the Acadian way of life.

"They Lavish, Eat, Drink, and Play all away as long as the Goods hold out," wrote one colonial official, "and when these are gone, they e'en sell their Embroidery, their Lace, and their Clothes." Instead of settling down on the farm, complained another, the young men head off to unsettled regions along the coast where they "do nothing but hunt or negotiate with the natives." Another tried in vain to enforce a decree forbidding "licentiousness [with native women] and ranging in the woods." The British even complained that the Acadians were too lazy to go out and clear some real forest for farms, the way they did it down in New England, but relied instead on the diking and draining of the tidal marshes for their fields.

L'Ordre de Bon Temps—"The Order of Good Times"—had set the tone in Acadia from the start, as did their intermingling with the Micmac who lived in the forest, hunting, making war, living intensely in the moment. The party in Acadia ended, however, at 3:00 p.m. on the fifth of September in 1755. In the epic ongoing struggle between Britain and France for the North American continent, certain British generals, as tensions built and suspicions flared, unfairly decided that the Acadians could no longer be trusted to remain neutral. On that September day Colonel Winslow of the British summoned the Acadian men and boys of Grand Pré to meet at the church, and once inside had his soldiers bar the doors while an interpreter read aloud the eviction notice to the shock of those trapped within.

Six days later, on September 11, 1755, with bayonets fixed the British troops marched the Acadian men and boys out of the church, down the cart path a mile and a half to the harbor. Women and children lined the road, wailing and praying, singing religious dirges, never expecting to see their fathers and husbands, brothers and sons again. Soon the women and children were rounded up, too, and packed onto other cargo ships—two people to a cell four feet by four feet by six feet. Smoke rose from the hundreds of squared-log Acadian homesteads set afire by British troops—to destroy the incentive to return. By the end of October twenty-four ships had sailed away, dropping the fragmented Acadian families in ports up and down the East Coast—Massachusetts, New York, Virginia and the Carolinas, Bermuda.

Some six thousand Acadians were deported in all, and, by some accounts, half died of disease and hunger. Some were made into indentured servants to the British colonists. Some returned to France. Others ended up in the French West Indies. One group eventually moved to New Orleans and the Mississippi Delta country—French territory, with a lot of wilds still left in it. Those Acadians in Louisiana invited their scattered relatives to join them. Thousands finally showed up. The name "Acadians" in Louisiana became "Cadians" became "Cajuns." In the Mississippi River bayous, they carried on their traditions of hunting and fishing and "ranging in the woods" and letting the Good Times roll.

Some—no one knows just how many—escaped Le Grand Dérangement ("The Great Disturbance") and hid in the woods of Acadia or fled to nearby Quebec. Over the years, some trickled back. They settled in unclaimed pockets on the fertile lands of Acadia.

Thirty years after that first expulsion in 1755, a small party of Acadian families who had been living quietly in the lower St. John River

Valley, once again, during a period of tense relations between empires, came under pressure by the British to leave. In 1785, they boarded small boats and headed up the St. John, past the Grand Falls. After ten days of traveling they pulled ashore at a broadening of the valley and a fertile flat that they named St. David, and where Joseph Daigle built a wooden cross that first evening. In some ways, it is an Acadian version of Plymouth Rock. Their settlement on the banks of the St. John—deep in what was then a wilderness—probably escaped detection by the fledgling United States for a number of years and was largely ignored by the British. The Acadians had found a perfect hiding spot.

This was the spot where I now stood. There was no one around. Green wooded hills and meadows rolled up and down the river valley. I could see prosperous farms in the distance. A warm summer breeze blew and the sun sparkled on the riffled water of the St. John. I would have chosen this spot, too.

I got back in the car and drove down the highway to the little town of Van Buren, Maine. It was still before noon, but I was hungry, and so I walked into Josie's Diner. A roundish, friendly man with dark hair and a mustache, a gravelly voice and an apron, took my order. As I sat at the lunch counter, I realized he was speaking in a language unintelligible to me, and with a kind of guttural intonation, with the man sitting two stools down.

"Is that French?" I asked as he came by again, wiping the counter.

"That's right," he replied. "I speak French to the people who want to speak French and English to the people who want to speak English. French or English, as long as everybody is happy, I don't care, right?"

It was the perfect Acadian response. He laughed, deeply and easily. We talked. His name was Gil Thibodeau—an old Acadian name, like the names of most people in Van Buren, Maine. Two hundred and fifty years ago, his family had been evicted from Acadia during *Le Grand Dérangement*. Some had ended up in Louisiana—today the town of Thibodeaux in bayou country west of New Orleans bears the family name. Another ancestor, Baptiste Thibodeau, had arrived here on the banks of the St. John with Joseph Daigle, who erected the Cross of St. David in the summer of 1785.

Sitting there at Josie's Diner with my cheeseburger and cup of tomato soup, I had arrived where the Acadians disappeared.

PART II

THE WILD
LANDS OF
WESTERN
PENNSYLVANIA

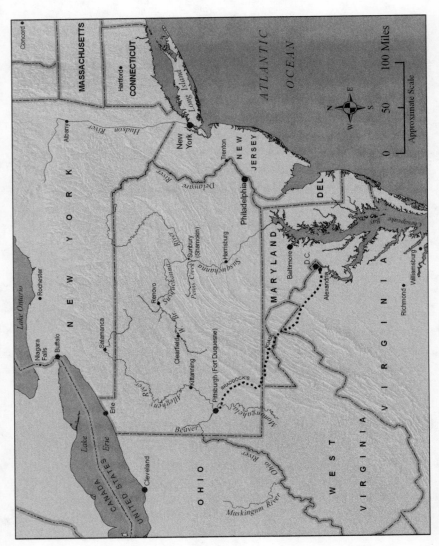

Map of Pennsylvania and surrounding region, with Braddock's Road (1755) to Fort Duquesne (later Pittsburgh) in what was then the Ohio Valley wilderness.

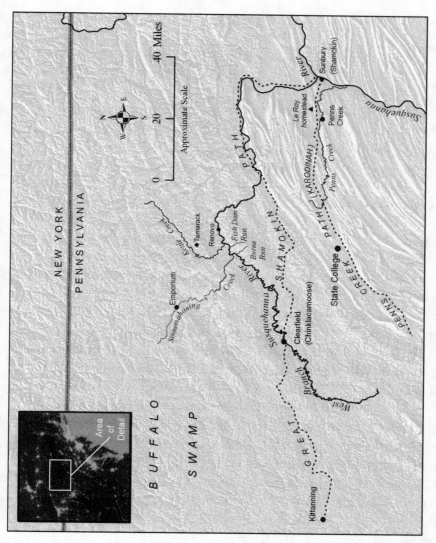

Detail map of Pennsylvania, showing Indian paths of mid-1700s, Le Roy homestead, and present-day Renovo (center) with Fish Dam Run and Burns Run nearby. Inset shows lights of region at night, with New York, Philadelphia, and Washington at right.

*E*arly on October 16, 1755, Jacob Le Roy's hired man had gone out to the pastures and woods of the family's farmstead in the Buffalo Valley on the Pennsylvania frontier to herd the cows back for milking. Le Roy's wife was away on some morning errand. It was right after autumn harvest and there was much work to be done. But Le Roy himself was home that morning. So were the children, Marie and John, and a girl visitor from a neighbor's homestead, as a band of eight Allegheny and Delaware Indians moved silently down the ancient trail that followed nearby Penn's Creek—Karondinhah, as the Indians knew it—having traveled nearly two hundred miles from the deep wilds of the Ohio River Valley. With their torsos blackened and facial features emboldened in the geometric red and black designs of war paint, it happened that the Le Roy place, on the very farthest western edge of the frontier, was the first white homestead the Indians encountered as they moved east toward the white settlement burgeoning from the British colonies of the Eastern Seaboard onto tribal lands.

The band of Alleghenies and Delawares found Jacob Le Roy fetching water in a leafy glen beside his cabin where a bountiful artesian spring burbled up. They either shot or tomahawked him. It's not quite clear which. They then dragged his body to the cabin, laid it half inside the doorway, buried two tomahawks in the skull, and set the cabin afire. After taking his two children, Marie and John, as well the visiting little girl, they disappeared.

Simultaneously, two Indians arrived at the cabin of the Leininger family, German immigrants who had settled in the Buffalo Valley a half mile from the Le Roy homestead. Mrs. Leininger had gone off that morning to the grist mill and left her three children at the cabin with her husband. At first they had no cause for alarm, as it was not unusual to have occasional Indian visitors at white cabins on the Pennsylvania frontier in the mid-1700s. The two Indians asked Leininger for rum, the strong drink available in colonial America brought from the West Indies. He said he had none. They asked for tobacco instead. Leininger gave them a plug. The two Indians filled a bowl, and finished smoking their pipe.

"We are Allegheny Indians, and your enemies!" they suddenly declared, according to an account the girls later gave. "You all must die!"

They shot the Leininger father, and tomahawked his twenty-year-old son. Once they'd dispatched the adult males, the Indians captured Barbara Leininger, aged twelve, along with Barbara's little sister, Regina, aged nine, and fled into the forest that covered the rounded ridges.

"THIS IS THE OLD LE ROY PLACE," said Kim Mattern, climbing out of his battered pickup and shaking my hand.

We were standing in front of a weathered red barn on a warm Sunday morning in July. A slender middle-aged man, Mattern wore shorts and a T-shirt and had long, grayish hair protruding from under his baseball cap. His casualness contrasted with the occupants of an Amish horse-drawn buggy that clip-clopped down the country road nearby—women and girls wearing bonnets, men and boys in white shirts and dark vests, going Sunday visiting. Green pastures and lush cornfields spilled up from the valley bottom to break gently against the rising wooded ridges. The old farmhouse stood beside the barn, looking both cheery and lonely out here, in the middle of the bucolic Buffalo Valley, with no other dwelling around.

He first checked for permission at the house's front door.

"Follow me," Mattern said.

I followed him across the grassy front yard. Mattern spent part of his childhood in the nearby hamlet of Penn's Creek, and at the age of eight discovered his first Indian artifact. Now working by day doing building maintenance in nearby Lewisburg, he spends his off hours scanning the countryside for new Indian sites as an amateur archaeologist, reporting his findings to the state. His artifact collection currently numbers about fifteen thousand pieces.

A hundred yards from the farmhouse, we descended into a beautiful little glen filled with the sound of dripping water and shaded by overhanging trees. A spring burbled out of the ground into a pool formed by a miniature dam, and cascaded over the dam's edge in a tiny waterfall that gathered into a stream, meandering through the grove toward Penn's Creek.

Mattern squatted down beside the pool, and scooped up some water in his palm. He drank.

"The Indians came from the west," he said, taking another scoop of water. "They were incited by the French to take back their lands from the settlers coming from the British colonies. Le Roy was the first settler here. My irony is that he was the first guy here and the first one killed."

Here, at this spring where Mattern drank, the Indians had come upon Le Roy on that October morning in 1755. And so one thread of the story began.

THE BRITISH AND FRENCH EMPIRES of the mid-1700s acted like two giant rival corporations battling for market dominance in a globe whose vast entirety had just been revealed. The French and Indian War, as we know it—or the Seven Years' War, as Europeans call it—was one major fight in this battle for global dominance. Far more than the Revolutionary War, which followed it by two decades, the French and Indian War shaped the cultural geography of North America. Had it gone the other way, and the French and Indians won instead of the British, the "blank spots" of which I write in North America—including those of Pennsylvania—might be larger and emptier today, given the difference in the two empires' cultural interaction with the Indians and their differing settlement practices.

The mid-1700s were also a time of tremendous intellectual ferment. As the French and British empires struggled for global ascendancy, the thinkers and writers who were hunkered down within them, oppressed by the heavy discipline imposed from above by king and church, embarked on their own struggle for individual rights. They heard explorers' accounts, now coming in from all over the globe, of how humans in their "natural" state—without the iron-fisted institutions of church and king—could live in dignity and freedom. For these and many other reasons, they began to cast aside their ancient bonds to biblical scripture and strict fealty to one's sovereign. Their view of the world and of the state, coming unmoored from these linchpins, shifted dramatically.

With it shifted their view of nature—or "Wild Nature," as some of them called it, or wilderness, as we think of it, in contrast to, say, the genteel and cultivated countryside of Britain or France. The wider world had grown far more accessible by the mid-1700s via sailing ship and carriage. Confronted with the vast and wild landscapes of the Alps or North America—or even the Sahara Desert or the Amazon forest or the Arctic—these city-dwelling thinkers groped for a vocabulary to describe Wild Nature's awesome power. A century or so earlier, Europeans, seeing some of them for the first time, portrayed these landscapes with the biblical imagery that flowed so easily from their pens. They cast the wild, unfamiliar spots of the earth in terms either black or white—either an Eden-like Paradise or a Satanic Hell.

But now, starting in the mid-1700s, Europe's intellectuals sought a more nuanced, insightful way to comprehend these powerful landscapes. Some of the thinkers had made youthful sojourns—even run away—to the Alps while others kept up with the wider world through the literature of exploration. We think of North America as very isolated from Europe then. It wasn't at all. A kind of intellectual volley began back and forth across the Atlantic over how to understand Wild Nature, a kind of serve and return, enabled by the merchant ships constantly sailing to and fro bearing letters, journals, books, and pamphlets, and keeping the drawing rooms of London and salons of Paris in touch with the North American wilds.

Philadelphia in the mid-1700s stood at the intellectual center of British North America, and near to the edge of its wilds. Only 150 miles west of this busy little city on the Eastern Seaboard and over the rounded wooded crest of the Allegheny Mountains began the great watershed of the Ohio Valley—so large it takes in present-day Ohio, Indiana, West Virginia, western Pennsylvania, and parts of other states, including Kentucky, Tennessee, and Illinois. For the British on the East Coast in the mid-1700s, almost all the Ohio Valley was a blank spot.

Parts of Pennsylvania—especially the northwest—remain remarkably blank today. This unexpected wildness in a state usually associated with the urban East is what drew me to it. Pennsylvania is compelling for the pivotal role it played, by way of the French and Indian War, in molding the cultural geography of North America. Even more, I was fascinated by the part that little Philadelphia, with its intellectual ferment of the mid-1700s, with its scientists, botanists, and poets, had played in changing the way Americans came to think about wilderness.

I started in eastern Pennsylvania at the Le Roy homestead, where the children were captured by Indians. I wanted to trace their route as prisoners over the Alleghenies to Pennsylvania's western sector and what was then the remote wilds of the Ohio Valley. Along the way my self-appointed mission was to seek out the blankest spots in Pennsylvania that I could find.

IN THE AUTUMN OF 1753, two years before the Indians arrived at the Le Roy cabin, George Washington, then an obscure twenty-one-year-old Virginia planter, left the British colonies of the East Coast and crossed the Allegheny Mountains into the remote Ohio Valley carrying a letter from Virginia's lieutenant governor, Robert Dinwiddie. A ham-handed and impetuous man, Dinwiddie, of course, represented British interests in colonial America as well as perhaps his own. He had selected the young Washington as his wilderness courier due to Washington's smattering of backwoods experience from his surveying work as a teenager, and to his political and family connections in coastal Virginia. Washington, seeking respectability as the new proprietor of a plantation he had inherited from his half-brother, eagerly took on Dinwiddie's mission.

Stumbling through the snow, Washington and his backwoods guides reached Fort Le Boeuf, near Lake Erie, on December 11, 1753. The French had recently constructed the fort along one of their key fur-trading routes that linked the Great Lakes and the Ohio Valley. The fort's commandant, Captain Jacques Legardeur de Saint-Pierre, greeted Washington's ragtag and travel-worn party with formal hospitality and invited Washington to dine with him that night. A formal dinner in the backwoods outpost might include candlelight and venison roasts and French clarets served before the roaring fire in rough-planked officers' quarters. A professional French officer thirty years Washington's senior, Saint-Pierre had decades of experience in the fur trade of the North American wilderness.

Washington handed over the letter from Dinwiddie.

"The lands upon the River Ohio," Dinwiddie had boldly penned, "are notoriously known to be the property of the Crown of Great Britain. . . . I must desire you to acquaint me by whose authority and instructions you have lately marched from Canada with an armed force, and invaded the King of Great Britain's territories. . . . it becomes my duty to require your peaceable departure . . ."

The French Canadians, their Indian associates, and their canoe-paddling voyageurs had carried packets of pelts through these parts of North America for nearly two centuries. The Ohio River and its tributaries provided a wilderness highway between their fur posts on the Great Lakes and their fur posts on the Mississippi River.

The problem was that both Britain and France exerted dim, sketchy claims to the Ohio Valley, rooted in the earliest days of European exploration in North America. Armor-plated explorers had planted their respective nation's flags on East Coast headlands and seized in name of God and King and Queen vast stretches of territory extending hundreds or thousands of miles inland. These vague, competing claims hadn't really mattered for nearly two hundred years. By the mid-1700s, however, the British colonial population of East Coast planters had swelled and new settlers jostled for farmland.

Just over the Appalachian crest lay the rich Ohio Valley, beckoning to the British colonials as an untamed wilderness to be settled, fields to be cleared and towns built, a vast area to be civilized and made bountiful through agriculture. But for the French who passed through the Ohio Valley in canoes and the Indians who lived there, hunted its forests, fished its streams, and planted small plots of corn beside their villages, the Ohio Valley already was bountiful and beautiful. It needed no improvement.

In the years before the capture of Marie Le Roy and Barbara Leininger, the Indian tribes living in Pennsylvania, the Ohio Valley, and elsewhere in the region had lost millions of acres to shady "treaties" concocted by British colonial authorities. William Penn, the Pennsylvania colony's Quaker founder, was famous for his fairness to Indians and desire to harmoniously live side by side. But once Penn died, his sons grabbed all the land they could lay their hands on. What each Indian tribe really needed, looking at these deals from the distance of two and a half centuries, was a strong team of lawyers and appraisers.*

---

* The British used remarkably innovative ways to cheat the Indians out of their lands. For instance, there was the bitter "Walking Purchase" of 1737. While accounts differ in exact details, a document, possibly forged, appeared in the 1730s purporting that years earlier the Indians had agreed with the Penn family to sell a tract of land that could be paced off in "a day and half's walk." Colonial authorities recruited the three fastest white "runners" they could find, cleared a path to speed their way through the forest, and set them off sprinting for a day and a half. Two of them collapsed from exhaustion; the other managed to cover fifty-five miles. And so the boundary was drawn, giving two thirds of a million acres of Indian lands to the Penns and displacing the Delaware tribe from eastern Pennsylvania.

To lay their dubious claim to Indian lands in the great blank spot of the Ohio Valley, the British colonials played tribes against each other and used clever geographical obfuscation. It worked like this: The British had managed to strike an allegiance with the Iroquois Confederacy, a powerful group of five or six tribes in what's now upstate New York. The confederacy claimed to have conquered other tribes far distant from its power base and thus to control the lands of those tribes, which it then sold in pieces to the British. In 1744, the Iroquois Confederacy sold off—for a few hundred pounds—what the Iroquois believed was only the Shenandoah Valley in Virginia. The fine print in the contract, however, said that the Iroquois were giving up all the remaining Indian lands in Virginia. The Indians understood the western boundary of Virginia as being the "place of the setting of the sun"—the crest of the Allegheny Mountains. However, Virginia's founding charter put the colony's western boundary all the way at the Pacific Ocean—a different "place of the setting of the sun."

By Virginia's way of thinking, the Iroquois Confederacy had just signed over the entire Ohio Valley to the British colony. Virginia land speculators immediately jumped in. A group of wealthy planters from the Northern Neck area—including George Washington's half-brother Lawrence—set themselves up as the Ohio Company and acquired from Virginia's House of Burgesses almost a third of a million acres of these very shakily gotten lands along the Ohio River in order to sell to homesteaders. The Ohio Company then gave stock to Lieutenant Governor Dinwiddie in the hopes it would prove politically expedient. They apparently were right. Dinwiddie penned his outrage at what he claimed were French incursions on Virginia land and dispatched his letter with young George Washington to Saint-Pierre at Fort Le Boeuf.

After his formal dinner with Saint-Pierre that December night in 1753, and as Saint-Pierre wrote his reply to Dinwiddie, Washington and his little party hung around Fort Le Boeuf, surreptitiously checking it out. They counted several hundred canoes that the French were building and preparing to descend to the main Ohio River in the spring. The land jealousy flared between the two rival empires, and Washington's own sense of indignity grew.

Saint-Pierre presented his written reply to Washington, and four days after his arrival at Fort Le Boeuf, Washington and his few guides headed back to coastal Virginia bearing the letter. After almost drowning when he fell off a log raft into an icy river, Washington arrived a month later at Dinwiddie's offices in Williamsburg. He handed over Saint-Pierre's letter.

The veteran French officer had replied coolly to Dinwiddie that the king of France held "incontestable" rights to the Ohio lands. Nevertheless, he would send Dinwiddie's letter to his superiors so they could judge for themselves the king of Great Britain's "pretensions."

"As to the summons you send me to retire," Saint-Pierre wrote, "I do not think myself obliged to obey it."

"I SHOULD MENTION that the French were traders," said Kim Mattern, as we hiked out of the shady glen and walked back to his pickup at the old Le Roy farmstead. "They were not interested in land. They were not interested in 'civilizing' the natives. But in the wars between the English and French, both French and English vied to have the natives on their side."

Mattern reached into the bed of his pickup for what looked like a stack of large picture frames. He held the first up for me to see in the bright Sunday sunlight. Mounted on white cottony material covered by glass lay dozens upon dozens of tiny arrowheads. Their makers had crafted them so precisely they looked sculpted from glass rather than chipped from chert, quartz, and rhyolite.

"These are Late Woodland points," Mattern said.

He lifted up another tray in the warm morning sun.

"I didn't know what you wanted to see, so I just brought a selection of some," he remarked. "These are from the Early Woodland period."

These points were finely worked, too, but heavier. Early Woodland meant archaeologists dated them from the era between 1000 B.C. and A.D. 1.

Then he lifted up a tray from the Archaic Period, and then fifteen more trays. Each represented a step deeper into the countless generations of Indians who inhabited this region today known as Pennsylvania but that surely had hundreds of other place-names that will never be spoken again.

"Do you know what *bifurcated* means?" Mattern asked me. "Like a tooth that has two roots," he said, forking his fingers downward. He held up a tray of the bifurcated spear points. Considerably larger than the others, their cutting edges had been worked in a jagged fashion with tiny stone teeth like the edges of a serrated knife.

"These are eight thousand years old," he said, holding up another tray from the Archaic.

Some had come from the Buffalo Valley. This spot where we stood had been hunted by humans for at least eighty centuries before the Le Roys arrived. It had been a blank spot—wilderness—only to European eyes. At thirty years per generation, that was roughly 270 generations who had lived here before the Le Roys built their farm.

Seeing the incredible detail of those thousands of years' worth of points that were part of Kim Mattern's collection of fifteen thousand, I suddenly understood why it was so important to the French and to the British colonials, once the hostilities broke out between them during the French and Indian War, to each have the Indians on their side. They knew how to hunt here, they knew how to live here, and they knew how to fight here. The only participant who seemed not to care a whit for Indian help was Major General Edward Braddock, who would come across the Atlantic to command British forces in North America. His soon-to-be aide, the eager young George Washington, would learn by his poor example. Singlehandedly, Braddock did much to invent the stereotype of the arrogant British commander who was utterly ignorant—and willfully dismissive—of the local culture.

WHEN WASHINGTON RETURNED from his wintry mail-delivery mission to Fort Le Boeuf, an indignant Dinwiddie presented to the Virginia legislature Saint-Pierre's cheeky reply—"I do not think myself obliged to obey." Though wary of Dinwiddie's personal motives and Ohio Company connections, the legislators did cough up ten thousand pounds to build forts in the Ohio Valley to counter the French moving in there. Washington had hardly returned home when Dinwiddie again dispatched him, in early April of 1754, back over the Alleghenies, heading a disheveled army of 160 volunteers drawn forward by the promise of free settlement land at the Forks of the Ohio.

Britain and France now raced each other through the wilderness for the same coveted strategic spot. This is where the Allegheny and Monongahela rivers meet to form the main Ohio—the site of today's Pittsburgh. In February, an advance party of forty Virginian volunteers had managed to reach the Forks and started erecting a fort. On April 17, however, they looked out from their crude ramparts to see a giant flotilla of canoes and pirogues paddle down the Allegheny River from the north, beaching at the Forks. From the boats, which were those Washington had seen being built back in December at Fort Le Boeuf, stepped five hundred professional French troops hauling eighteen cannons. They marched to the walls of the makeshift British fort with its undernourished complement of Virginia volunteers and demanded immediate surrender. Guaranteed by Captain Contrecoeur safe passage back to the Tidewater, Commander Ward readily gave in, and the French, in gentlemanly military tradition, laid on a feast that night for the hungry Virginians.

Meanwhile, George Washington and his motley band of 160 was advancing hard through the wilderness to the Forks from the east. While an older and more confident commander might have considered his options at this point, the determined young Washington kept advancing on orders issued to him by the militarily inexperienced Dinwiddie—and without London's approval.

"You are to restrain all such Offenders [who attempt to interrupt British settlement], & in Case of resistance make Prisoners of or kill & destroy them."

These orders, observes one historian, "amounted to an invitation to start a war."

Which is just what happened. Accounts generally agree on events leading up to the fateful moment. Learning of Washington's approach toward the Forks, Captain Contrecoeur sent out a small party headed by a distinguished French officer, Joseph Coulon de Villiers de Jumonville, to converse with them and read a summons warning them to stay off French territory. When Washington got word of the French advance party, he assumed it was an attack. He roused his men, marched them through a rainy night for seven miles, and at dawn surprised the waking French party in a woody bottomland—since known as Jumonville Glen. The French jumped up in alarm; one of them apparently fired a shot. Washington ordered a volley in return. The French tried to retreat but their way was blocked by Washington's Indian guides. There was a pause. Washington held fire to let the French leader, Jumonville, through a translator, read the letter he carried aloud.

Then the accounts vary wildly from eyewitnesses on each side.

Washington's official account is apparently a whitewashed version of events, written by a young officer covering up his lack of control of the situation. It stated that Jumonville was killed in combat and so were nine others, and the Indians scalped them.

But a careful reconstruction based on several other eyewitness accounts, English, French, and Indian, paints a far different drama. Jumonville was wounded and had fallen in the initial volleys. During the cease-fire, Washington took the letter Jumonville carried and walked off to have his own translator read it. While Washington read over the letter, an Indian ally of the British from the Iroquois Confederacy approached the fallen Jumonville. Known as Tanaghrisson, or the "Half-King," he had his own motives to start a conflict between French and British—he had been trying to rally his own following of Indians, without much success, to join him with the British, in order to keep himself in power.

"Thou art not yet dead, my father," said Tanaghrisson.

With that, Tanaghrisson split open Jumonville's skull with several blows from his hatchet. Then he plunged his hands into the cranium and squeezed Jumonville's brains through his fingers.

Tanaghrisson's well-aimed hatchet blow was a shrewdly calculated political move on his part. If he could provoke the French to attack the British—his allies—and the British responded with war, it could help him, and the Iroquois Confederacy, to maintain some influence over the separate Indian tribes of the Ohio Valley. Tanaghrisson's hatchet murder of Jumonville was just enough of an outrage, in this sodden, brushy creek bottom in the Ohio wilderness with an uncertain twenty-one-year-old George Washington in charge, to spark what has been called the first global war. Starting here at Jumonville Glen, near modern-day Farmington, Pennsylvania, it lasted for seven years, brought in many countries of Europe, and was fought in North America and Europe as well as India and the Caribbean, where Britain and France had colonial territories.

Ultimately, the French had to give their claim to North America over to Great Britain. It was thus a war that defined America's boundaries, and its lack of boundaries, its open spaces for westward expansion, its cities, its affiliations to which nations of Europe, as well as its sense of independence from them all. It gave Americans a sense of their own destiny. And it fostered the notion that there is always more land to settle—more open space, another blank spot—just over the next hill.

WITH THE SPLITTING OPEN of Jumonville's skull, chaos quickly spread on the American frontier. A thousand more French forces quickly arrived by canoe at Fort Duquesne, which is what France named its outpost-under-construction at the Forks of the Ohio. Captain Contrecoeur sent out a party under Jumonville's revenge-minded older brother, Captain Louis Coulon de Villiers, to run down the retreating George Washington. Washington and his exhausted men holed up in a small, crude British outpost, the aptly named Fort Necessity, huddling in muddy trenches in a powder-dampening downpour as the French and their Indian allies showered them with musketballs from the surrounding forest. In the gloomy dusk Coulon de Villiers offered Washington surrender terms—he could take blame for the "assassination" and walk freely out of the Ohio Valley with his troops, pledging not to set foot in it again for a year. Or he and his men could be destroyed.

At midnight on July 3, 1754, Washington accepted the terms in the outpost's leaky blockhouse.

Daybreak brought the worst of the humiliation. Washington and his fellow Virginians now were able to identify the French allies.

"[W]hat is most severe upon us," lamented one of Washington's party, "they were all our own Indians, Shawnesses, Delawares and Mingos."

The Indians whom the British thought were their allies had switched over to the French.

The buildup led to all-out warfare between the two great empires. By early September, the alarming news of Washington's humiliation by the French in the wilds of the Ohio Valley had traveled back across the Atlantic to London.

"All North America will be lost if These Practices are tolerated," wrote the aggressively minded Duke of Newcastle, who, through his acquaintance with King George's son, had the ear of the royal court and convinced it to block the French from building forts in the Ohio Valley.

With King George's blessing, two infantry regiments set sail from Ireland bound for the wilderness of the Ohio Valley. They were under the command of Major General Edward Braddock, who was also given authority over the ten existing British regiments in North America plus the power to summon up deactivated ones. Braddock, who had trained on the orderly battlefields of Europe and was utterly ignorant about wilderness guerrilla fighting, planned to crush the French not only in their Ohio Valley strongholds, but on three other fronts at the same time—their forts on Lake Ontario and on Lake Champlain, as well as the forts the French had recently built on the peninsula leading to Nova Scotia. This was Acadia, now in British hands, but still heavily French in population.

Braddock's contempt extended both to Indian warriors and to the fighting ability of American colonial troops—they could not drill with the same precision that the British regulars displayed in London's Hyde Park.

"[I]t is impossible that [savages] should make any impression" on disciplined British troops, he told Ben Franklin upon arriving in America.

Franklin wasn't so sure.

Braddock alienated the Pennsylvania Assembly by calling it "pusillanimous" because its pacifist Quaker members wouldn't appropriate money for his troops to fight the French.

Nor did he warm to Indian diplomacy. Chief Shingas, the head of the Ohio Delawares, approached Braddock and offered to rally other Ohio Valley tribes to help the British drive the French out of the Ohio Valley. The chief then asked him, "What would the British do with the land once they controlled it?"

Braddock replied, "The English should inhabit and inherit the land."

The chief asked whether the Indians who were friends of the British could live and trade among the British settlers of the Ohio Valley and have hunting grounds there.

"No savage should inherit the land," answered Braddock.

If the Indians wouldn't be free to live on the land, Chief Shingas responded, they wouldn't fight for it.

Braddock answered that he did not need their help and he had "no doubt of driveing the French and their Indians away."

These Indians led by Shingas, who had been ready to join the British against the French if it meant they were given back their hunting rights in the Ohio Valley, abandoned Braddock in anger and returned from the colonized East to the wilds of the Ohio. Many of them now eagerly sought to go to war on the side of the French, after being so high-handedly rejected by the British in the person of Major General Braddock.

"If it hadn't been Le Roy, it would have been someone else," Mattern mused as we climbed the wooded ridge overlooking the old Le Roy farmstead.

He swung the shaft of an old golf club, like a riding crop or machete, to knock aside the underbrush, probed around with it at exposed tree roots and amid the excavated dirt piles from gopher holes to turn up Indian artifacts. Occasionally he poked a little more intently at one chip of rock or another. "I see what *should* be on the site and then block it out and see what *shouldn't* be there," he explained. He reached down and plucked leaves of native plants that the Indians ate: wild strawberry, native garlic, Jacob's root.

It was Mattern's belief, derived from written accounts and his knowledge of the local geography, that the Indian raiding party, after attacking the Le Roy and Leininger homesteads, regrouped at the top of this wooded ridge.

"They rendezvoused up here and then headed west," Mattern told me. "They had done their deed. They had gained their power. That was their belief, they gained power from the enemy. You have to understand that it was more important to take captives and to return home with them, not to kill everyone. They believed in counting coup. Basically, it means hitting your enemy and not getting hit back. Not hitting them with an arrow but *striking* them with the hand. It was better to scalp them alive than dead. Hair was sacred—you really took power."

He probed with his golf shaft at the bare soil around some exposed tree roots, and identified the edible plant known as poke.

"The natives believed that everything had spirit or power. A tree growing up through the rock, standing up to the wind, that has power. The bear has power, the wolf has power, the rock has power.

"Everything has power—that's why so much was sacred to them.

Their belief system was *so* different from ours, and we called them pagans. The English and Dutch didn't understand the intricacies."

GENERAL BRADDOCK, SURELY, did not understand the intricacies, nor fathom the deep and ancient Indian attachment to the earth. After telling Chief Shingas that "no savage should inherit the land" and that he didn't need Shingas's help to drive the French from the Ohio Valley, Braddock and his column of 2,200 men left Fort Cumberland, Maryland, near the headwaters of the Potomac, in late May 1755. They were marching with purpose toward the new French Fort Duquesne at the Forks of the Ohio, 110 miles away through the wilderness. The British claimed that the French fort had been placed illegally on lands that belonged to the British crown—the entire Ohio Valley. Three hundred light infantry headed the column, backed up by 250 frontiersmen chopping a road through thick forest for the column's bulk, which included more soldiers, cannons to siege the fort, supply wagons (one driven by Daniel Boone), and a contingent of camp women. In addition to seven Mingo (or Iroquois Confederacy) Indian scouts, though no Indian warriors, the column included a large complement of American "provincials"—essentially colonial farmers—who, in Braddock's view, were of dubious worth compared to his crack British troops.

Making agonizingly slow progress through "uninhabited Wilderness over steep rocky Mountains and almost impassable Morasses" because Braddock had insisted on using wagons instead of pack horses, the column had just forded the Monongahela River early on the afternoon of July 9. It was now within ten miles of Fort Duquesne. The head of the column and scouts started up a draw into the higher terrain that rose on the opposite bank. The soldiers noticed that, instead of the thick underbrush they had been pushing through on the other side of the river, the forest understory here was open and had been burned to encourage grass to grow—a sign the Indians had used these lands recently as hunting grounds.

Through the open trees, only two hundred yards away, the British scouts suddenly spotted humans. This, it turned out, was the head of a party of nearly a thousand Indians and Canadian soldiers, sent out from Fort Duquesne by Contrecoeur to intercept the advancing British.

It was with surprise on both sides that the two parties met, but each had a totally different response. Braddock's British troops lined up in formation in the crude road and began to fire coordinated volleys at the Indians and French Canadians. The first few volleys dropped the French commander, Beaujeu, as he waved his hat to direct his trained troops. The seven hundred Indians with Beaujeu, however, instantly took cover behind trees and in the ravine, lay prone on the ground, and otherwise hid from the volleys, then ducked through the forest to surround the British column.

As the Indians opened fire from their hiding places, the British advance party fell back, running into the main group, which continued to move forward. The column of redcoats was jammed into the road as fire poured in on them from the Indian hiding places. They couldn't even see where to fire their organized volleys. Virtually all the British officers in the advance column were wiped out in the first ten minutes. The American forces who accompanied the British troops attempted, like the Indians who were attacking them, to hide behind trees. But Braddock, charging ahead from the rear of the column, fiercely urged his British troops and the American provincials to keep formation and fire coordinated and disciplined volleys, which he knew to be effective from the wide-open, chessboardlike battlefields of Europe.

According to one witness, "Whenever he saw a man skulking behind a tree, he flew at once to the spot, and, with curses on his cowardice and blows with the flat of his sword, drove him back into the open road."

The Indians and French shot four horses from under Braddock, while Washington, who'd gone into battle severely weakened by illness, lost two. The fight raged for three hours—lead flying from the woods at the orderly rows of redcoats in the crude road and the unseen Indians sounding to British ears as "ravenous Hell-hounds . . . yelping and screaming like so many Devils."

Braddock—perhaps mercifully for his men—finally took a musket ball through the arm and lungs and fell from his horse. No longer forced to stand their ground in formation, his troops fell back toward the river, then broke and fled in terror—running for miles through the woods—as the Indians began scalping the fallen. For decades, a story persisted that Braddock had been shot by one of his own troops—an American provincial named Thomas Fausett of Pennsylvania. Years later he admitted to cutting down his own general because if he hadn't, all the men would have been killed.

It was an utter slaughter. Of 1,460 British and American troops that had actually gone into combat, 456 were killed and 421 wounded. Of the 89 commissioned officers, 63 were killed or wounded.

General Braddock, the architect of this disaster which would forever bear the ignominious name Braddock's Defeat, managed to survive for four days. His men ferried their wounded leader back across the Monongahela, and began the long, stumbling road toward Maryland.

"Who would have thought it?" Braddock said quietly, as he lay dying. "We shall better know how to deal with them next time."

His surviving officers buried Braddock in the center of the crude, muddy path named "Braddock's Road" that he had pushed through the Pennsylvania wilderness. After interring Braddock under his road, the officers marched the remaining straggling, retreating troops and horses over his freshly dug grave to hide it, fearing that the Indians would desecrate his body.

"He looked upon us as dogs," said Chief Scaroudy, explaining why the Indians had abandoned the British and allied themselves with the French in the battle for the Ohio Valley, "and would never hear anything that was said to him."

Word quickly spread through the British Empire of Braddock's crushing defeat in the Ohio Valley. British and French troops already in North America mobilized toward the Great Lakes border area and surrounding uplands and more were dispatched from abroad. These had been hazy regions of possession from the first colonial arrivals in the New World—the French colonized to the north and the British, in much greater numbers, to the south. But where was the line that separated them?

THESE KINDS OF HAZY BORDERLANDS still exist all over the world. Political no-man's-lands where there is a vacuum of international power, they often occur in rugged, remote regions, in mountainous highlands, and at the headwaters of river systems. The historian Owen Lattimore, writing in the mid-1900s, and referring to places such as Manchuria, Tibet, and Afghanistan, called these regions "storm centers of the world." In the mid-1750s the wild Ohio Valley, and the mountainous borderlands around it, was the storm's epicenter.

With Braddock's Defeat, London and Paris both quickly sent ships westward across the Atlantic, laden with men and supplies. The stakes now clearly had soared: which empire—French or British—would control the North American continent? Three months after Braddock's Defeat in July 1755, British authorities questioned the loyalties of the French-speaking Acadians to the British crown, summoned them to the church at Grand Pré, locked the doors, read their eviction notice, torched their homes, and loaded them on ships.

Barely a month after the British started the "grand deportation" of the Acadians, the French, using their Indian allies, counterthrusted in Pennsylvania by "carrying terror" to the British settlers. That morning of October 16, 1755, the raiding band of Delaware and Allegheny Indians attacked the Le Roy and Leininger homesteads and captured the children—the first of many Indian raids on settlers of the Pennsylvania frontier, in addition to raids already under way on settlements in Virginia and Maryland. Many of these were led by the Delaware chief Shingas—he who had been rebuffed by Braddock—and the great warrior Captain Jacobs.

It was terror with a very specific purpose.

"Nothing is more calculated to disgust the people of those Colonies and make them desire the return of peace" than these random attacks on the settlers' homesteads, wrote the Marquis de Vaudreuil, the governor-general of French Canada, who had many years' experience in the North American wilds.

As panic and terror spread on the news of the multiple murders, kidnappings, and scalpings, such as the Le Roy and Leininger families suffered, the British settlers fled the frontier for the safety of the cities. One such haven for traumatized refugees was Philadelphia, sitting at the edge of this great swath of blank terrain.

That tumultuous autumn of 1755, Billy Bartram had begun his fourth year of studies at the prestigious Philadelphia Academy. A poetry-besotted youth of sixteen, Billy surely watched these developments on the frontier with great interest. Despite the wave of Indian-hating that engulfed much of Philadelphia as terror spread, Billy Bartram came to respect—even idolize—Indians.

Billy, writing under the name William Bartram, would eventually be a key player in the intellectual volleys across the Atlantic. While failing at many endeavors—merchant, planter, suitor—he spent years as a starry-eyed wanderer in the American wilderness, far ahead of his time, nearly a century before Thoreau. His book *Travels,* published in the late 1700s, would deeply influence the Romantic poets coming of age in Britain around 1800, and inspire the love for Wild Nature that later would be absorbed and refined by American wilderness writers—most notably Emerson, Thoreau, and Muir. Our vision of wilderness today, in other words, derives in good part from this poetic lost soul, Billy Bartram of Philadelphia, stumbling about in the American woods in the mid-1700s.

This is all the more remarkable because Indians killed Billy's Quaker grandfather, who emigrated from England to Pennsylvania in 1682 when William Penn founded it as a Quaker colony. Billy's father, John, was raised by his Philadelphia grandmother and started out as a Quaker farmer, but, falling in with a crowd of young Philadelphia intellectuals that included Ben Franklin, soon displayed prodigious skill as a self-taught botanist.

Botany had just arrived as a European science. For centuries, herbalists, "physicks," and alchemists had studied and cultivated plants for their medicinal benefits. But with the dawning of the "Age of Sail" and global exploration, European ships in the sixteenth and seventeenth centuries brought back exotic plant specimens from distant lands. The invention of the compound microscope in 1590 allowed Robert Hooke to identify the cell structure of plants and Stephen Hales to trace the movement of water in them—the start of experimental plant physiology. The European aristocracy planted botanical gardens on their estates, showcasing rare plants in the manner that today's wealthy collect expensive works of art.

John Bartram learned how to use a microscope and the Latin plant classification system then being worked out in the 1730s by Linnaeus in Sweden. He was invited to join Ben Franklin's new "Junto"—a club of young men started in 1727 who met every Friday evening in Philadelphia to debate "morals, politics and natural philosophy" (and provide a handy forum for the drinking songs Franklin liked to invent). Bartram's farm—really a very shaggy botanical garden—on the banks of the Schuylkill River just outside Philadelphia soon became widely known in scientific circles. European plant collectors commissioned Bartram to travel throughout the colonies—including the Pennsylvania wilderness—to gather new botanical specimens that had never before been seen in Europe.

It was no doubt through the Junto and the worldly Ben Franklin that Bartram received his first exposure to Deism and drifted from pure Quakerism. All those European expeditions around the globe had brought back accounts of religious practices in Africa, Asia, the Pacific Islands. Scientists like Isaac Newton and thinkers like Descartes, meanwhile, had demonstrated a universe that operated according to rationalistic principles. Applying this rationalism to religion, European intellectuals now isolated the basic principles that they perceived united all religion—such as belief in a supreme being and that living a virtuous life was the highest form of worship. They shunned the literal word of the Bible, questioned miracles as "proof" of God's existence, and rejected the Holy Trinity in favor a single divinity.

These beliefs eventually got John Bartram kicked out of the Darby Friends Meeting. While deliberating his case for fifteen months, the Meeting Overseers visited Bartram—who comes across as gentle and friendly in manner but firm in belief—at his house. They then reported back to the Meeting.

"[He] still persists therein to say the longer he lives the stronger he is in the disbelief of the divinity of Jesus Christ."

At the time of his disownment by the Meeting, Bartram, in addition to his botanical reading on fruit trees, mosses, and herbs, was taking extensive notes on *The Morals of Confucius*—a favorite philosopher of the Deists. He was also a fan of the British poet Alexander Pope, a dwarfish and sharp-tongued gardening devotee who celebrated nature in his verse and whose spiritual views—though he was a Catholic in name—leaned toward Deism. Above the entrance to his greenhouse, Bartram inscribed a couplet from Pope's "Essay on Man":

> *Slave to no sect, who takes no private road*
> *But looks through nature, up to nature's God!*

John Bartram's own vision of spirituality, one that would prove pivotal in how we view nature today, developed from many influences—a kind of amalgam of science, Deism, and his precise plant observations, all of it perhaps leavened with a little medieval cosmology and Chinese *qi:* God is manifest in all nature. All nature is animated by a divine spirit.

In particular, Bartram cited an "intelligence" in plants as evidence of divinity in nature—the same divinity that is present in all humans. Plants, he observed in letters to friends, respond to heat and cold, light and dark, and the petals of many flower species close up in rainy weather or as evening approaches. He especially mentioned the Tipiti-witchet of the Carolinas and the mimosa tree, a native of Asia, whose leaves fold up on cool evenings.

"[I]f we won't allow them real feeling, or what we call sense, it must be some action next degree inferior to it, for which we want a proper epithet, or the immediate finger of God. . . . I have queried whether there is not a portion of universal intellect diffused in all life & self motion adequate to its particular organization."

"It is through the telescope," he wrote on another occasion that would echo through the centuries, "that I see God in his glory."

Such was the unorthodox religious atmosphere and intensely botanical household in which young Billy Bartram, born in 1739, grew up. He seems to have been a moony, introspective youth, passionate about drawing and poetry. In 1752, at the age of thirteen, Billy entered the Philadelphia Academy—a progressive liberal arts school founded by Ben Franklin in an era when most schools focused on ministerial training. At this innovative school, Billy and his teenaged friends fell under the influence of the brilliant and fiery provost, William Smith, who had recently studied at Scotland's University of Aberdeen.

Smith brought the latest European literary trends to little Philadelphia. These adolescent sons of the city's leading merchants and scientists now became smitten by British pseudo-classical verse. With Provost Smith as their adviser, they founded a publication, *The American Magazine,* which showcased their poetry written in strict rhymed couplets and studded with references to ancient gods and bucolic landscapes.

Billy's friend and classmate, sixteen-year-old Nathaniel Evans, published a poem wondering if the "sylvan muse" that inspired the great ancient Greek and Roman poets would ever appear in the New World or along Schuylkill's banks—presumably among one of the circle of friends.

Shall fam'd arcadia own the tuneful choir
And fair Sicilia boast the matchless lyre?
. . .
O Pennsylvania, shall no son of thine
Glow with the raptures of the sacred nine?

Billy didn't publish in *The American Magazine* but he clearly absorbed the lush, yearning spirit of its verse. His greatest passion was drawing pictures of birds, plants, and flowers, a talent he honed at age fourteen on plant-collecting expeditions with his father such as to the Catskill Mountains, the Hudson Valley, and to visit the New York botanist Cadwallader Colden. But that fall of 1755 their plans for more expeditions—especially to Carolina to observe its rich subtropical vegetation—were disrupted by the outbreak of full-on warfare in North America for possession of the Ohio Valley.

The "treacherous" Indians, wrote Billy's father, John Bartram, to a correspondent in Carolina, where his own father years earlier had apparently been killed by natives while traveling there, "have destroyed all our back inhabitants. No traveling now, to Dr. Colden's nor to the back parts of Pennsylvania, Maryland, nor Virginia."

AFTER EXPLORING THE WOODED RIDGETOP above the old Le Roy place where the Indians had hidden their hostages, I said goodbye to Kim Mattern that sunny Sunday morning. I then traced the route of the young captives of the Le Roy and Leininger families, heading exactly into those "back parts" of Pennsylvania mentioned by John Bartram that the events of autumn 1755 had put off-limits. While the long, fertile valleys had been cultivated two centuries ago into rolling greenswards, the great northeastern-trending mountain ridges of these northern Alleghenies still rise up as thickly forested and nearly unsettled as in Bartram's day.

Taking Mattern's directions on back roads out of the charming Buffalo Valley, I soon connected with a four-lane highway that hugged the placid, languorous Susquehanna River and drove a few miles north, past the old river town of Sunbury, at the confluence of the river's North and West branches. Here—although there was no evidence remaining—is where the ancient Indian village of Shamokin had stood.

From Shamokin I took to smaller roads again, trying to pick up the route on which their Indian captors led Marie Le Roy and Barbara Leininger westward, into what was then a massive blank spot for the European settlers of North America.

Mattern had told me that the retreating raiding party probably avoided the Great Shamokin Trail, a kind of ancient, foot-trodden superhighway connecting Shamokin on the Susquehanna, which flows to the Atlantic Ocean, to the Indian towns to the west. These villages sat on the Allegheny River and other Ohio Valley tributaries, which flow to the Mississippi and then to the Gulf of Mexico. In the millennia before European settlement this route served for long-distance, cross-country travel much as today's Interstate 80 does, and connected the great watershed of the Atlantic Coast to that of the Mississippi Valley. In fact, today's I-80 follows the Great Shamokin Trail through a good deal of Pennsylvania.

By avoiding the Shamokin Trail, the captors stayed off the obvious route white searchers would follow when looking for the girls. The Indian captors probably took the smaller Karondinhah, or Penn's Creek Trail. I followed this more obscure route, the captors' route, by driving along Pennsylvania Highway 45. The highway rolled atop a gentle ridge in beautiful green farming country dotted with enormous Amish barns that resembled stoutly built country inns with shuttered windows, the wooded ridges rising as backdrops. Corn grew in thick, even rows, and herds of black-and-white-spotted Holstein cows grazed. On this Sunday afternoon Amish buggies trotted up the road with their bonneted women and vest-jacketed men in bushy beards, going Sunday visiting to their neighbors' farms. Small boys in their vests played on shady lawns while parents chatted on porches. I wanted to stop at the prosperous farmsteads offering eggs, cheese, raw milk for sale, but the hand-lettered signs all said, "No Sunday Sales."

I felt that thrill of discovery that comes from unexpectedly stumbling upon someplace very different from one's own culture. I was swept up by the beautiful landscape, the elaborate barns that showed so much craftsmanship, this place so rooted in the fertile earth and in the work of one's hands compared to modern strip-mall America. I was reminded of a larger-scale version of the rolling Wisconsin dairy-farming country of my childhood. It was clear why, as the events unfolded on October 16, 1755, the day of the attack on the Le Roy and Leininger farmsteads, the white settlers coveted these rich, productive valleys and graceful, wooded hills—and why the Indians were not ready to forsake them.

Immediately after their capture, the Indians had led the girls to the top of a nearby high hill—no doubt the one beside the Le Roy homestead where Kim Mattern had led me poking for artifacts with his golf-club shaft. The rest of the Indian raiding party arrived toward dusk, the girls reported later, and tossed six fresh, bloody scalps on the ground at the girls' feet, saying they'd had a good hunt that day.

The Indians conducted more raids on settlers the next day, returning with nine scalps and five more prisoners. On the third day they divided up the spoils, reported the girls, which totaled ten captives, fourteen horses, and abundant food taken from the farmsteads. The two girls—Marie Le Roy and Barbara Leininger—went to an Indian named Galasko, along with two horses. As they later described it:

> We traveled with our new master for two days. He was tolerably kind, and allowed us to ride all the way, while he and the rest of the Indians walked. Of this circumstance Barbara Leininger took advantage, and tried to escape. But she was almost immediately recaptured, and condemned to be burned alive. The savages gave her a French Bible, which they had taken from le Roy's house, in order that she might prepare for death; and, when she told them that she could not understand it, they gave her a German Bible. Thereupon they made a large pile of wood and set it on fire, intending to put her into the midst of it. But a young Indian begged so earnestly for her life that she was pardoned, after having promised not to attempt to escape again, and to stop her crying.

As I drove west on Highway 45 dark clouds swept in. Somewhere along here, west of modern-day Lewisburg, the Indian raiding band had split into two groups, apparently to avoid detection by white searchers, with the girls' group heading toward a Delaware Indian town called Jenkiklamuhs (now Clearfield), which sat on the West Branch of the Susquehanna. The farming valley along Highway 45 looked peaceful and prosperous. A shimmery curtain of rain briefly veiled the wooded ridges. The sun returned and the narrow, sinuous strip of asphalt glistened, my tires zipping over it. The road wound upward, over a mountain ridge, through remnant groves of big white pine trees—the species that once cloaked much of this mountain landscape before it was logged. Here ran one of the long fingers of the northern Allegheny Mountains like a great curved claw. I guessed Galasko had led Marie and Barbara on his stolen horses through this same mountain pass. I descended again into farm country. Villages eventually yielded to subdivisions. Highway 45 fed into a four-lane. The four-lane roared into the town of State College, home of Pennsylvania State University. Here, in the collections of Pennsylvania Archives, I hoped to find what I needed to retrace Marie and Barbara's captivity. Maps. Old, old maps.

At the same time that Galasko led Marie and Barbara westward through the Pennsylvania wilds, in October 1755, back in Philadelphia, John Bartram started thinking that his son Billy should get a job. A *real* job. Enough dallying in the arts. By then, Billy had attended the Philadelphia Academy for about three years, with its poetry and classics, its playwriting and liberal arts (the school would eventually become the University of Pennsylvania). He'd become very proficient at drawing, but his father wanted him to have a means to make a hardearned, decent living beyond what he considered these leisured—and unprofitable—aristocratic pursuits. He didn't want Billy to be "what is commonly called a gentleman," he wrote in a letter to his London botanical friend Peter Collinson. In turn, Collinson, who had much admired Billy's botanical drawings, now advised Billy "to leave off his Darling Delights to qualify himself to live in the world."

When he turned sixteen, John presented Billy with various career options. Billy shunned each one, struggling to find his place.

Medicine, thought John. He purchased medical texts for Billy to study, but then he complained that Billy didn't turn a single page.

Surveying, thought John, as it would allow Billy the chance to study and draw plants. Then he reconsidered, remarking, "We have five times more surveyors already than can get half employ."

John consulted with his friend, the ever-practical Ben Franklin. Like the confused Dustin Hoffman character in *The Graduate* who is told by his father's friend to go into the fast-growing field of plastics, the at-loose-ends young Billy heard only one word of advice from Ben Franklin—"Printing."

John nixed it, knowing that "as [Ben] well knew, he was the only printer that did ever make a good livelihood by it, in this place."

Ben thought it over a bit, then suggested engraving. That didn't work out either. What Billy really liked was botany and drawing—pursuits that John worried "won't get him his living."

Finally, the practical-minded father took the initiative for the moony son and apprenticed him to a prosperous Philadelphia merchant, Captain Child, to learn how to trade in cargoes of goods. Billy spent four years with Captain Child—who felt toward him like a father to a son—and then set off to Cape Fear, in Carolina, where his uncle lived, to go into business as an independent merchant himself.

Billy's entrepreneurial foray soon failed. He endured the ocean voyage to Cape Fear badly seasick, then floods ruined much of the Carolina countryside, he reported in a letter home upon his arrival, undermining the chances of selling much merchandise. He did manage to sell one shipment of thirty-five barrels of turpentine, but no evidence exists of any merchant trades beyond that. In fact, there is little evidence of Billy of any kind during most of this period. What survives is an absence of Billy—a kind of blank spot of Billy. His father and Peter Collinson wrote him repeatedly, their surviving letters displaying a growing annoyance that Billy doesn't respond to them, nor to their requests to send back a few plants or seeds from Carolina's warm coastal climes.

"[T]hee need not hinder half an hour's time to gather them," father admonished son for his laziness, "or turn 20 yards out of thy way to pluck them."

John began to lose faith in Billy, especially compared to his two other industrious sons, John Jr. and Moses.

"I doubt Will," he wrote to Collinson. "He will be ruined in Carolina. Everything goes wrong with him there."

"Billy, so ingenious a lad," wrote Collinson to John, "is as it were lost in indolence and obscurity."

Billy may have started drinking heavily. His father's letters to him of this period are filled with references to "temperance." Or he may have fallen secretly in love with his first cousin, Mary Bartram, on whose family's estate he lived at Cape Fear, perched high on a river bluff that offered stunning views of forest and cane meadows spreading below. Letters written years later point to that possibility, as does family tradition. Whatever the case, Billy certainly seems to have been intoxicated by the sheer, flowering lushness of Carolina compared to spare Pennsylvania.

And so Billy idled at Cape Fear, with cousin Mary, in the climate's "eternal spring." He got along well with his uncle. He drew. He studied plants. He worked lackadaisically at trading. His business affairs deteriorated, and he fell deeper into debt to creditors back in Philadelphia.

Meanwhile his father, thanks to diligent letter-writing by his friend Collinson to the duke of Northumberland, was appointed as the King's Botanist for America. The appointment came to John with a stipend of fifty pounds a year. Collinson proposed to the king that John Bartram travel through the wilderness of the Florida interior to send back to Britain exotic and wonderful plant specimens.

Thus appointed, John Bartram wrote to Billy proposing that he join him as assistant on the Florida expedition. He should sell off his remaining trade goods, John advised, and put his financial affairs into the hands of an attorney. Happily bailing out on the merchant's life, Billy accompanied John through eastern Florida on a journey that was supposed to last one month but extended to more than five, so engrossed were the Bartrams with the flowering plants, the swamps and pine barrens, the gushing springs and bellowing alligators.

Not wishing to leave the tropical exotica to return to the dull merchant's life, Billy fixated on the notion that he'd like to set up as a rice planter on a remote, swampy stretch of Florida's St. John's River. Although his father considered this another "frolic" of Billy's, John staked him to the necessities, which were dispatched from Charleston to Florida as John headed back north, for Billy to start a plantation in the wilderness. These necessities included four slaves to clear the land, an iron pot, axes, seeds, barrels of corn and pork, and a pot of sugar.

Six months later, a Charleston acquaintance of the senior Bartram's, Henry Laurens, visited Billy at his so-called plantation and reported to John back in Philadelphia that Billy was living in a leaky hovel beside a stinking malarial swamp. He was sick and feverish, out of food, and the labor of clearing a plantation was clearly beyond his "tender and delicate frame of body and intellect."

"[N]o colouring," he wrote, "can do justice to the forlorn state of poor Billy Bartram."

Billy returned to Philadelphia by year's end, working as a day laborer despite his expensive education in the classics and poetry. He then suddenly bolted and disappeared from Philadelphia after his creditors apparently threatened him with physical harm if he didn't make good on his debts. After several months, he eventually showed up at Cape Fear again, reestablished communication with his family, and John paid off the creditors with "one hundred pounds ready cash."

Billy lingered at Cape Fear for another two years despite the death of his uncle. It was as if he were taken with some spirit of the age, some intangible zeitgeist of his generation that he couldn't name, wandering about seeking a place, or simply the start of his path, in the world.

That path finally arrived in the form of Dr. John Fothergill, a renowned London physician who was creating a large botanical garden on his Essex country estate. The ubiquitous Collinson had shown him Billy Bartram's impressive drawings of American turtles made at Cape Fear. Fothergill commissioned Billy for more drawings, and Billy eventually suggested Fothergill stake him to another botanical excursion through Florida. Fothergill hesitated—was he sober and diligent? wrote Fothergill to Bartram senior—but the doctor finally offered Billy fifty pounds per year to go exploring on his own, which was the start of Billy's remarkable journey that would shape the way we look at the wilds.

It was another beautiful July morning the next day as I jogged along the pathways and green lawns of the Penn State campus. Rummaging through library card catalogues and computer records, I found on microfiche the map I sought. It had been compiled by Paul A. W. Wallace, who spent a lifetime researching the old Indian trails of Pennsylvania. Wallace's central map showed the entire state—or what's now the state—etched with an intricate spiderweb of ancient trails. There were dozens and dozens of them, a kind of shadow image of how intimately the region was known to Indians. One of the most prominent trails, the Great Shamokin Path, ran east-west across the network like a spine. Just to the north of the Shamokin Path several big holes showed in the web—"blank spots" even on this Indian traveling map. One especially large blank spot was labeled "Buffalo Swamp." If I had hostages, and were hiding from white pursuers, this is where I'd head.

I veered north. I drove with a Starbucks coffee—purchased from an outlet near the Penn State campus and its archives—in the cup holder and the modern *Rand McNally Road Atlas* opened on the passenger seat of my rental car. Even the Rand McNally map showed big blank spots, which happened to correspond with the blank spots of the Wallace map. Some now bore the designation of "state forests" and were shaded a light green, while some remained simply white and empty.

Some months earlier I'd met a young forester at a conference in Santa Fe. Although now based in the Southwest, he'd worked for several years in Pennsylvania.

He'd scrawled "Renovo" on the back of his card and handed it to me.

"Go to Renovo," he'd told me. "You won't believe there's a spot that remote in the East."

I still had his card. So now I headed for Renovo.

I exited I-80 at the old river town of Lock Haven. As late afternoon slipped toward evening, I twisted along a two-lane road, overhung by dense forest, that hugged the West Branch of the Susquehanna. Glimpsed through the trees, the river slid by smooth and quiet and dark. There were no houses. The air felt cool. Steep, wooded mountainsides slanted upward from both banks. Starbucks belonged to a different civilization, a distant dot whose buzzing and sparking couldn't penetrate these quiet, dark forests. Ahead, there would be no designer coffee bars, no *New York Times,* no Internet access.

It felt lonely. I missed my family back in Montana. It occurred to me that one definition of remoteness—a blank spot—has to do with accessibility to distant information. Crouched low, studying flower petals and leaf structures, the Bartrams collected information that was profoundly local. An Indian hunter along this river studied the soil, the grasses, the wind, the weather, for signs—signs of bear, or deer, or elk, or enemies, or berries that were about to ripen. They were far better informed than we could ever be on the minutiae, the details, the subtleties and profundities, *of this place.* Instead, I lived in a world where information—much of it—came from afar. In my world, information had become a *commodity*—a raw material traded in great quantities. Its details might or might not apply to my immediate surroundings. It arrived in huge dollops and I had to sieve through it at high speed to determine if any bits of it applied to my circumstance, discarding the vast majority of it. But out here, for a Delaware Indian studying animal prints, or a John or William Bartram bent to a flower's petals, all information was local and specific. All of it counted. All was useful and thus valuable.

A whole corridor of modern American life—Interstate 80—a giant coast-to-coast pipeline through which washes our commerce and what we call our culture, lay only twenty or thirty miles south of me, linking New York and San Francisco. Goods and information—semi-loads of freight and electromagnetic signals bouncing between cell-phone towers—followed the roaring highway across the continent. But just north of it lay this kind of blackness of information, a blank spot. So-called civilizations—including ours—judge their state of "advancement," in one measure, by the speed and accessibility of information traveling within their borders: Phoenician ships. Roman roads. Incan runners. The British postal system. Our Internet . . . as if civilization were a giant organism that processed information instead of food. I thought of those computer-chip makers engaged in their titanic engineering wars to design the fastest systems.

But there was no system here. Or if there was a system, it was so ancient I didn't understand it.

I pulled off the road at a small clearing in the forest along the river. A historical marker stood there.

SINNEMAHONING PATH
An ancient Indian trail connected the West Branch of the Susquehanna with the Upper Allegheny. . . . [leading] to the Seneca country.

Here was a key spot on that ancient map. Here, in these mountains, the headwater streams of the Susquehanna reached up from the East Coast, while the headwaters of the Allegheny reached up from the Ohio Valley. With a short carry of their canoes at Portage Creek, the East Coast tribes met the Great Lakes tribes, bridging two large chunks of the continent. Every day we move unknowingly through thousands of "links" scattered across the Internet. The Sinnemahoning trail was a link, too, but one both local and profound at the same time, a path through the forest that connected cultures.

The road finally emerged from the woods. Narrow, grassy flats lined the river. A cabin or a house sat here and there, mountains rising steeply behind them. I passed a sign announcing the town of Renovo, "Home of the Pennsylvania Railroad." The tracks traced the river valley. This, too, had once served as a major high-speed link across the continent, the tracks tracing the Susquehanna River valley through these mountains, tying the East Coast to Chicago and St. Louis.

Renovo's population, currently 1,232, was now shrinking by about 1 percent per year. The town possessed that one-car-at-a-time-down-the-street feeling of boomtowns from which the action had moved on decades ago. Stretched out along the rail line that paralleled the river were small, faded frame houses. Unlike the older river towns I'd seen, such as Sunbury, which centered on the river, the houses faced the Penn Railroad tracks instead of the Susquehanna. I could see parallels between this area and the blank spot of northern Maine. During the height of the timbering era, the St. John River had been a major thoroughfare for logs. Now only wilderness existed along its banks. Here in Renovo, the era of the railroad was passing and the town shrinking, and around it lay hundreds of thousands of acres of steep, wooded mountains.

I pulled into the Sportsman's Motel on the east edge of town, checked into a room, and sat at the motel's bar for a steak dinner and cold mugs of the local beer. Savoring the warm and lively atmosphere, the locals and visitors mixing, I spread out my maps on the bar. On some of the modern maps, this section of the state, blanketed with mountains and several state forests, was marked "The Pennsylvania Wilds."

The owner, Cindy, sat kitty-corner from me at the bar, sipping a martini while waiting for her friend Kim. I thanked her for the delicious dinner.

"Where are you from?" she asked.

"Montana."

"So what are you doing here?"

"It's a long story," I replied. "I'm searching for the emptiest places on the map."

"Well, you're here." She laughed. "We're still trying to get cell-phone coverage."

"With all these mountains, I believe it," I said. "You'd need a tower every fifty feet. With so few people, it couldn't be worth the expense for the telephone company."

"I've met with Verizon about it," said Cindy. "They just laugh."

MARIE LE ROY AND BARBARA LEININGER, with their Indian captor, Galasko, passed close to the south of this remote area—the blank spot—of state forests now centered around Renovo. Joining the Great Shamokin Path, the party traveled west across the divide between the Atlantic and Ohio watersheds. After two months of travel, they arrived in December 1755 at Galasko's destination—the Indian village of Kittaning, located at the present-day town of the same name but slightly different spelling. Kittaning sat on the Allegheny River about forty miles upstream from the strategic Forks, where the Allegheny joins the Monongahela River to form the Ohio. Reported the girls:

> As [Kittaning] was to be our place of permanent abode, we here received our welcome, according to Indian custom. It consisted of three blows each, on the back. They were, however, administered with great mercy. Indeed, we concluded that we were beaten merely in order to keep up an ancient usage, and not with the intention of injuring us.

The village consisted of about thirty houses of the Ohio Delaware tribe, and was the stronghold of Chief Shingas and Captain Jacobs. These were the two Delaware warriors and leaders who had repeatedly approached the British with offers to help drive the French from the Ohio Valley but were repeatedly rebuffed, most arrogantly by General Braddock, who had told them the British didn't need their help.

In response, the enraged chiefs and their people had allied themselves with the French, who had built their Fort Duquesne at the Forks, only a few days' travel downstream from Kittaning. Braddock, meanwhile, had come to rest under the muddy road he and his now-slaughtered men had chopped through the wilderness. The fruits of his arrogance—the spoils of Indian raids on British settlements—were now returning to Kittaning and other villages in the form of hostages such as Marie and Barbara.

Galasko put the girls to work at Kittaning as domestics. They tanned leather for moccasins, cleared land and planted corn, cut down trees and made huts, washed clothes and cooked food. There were times of deprivation, however. The village was forced to subsist at periods on acorns, bark, and roots.

In the summer of 1756, six months after their December arrival at Kittaning, political shock waves roiled out around the entire globe from this remote forest of the Ohio Valley. A delicate web of alliances that had prevented hostile European empires—Britain, France, Prussia, Austria, Russia—from attacking one another now began to shred.

France looked for some diplomatic or military threat to use against Britain in Europe in order to force Britain to back off from its claims in North America—the Ohio Valley in particular. But Britain had forged such a tight web of European treaties and alliances that France could find few chinks in its armor in Europe. Seeking a vulnerability, France finally dispatched warships from its Mediterranean ports to attack the British military stronghold on the Mediterranean island of Minorca. Britain responded poorly by sending a barnacle-encrusted and ill-commanded fleet under Admiral Byng to "defend" Minorca. The island's St. Philip's Castle fell to French siege. The defeat so humiliated the militant duke of Newcastle and other authorities back in London that Admiral Byng was not only court-martialed but executed by firing squad.

"In England," cracked the French philosophe Voltaire, "it is good to kill an admiral from time to time, to encourage the others."

Frederick of Prussia chose this delicate moment to attack the Austrian Empire of Empress Maria Theresa. As Frederick was allied with Britain and Maria Theresa allied with France, France now had to come to the empress's defense. This caused Russia to bail out of its treaty with Britain, since Russia didn't want to confront France in helping Britain help Frederick of Prussia fight the Austrian Empire of Maria Theresa . . .

The whole web unraveling . . .

It was just as messy back in Philadelphia in late 1755 and early 1756. In the Pennsylvania Assembly chambers, the traditionally pacifist Quakers wanted to negotiate with the Indians instead of fight them. Quakers in the assembly didn't think it right that the regular farmers should pay a tax to fund fighting the Indians while the enormously wealthy Penn family was exempt from paying taxes on its vast land holdings. The shady land dealings of William Penn's sons had helped ignite the Indian anger in the first place.

The all-purpose fixer Ben Franklin finally ironed out a deal in which the Penns ponied up what they delicately called a "gift" of five thousand pounds sterling so it wouldn't set a tax precedent on their lands. Governor Morris of Pennsylvania then formally declared war on the French and Indians and appointed a defense commission. The commission promptly threw the assembly, with its many Quakers, into chaos when it advertised bounties on the scalps of any Indian over ten years old, male or female, and a special bounty of seven hundred dollars each for the scalps—or rather the heads—of Chief Shingas and Captain Jacobs. The horrified Quakers at this point withdrew from assembly politics and negotiated informally with the tribes.

Still the Indian raids continued. Settlements were torched and forts overrun frighteningly close to Philadelphia itself. Virginia mounted a regiment under the young George Washington—who might have stopped the fighting before it started back at Jumonville Glen—while Virginia's terrified frontier settlers fled to the cities. The one military bright spot of 1756, if you could call it that, was a bold raid by Colonel John Armstrong and his three hundred provincials on the village of Kittaning, the stronghold of Chief Shingas and Captain Jacobs and where a number of captives were held. The Le Roy and Leininger girls, however, were spirited away as his men attacked. As recounted by the girls:

> In the month of September Col. Armstrong arrived with his men, and attacked Kittanny Town. Both of us happened to be in that part of it which lies on the (right) side of the (Allegheny) river. We were immediately conveyed ten miles farther into the interior, in order that we might have no chance of trying, on this occasion, to escape. The savages threatened to kill us. If the English had advanced, this might have happened. For, at that time, the Indians were greatly in dread of Col. Armstrong's corps.

Armstrong's dawn attack surprised much of Kittaning village, leading to a bloody shoot-out. While some of the Delawares escaped the village, others, like Captain Jacobs, held out in their houses. Captain Jacobs fired from his window with great accuracy, witnesses reported, as his wife quickly reloaded muskets for him. But, despite heavy losses, Armstrong's men closed in on the holdouts.

They called for Captain Jacobs to come out—he who had spoken before the Pennsylvania Assembly with an offer to help the British colonials fight the French. The alternative, they said, was being burned alive in his house.

"I can eat fire," he shouted back to the Pennsylvania militiamen.

Despite his deadly musket fire, they managed to set his house alight. Captain Jacobs's powder kegs ignited and the house exploded with a tremendous roar.

"[T]he Leg and Thigh of an Indian with a Child of three or four years old," reported an eyewitness with Armstrong, flew to "such a height that they appeared as nothing and fell in the adjacent Corn Field."

Armstrong had lost about forty men killed or wounded, and the Delawares lost ten or twelve, whose scalps were taken by Armstrong's troops for bounty back in Philadelphia. Armstrong also managed to rescue eleven of the English captives. But Marie and Barbara were not among them. Reported the girls:

> After the English had withdrawn, we were again brought back to Kittany, which town had been burned to the ground.
>
> There we had the mournful opportunity of witnessing the cruel end of an English woman, who had attempted to flee out of her captivity and to return to the settlements with Col. Armstrong. Having been recaptured by the savages, and brought back to Kittany, she was put to death in an unheard of way. First, they scalped her; next they laid burning splinters of wood, here and there, upon her body; and then they cut off her ears and fingers, forcing them into her mouth so that she had to swallow them. Amidst such torments, this woman lived from nine o'clock in the morning until toward sunset, when a French officer took compassion on her, and put her out of her misery.

And so it went with the French and Indians' War of Terror—and the Americans' first War *on* Terror—in that autumn of 1756.

"WHAT'S THE WILDEST, emptiest, blankest spot you know of around here?" I asked Richard Kugel.

I tried to phrase my question simply. I didn't go into all the reasons *why* I wanted to find this wildest, blankest place. But I asked the question with a certain excitement that no doubt grew from those long-ago jaunts into the secret places of the Wisconsin woods around my home, from my love of them and the perpetual wish to find more.

Kugel seemed to understand without my explaining further. He was the assistant forester at Sproul State Forest, one of the state-owned preserves that surround the town of Renovo like the Pacific Ocean surrounds Hawaii. Kugel wore his hair in a long red ponytail that looked improbable against the corporate-style conference room at the modern

Sproul Forest headquarters just outside town. He'd been telling me that when people don't manage to shoot a deer during hunting season here they'll call their state representative to complain about forest management causing the deer to go extinct. In answer to my question about blank spots, he now pointed to a certain place on the big forest map spread out on the conference table. I could see tight, spaghetti-like whorls of topographic lines that indicated extreme relief in the terrain.

"Fish Dam Run," he said, with his finger on the whorls. "There's no trail down there and it's rough going but it's plenty wild."

THERE WERE NO BOX STORES in Renovo. I bought some dry flies at an old-fashioned sporting goods place, a few snacks at the small supermarket, and drove across the Susquehanna River on the Highway 144 bridge. The two-lane road snaked briefly along the river past some old railroad workers' houses, then, springing out of the river bottomlands, suddenly curled up a steep draw. It entered a pretty forest, quite open underneath.

After climbing a long way, the road finally reached the top of a miles-long rolling ridge that trended northeast like so many of the Allegheny ridges, and traced the crest. I was far above the surrounding countryside. The ridge's northwestern edge was scalloped with steep gullies—as if a great cantaloupe scoop had sliced away giant balls from the ridge. The gullies dropped away on my right, deepening and lengthening, the forest within them thickening as it spilled down the ravines' sides, until they fell into the Susquehanna some five miles away and nearly two thousand feet below.

The clerk at the sporting goods store, who'd moved here from what Renovo residents call "the flatlands," had described to me the first time she'd driven this ridgetop road in winter.

"I said, 'God, just get me off this mountain.' "

I stopped at a scenic pullout along the highway that perched on the edge of one great ravine. I looked out over miles of hazy ridgeline cut by other deep ravines. The ridgetops were the ancient folds of mountains—the Appalachians and its Allegheny chain—forced up 250 million years ago when the rock plate now holding Africa shoved inexorably into the North American plate. These mountains were once joined to Morocco's Atlas Mountains. Some of the hazy, rounded ridges

I could see, now about 2,200 feet above sea level, once stood at least another ten thousand feet higher—and perhaps taller than Everest—worn down just as inexorably by water and wind and ice in those hundreds of millions of years since. What was once these Himalaya-like mountaintops has washed away as silt and rock to form the Eastern Seaboard of North America, where major cities sit.

A sign explained that, due to the lack of city lights here at night, it was possible from this point to see six thousand objects in space—planets, stars, supernovae, distant galaxies. Here, I thought, was yet another measure of "blank spot"—a place on this heavily wired Earth where you could clearly see the clouds of brilliant stars. Ten thousand years ago—even a mere thousand years ago, before lamplighters walked the growing cities with their torches at dusk—that particular blank spot existed virtually everywhere on Earth. It dismayed me that it had vanished from so much of the planet. How psychologically healthy it would be for all of us to live in it—to be reminded, with a casual glance up at the clouds of stars, of our own insignificance.

Turning off the pavement, I followed a gravelly road called Jews Run along an outlying ridge defined by a deep ravine on each side. To my left dropped away Burns Run and to my right Fish Dam Run. Both were marked "wild areas" on my Sproul State Forest map. I parked alongside a trail marker for the Chuck Keiper Trail, named after a well-known wildlife conservation officer. This inscribes a huge loop through the state forest, and drops into and then climbs out of both ravines. I couldn't decide which ravine looked more promising—richer in its "blankness," its "wildness," in those elusive qualities I sought. It was late in the day—after 2 p.m. I decided to hike down into Burns Run today, and come back tomorrow, with an earlier start, and try Fish Dam Run.

From an open, meadowy area on the ridgetop, the trail plunged quickly over the edge, switchbacking downward. The deeper I went, the tighter the forest canopy closed overhead. The forest felt damp and twilighty, the air moist and fragrant, the leaves broad and soft and still, the floor damp and spongy, so unlike the bone-dry, crackling, wind-sighing Montana forests I'd hiked for years. I recognized some tree species, like maples, from my Wisconsin upbringing but not all. Unlike dense Wisconsin, however, little undergrowth appeared here, except occasional leafy carpets over the floor. In places, the naked, columnlike tree boles and thick overarching canopy lent the forest a hushed, cathedral feeling.

After perhaps a half-hour's descent, I reached the ravine's bottom, where a small stream trickled over mossy rocks in little rills. I followed the trail along the rills as the ravine deepened, swishing through ferny patches and mossy evergreen groves. Then, on the left wall of the ravine, I spotted something shimmering through the tree trunks. As I drew nearer, I realized it was a clump of giant rhododendron bushes, way taller than I could reach, with big pink and white blossoms the size of my hand that glistened in a single beam of sun penetrating the thick forest canopy. I noticed other clumps of big pink and white rhododendrons dotting the steep, woody hillside farther up. In dozens of years hiking forests, mostly northern ones, I'd never before walked a flowering woods.

There was, as some of the earliest travelers to North America's Middle Latitudes reported, an Edenesque quality to these woods. They were both wild and flowering at once, unfettered in their luxuriant growth yet somehow benign and welcoming in their carpets of moss and bright flower blooms. A sense of excitement sprung from the sheer *fecundity* of it, the richness and variety of life pushing up from the rich, black soil.

I knew well the gloom of northern forests—the dark fir and spruce boughs crowding against one another, the scaly barks, the mats of decaying needles underfoot. Those northern forests harbored so few tree species that even at their thickest and richest, even on a sunny day, they spoke of spareness. They spoke of a need to gird yourself, to prepare yourself, to be deprived.

John and William Bartram embraced the rich Middle Latitude forests like the one into which I descended in Burns Run. They'd traveled some of these same Pennsylvania forests. But for William, this was only an introduction. I could imagine William's ecstasy, as an artistic and wandering and lovelorn young man, at first encountering the even more extreme blossoming fecundity of, say, a South Carolina wilds, or Florida's.

DESPITE QUESTIONS ABOUT BILLY'S CHARACTER, the wealthy Dr. Fothergill of London offered to fund his botanical explorations to the Southeast and Florida to the tune of fifty pounds a year. At thirty-four years old and having spent most of his adulthood at loose ends, Billy left Philadelphia in 1773 as if it were the husk of a former life. He sailed as far as Savannah, carrying letters of introduction to gain him entry to governors, prominent families, and planters, and promptly spent forty pounds to buy a good horse. On horseback, he set out south down the coastline, crossing the estuaries on small ferries and stopping by evenings at hospitable plantations, many of which grew rice in the coastal wetlands. Then he cut inland to meet the St. Mary's River and trace it upstream to its source in the Okefenokee Swamp, which straddles today's line between Georgia and Florida.

On his first day traveling up the St. Mary's toward the swamp, Billy had one of his life's most revelatory experiences. As he left the white settlements and headed into the blankness that lay beyond, he spotted a Seminole Indian armed with a rifle, riding his way.

> . . . the first sight of him startled me, and I endeavoured to elude his sight, by stopping my pace, and keeping large trees between us; but he espied me, and turning short about, sat spurs to his horse, and came up on full gallop. I never before this was afraid at the sight of an Indian, but at this time, I must own that my spirits were very much agitated: I saw at once, that being unarmed, I was in his power, and having now but a few moments to prepare, I resigned myself entirely to the will of the Almighty, trusting to his mercies for my preservation; my mind then became tranquil, and I resolved to meet the dreaded foe with resolution and chearful confidence. The intrepid Siminole stopped suddenly, three or four yards before me, and silently viewed me, his countenance angry and fierce, shifting his rifle from shoulder to shoulder, and looking about instantly on all sides. I advanced towards him, and with an air of confidence offered him my hand, hailing him, brother; at this he hastily jerked back his arm, with a look of malice, rage and disdain, seeming every way disconcerted; when again looking at me more attentively, he instantly spurred up to me, and, with dignity in his look and action, gave me his hand.

Arriving at the trading post upstream by following the Seminole's directions, Billy was warmly received and heard from the white traders that the Indian was "one of the greatest villains on earth." The previous night the traders had broken his rifle and beaten him so severely that he left the post pledging to kill the first white man he saw.

"My friend, consider yourself a fortunate man," they told him.

But Billy didn't see the incident as an example of good luck. While his father, John, hated Indians, and called them "the most barbarous creatures in the universe," Billy interpreted the encounter with the Seminole as an example of an inner goodness that inhabits all humans, whether "savage" or "civilized."

"Can it be denied, but that the moral principle, which directs the savages to virtuous and praiseworthy actions, is natural or innate?"

Billy had grown up in an entirely different generation. He'd been exposed to the new ideas crossing the Atlantic from Europe about the arts, about human liberty, and about the natural goodness of man. During his time at the progressive-minded Philadelphia Academy, he'd been a protégé of the faculty member Charles Thomson. A professor of Latin and Greek, Thomson was also a student and a friend of the Delaware Indians during the turmoil of the French and Indian War. He spoke out boldly against unfair white treatment of the Delawares in land dealings and treaty-makings with the colonials. He condemned the way the whites had conspired to keep the Delaware chief Tedyus-cung drunk during the entirety of a key treaty conference at Easton, Pennsylvania, in 1757 which Thomson personally attended as a Quaker observer. In that treaty conference, conducted at the height of the war, the Delawares had gained the promise from the colonials of a place in Pennsylvania's Wyoming Valley—land previously taken from them—where they could settle.

The Delawares called Thomson "the man who tells the truth."

Now Billy began to see firsthand what Thomson had spoken out against.

Continuing up the St. Mary's, he noted in scientific detail the flowers and shrubs along the riverbanks and in the nearby savannas. When he arrived at the great Okefenokee Swamp with its labyrinth of waterways and islands of high ground, he doesn't appear to have ventured into the swamp itself, but he was fascinated by the stories told about it. In particular, he related a legend told by the Creek Indians, that a band of their stray hunters venturing into the swamp once encountered a race of beautiful and generous women who lived deep within this "terrestrial paradise." But the women could not tarry with the Creeks, as their jealous men would miss them. The Creek hunters had returned many times into the maze of waterways looking for them, and seen footprints and traces of settlement, but after that first clandestine meeting never again had found the beautiful women.

Billy also heard from the Creeks that these people might be the remnants of an ancient Indian tribe, the Yamases, that the Creeks had conquered long ago and who took refuge deep in the swamp.

Heading back to the coast and the M'Intosh plantation, where he'd stayed earlier, Bartram took fifteen-year-old Jack M'Intosh on as a traveling companion—"a sensible and virtuous youth." Together Billy and Jack then headed up the Savannah River, taking notes and gathering specimens for Dr. Fothergill, with their destination a congress—a large meeting—between white traders and Creek and Cherokee Indians.

The white traders were demanding two million acres of Indian lands. Presumably, this was to settle debts in trade goods that the Indians had run up at trading posts. The young Creek warriors wanted to fight instead of cede their lands, but, after days of negotiation, the older chiefs finally convinced the young warriors not to fight, and the tribes gave over the lands to the whites. Bartram and Jack M'Intosh then joined a ninety-man surveying party to stake out the two-million-acre claim, which pushed Billy's sympathies further toward the Indians. After walking through the most magnificent forest he ever saw, in a fertile vale that hosted black oaks ten and eleven feet in diameter at breast height, he witnessed how a white surveyor standing on a hilltop misread a compass in order to cheat the Indians out of more of these lands. Finally, a chief raised his arm, pointed toward the correct river confluence in the distance, and said that the "wicked little instrument was a liar."

And so Billy Bartram, as he ventured farther from Philadelphia and his father and deeper into the wild lands of the Southeast, grew emotionally closer to the Indians. He began to grasp their way of looking at the world and to reconcile it with his.

MARIE LE ROY AND BARBARA LEININGER showed little evidence of embracing the Indian way of looking at the world—at least not the Indian warrior way. They showed even less of embracing the French way. After General Armstrong torched the Indian village of Kittaning and blew up Captain Jacobs in his house, the Indians brought the two captives to Fort Duquesne—the French stronghold at the Forks of the

Ohio. Here the girls labored for several months as servants for the French, who paid wages to the girls' Indian masters. Pleased to eat bread again (although they didn't like the French bacon), they felt, in some respects, better off than in the Indian villages.

> [W]e could not, however, abide the French. They tried hard to induce us to forsake the Indians and stay with them, making us various favourable offers. But we believed it would be better for us to remain among the Indians, in as much as they would be more likely to make peace with the English than the French, and in as much as there would be more ways open for flight in the forest than in a fort.

It's easy to think that Marie and Barbara couldn't "abide" the French because the French soldiers may have been interested in something more intimate than a simple housekeeping arrangement. Or perhaps, in fact, the girls made a coldly calculated strategic decision. Whatever the case, their Indian masters took the girls from the French at Fort Duquesne and brought them to the Indian town of Kaschkaschkung (or Kuskuski), on Beaver Creek, a river that flowed into the Ohio about twenty-five miles west of the Forks.

The girls remained at the Beaver Creek village, clearing fields for the Indian nobility, planting corn, tanning hides, through the year of 1758. On August 18 of that year, a white visitor—a German Moravian minister and cabinetmaker by the name of Frederick Post—suddenly appeared at Kaschkaschkung and gave Marie and Barbara, then in their mid-teens after three years in captivity, hope. Emigrating from Prussia to America as the disciple of a religious visionary, Post had married an Eastern Delaware woman and learned the Indian languages. He then had worked to convert the Indians to Christianity. Given his rapport with the Delawares, he'd now been tapped by Governor Denny of Pennsylvania to try to convince the Ohio Valley Indians, who included the Western Delawares, to leave the French and make a separate peace with the British colonials.

As soon as he had slipped into the Ohio Valley, word spread through Indian and French networks that Post was somewhere in the territory. The French sent out search parties to find him and, according to Marie and Barbara, threatened to roast Post alive for five days should they catch him. Well versed in native ways, however, Post enjoyed Indian protection during his mission and was personally guided into the Ohio Valley by Pisquetomen, the older brother of Chief Shingas.

That August of 1758, both sides well understood, was an opportune moment for reconciliation between the British and the Indians of the Ohio Valley. The British, after their initial setbacks in the war, were now striking powerfully against the Indians' French allies at Fort Ticonderoga (where, despite their attack with fifteen thousand men, they were forced to retreat), Louisbourg, and Fort Frontenac. Earlier that summer, the British started building another road through the wilderness and a string of supply forts to stage a major attack on Fort Duquesne at the Forks. But the British knew they would badly need the Ohio Valley Indians on their side in order to attack the French at Fort Duquesne. The Indians, meanwhile, sensed the momentum of the war shifting to the British.

Frederick Post spent two days at Kaschkaschkung, meeting with various Ohio Valley chieftains, before taking his offer to other villages along Beaver Creek and the Ohio River. Marie and Barbara described the excitement stirred by Post's visit:

> We and all the other prisoners heartily wished him success and God's blessing upon his undertaking. We were, however, not allowed to speak with him. The Indians gave us plainly to understand that any attempt to do this would be taken amiss. He himself, by the reserve with which he treated us, let us see that this was not the time to talk over our afflictions.

Post found a receptive audience among the chieftains, who wished to end the fighting. Post reminded them of the promise made by the colonial authorities at the Easton conference the previous year, that the Delawares could have lands to settle in the Wyoming Valley. He said the British didn't want to settle the Ohio Valley. The British only wanted to push the French out of the valley.

Still, the Indians remained skeptical. It was difficult to argue with the chieftains' logic:

> It is plain that you white people are the cause of this war; why do not you and the *French* fight in the old country, and on the sea? Why do you come to fight on our land? This makes every body believe, you want to take the land from us by force, and settle it.

THE DAY AFTER MY HIKE down into Burns Run, I went looking for a link between that period in the mid-1700s when the wild Ohio Valley's fate hung in the balance, and the Ohio Valley now. Specifically, I sought a local historian who could tell me about the earliest settlers around Renovo. While most of the area surrounding Renovo remained blank—wild and unpopulated and mountainous—a few hamlets lay scattered about.

It was raining in the morning as I left my things in my room at the Sportsman's Motel and drove north from Renovo along Highway 144. The road climbed through misty, wet, forested mountains until topping out on a grassy, shorn plateau.

At first I thought it was a golf course planted out here in the forested mountains. Then through the mist I noticed that in the middle of the broad greensward squatted a modern industrial complex. Large pipes curved out of the ground and into the complex, like the legs of some great metallic insect sitting on a lawn. Later I learned it was a natural gas storage plant. This corner of Pennsylvania had been drilled for oil and gas over a century ago. Now the empty wells were used in reverse—natural gas was piped from Texas and Mexico, and with 25,000 horsepower pumps, injected back into the old wells here in the mountains of Pennsylvania, and stored underground until needed; for instance, to heat the homes of East Coast residents. It was the largest gas storage facility east of the Mississippi River. While the surface was forest or grass, underground, at least right here, was hardly blank—rather, it was the subsurface natural gas tank for New York City.

Winding on back roads into the forest, I reached my destination—an old frame house on a broad lawn surrounded by the dripping forest. This was the home of Eric and Peggy Lucas, whose late mother, Dorothy M. Bailey, was a prominent local historian.

"You came two years too late," Peggy told me. "My mother knew everything about the area."

As we sat in the Lucas's living room, chatting amiably, they periodically dug into one of Dorothy's files or another, photocopied its contents, and handed it to me, such as the brief biography of Simeon Pfoutz, the first settler on the fertile flats along Kettle Creek, now a well-known trout stream just off the plateau. He'd arrived by canoe in 1813 with his wife, Susannah, fathered nine children, raised several baby mountain lions, and, after anointing himself the valley's feudal lord, appropriated a share of the crops of later British settlers. This lasted until the British settlers, out of frustration with his bullying, brought in a tough Irish settler by the name of Ikey Corn who put a quick end to Pfoutz's feudal pretensions. Pfoutz died abruptly in 1856 while showing off his parlor trick in which he slipped his "pet" rattlesnake down his shirt collar to show how it could crawl out his sleeve. On this particular occasion, the pet rattler chose to nail the radial artery in Pfoutz's arm. He was dead within nine minutes.

Eric Lucas had worked at the gas plant that I thought was a golf course. He told me that decades ago, before the gas wells, Cross Fork had a booming lumber industry.

"All these mountains were covered with virgin timber. Some of that lumber built this house."

They pulled out more photos from Dorothy's files. One from 1905 showed dozens and dozens of houses in Cross Fork. Big stumps dotted the bare, surrounding hills where the loggers had cut. The next photo, from 1937, showed only about six houses sitting on big pastures where the rest of the town had once stood. Young forest sprouted from what had been the stump-dotted hills.

Originally erected as a four-room bunkhouse and cookhouse for a lumber camp, the Lucas's house had later been expanded to ten rooms and was Dorothy Bailey's childhood home. Born in 1915, the local historian, her daughter told me, had traced her ancestry back to Robert Campbell, who served as a piper and drummer for George Washington's army during the Revolutionary War. It was through fellow soldiers in Washington's army—though not Robert Campbell—that much of the Indian land in these parts of Pennsylvania ended up in white hands.

I drove from the Lucas's house back to Sproul State Forest headquarters, where I learned more about these Revolutionary War land transfers. Two decades later, due in part to his military experience gained in the French and Indian War, George Washington would, of course, head the American army against the British during the Revolutionary War. The American Continental Congress didn't have much money to feed or pay its soldiers to fight the British, but the new nation did have access to land—and, at least in Pennsylvania, a lot of it.

The Sproul Forest headquarters now manages 300,000 acres of land around Renovo, and the foresters unfolded old land maps for me.

They were crosshatched with an out-of-kilter checkerboard pattern—almost a jigsaw puzzle—of "warrants" of from 100 acres to 1,000 acres or so each. The first warrants dated to the years just after the Revolutionary War, and each still bore the name of the original soldier who had received it as pay from the Commonwealth of Pennsylvania.

"In most cases, the soldiers didn't even know where it was," District Forester Doug D'Amore told me. " 'We owe you "x" dollars from the war—here's your land.' "

The great majority of the land, as it turned out, was steep, mountainous, and rocky. Only very small fertile strips in the river bottomlands made decent farmland. That's where the few settlers stayed. The rest was virtually worthless to these war veterans and simply abandoned. This reconfirmed what I'd found in Maine—that fertile land is settled quickly. Wherever the land is not suitable for farming, you're most likely to find a blank spot.

"Some of these warrants sold numerous times at tax sales," said D'Amore, who works closely with the Sproul State Forest's landholdings and warrant issues. "Ultimately the warrants got in the hands of the early lumber companies. This valley was logged three or four different ways. They started probably in the 1830s cutting Kettle Creek for the big, fat white pine."

The timber cutting lasted, off and on, for nearly a century—from the 1830s to the early 1900s. The early loggers rafted the logs down the streams and rivers. Later, company railroads were pushed into the forest to haul out timber left over from the first cut—hemlock trees to extract tannin for leather tanning, hardwood saw timber, and finally the small pulpwood to be ground up and made into paper. This forest cut, the railroads and logging companies then pulled up the tracks and moved on to a new forest.

By World War I, the region's forests were all logged out. The timber companies no longer had any use for those Revolutionary War land warrants they'd assembled. They sold off the warrants cheaply to the state.

"Basically, you just take the resources off and let them go," said D'Amore.

"You can't farm rocks," added the assistant forester Rich Kugel. "With the logging, everything was sucked out of it. In the 1930s the Commonwealth got most of the state forest land for a buck an acre."

Not much had changed since the 1930s. With the logging lands up for grabs at so low a price, Pennsylvania purchased massive acreages and assembled its vast state forests in these western mountains. These are what showed up on my Earth-at-night photo as "blank spots." Instead of a sea of stumps, trees now had regrown as a second-growth forest. This is the forest that exists today, and that I visited during my hikes down into various "runs" and along ridges. The manufacturing—what little had existed in some of the small towns—had largely died out. As a way to market its attractions to tourists, the state had recently re-branded this big, empty region the "Pennsylvania Wilds."

Tourism, however, has remained slim.

"Right now," said D'Amore, "the mind-set is we don't want for-eigners coming in hunting our deer, catching our fish, drinking our beer, chasing our women . . . and anybody who isn't from this county is a foreigner. An 'Influx Flatlander.' "

D'Amore, though raised in a still more mountainous region of Pennsylvania farther north—and at a higher elevation—said he is still considered a "Flatlander" here, while Kugel lives on Kettle Creek but is not considered a true "Cricker."

"We'll always be outsiders," D'Amore said.

I LEFT THE SPROUL FOREST HEADQUARTERS and drove back up into the mountains to Jews Run Road, where the previous day I'd ex-plored the deep ravine called Burns Run. Today, I planned to descend into Fish Dam Run—the place that Rich Kugel had recommended as the wildest of the wild in these parts. Leaving the car parked on the same open, grassy ridgetop, I followed the path to the right instead of the left as I had the day before, dropping over the ravine's steep brink into Fish Dam Run. The afternoon already had grown late. Dark rain clouds blew over, lending a heavy gloom to the forest. I kept onward, more dutifully than enthusiastically. As I hiked down deeper into the forested ravine, I thought longingly of the cheery warmth of the Sports-man's Motel back in Renovo. I'd come this far to seek out blank spots. Now I was in one.

The path wound down, down, down, crossed the ravine's bottom, and began to ascend the other side. Instead of following the path up again, I left the trail and struck off on my own still deeper into the ravine, which ran several more miles down to the Susquehanna River.

While on the path my mind wandered, but once I stepped off the trodden path, I concentrated exactly on what I was doing. I stepped carefully across the forest floor, over fallen logs and across carpets of leafy ground cover. I looked behind me periodically to identify landmarks and side gullies to mentally mark my return route. Crossing the little creek on boulders and logs, I left footprints in the mud in the event I got lost and searchers needed clues—or I needed clues. I crossed the fresh trail of a bear—I was quite sure it was bear—that had crushed large, broken-stemmed steps through the leafy patches.

As I had in Burns Run, I thought again of the acute awareness a young Indian hunter would bring to this spot, right here, three hundred years ago. But now I asked myself a different question. What was I hunting for down in this deep, obscure ravine? I wasn't looking to kill a bear or deer, or to gather plants, as an Indian hunter might have been. Nor, unlike an early American Puritan, was I alarmed at the devilish quality of these gloomy deep woods. Nor did I seek to clear a farm and build a homestead, nor chop down the forest and sell the timber. I didn't seek any practical use for this wilderness. I searched solely for the experience of wilderness. I hunted for the transporting aspect of wilderness. I hoped to experience some grand emotion here, to experience it and take it back with me. I sought the *romance* of wilderness.

For this notion I had Billy Bartram to thank. And channeled through Bartram, I had Rousseau to thank and Edmund Burke, and Denis Diderot and Lord Shaftesbury, and the Deists, and before them, way before, the Greeks and the Romans whose paeans to Arcadia—to the idealized rural life away from cities (which also may have been the source of the name Acadia given to that bountiful region those early French settled)—were read avidly by these eighteenth-century writers.

After traveling with the surveying party divvying up Indian lands, Bartram and young M'Intosh returned to the coastal lowlands of Georgia, borrowed a canoe carved from cypress, and paddled up the Altamaha River—one of the largest rivers on the East Coast, flowing from the Appalachian highlands to lowland coastal swamps and then out to sea. Here's how Bartram would come to describe the Altamaha.

I ASCENDED this beautiful river, on whose fruitful banks the generous and true sons of liberty securely dwell, fifty miles above the
white settlements. HOW gently flow thy peaceful floods, O
Alatamaha! How sublimely rise to view, on thy elevated shores, yon
Magnolian groves, from whose tops the surrounding expanse is per-
fumed, by clouds of incense, blended with the exhaling balm of the
Liquid-amber, and odours continually arising from circumambient
aromatic groves of Illicium, Myrica, Laurus, and Bignonia. WHEN
wearied . . . I resigned my bark to the friendly current . . . THUS secure and tranquil, and meditating on the marvellous scenes of primitive nature, as yet unmodified by the hand of man, I gently
descended the peaceful stream, on whose polished surface were de-
picted the mutable shadows from its pensile banks; whilst myriads of
finny inhabitants sported in its pellucid floods.

This is just one typical passage in his book, based on what would
become a four-year wilderness expedition, titled *Travels through North
and South Carolina, Georgia, East and West Florida, the Cherokee Country, etc.* by William Bartram.

In this Altamaha passage the word *sublime* appears twice—a word
that puckers the lips before sliding so liquidly off the tongue like Billy's
cypress canoe down the river's waters. It appears with remarkable fre-
quency throughout the *Travels*. It was a word—a broad concept,
really—that finally defined an inchoate feeling about the glories of nature that had swirled in the minds of early and mid-eighteenth-century
European thinkers—thinkers who had ventured into the Swiss Alps,
the English hill country, as well as into the woody British clubs and
trendy, glittering salons of Paris amid the rustling silks and tinkling
china and witty conversation of the philosophes. Bartram was one of
the first—if not the first—to apply this concept to the American
wilderness, and did so with long-lasting impact.

To understand where the concept originated, it's helpful to return
to Europe—the other half of this intellectual rally across the Atlantic—
and especially to the Frenchman Jean-Jacques Rousseau.

A great con man, passionate writer, and adventurer rolled into one,
Rousseau imparted the spirit of "wild nature" and the "natural man" to
a whole generation in Europe. After his mother's early death, Rousseau
ran away from his home in Geneva, drifted south over the Alps to
Savoy, and, at age sixteen, was taken in by a twenty-eight-year-old

baroness, Madame de Warens, who had a penchant for collecting young men. It was from Madame de Warens that Rousseau got his first education in the natural world, and, as result, we have been handed down part of ours.

Despite ties to the Catholic Church, Madame de Warens was a committed Deist. She believed in the spiritual goodness of all humans and put great faith in the power of the natural world, as well as dabbled in herbalism and alchemy. Over the course of several years in residence at her estate at Annecy—the most delightful period of his life, he described it—Madame de Warens introduced Rousseau to great works of literature and philosophy, refined his manners, his conversation, his ways in the arts of love, and imbued in him a sense of the power of the natural world.

Eventually Rousseau showed up in Paris in the city's exploding literary scene of the mid-1700s, at the height of the Enlightenment, as French thinkers leveled the weapon of reason against king and church. It was while walking to Vincennes prison one hot summer day to visit his friend the philosophe Denis Diderot, who had offended the church with his proto-evolutionary theories, that Rousseau had his central inspiration about man and nature.

Lying under a shade tree to rest and read a newspaper, his eye fell on a notice that the Academy of Dijon was offering a prize to the best essay addressing whether advances in the sciences and arts had helped to refine or corrupt morals. Like all great con men, Rousseau possessed a remarkable talent for sniffing out the spirit of the moment and making it his own. Hot, agitated, en route to visit his imprisoned friend who'd spoken out, he embraced a spirit of the age that was much alive in Paris intellectual circles—a rising, radical voice against the oppression of church and state—and melded it with a new, and equally heretical, belief in the inherent goodness of "natural" man. Rousseau's short answer to the essay question was that advances in "civilization" *hadn't* helped purify morals.

When Rousseau arrived at the Vincennes dungeon, the incarcerated Diderot helped him shape his ideas about man and nature. Diderot knew well the work of the English philosopher Lord Shaftesbury, whom he'd translated into French, and who strongly believed in the inherent goodness of "primitive" man—a goodness that could be perverted by exposure to poor morals, religious fanaticism, and other supposed "civilized" influences. For these observations, Shaftesbury drew on reports coming into London from sailing expeditions all over the world in the late seventeenth and early eighteenth centuries.

"Turn [your] Eye toward remote Countrys," Shaftesbury wrote in his *Advice to an Author.* "[S]earch for that simplicity of manners, and innocence of behaviour, which has often been known among mere savages; ere they were corrupted by our commerce, and, by sad Example, instructed in all kinds of Treachery and Inhumanity."

The notion of the goodness of the primitive man and the simplicity of nature resonated with Rousseau. He'd witnessed firsthand the artificiality and intrigues of the "civilized" life in Italian noble houses and Parisian salons. He fondly remembered his simple days of wandering through Savoy and the Alps, subsisting only on a sturdy chunk of bread and a bit of wine. The natural and uncorrupted man in the natural and unurbanized landscape now became for Rousseau an icon of goodness—and of freedom.

Sending off his impassioned essay, Rousseau, to his great surprise, won the Dijon Prize, and instant and widespread acclaim.

Always quick to seize the moment, Rousseau then personally resolved to strive for the simplicity and goodness he believed lay within all men. Growing a beard, and selling off his lace shirts and white stockings, he cut a wild and celebrated figure in the Parisian salons—a kind of French intellectual proto-hippie. Finally Rousseau retreated to the French countryside and to his native republic of Geneva to write, including his book *The Social Contract,* which helped trigger the American and French revolutions. But it was his novel *Julie, or The New Heloise,* published in 1761 and a resounding bestseller throughout Europe, that helped trigger the Romantic movement and captured a new passion between Man and Nature. Consisting of a series of letters between a young tutor and the daughter of a nobleman in the Alps who are in love but forbidden to marry, it brimmed with soulful emotion instead of cool reason. Instead of the bright city life—Paris was portrayed as an endless desert—*The New Heloise* celebrated the pastoral villages and wild mountain landscapes of the Alps. It spoke of nature—and of wildness—as exerting a transformative effect on the human soul. An emotionally confused St. Preux, in love with Julie, now a wife and mother, describes how he found hope by climbing a peak in Switzerland's Upper Valais:

Meditations there take on an indescribably grand and sublime character. . . . It seems by rising above the habitations of men one leaves all base and earthly sentiments behind, and in proportion as one approaches ethereal spaces the soul contracts something of their inalterable purity.

Here in Rousseau's description of the Alps appears that word *sublime*—which would become a touchstone in Billy Bartram's writings about the wilderness. The word itself was philosophically explicated a few years before Rousseau's novel by a young Edmund Burke, who later gained renown for his political essays: Explained Burke in his early treatise, *A Philosophical Enquiry into the Origin of Our Ideas of the Sublime and Beautiful:* "Whatever is fitted in any sort to excite the ideas of pain and danger, that is to say, whatever is in any sort terrible . . . is a source of the *sublime* . . ."

Small, smooth objects fell in the realm of the beautiful, while wild, craggy mountain landscapes gave rise to these feelings of the sublime— that sense of being overwhelmed by vastness, by power, by infinity. Beyond raw terror, the sublime, according to Burke, provokes a certain *delight.* But it isn't found simply anywhere in the presence of power or terror or danger. The tremendous power of a draft horse, for example, doesn't inspire the sublime.

"[I]t comes upon us in the gloomy forest, and in the howling wilderness, in the form of the lion, the tiger, the panther, or rhinoceros."

It was all of a piece—a crystallized moment when the Western outlook on Wild Nature started a dramatic transformation. For so long the concept of "Wilderness" and "the Wilds" had, in Western eyes, been viewed through the lens of the Old Testament. It was either a Paradise or a Hell. But Burke, Rousseau, and their contemporaries finally saw in Wild Nature a world that had its own spiritual value and transformative power. Burke succeeded in putting a name and definition to it— the "sublime." In a way, it acknowledged the presence of God in the power and infinity of those towering mountains, those turbulent seas, those depthless heavens.

When you read Burke's essay, and you read Rousseau, and then you read Bartram's *Travels,* you realize that Billy Bartram saw his four years in the American wilderness as a kind of grand quest for the sublime. He knew botany. He'd read British poets like Mark Akenside, whose *The Pleasures of the Imagination* celebrated Nature as a touchstone of the imagination. Surely he'd read Burke on the sublime, and probably Rousseau on the natural man. Now Billy Bartram—or William, this "son of Pennsylvania"—would "glow with the raptures of the sacred nine," as his yearning classmate had once written. Billy would write his own epic poetic account of his travels in the American wilderness in search of those wild animals, those strange plants, those exotic tribes whose inherent goodness should be the envy of civilized man, those grand emotions.

> [We] enjoyed a most enchanting view; a vast expanse of green meadows and strawberry fields; a meandering river gliding through, saluting in its various turnings the swelling, green, turfy knolls, embellished with parterres of flowers and fruitful strawberry beds, flocks of turkies strolling about them; herds of deer prancing in the meads or bounding over the hills; companies of young, innocent Cherokee virgins, some busy gathering the rich, fragrant fruit, others having already filled their baskets, lay reclined under the shade of the floriferous and fragrant native bowers . . . disclosing their beauties to the fluttering breeze, and bathing their limbs in the cool fleeting streams; whilst other parties, more gay and libertine, were yet collecting strawberries, or wantonly chasing their companions, tantalising them, staining their lips and cheeks with rich fruit.

Just as Bartram had embarked on a grand quest for the sublime and the inherent goodness of "natural man," the deeper I hiked into the pathless ravine of Fish Dam Run that rainy late afternoon and the denser the ravine grew with fallen logs, mossy rocks, rhododendron bushes, undergrowth, the more I considered my travels to this "blank spot." I jumped back and forth across the little stream, seeking the easiest way. The whole concept of "blank spots" implied a romance in these wild places. It implied that in the spaces left undescribed by the map I would discover something extraordinary, something powerful, something that would transport me, as the wild places had transported Rousseau and other eighteenth-century European urban sophisticates who climbed in the Alps. For much of my life, I realized, I had been searching, in one way or another, for those blank spots on the map, for those places Billy Bartram discovered for himself, while Cherokee maidens frolicked in the strawberry fields.

Marie Le Roy and Barbara Leininger had been taken to a "blank spot," too, but they gave no indication of seeking the Sublime in Nature or valuing the inherent goodness in "natural man." For them, this blank spot meant captivity rather than emotional freedom. At the same time that Burke was laboring on his essay distinguishing the Beautiful and the Sublime, and Rousseau was retreating from the artificiality of Paris to the Alps to write, the girls were laboring as slaves in the Indian village on Beaver Creek, clearing fields, tanning hides, and planting corn.

In late winter of 1759—three and a half years after their capture at Penn's Creek, and once Indian alliances had shifted—Marie and Barbara plotted their escape. As the British advanced in the Ohio Valley by chopping another road through the forest toward the Forks, the Delaware leaders, in late autumn of 1758, decided to accept British peace offers, which included promises that the Ohio lands would remain in Indian hands. The Delaware Indians abandoned their alliance with the French. They moved their families—and their captives, including Marie and Barbara, now in their mid-teens—out of harm's way, heading about 150 miles westward to a village called Moschkingo, located in present-day Ohio.

The French, left at Fort Duquesne and knowing they couldn't hold it against the British advance without the help of the Indian warriors, planted sixty barrels of gunpowder in its walls and ignited the fuse. The fort exploded into bits with a roar heard ten miles away by the British front guard. The French then retreated, sending their cannons by boat down the Ohio and Mississippi to Louisiana. The British marched in to the Forks of the Ohio the next day, renamed the strategic outpost Pittsburgh, and erected their own fort among the shattered French ruins.

A little more than two months later, in February, the Delaware Indian men left their new camp at Moschkingo to travel back east to the new British post at Pittsburgh to trade furs. The Indian women and the captive girls remained at Moschkingo to gather roots. Among the other captives at Moschkingo were two boys, apparently in their late teens,

David Breckenridge and Owen Gibson. It was with David and Owen that the girls planned their escape.

Barbara feigned sickness—probably claiming she had her period—and was allowed to build a separate hut. Another captive woman, a German named Mary, had been secretly hoarding provisions for just such an escape attempt but then injured her leg and couldn't go. She gave her hoard to the girls—two pounds of dried meat, a quart of corn, and four pounds of sugar. On the night of March 16, 1759, Marie, Barbara, David, and Owen rendezvoused at Barbara's hut. They slipped out of the Indian town as it slept, creeping past more than a dozen dogs without alarming them.

Once beyond the village, the four adolescents grasped the direness of the situation. They had to avoid the skilled Indian hunters who would surely come searching for them. Without compass or maps, and with only the sketchiest knowledge of the trails, they had to find their way through nearly two hundred miles of wilderness—a blank spot to them—to the nearest British outpost, which was Pittsburgh, while avoiding the main trails on which they might encounter Indians.

Just beyond the village that night, they reached the bank of the Muskingum River and desperately looked for a means to cross it before they were discovered missing. Barbara improvised on an old hymn and softly sang it on the Muskingum shore. It was not a hymn that passionately embraced the new concept just gaining currency in Europe of the Sublimity of Wild Nature and the Inherent Goodness of Primitive Man.

> *O bring us safely across the river!*
> *In fear I cry, yea my soul doth quiver . . .*
> *Alas, what great hardships are yet in store.*
> *In the wilderness wide, beyond that shore!*
> *It has neither water, nor meat, nor bread,*
> *But each new morning something new to dread.*
> *Yet little sorrow would hunger me cost*
> *If but I could flee from the savage host,*
> *Which murders and fights and burns far and wide,*
> *While Satan himself is array'd on its side.*

Searching about in the darkness, the four youths discovered a raft that the Indians used to ford the river. Clambering aboard, they pushed out. The current swept them downstream nearly a mile before they landed on the far shore. Jumping off the raft, they ran through the woods all that night. They kept on running through most of the next day. Finally, on the second night, they stopped to rest. They didn't dare light a fire for fear of attracting notice.

Rising the next dawn, Owen Gibson spotted a bear. He and David each carried guns—apparently they had been trusted by their Indian captors as reliable hunters—and Owen fired on it. The bear fell, wounded. As Owen approached with a tomahawk to dispatch it, the bear jumped to its feet, charged at Owen, and bit him in the foot, leaving puncture wounds. It then fled into some rocky grottos. Hungry for meat, the foursome attempted to track the bear but soon lost its trail amid the rocks.

All that day they walked onward through the forest, despite Owen's punctured foot, worried about their dwindling food cache. On the following day—their third in flight from the Indian village—Owen managed to shoot a deer. Cutting off its hindquarters, they carried the meat with them that day and roasted it over a fire that night, ravenously consuming all of it. On the fourth day they reached the Ohio River, having made a circuitous loop of over one hundred miles in four days in order to avoid the most well-traveled trails. But Pittsburgh, the haven occupied by the British that they now sought, still remained far away.

The two boys worked most of the night to build a raft to cross the Ohio. Poling and paddling across to the far bank, they saw symbols left by the Indians indicating that the Forks lay to the east, still about 150 miles away. They determined to walk straight east—into the rising sun—until they reached it. For seven days they walked eastward, sometimes on a path and sometimes through the woods. On the seventh day they came to a watercourse that they recognized—Little Beaver Creek, where they had formerly resided as captives. They now knew they were about fifty miles from the Forks and safety with the British.

And now, that we imagined ourselves so near the end of all our troubles and misery, a whole host of mishaps came upon us. Our provisions were at an end; Barbara Leininger fell into the water and was nearly drowned; and worst misfortune of all! Owen Gibson lost his flint and steel. Hence we had to spend four nights without fire, amidst rain and snow.

On March 31, 1759—fifteen days after slipping out of the Indian village on the Muskingum River—the group reached the Allegheny River near the Forks. They were now three miles from Pittsburgh. Again, the foursome built a raft, and ferried themselves across the Allegheny, although Marie, as Barbara had before, fell in the river and almost drowned before the other three managed to pull her out. Landing on the Allegheny's far shore, they walked a short way to the banks of the Monongahela. The British post lay just on the other side. Shouting across the river, they heard an answering call. The commander, Colonel Mercer, sent over a boat to carry them across. Clad as the captives were in native dress, however, the boatmen mistook them for Indians and the youths had to convince the boatmen they were in fact captives before they were let aboard.

Colonel Mercer took in the foursome at the fort, where he fed them well, had clothes made for them—the girls each received new petticoats—and presented them with new knives. After two weeks of Colonel Mercer's hospitality, they joined a contingent of soldiers headed east, into territory firmly held by the British. Marie Le Roy and Barbara Leininger reached Philadelphia on May 6, 1759, about two months after their escape and three and a half years after their capture at Penn's Creek. It was then, on their arrival in Philadelphia, that they told their story to government and religious authorities, who wrote it down. *The Narrative of Marie Le Roy and Barbara Leininger* was quickly published in pamphlet form and avidly read, in part because it contained a list of several dozen British prisoners whom the girls had met over their captivity. The list was published at the end of the pamphlet to let the families know they were still alive. Barbara's younger sister, Regina, however, who had been captured with Barbara and Marie at Penn's Creek, had married an Indian man during captivity and adopted their ways. She didn't emerge from the forest for another five years, after the French had finally given up all their claims in North America to the British, and peace prevailed between the British on the one side, and the French and Indians. Regina then reunited with her family.

MARIE LE ROY AND BARBARA LEININGER's account has endured these last two and a half centuries mainly as a curiosity and a vivid and dramatic historical document of an era. Bartram's *Travels,* on the other hand, unconsciously reverberates with us every day.

By the time Billy Bartram returned to Philadelphia, in winter 1777, from his four years of wilderness travel, his father was elderly and frail, and John died the following September as British troops advanced on Philadelphia to attack the American rebels during the War of Independence. (It was said that he worried himself to death that the British troops would trample his precious gardens.) John willed his botanical estate to his more businesslike and less peripatetic son, John Jr. Billy took up residence on the family estate, helping to manage its nurseries, which sold plants commercially.

He spent about a decade at the farm quietly writing his account of his years wandering the American wilderness. Visitors to the Bartram botanical estate, who included Thomas Jefferson and other luminaries, sometimes found him in the garden, barefoot with hoe in hand. Bartram's *Travels* was published in Philadelphia in 1791, and, in its American edition, was greeted with mixed reviews and modest success.

The previous year, however, another epic account of travel in wild and exotic places had captured the rapt attention of a British audience—James "Abyssinian" Bruce's *Travels to Discover the Sources of the Nile*. After its American debut, Bartram's *Travels* was quickly published in England, where it found a large and enthusiastic audience. In rapid succession came an Irish edition, another one in English, then German, Dutch, and French. Clearly, Bartram's *Travels,* celebrating the "sublime" in the American wilderness, had struck some kind of nerve in Europe. It had appeared at a key moment, as Europe's intellectual climate shifted beyond the smooth cusp of Enlightenment rationalism toward the grand, jagged emotions that would soon become the Romantic movement—epic quests undertaken by heroic loners . . . scenes of wild nature that provoked the sublime . . . powerful passions deep within the soul, exposing the boldest truths.

The young British poet Samuel Taylor Coleridge was deeply smitten by Bartram's *Travels* and copied passages of Bartram's prose into his notebooks. He appears to have been fascinated not only by Bartram's exotic, poetic descriptions of the American wilds but also by Bartram's passionate belief in a kind of soulful "life force" that animates all things. Coleridge, who read widely in other visionary and philosophical works, including Eastern religions, now embraced this Bartramian notion. As a poet, he further believed that in humans this "life force" expressed itself in creative genius.

One night in the summer of 1798, Coleridge, unhappily married, father of small children, sat in an armchair in a lonely farmhouse in Somerset, having ingested—for an illness, he claimed—an opium extract. Among the images fleeting through his opium dreams were both fragments of Bruce's *Sources of the Nile* and the natural wonders William Bartram had described in his *Travels*. Coleridge envisioned especially vividly a powerful, geyserlike spring Bartram had discovered in central Florida that churned up great boils of white sand and bits of shell. The spring, intimately described by Bartram, then settled into a beautiful, clear pool, out of which meandered a stream that ran five miles through grassy meadows, finally emptying into Florida's Lake George.

Coleridge awoke from his opium visions three hours later, still in his armchair, having composed in the course of his visions what he estimated were between two hundred and three hundred lines of poetry. He immediately took up pen and paper and scrawled down all he could recall. This "fragment," as he called it, became his visionary "Kubla Khan." Now one of the most famous poems in the English language, this work helped touch off what became the Romantic movement. It is a profound rhythmic incantation of the power of that creative genius as it manifests itself in humans and nature.

> *And from this chasm, with ceaseless turmoil seething,*
> *As if the earth in fast quick pants were breathing,*
> *A mighty fountain momently was forced:*
> *Amid whose swift half-intermitted burst*
> *Huge fragments vaulted like rebounding hail,*
> *Or chaffy grain beneath the thresher's flail;*
> *And 'mid these dancing rocks at once and ever*
> *It flung up momently the sacred river.*
> *Five miles meandering with a mazy motion*
> *Through wood and vale the sacred river ran*
> *Then reached the caverns measureless to man,*
> *And sank in tumult to a lifeless ocean . . .*

Coleridge then turned his friend William Wordsworth, also an aspiring poet, on to Bartram's *Travels*. Suffering from a broken love affair in France and seeking his path in the world both poetically and personally, Wordsworth and his sister, Dorothy, lived in a cottage not far from Coleridge. During long walks through the beautiful hills of the West Country, the threesome theorized about poetry and nature. Mindful of John and William Bartram's observations that a kind of intelligence or spirit animates plants, Wordsworth began to understand nature as infused with a conscious and moral purpose. He substituted, in the words of one Wordsworth critic and biographer, "the idea of Nature for the idea of God."

> *A motion and a spirit, that impels*
> *All thinking things, all objects of all thoughts,*
> *And rolls through all things.*

Wordsworth wrote of the need to look to Nature for instruction in that wisdom and moral purpose that he believed lies within all living things—partly due to the Bartrams' descriptions of the intelligence of plants and the sublimity of wild landscapes. Wordsworth urged his readers, as in his "The Tables Turned," to abandon the strict study of books and strike out into the natural world and learn from it. "Up! up! my Friend, and quit your books . . . Let Nature be your teacher."

Attitudes had changed so quickly. In 1759, Barbara Leininger, standing on the bank of the Muskingum River with Marie Le Roy and David and Owen and searching for a way to cross before being discovered by the "savage host," composed her own hymn about wild Nature, where she found "Each new morning something new to dread." Two decades after Barbara's hymn, William Bartram, on his travels, sings a kind of prose hymn to the rising of the sun in the wilds. "[T]he pulse of nature becomes more active, and the universal vibration of life insensibly and irresistibly moves the wonderous machine; how cheerful and gay all nature appears." And, two decades after Billy Bartram's sublime wilderness experience at dawn, William Wordsworth rhapsodized about Bartram's "pulse of the machine" and the "impulse" of nature:

> *One impulse from the vernal wood*
> *May teach you more of man*
> *Of moral evil and of good*
> *Than all the sages can.*

In those forty years—from Barbara and Marie's 1759 escape through the Pennsylvania wilderness to Wordsworth's 1798 poem "The

Tables Turned"—the thinking radically transformed about Nature and the Wilds. It was a shift midwifed—channeled—by that "gentle, mild, young man," Billy Bartram. The wilds became, instead of a place to fear, a place of reverence. Instead of a place of ignorance, they became a place of wisdom. Rejecting a sterile citadel of learning like Cambridge, Wordsworth wrote longingly of a wild place where one could think deeply, "a sanctuary for our country's youth . . . a primeval grove . . . [that] should bear a stamp of awe . . ."

But Wordsworth was just the beginning. Other thinkers in the decades ahead would refine this romantic notion of Wild Nature and further develop its spiritual benefits, eventually melding this with a deepening grasp of Wild Nature's scientific complexity and integrity—as represented in ecosystems—until arriving at our understanding of it today.

I DROVE A LONG LOOP—it took me two days—up through northwestern Pennsylvania in search of the Buffalo Swamp and the last sliver of Indian land left in Pennsylvania, known as "Cornplanter's Kingdom." I rolled along for hours on winding highways through small towns and cornfields, through mountain valleys, through the Allegheny National Forest. At Warren, almost to the New York border, I crossed the Upper Allegheny River.

I was now close to Cornplanter's lands. A Seneca chief, he and his followers in 1784 had been given "as an act of mercy" by the newly constituted United States of America a few hundred acres along the Upper Allegheny. The United States, soon after its founding as a nation, took all the remainder of the Indian lands in Pennsylvania for a mere five thousand dollars. The Americans argued that since the Indians had sided with the British during the Revolutionary War and attacked Americans, they had given up any right to their lands in the Ohio Valley. The Americans announced the Ohio Valley would now be open to white settlement. This was a mere twenty-five years after British assurances, delivered by Frederick Post to the village on Beaver Creek where Marie and Barbara were held captives, that the Indians could keep their Ohio Valley lands.

And so—just like that, on the receiving end of yet another legalism—the Native Americans lost another large chunk of the North

American continent. After following the history of these Pennsylvania and Ohio Valley transactions of Indian lands, it was abundantly obvious to me that the Indians, from the start, should have heeded Shakespeare's character's advice: "The first thing we do, let's kill all the lawyers."

I drove north along the Upper Allegheny, to what should have been the borders of Cornplanter's tiny reservation. Instead, I was greeted by signs for golf courses, suburban houses, and a huge blue lake—actually a reservoir—surrounded by green hills. Jet Skis zinged across it in the July sun, leaving sparkling white wakes. There was no sign of an Indian reservation.

Up the road a short way, I crossed into New York State. Just over the border, I spotted a roadside stand. The sign adverted "Ohi:Yo Smokes." I was now on the Seneca Reservation, but not Cornplanter's.

I pulled over on the gravelly shoulder. I struck up a conversation with two Seneca Indians who ran the stand, Les McComber and Dennis Lytel, under a shady awning outside, while Dennis carved a walking stick and we all sipped ginger ale.

They told me that Ohi:Yo means "Beautiful River," which refers to the Allegheny. The Seneca were a warrior tribe—the most feared, they said, of the Iroquois Confederacy—and a tribe in which women have a powerful role. ("The mothers have the last say," as Les put it. "With the Mohawks, the fathers have the last say.") With their lands on the western edge of the confederacy, the Senecas were known as "Keepers of the Western Door" while the Mohawks were "Keepers of the Eastern Door."

"They didn't do a very good job," cracked Dennis about the Mohawks. "They let the Pilgrims in."

"How far does the reservation extend to the south?" I asked, wondering if it went into Pennsylvania.

"From sea to shining sea," Les replied with a smile.

"I'm interested in Cornplanter's village," I said.

"It's all underwater now," he said. "The old people still remember it."

Then they told me the story of how in the 1960s the dam came in. The Indians in Cornplanter's old village were forced out of their homes, and the homes then were burned by the Army Corps of Engineers. They said the tribal leader at the time sold out the Senecas for $795 per person. They spoke for a long time of internal tribal politics, and how the "businessmen" were in charge now.

Indian lands were taken by deceit for the first 450 years of European arrival in America, and, at least until the 1960s, the pattern still prevailed. It was encouraging to hear Les and Dennis speak of Salamanca, New York, a larger town about ten miles to the north. All along, the Indians have owned the land that lies under Salamanca's downtown, and have leased it—rather than sold it—to the whites since the days of George Washington.

For the first two centuries, the Indians leased the land at nominal rates. "But in 1999 when it came time to renew the lease," Les and Dennis told me, "the Senecas consulted a property assessor like the white man. We had it assessed at value. Then we started charging what it was worth."

Some of the white businesses renewed their leases at considerably greater expense. Some, they said, had to be escorted off the property by federal marshals.

And so, I thought, the wheel finally turns.

I DROVE THROUGH SALAMANCA on a four-lane highway lined with big new casinos, then circled back down into Pennsylvania. I now sought the "Buffalo Swamp." My road atlas showed a big white roadless area that approximated the location of the Buffalo Swamp that I'd seen on maps dating to the eighteenth century. After spending the night at the small town of Kane, the next day I drove an arc around the swamp's northern and eastern edges on State Highways 46 and 146.

I passed few towns or development of any sort. There were a few abandoned hamlets, an old church, what looked like abandoned fields. I skirted marshy flats that sprouted islands of white pine. The whole area felt high in elevation—kind of a plateau—yet swampy. No major watercourses ran through it. The Indians, traveling by canoe along free-flowing streams, would have skirted it if they were trying to get anywhere fast, and yet the buffalo (or the elk) may have liked its rich grasses. Thus the ancient name Buffalo Swamp?

In the little town of Clermont, I idled past the annual picnic of the Volunteer Fire Department, where I heard the clank of horseshoes ringing on metal stakes. The old Clermont School was abandoned. Old barns and pastures stood about. A cemetery displayed a prominent headstone facing the road: "Mangrate 1810–1850." This, no doubt, was when Clermont thrived.

East on Highway 46—empty of humans, and their houses. Only forest along it. It reminded me of a very empty New England. Then south on 146. Big wooded bluffs overlooked a long, narrow valley dotted with old farms.

I turned due west at the town of Emporium—and now aimed straight into the heart of the old Buffalo Swamp. A narrow paved road followed the Driftwood Branch of Sinnemahoning Creek upstream. Wooded hills skirted a pretty valley of fields and farms. Several suburban-style houses with neat green lawns bordered the road— I speculated these were the "suburbs" of Emporium and imagined the town's bankers living here. I passed a lumber mill, Lewis & Hockenberry, that makes furniture-grade hardwoods from the surrounding forests of the Allegheny Mountains. My "blank spot" was not feeling very blank.

The road narrowed. The creek danced in late afternoon sun. The houses grew smaller—now bungalows and cabins. Signs posted over their entrances named them as "camps." "Maple Camp." "Love Wolf Camp." "Little Round Top Camp." "Camp Cozy Aire." These, I realized, were family-owned deer hunting camps and summer cabins. I passed an older couple sitting on the front porch of a log cabin, overlooking a pond.

Six miles up, I bumped off the pavement and crossed the Driftwood Branch on a small bridge. Climbing with the creek, the gravel road now ascended into the woods. The creek pooled and splashed through pretty emerald glens, overhung by leafy green bowers and sparkling in the sun. At the prettiest spot a sign read "Posted." It made me angry, as if to say here is a bit of paradise and you can't come in. The fine print said it was owned by a logging company that rented the lands out for hunting and fishing, which made it a bit more understandable why would-be wanderers were told to go away.

A few miles farther, twisting higher into the woods, where hemlock and maple groves lined the creek, a sign announced I'd entered state forest. The road abruptly left the creek and twisted sharply upward, climbing a steep hillside on tight switchbacks. Sensing the terrain was about to top out, I kept going.

The road suddenly leveled. I'd now driven about fifteen miles from Emporium into the old Buffalo Swamp. I'd reached a kind of ridgetop plateau. Maples and pines and tamaracks stood in open groves, sunny glades between them. A glistening carpet of tall ferns covered the entire forest floor.

I stopped the car and got out. After the rumble and thunk of tires over the dirt road, it was quiet except for the slight sigh of wind in the boughs. The place exhilarated me. Here was the blankest of the blank spots I could find on the western Pennsylvania map. I'd chosen it mostly at random. Yet I couldn't imagine stumbling onto a lovelier place. I waded hip-deep into the swishing ferny glades, marveling at the spot. That I had discovered it on my own, without someone pointing it out to me—unlike the wild ravines at Fish Dam Run, where I'd been directed by a forester—made it all the richer. That sense of discovery, I'd learned in childhood in the Wisconsin woods, could be intoxicating.

I *could* have felt a sense of dread out here. That something sinister lurked in the remote landscape, in these wilds, so far from a town, that something bad could happen to me here, my sense of unease left unchecked blossoming into panic. But I had Pennsylvania's own Billy Bartram to thank that I didn't feel anything approaching dread. Instead I felt a sense of celebration and marvel. I had Bartram to thank, and Coleridge, and Wordsworth. And, of course, Emerson and Thoreau, and my own father, who had seen romance in living in a log cabin in the woods.

Many other thinkers and writers, naturalists and philosophers, had helped generate the concept, but these were the direct ancestors that I could acknowledge for how I felt, standing there in the glistening ferns in the midst of the ancient Buffalo Swamp. It had taken them centuries, but they had finally managed to transcend the way of thinking about wilderness, about Wild Nature, rooted in the Old Testament. It didn't have to be an Eden-like Paradise. Nor did it have to be a Satanic Hell. Rather, it had its own spiritual value.

I wished Bartram was with me in that ferny glade. I imagine him crouching low to pull the fern fronds to his face, reflecting on the life forces running through them, then sitting down, as if nesting among them, and taking out his sketchbook and notepad. I'm quite sure Bartram wouldn't have done what I did. I looked at my watch. I had a "schedule" to keep. I estimated whether I could make the next spot on my itinerary before dark. This was the elk-viewing area on Highway 555 along the Bennett Branch of the Sinnemahoning. Once native to these mountains, elk had been wiped out long ago, but recently were reintroduced and were now thriving. I hoped to see them—as well as stop at Kittanning on the Allegheny, where Marie and Barbara had been held—before I had to get to Pittsburgh to catch a plane home to Montana.

I climbed back in the car and, within ten minutes of arriving in the ferny glades in the center of the blank spot of the ancient Buffalo Swamp, drove back down the way I'd come toward Emporium.

I immediately regretted it. But it felt too late, and I was in too much of a hurry, to turn back.

Brooding as I drove the long, thumping dirt road out, I realized that, paradoxically, blank spots exist in direct proportion to our modern sense of time and are just as relative as time. The longer it takes to reach a place—the larger of a valuable chunk from our schedule we have to spend in transit—the blanker that spot will most likely be. In relation to the rest of our crowded world, the more time it demands from us, the more precious that spot will become.

PART III

THE LOST
COUNTRY OF
SOUTHEAST
OREGON

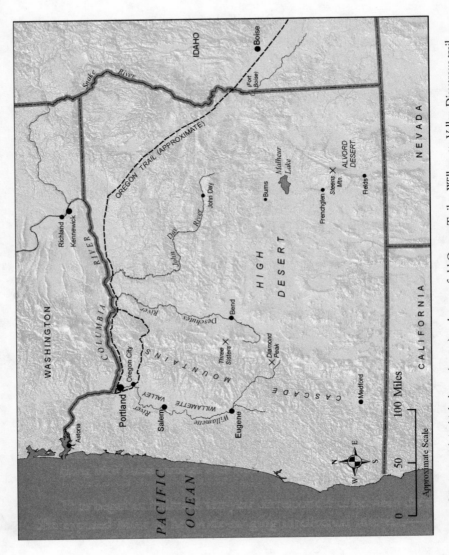

Map of Oregon with its high desert (center) and route of old Oregon Trail to Willamette Valley. Disastrous trail "Cut-Off" went from Fort Boise, past Malheur Lake, toward Diamond Peak.

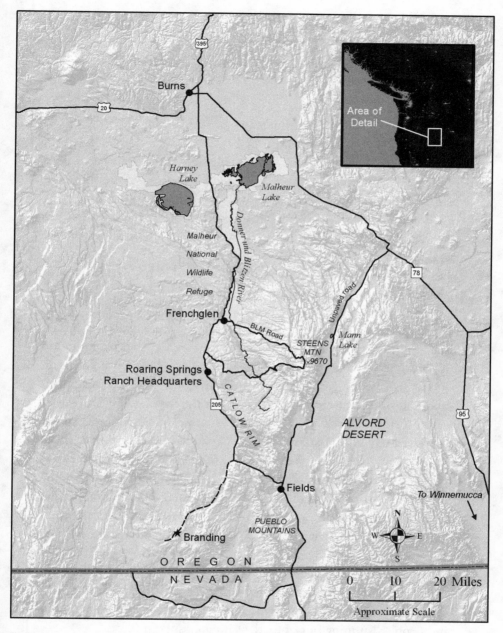

Steens Mountain area in southeast Oregon and Roaring Springs Ranch. Inset shows lights of region at night, with Vancouver/Seattle/Portland at left, Boise at right.

*T*he first one to stumble out was Martin Blanding.

He was found in mid-October 1853, by a thirteen-year-old boy, Dave Mathews, who'd been out herding cattle near Disappointment Butte, in Oregon's Willamette Valley, when he spotted a smoldering campfire. Dave Mathews discovered Martin Blanding lying on the ground beside the fire, so weak he could barely move to acknowledge Mathews. He'd clumsily jammed a stick in the earth suspended over the fire on which he'd skewered a hunk of "slunk colt." He'd hacked it from the hindquarters of a foal that had just been born from the mare he'd been riding. Blanding, barely able to lift the gun, had killed the foal the evening before.

Mathews told Blanding that there was a house nearby. Blanding "cried for joy" and, when they arrived at the dwelling, stuffed food into his mouth so fast that the hosts forced him to stop before he became ill.

He managed to get out his story. A party of 250 wagons had taken a shortcut on the Oregon Trail. They'd left the main trail weeks earlier near Fort Boise. The "Cut-Off" led them across the huge, empty spaces of modern-day southeastern Oregon. They'd become disoriented amid the great untracked valleys, the mountain ranges, the deserts, the alkaline lakes. They couldn't find water. They'd run out of food except some flour and the stringy flesh of near-dead cows. After weeks of wandering, they'd discarded bedsteads, buckets, starving cows, and even left their wagons behind. The party fragmented. Finally Blanding and another man struck westward to seek help.

The rest of them are all still out there, the starving Blanding told his hosts. Out there in the wild empty spaces. The women, the children, the babies. A whole train of them, 250 wagons and more than a thousand people. Running out of food. Winter closing in. Lost.

I HEADED TOWARD SOUTHEAST OREGON at the end of May. It was a good time of year to visit, I'd heard, when birds migrated through desert-ringed marshlands and the mountain grasses still kept their spring green. I bade goodbye to my family, climbed into my battered, twenty-year-old Isuzu Trooper at our home in Missoula, Montana—the rig had a rugged undercarriage and powerful four-wheel drive that I anticipated I might need—caught the entrance ramp to Interstate 90 four blocks from our house, and drove west into the Bitterroot Mountains.

It was hot—very hot for late May—in the mid-nineties down in the valleys. Yet high on the peaks of the Bitterroots the deep, melting snows lingering from a long winter glistened temptingly against a cobalt sky. On days like this, I love to drive with all the windows down, hot breeze blasting through the unair-conditioned car, sun burning my bare forearm resting on the open window.

Interstate 90 spilled me from the minty Bitterroots onto the dry, rolling, beige wheatlands of eastern Washington. Trying to make time on the four-lane roads while they lasted, I sheared south on Highway 395, crossing a sweeping bend of the Columbia River at Pasco and Kennewick. The river swirled with muddy snowmelt running off ten thousand mountains and now shoving against the massive pilings of the highway bridge. The little creek that gurgled past our front door in Missoula several hundred miles upstream, in the mountains, ended up here.

Across the Columbia, I entered Oregon. For much of the country, Oregon conjures mossy rainforests and Pacific waves crashing on rocky headlands. That version of Oregon certainly exists—on the *west* side of the Cascades. The mountain range creates a wall separating the two climates and two halves of Oregon. Wet air masses sweep in from the Pacific, climb up that wall, cool in temperature, pour down the rain that "cascades" back to the Pacific in salmon-filled streams. That air has been squeezed dry by the time it makes it over the range and reaches eastern Oregon. That half of the state has a desertlike, semiarid climate. The two halves are like black and white—or rather, emerald green and dusty beige.

Rumbling west, the Oregon Trail pioneers hungered for those green and fertile lands on the *west* side of the Cascades—especially the famously lush Willamette Valley, the final destination sought by many of the wagon trains. But to reach it, they had to get past high, dry eastern Oregon. The safest, and by far most common, route was simply to skirt northward around it in a long detour that followed the Snake and Columbia rivers until the Columbia—and the wagon trains—reached the moist side of the Cascades. This kept the emigrants along good, sweet water the whole way.

But the *shortest* route to the Willamette aimed straight across the high deserts of southeastern Oregon. Over their two-thousand-mile journey from Independence, Missouri, to the Willamette Valley, which took four to six months, the pilots of the prairie-schooner caravans constantly looked for "Cut-Offs"—shortcuts—that potentially could save many days of grinding travel. Most of these cutoffs they discovered did, in fact, save miles and time. But the one across southeast Oregon proved, over several attempts, to be an unmitigated disaster. As I read the old diary accounts by emigrants who survived it, I came to think of southeastern Oregon as the Bermuda Triangle of wagon trains.

The southeast was the last part of Oregon to get settled, and even now, it's not "settled" in the common sense of the term. This is ranch country—*big* ranches. A small ranch here covers 25,000 acres. The large ones encompass holdings beyond anything that we consider conventional "ownership" of land. They are their own territories, sovereignties of open spaces.

You can still get lost here, and people do, willingly and not. They get lost in a different way of life, a different rhythm, a different sense of boundaries and space. Once you've been there, it's easy to see why it attracted those who wished to live a life of adventure, those who did things their own way, and those whose preferred, by their own sense of necessity, or the sheer thrill of it, to live outside the conventional boundaries of the law.

Some of the Old West still lives here today, bumping with increasing force into the "New West." Or maybe it's vice versa. As ever, it centers on who controls—and how to treat—the land. Maybe that Old West was never more than a mirage. In our mythology it implies the ultimate freedom to do whatever you wanted. Maybe it was true in the West—as long as you possessed the land. But possessing the land—these vast acreages—was never easy and always temporary.

As one of America's first naturalists to move west, John Muir understood this. He intimately grasped the importance of controlling the land. Having spent his youth clearing his family's farm in the wilderness of Wisconsin, he was attuned to the motives of those who coveted land for profit and to the benefits of keeping land in the domain of the public. You could argue that Muir, starting in the 1870s when he came to Yosemite, represented the first crusader for a New West. He traveled through much of the West, including Oregon and the Nevada basin country near my destination. To this day, Muir's voice remains one of the most powerful to advocate wilderness and empty spaces.

At Pendleton, Highway 395 shrank to two lanes and climbed out of the Columbia River Valley up a long draw. In a narrow valley among grassy hills, I glided through the tiny burg of Pilot Rock, where a large basalt cliff hefted above a clump of houses and cottonwood trees. The cliff had served as a navigation point for pilots guiding their wagon trains along the main stem of the Oregon Trail, the route that followed the Columbia and skirted around the high deserts of southeastern Oregon. As I drove out of Pilot Rock, I scanned the pastures along the road for traces of wagon ruts—still existing in places along the Oregon Trail—but saw none.

It was early evening now. The sunlight mellowed to a deep gold. The temperature cooled and I brought my bare arm in, rolled up the window partway. The swerving road climbed another long grassy draw, still farther from the broad Columbia. Western meadowlarks trilled. I passed almost no other cars. I'd left the Interstate system, with its nodal interchanges that serve as our own landmarks, our own Pilot Rocks— these places we regard as safe ports of familiarity and sustenance and shelter with their Denny's and McDonald's and Burger Kings, their Texacos and Citgos, their Starbucks and Wal-Marts, their Hampton Inns and Motel 6s and Super 8s. I felt a thrill to leave that easy, familiar world and strike out into the realm of twisting roads and small dots of towns, with evening approaching, unsure where I'd stay the night.

The road climbed over a small, forested mountain range still holding on to a few dirty patches of winter's old snow. A historical marker at the summit called it "Battle Mountain," where the last significant fight against Indians in the Pacific Northwest occurred on July 8, 1878. They were, predictably, protesting against white encroachment.

They lost.

From the 4,200-foot summit of Battle Mountain, I descended into a broad valley, rimmed by distant wooded hills like a far-off shoreline and specked, as if they were islands on the sea, by stands of ponderosa pines and patches of wet green meadow. There were virtually no houses. I sensed that this resembled the landscape the way it looked before white settlers arrived here. I sensed I was now entering the big country. It excited me the way all new and big country excites me with the desire almost literally to reach out and embrace it.

I swung down the canyon of surging Camas Creek, rose over another summit, down across another broad valley, climbed another summit, down across another valley, crossing the fingers of the Blue Mountains and forks of the John Day River, as if I were an ant running over a set of knuckles. Still I headed south on Highway 395. Finally, well after dark, after a fat yellow full moon rose over piney mountain ridges, I pulled into the small town of John Day. I found a motel and—with the town's restaurants darkened at 10 p.m.—gratefully ate a take-out burger in my room and drank a beer.

TALL, CHEERFUL—and perhaps mentally unstable—John Day was a forty-year-old Virginian and crack rifle shot who, in 1811, joined the "Overland Party" that John Jacob Astor of New York City sent across the West to found a fur-trading empire on the Pacific Coast.

Astor had emigrated from Germany in the 1780s and, virtually upon stepping off the boat from Europe and with the advice of a fellow passenger, started a New York City fur shop. He then expanded into the Great Lakes fur trade, as well as New York real estate, and grew very wealthy. With the acquisition of the Louisiana Purchase and Lewis and Clark's exploration to the Pacific in 1804–06, the ever-shrewd Astor saw the opportunity to massively expand his Great Lakes fur-trading business all the way to the West Coast, and beyond. This ambitious—even audacious—plan involved trading New York manufactured goods with the West Coast Indians for furs, trading the American furs in China for porcelain, and trading the Chinese porcelains back in New York for good money.

Astor sent a ship around Cape Horn with orders to establish a post at the Columbia's mouth, soon to be known as Fort Astoria. He also sent the Overland Party to join up there with the shipboard group. In December 1811, while crossing the Rockies, the Overland Party ran low on food and one of its members, John Day, the crack Virginia hunter, fell ill and emaciated along the banks of the Snake River in today's Idaho. Too weak to travel farther, he dropped behind the party's main body, kept company by his former boss, Ramsay Crooks, who liked and respected Day and wouldn't leave him behind alone.

After three weeks recuperating, Crooks and Day started west again toward the Pacific Coast, at first following the main party's tracks in the snow. Eventually they lost the trail. For several weeks, they wandered aimlessly in the mountains, eating horsemeat and beaver and roots. As winter gave way to spring, they finally stumbled over the last ridge of the Blue Mountains, and, with food and directions provided by a friendly tribe of Walla Walla Indians, reached the Columbia River.

They followed the Columbia downstream toward the Pacific Coast and their companions at Fort Astoria. After one hundred miles of traveling the Columbia's banks, they reached the Mau Mau River and another band of Indians who gave the hungry twosome food. But as Day and Crooks stuffed themselves with nourishment, the Indians took their rifles. They then took Crooks and Day's fire-making flints and steels.

"They then stripped them naked," recounted Washington Irving, who was commissioned by John Jacob Astor to write the history of Astor's fur-trading enterprise, "and drove them off, refusing the entreaties of Mr. Crooks for a flint and steel of which they had robbed him; and threatening his life if he did not instantly depart."

Reversing course and struggling—naked—back up the Columbia banks, they attempted to return to the villages of the friendly Walla Walla Indians. Day and Crooks had made roughly eighty miles and were about to veer from the river inland when they spotted a party of canoes of Astor's fur traders descending the Columbia. They shouted out from shore and the canoes steered toward them. Rescued at last, they were taken down the Columbia by canoe and arrived, in May 1812, at the newly founded Fort Astoria on the Oregon Coast.

The haggard and exhausted Day convalesced only a few weeks, however, before he was dispatched back east as a member of a party carrying messages to Mr. Astor in New York City. This meant traveling by canoe, foot, and horseback the same way he had just come with such difficulty, two thousand miles back to St. Louis, whence the messages would be sent on to New York.

The messenger party and Day left Fort Astoria on June 29, 1812, according to Washington Irving's book *Astoria*. To the surprise of the group, which knew only his usual manly cheer, John Day immediately showed signs of uneasiness and "wayward deportment."

"It was supposed," Irving reported, "that the recollection of past sufferings might harass his mind in undertaking to retrace the scenes where they had been experienced."

Today we'd say it with an acronym. John Day was suffering from PTSD—post-traumatic stress disorder.

As they progressed up the Columbia, Day became wilder and more incoherent. His companions tried to calm him without effect. The sight of Indians "put him in an absolute fury" and unleashed from him a barrage of epithets. The party had been under way from Astoria only four days, when, on the night of July 2, while camped at Wapato Island in the Columbia River, John Day made an attempt to kill himself, presumably with a gun. The others stopped him. He calmed down. The camp went to sleep. Sometime before dawn while others slept, he grabbed a pair of pistols, aimed them at his head, and pulled the triggers. He somehow missed, aiming too high. It was then his companions sent him back, in the company of friendly Indians headed downriver by canoe, to his comrades at Astoria.

"[B]ut his constitution," Irving writes, "was completely broken by the hardships he had undergone, and he died within a year."

And so Day's companions renamed the Mau Mau River, at whose mouth he had been stripped naked and driven away into the wilds, the John Day River.

I HAD A LATE, QUICK BREAKFAST of eggs and bacon at a café on John Day's main street before heading south again. The town felt small and far removed, like a mountain village, tucked in a narrow river valley and surrounded by steep piney hills. The date was May 20, 2008, and Hillary Clinton and Barack Obama were feverishly fighting each other for the Democratic presidential nomination. Today was the day of the crucial Oregon primary, and yet, as I drove out of John Day, I saw no indication whatever of this Election Day. No yard signs for Hillary Clinton or Barack Obama. No billboards. Nothing.

I recalled that "blank spot" feeling I'd had in western Pennsylvania. One definition of "blank spot," to me, is the absence of outside communications. You move away from terrain where messages constantly zip in from far away and where you must constantly filter out that information which is exterior and extraneous. In a blank spot, you move into terrain where all messages are local and all, in some way, are significant. Hillary Clinton and Barack Obama were not—it appeared—significant here. Or, conversely, their campaigns didn't think John Day significant.

I drove south, over more low mountain summits and across more broad valleys. The terrain grew more arid—juniper trees instead of ponderosa pines. I saw men in pickups and cowboy hats. I saw cows—lots of cows—in distant herds scattered like flecks of pepper over the green pastures. I'd entered the big rangelands, and I'd left urban America, and the Interstate nodes that connect it, far behind.

Burns felt like an old cow town, with its broad streets and low stone buildings and an airy sense of spaciousness that began just beyond the edge of town. To freshen it up, they'd planted young trees along the sidewalks—apple, I believe—which were blossoming pink and white in late May. As I drove into town a cold, wet front suddenly hit from the coast. Low gray clouds swept over Burns, gusting a cold rain over the arid terrain that receives only six inches total moisture per year. I walked along the storm-darkened main street toward a brightly lit café for a sandwich while the rain blew confetti showers of the pink and white apple blossoms from the branches and plastered them in a wilting mosaic to the wet sidewalk. Burns reverted a notch closer to the high-desert town that it is.

I asked the waitress about the election and lack of activity.

"Some people voted," she said.

I took that to mean it didn't include her.

At the Harney County Library, around the corner, the cold rain gusted on the big windows. I sat at a research table in its Claire McGill Luce Western History Room, named after its benefactor. She'd grown up on a ranch near Burns, went to New York City for finishing school, met and married Henry Luce III, son of the founder of *Time* magazine, and who eventually became *Time*'s publisher like his father. When she died of cancer at forty-seven, she left funds for these Western collections.

A kind research librarian, Karen Nitz, combed file drawers and pulled folders of material on the "Lost Wagon Train," piling them in front of me on the table near the rain-splattered windows. It turned out that several different wagon trains had gone "lost" right around here.

A former mountain man by the name of Stephen Meek piloted the first wagon train to attempt the cutoff across southeastern Oregon, in 1845. Meek knew the old Hudson's Bay Company fur-trading trails, which tended to follow Indian trails, and planned to lead the emigrants to the Willamette Valley along them. But the emigrants lost faith in his guidance, departed from his proposed route, ran out of food and water, and, as the weakest among them started to die, nearly hanged Meek from a tripod of upraised wagon hitches. He hid inside a covered wagon, piloting from within, while the train veered due north toward the safety of the Columbia, leaving dozens of graves along the way.

Eight years after Stephen Meek's 1845 debacle another Oregon Trail party, which included Martin Blanding, made the same shortcut attempt, lured by the promise that a road had been cleared from the Willamette Valley over the Cascades to meet them. Their pilot, one Elijah Elliot, had been paid five hundred dollars to bring in a wagon train over the new route by settlers in the Willamette who stood to profit by it. But Elliot, apparently, was personally unfamiliar with this country. Rather, he carried a set of written directions. When the makeshift gallows went up and death threats were uttered, he admitted outright that he was lost.

The distances had been wildly underestimated. Near today's Burns, the party believed it had almost reached the lush farms of the Willamette Valley, still deserts and mountain ranges away. In the arid country west of Burns they had to travel fifty or seventy-five miles between watering holes.

It's hard to exaggerate just how much water these wagon trains needed daily, these traveling villages where babies were born and people died, all the while moving, moving every day.

A seven-man "advance party" set off on horseback to summon help from the Willamette, thinking they'd return in ten days with relief. A month later they still stumbled through high country in the Cascades, having mistaken the peaks of the Three Sisters areas for their landmark, Diamond Mountain, where they were supposed to find the new road.

One by one, the advance party's horses collapsed, and the men ate them. Then the men weakened, too. The four strongest went ahead— still farther in the wrong direction—while cold October rains fell in the

Cascades. The three weaker men at the rear couldn't start a fire with their usual tinder—bits of cotton plucked from the lapel of Andrew McClure's coat, the cotton set aflame by loading it into a pistol and firing into a hat to catch the flaming bits.

> Mc[lure]. was Sick. & discouraged, and Said Boys I don't think I Shall ever be able to get into the Valley. But I want you to Save yourselves. Because While you are Stout enough to travel I think, it would be wrong for you to perish, on my account. I said No, Mc. I'll Never leave you in these woods, as long as there's a Button on your old coat, & Bob Said No Mc. We will never leave you as long as there is a Button on your old Coat & he was fairly overcome, & Said as he Wept, Boys, if you are not my true friends, No one ever had friends.

Down on the desert country west of Burns, the main party struggled to find water. Only a little flour and salt remained for food. As the beasts broke down from hunger and exhaustion, the emigrants slaughtered their cattle, which they'd brought to farm the Willamette. Observed Mrs. Esther Lyman, trying to feed the stringy meat to her hungry children, the cattle were so emaciated that "there was not enough [fat] on the whole Beef to greace a griddle."

The main party knew the Deschutes River lay somewhere ahead near the base of the Cascades. But they didn't know just where nor how far. Finally, they decided their only hope was to let loose their cows and hope the animals would sniff out water. Many years later, Hanks Neville Hill recounted to his grandchildren that he was one of the small group of men who followed on horseback after the set-loose stock, while the main party stayed put. After the first long, dry day, unable to eat because they had no water, the men were making camp for the night when a fourteen-year-old boy came riding up on a buckskin pony, having tagged along from the main camp. He was Isaac Darneille, who would one day marry Hill's daughter and be father to the grandchildren to whom Hill was telling the story:

> Bright and early next morning we struck out with the boy and pony in the lead. . . . [L]ate that evening as we were moving wearily along, our jaded beasts, which we had to whip heretofore to keep in a walk, began to show signs of life by picking up their ears and sniffing the air, while the buckskin pony almost raised a trot. We knew what it meant and urged them on till the pony was in a lope away ahead and

the rest in a trot. Suddenly the pony stopped, the boy disappeared, and on coming up we found ourselves gazing down fifty feet or more into the rushing waters of the DesChutes river. And there halfway down the almost perpendicular banks was that madcap boy, tearing along. . . . [F]inally with a tumble and a roll he lands at the bottom, flat on his stomach, face down in cold water, trying in that first drink to quench the thirst that had been burning him up for three days.

Hill had left his pregnant wife and children back in the main camp. After finding the Deschutes and its precious water, he started back to them the next day, bearing two twelve-gallon kegs lashed on horseback. He traveled all that day and into the night.

About 10 o'clock that night I sighted the campfire. When I reached it every thing was still, the lights out in all the tents except mine. I hastened inside and up to my wife's bedside. She looked up with a sad smile and said, "Don't hurt the baby, dear." Oh, how I felt! Sure enough, there lay the little stranger as contented as if on a bed of down in a cozy home. We then and there named him "Hardy." Your Grandma had during all that time, for herself and four children, about a quart of water. . . . One of my little girls was lying there fast asleep with her tongue swollen out of her mouth. Strange as it may seem, children complained the least and would keep where strong men would faint.

Scouts now searched the far bank of the Deschutes for the newly blazed road, and, some thirty miles upstream, discovered the terminus of the Free Emigrant Road. This, they hoped, would lead them over the Diamond Mountain pass of the Cascades and down into the fertile Willamette Valley. Another advance party—the first one having disappeared some weeks earlier—hastened up the road to summon help from the Willamette.

The wagons slowly rolled up the road, chunking over stumps and logs left by the seven young men of the road-blazing crew, which felled the trees but returned to the Willamette without clearing them away. It was supposed to be twenty miles up to the Diamond Pass summit, but, Esther Lyman recalled, it turned out to be "a long forty." Her husband had gone ahead with the second advance party. Unable to drive her wagon alone, she'd left it, their team of oxen, and her featherbed behind, with the hope of retrieving them when her husband returned. Another emigrant carted them off.

The train's cattle had no grass on the long, slow haul up Diamond Mountain. Wagonless, Esther Lyman and her children slept on the ground under a covering that, in the mornings, would be drenched with cold rain or thick with frost. Breakfast meant a scrawny piece of boiled meat. It was now approaching mid-October. The emigrants feared the arrival of early mountain snows that could trap them. They well knew the story of the snows that had trapped the Donner Party seven years before in the California Sierras.

The last pitch to the summit of Diamond Pass they found excruciatingly steep, muddy, and difficult. The men linked multiple teams of oxen together and pulled the wagons over one by one while the animals' hooves slipped in cold mud. Snow fell lightly that day at the summit. Some wagons didn't make it over before dark. The men chocked the wagon wheels with logs to prevent them from rolling backward, and the oxen slept where they stood while the emigrants pitched tents on a piece of flatter ground at the top.

"Oh what visions of Bred butter pies Cakes and other good things to eat visited us by night," recalled Esther Lyman, "making awakening reality still more dreadful."

No one struggling over Diamond Pass realized that, two days earlier, young Dave Mathews had discovered Martin Blanding, member of the second advance party, lying emaciated beside a smoldering campfire. Blanding was the first to stumble out to the Willamette. Following the crude Emigrant Free Road, he'd made it ninety miles down the far side of Diamond Mountain, and, keeping to the twisting pathway, forded and reforded and forded again—some thirty times—the Middle Fork of the Willamette River to the edge of civilization.

The alarm spread through the newly settled farmsteads of the Willamette Valley. Settlers—some of them promoters of the new road, and surely horrified at the prospect of its first users starving to death—quickly loaded up horses and wagons and headed up the crude trail toward the top of Diamond Pass, bearing more than 20,000 pounds of flour and other goods.

The wagon train had now started the long, rough journey down Diamond Pass. Huge, dead-fallen firs in the thick rainforest lay across the road. Instead of clearing them away, the road-blazing crew had constructed crude ramps over the three-foot-thick logs. Esther Lyman and her children found it easier to walk ahead than to bump as passengers over them, with the risk of overturning.

One day as she walked along she heard the faint ringing of a bell. She thought at first it was the wagons that rumbled a mile behind her, or a stray cow that she might slaughter and eat, as she had just run out of meat. Then around the bend came a horse-mounted man leading two horses and a mule. Esther Lyman spotted the sacks of flour, potatoes, and onions that the animals carried.

> I think I was never so glad to see any human being in my life before. As soon as I could command my voice sufficient to speak I told him my situation. his reply was that I and my children must be got into the valley as soon as possible, and as I had no husband to see to me he would just take me and the children on his own animals and convey us to the settlements. . . . When we all got together you had better believe we had a time of feasting and rejoicing; Bread never tasted half so good before although it was made [of] flour salt and water. When we had partiality satisfied our appetites and turned to thank again our generous benefactor the tears were chasing each other down his cheeks. he hastaly dashed them aside and replyed that if he had relieved our wants he was amply rewarded. Oh he was a noble young man . . .

Esther Lyman and her children were rescued. Soon more provisions reached the struggling wagon train—a total of ninety-four laden pack animals and twenty-three wagons heaped with food, sent by the settlers of the Willamette Valley. It took nearly three weeks from the time Dave Mathews found Martin Blanding until all the parties of the Lost Wagon Train were safely led from the rugged Cascade crest down into the gentle Willamette. Once there, in that fertile green valley, some staked out farms and prospered. Others kept moving toward California. Some of the Lost Wagon Train descendants still live in the Willamette Valley today.

I THANKED KAREN NITZ for her help and walked out of the Harney County Library into the cold, gusting rain and the apple blossoms scattered on the wide wet streets. Burns was the last town for a long, long while. Bearing in mind the fate of the Lost Wagon Train in the country beyond Burns, I stocked up on canned goods at a local supermarket, and bought an extra five-gallon water jug at the hardware store. I then headed south again, on Highway 205, down the broad Harney Valley, which cradles Malheur Lake. Very shallow, this measures nearly twenty miles across but only ten feet deep. The shoulderless asphalt strip perched precariously on a dike as it crossed the lake's marshy arms, these oasislike desert wetlands brimming with the spring rains. It was right here that Elijah Elliot, pilot of the 1853 wagon train that included Martin Blanding and Esther Lyman, concluded he was lost. Unsure which direction to lead the prairie schooners around the lake, he spent a week wandering back and forth before heading west again, uncertain just where to aim, out into the dry country.

The emerald expanses of marsh grass held leggy flocks of white, flamingo-like egrets, and storky, gray sandhill cranes, which plucked at the water with their long beaks. This massive watering hole—as distinct from its surroundings as an irrigated putting green on a sere desert landscape—serves as a major stop on the migratory pathways between the Arctic and the subtropics. In 1908, Malheur Lake had been designated a federal bird refuge in order to protect the egrets, herons, swans, and other species from "plume hunters" who sold the feathers to hatmakers back in New York.

I CONTINUED SOUTH, aiming for the center of southeast Oregon's blank spot. I was in Harney County, the state's least populated. Highway 205 climbed a rise out of the rich, green Harney Basin and descended into another—this one huge and dry. The horizon receded far ahead of me. Instead of the lapping carpet of marshy swamps, sagebrush grew in a million separate clumps, as if the present had dissolved into a distant, grainy, black-and-white past.

There were no houses. There were no road signs. There was only the skinny strip of asphalt and the enormous spaces.

My mind wandered as I drove. I thought of dates. I thought of 1845 and of 1853—the two years, respectively, when Stephen Meek and Elijah Elliot "lost" their wagon trains in southeast Oregon's high deserts. It occurred to me those were *exactly* the dates that Thoreau built his cabin on Walden Pond, lived there, and labored on his manuscript. I sensed a kind of convergence in those years as the European

"Romantic" spirit about nature moved west, mingled with the American pioneer spirit.

The young "mountain men"—these hippies of their era—led the charge. Eager to cast aside convention and security, they left the constraints of the East and traveled up the Missouri River in the wake of Lewis and Clark's 1804–06 expedition—seeking freedom, adventure, wild places, and, almost incidentally, a fortune in furs. Many didn't want to go back, intermarrying with Indian women, supporting mixed-race families. I wonder how many had read one of the popular young British poets of their day, Lord Byron, who inspired a whole generation of European youth to seek the wild, lonely places of the earth with poems like his *Childe Harold's Pilgrimage* (1812–18).

> *There is a pleasure in the pathless woods,*
> *There is a rapture on the lonely shore.*
> *There is society where none intrudes;*
> *By the deep sea, and music in its roar;*
> *I love not man the less, but nature more.*

Washington Irving, "America's first man of letters," well knew Byron's *Childe Harold.* Born in New York City, Irving had moved to Britain in 1815 as an aspiring writer, entered its literary scene, and discovered his voice—"Rip Van Winkle," "The Legend of Sleepy Hollow"—by looking back on rural America through a Romantic lens shaped by Sir Walter Scott, Lord Byron, and other British writers. For seventeen years, during the height of the "mountain man" and fur-trade era in the American West, Irving lived amid British and Continental sophistication, among courts, writers, diplomats. From Europe, he read and heard stories of the mountain men opening up the unexplored valleys of the Rocky Mountains. The stories of the American wilderness clearly hit a romantic chord in the urbane Irving. When he finally returned to America in 1832 it was, he said, to see the West before it vanished.

"[While it was] still in a state of pristine wildness, and behold herds of buffaloes scouring the native prairies."

Irving joined up with a government commission trying to negotiate peace between Great Plains Indian tribes and tagged along on an extended camping tour of the Kansas and Arkansas territories. The

Continental cosmopolitan managed, after some effort, to shoot a buffalo, and came away touting the benefits of the "wild wood life . . . of a magnificent wilderness."

"We send our youth abroad to grow luxurious and effeminate in Europe," wrote Irving in *A Tour on the Prairies*. "[I]t appears to me that a previous tour on the prairies would be more likely to produce that manliness, simplicity and self dependence most in unison with our political institutions."

Expressed early by Irving, this sentiment that American wilderness shaped American character would resonate ever more loudly as America's wild spaces vanished. Even as the mountain men still roamed the West in the early 1830s, trapping beaver, holding their raucous annual rendezvous, marrying Indian women, there was a sense of something irreplaceable slipping away. The aging and cantankerous John Jacob Astor himself, looking back from the 1830s, saw romance in the early days in the Western wilderness. In 1834 he commissioned Irving, at a handsome sum, to write *Astoria*, the history of his fur-trading endeavor to the West Coast that had occurred only twenty-five years before, which Irving filled with high adventure and romance among mountain men and Indians, including the story of poor John Day.

By the 1840s, the fur trade had played out, due in part to a fashion shift away from beaver-skin hats. The first wagon trains of settlers in quest of cheap or free land to farm rolled west on the Oregon Trail, guided by ex–mountain men like Stephen Meek. The sense of loss intensified as farmers moved west. Francis Parkman, then an intense young man with a passion for history, lamented in his Harvard graduation address in 1844 that when Columbus came to America, it was "the domain of Nature . . . the sublimest object in the world" but now the "solemn poetry that breathed from her endless wilderness is gone . . ."

Following Washington Irving's lead, two years after his college graduation, Parkman traveled a part of the newly opened Oregon Trail in the course of his historical research about France's empire in the New World. The nervous, hyperintellectual Parkman, prone to migraines, didn't have much use for the Oregon Trail emigrants (nor probably they for him), finding them oxlike and oafish and dull. Picture Parkman's cringe upon meeting, say, the plain-talking Mrs. Esther Lyman: "There's not enough fat on that beef to grease a griddle."

For Parkman, the Oregon Trail experience was not the domain of Nature at her "sublimest." But there was an odd convergence in these years, the late 1840s, between the Romantic outlook on Nature of the Parkmans, and the practical pioneering spirit of the Esther Lymans. All at the same moment, Thoreau scribbled away in his cabin at Walden Pond, Parkman traveled the Plains in search of Romance, and emigration on the Oregon Trail surged toward its peak.

It's no coincidence, then, that during this convergence of time and attitudes in the late 1840s, a young boy named John Muir emigrated from Scotland with his family to chop a farm from the Wisconsin woods. He embodied both the pioneering spirit of an Esther Lyman and the Romantic take on Nature of a Francis Parkman. As he matured, he, too, would head west and become America's, and perhaps the world's, foremost advocate of saving wilderness.

AN HOUR'S DRIVE SOUTH of Burns on Highway 205, I spotted a green oasis of cottonwood trees nestled against a dry hillside, like a patch of moss at the base of a big rock. The road suddenly curved, slowing, easing from the hard sagebrushy landscape into the cozy green pocket. Six or seven houses were tucked pleasantly under the trees, along with a tiny general store, a schoolhouse, and an old frame building with a smooth green lawn. A sign identified this as the Frenchglen Hotel. I parked on the crunching gravel, climbed the thumping steps of the wooden front porch, opened the creaky screen door, and got a room for the night.

"Dinner's at six thirty," said John Ross, the manager behind the stand-up desk. "It's family style."

Three or four tables were laid with fifteen or twenty place settings in the combination lobby and dining room. The room had a warm, cluttered, woody feeling, and from the kitchen wafted the rich, browned smell of roasting meat. I hauled my duffel bag up the creaking steps to my room. Very small, maybe eight feet square, it had one bed, wainscot trim painted neatly in gray and white, and an old-fashioned sash window that looked onto the green lawn under the cottonwoods. I recalled, from similar hostelries in Montana, that this is what a typical Old West boardinghouse or stagecoach stop looks like. Simple wooden construction, narrow, creaking stairways and passages, doorknobs that rattled, rooms just big enough for a bed and for your boots and maybe a washbasin, with the bathroom down the hall.

Now owned by the Oregon state parks department, the Frenchglen Hotel was once known as "P Station"—stagecoach stop, guesthouse, supply depot—of Pete French's cattle empire, the P Ranch. French had grown up on his family's sheep ranch in California in the 1850s and 1860s, and was eventually hired on as a horse breaker with a much more prosperous California cattle rancher, Dr. Hugh Glenn. Diminutive in stature but fiercely ambitious, French learned how to work cattle with horses under the tutelage of the Spanish-speaking *vaqueros* of Glenn's ranch.

In the spring of 1872, Dr. Glenn financed Pete French and sent him north to rumored grazing lands in the Oregon Territory at the head of an entourage of 1,200 shorthorns, six *vaqueros,* twenty horses, and a Chinese cook. Where I stood at Frenchglen, Pete French had come upon a many-miles-long strip of wet, grassy marshland along the Donner und Blitzen—"Thunder and Lightning" in German—River that could be diked and ditched and drained to create rich hayfields, supplemented by the upland pastures of nearby Steens Mountain. It was just what he was looking for.

Single-mindedly, young French pieced together a cattle kingdom by whatever means he could, including fencing off lands that other ranchers considered their own and appropriating water rights. He defied the threats against him, small as he was physically, or perhaps because of it.

"I'll fight any man," he claimed.

The French-Glenn Cattle Co. and its P Ranch numbered some twenty thousand head by 1878. It survived an attack that year by Paiute and Bannock Indians, it survived several terrible winters, and it even survived the breakup of an eight-year marriage between Pete French and Dr. Glenn's daughter. What the P Ranch ultimately didn't survive was Pete French's in-your-face personality.

On the day after Christmas 1897, French, aged forty-eight, was opening a cattle gate on the P Ranch when a local rancher named Ed Oliver who'd had a land dispute with French rode up to him, fast. One account says that Oliver's horse slammed into French's. French responded by beating Oliver over the head with a willow whip, screaming, "I'll kill you." Oliver pulled out a revolver. He fired once at French.

The short, feisty cattle baron was dead. Ed Oliver, acquitted by a jury of his fellow homesteaders, walked free.

Two middle-aged men sat across from me at the breakfast table at the Frenchglen Hotel.

"If you're looking for blank spots," said one of the men, "I have just the thing for you."

As we chatted, John, the hotel manager, carried plates of bacon and eggs, pancakes and muffins, mugs of coffee and tea, to the table. The two had driven from western Oregon—the wet, green coastal Oregon—to camp on these high deserts. But the weather had suddenly turned so cold and rainy they'd opted for the comfort of the Frenchglen Hotel. Most other breakfast guests were birders, too—a group of three women, another party of five. Draped with binoculars, fitted with billed caps and birding books and notepads, they annually gathered here at this season, in late May, when the flocks migrate through the desert marshes soaked with spring rains.

The man went upstairs, and returned a minute or two later with a page torn from the alumni magazine of the University of Oregon. He placed it beside my plate of eggs and sausage.

Titled "Long Drive for a Latte," it was one of the coolest maps I'd ever seen. Created by the university's geography department, it showed the entire Lower 48 states of the U.S.A. in white with the states' borders outlined with thin black lines. The whole map, all forty-eight states, was white except for one small, heart-shaped black patch. It was labeled with an arrow:

"The only place in the lower forty-eight that is more than . . . 100 miles from the nearest general hospital; 150 miles from the nearest Starbucks; 100 miles from the nearest Wal-Mart."

I studied the heart-shaped shaded area and laughed. It was in southeastern Oregon. Here at the Frenchglen Hotel we sat just on its northern edge.

"Where's the nearest Wal-Mart?" I called out to John, the manager, still serving plates of breakfast.

"Bend or Winnemucca."

"How about Starbucks?"

"Probably Bend . . . and maybe Winnemucca has one, too."

"How far away are Bend and Winnemucca?"

"Bend is one hundred and ninety miles and Winnemucca is one hundred and seventy-five miles."

"How about a hospital?"

"That would be Burns. It's about an hour by ambulance, or you can get to the hospital in Bend by air flight. That's about an hour, too."

Much of the breakfast room now was listening in to the conversation.

"The point is," a woman called out from the next table, "don't get sick!"

I was more interested in finding blank spots than worried about getting sick. The map confirmed that I'd finally arrived at the blank spot that I'd sought, one as far removed as possible in these Lower 48 states from our usual points of reference, those nodes—the Wal-Mart, the Starbucks, the Super 8s—of instant communications, credit-card efficiency, and no-strain familiarity.

Still, I couldn't disengage myself entirely from that world.

"Anyone know the primary results?" I asked.

No one did. The birders from the coast were intensely interested— Hillary Clinton or Barack Obama?—but the local people didn't know and didn't really seem to care.

One of the birders, a retired doctor who had worked in rural Alaska, came through the creaking screen door and joined his friends at our big table. He'd just been sitting in his car, parked under the cottonwood trees out front, listening to its satellite radio.

"Hillary won Kentucky by thirty-five points," he now reported, "and Barack won overwhelmingly in Oregon, but they didn't give numbers."

Breakfasters shifted in and out of the room. I ate my sausage and eggs and asked John the names of some of the largest ranches in the area. He referred me to Mandy, on the hotel's staff, who had grown up on a local ranch.

I caught up to her in the creaky hallway, carrying a big armload of sheets, her small boy in tow.

"The Roaring Springs is by far the largest ranch right here," she said.

She gave me directions. These were a model of simplicity—drive straight south on the highway for twenty miles or so until I came to the first buildings. Those were the ranch headquarters. No, I didn't have to make an appointment. I could just show up.

I sensed how different this culture was, where our strict adherence to hours and minutes yielded to an attenuated sense of time that rode the rhythms of season or daylight.

"The pilots were here at the hotel last night for dinner," she said. "When the owner flies in, his pilots come up here sometimes to eat."

I returned to my seat at the breakfast table and sipped my tea. One birder group had left, and two neatly dressed men sat next to me. It turned out they were the pilots for the Roaring Springs Ranch owner, who'd flown in on his Citation jet for some fishing with his grandchildren.

"Where do you *land* a jet?" asked a birder.

"The landing strip is right beside the road," one of the pilots replied. "*Right* beside it. Sometimes we scare both the cars and ourselves."

"Do you think the owner would talk to me?" I asked.

"He's a really nice guy," said the other.

As I LOADED UP MY CAR at the Frenchglen Hotel, blackbirds trilled in the marshy ditches across the road, their lilt matching melodically with the sunny, cool, breezy morning. The Donner und Blitzen River flowed through these bottomlands like a rain gutter along the bottom edge of a gently sloping roof, carrying the water to Malheur Lake near Burns. As I looked to the east, toward the sun, the roof rose gently toward the sky—the long, easy slopes of Steens Mountain. This is a massive ridge running north–south that's roughly sixty miles long. While this side of the roof sloped down gently over several miles, the far side, which I couldn't see from here, dropped off in an abrupt escarpment that plunged some five thousand feet to the dry, dusty floor of the Alvord Desert.

Highway 205 south out of Frenchglen climbed a sage-and-juniper ridge and rolled down the other side into another huge sagebrush valley, far larger than any I'd seen before. To my left, Steens Mountain rose long and gentle, its sloping green meadows flecked with dark juniper groves, and to my right, cloud shadows raced across the sagebrush flats, the shadows seeming to blow so fast on the cool wind they kept pace with my car.

The road ran straight. I looked ahead for any sign of ranch buildings. There were none.

I was giddy at all the emptiness that surrounded me—the simple lack of humanity and its structures, the infinite arching vault of tan earth and blue sky. Growing up in the bounded spaces of Wisconsin's woods and fields and small lakes, I rarely could see as far as a mile to the horizon. Racing these cloud shadows down Highway 205, I gazed off to the west perhaps thirty or forty miles across the sagebrush flats to a languorous, distant horizon of bluish mountains.

Was that what first attracted John Muir to the West? Was it this sense of infinity striking him in the face that kept him in the West, after the closer embrace of the Wisconsin woods or Scotland?

When Muir was a ten-year-old boy—in 1849, while Emerson preached Nature in Concord and Thoreau scratched over multiple drafts of what became *Walden*—Muir's family immigrated to America. Young John and his brother and their father went in advance of the rest of the family, riding an oxcart through the trackless woods and marshes and prairie openings to a hill overlooking Wisconsin's beautiful Fountain Lake, where they built a house. Muir and his brother's life in a strict Scottish schoolhouse gave way to freedom.

"This sudden plash into pure wildness—baptism in Nature's warm heart—how utterly happy it made us!" Muir wrote in *The Story of My Boyhood and Youth*. "Nature streaming into us, wooingly teaching her wonderful glowing lessons, so unlike the dismal grammar ashes and cinders so long thrashed into us."

That glorious freedom, however, soon was leavened with the crushing work of clearing a farm. A strict authoritarian and Calvinist, Muir's father put his eldest son, John, behind the plow at age twelve. Working seventeen-hour days, John dug stumps out of fields and split oak logs into fence rails. The family worshipped together every night before going to bed at eight o'clock on their father's command, with little chance to do the leisure reading that John so loved.

For all his Calvinistic strictness, Muir's father viewed the natural world through the lens of God's work. Leaving aside Christianity, this was not so far from what Transcendentalists such as Emerson were advocating back in Concord—that spirituality infused all Nature. In his memoir, Muir described his father's ecstatic reaction to the Northern Lights shimmering over their farm one cold Wisconsin winter night.

"Come! Come, mother!" shouted Father Muir. "Come, bairns! and see the glory of God. All the sky is clad in a robe of red light . . . Hush and wonder and adore, for surely this is the clothing of the Lord himself, and perhaps He will even now appear looking down from his high heaven."

This sense of spirituality in the natural world shaped the way John himself would see Nature.

I recalled reading Muir's *The Story of My Boyhood and Youth* as a fifth- or sixth-grader in Wisconsin, and identifying with his many rambles in the woods like those around our own log cabin. But what I remembered most vividly was Muir's discovery that by waking very early in the morning—as early as 1:00 a.m., he claimed—he found the leisure to read Milton, Shakespeare, Mark Akenside (the British poet and Deist who had so influenced William Bartram), and the German explorer and naturalist Alexander von Humboldt, whose five years in South America captured Muir's imagination. On other predawn mornings Muir descended to the cellar and tinkered by candlelight with his beloved inventions. He rasped and filed bits of wood and metal into gears and dials to construct homemade clocks, thermometers, and an "alarm bed" that tipped him upright at a preset hour.

These inventions finally liberated Muir from the backbreaking work of the family farm, set him on the road to an education, and, eventually, the wilderness. At a neighbor's suggestion the twenty-two-year-old Muir strapped his inventions onto an old washboard, asked his brother to drop him via the family's wagon in a nearby village, and boarded the steam train to the state capital at Madison. Here he entered his inventions in the Wisconsin State Fair, which he hoped might lead to a machine-shop job. To his surprise, Muir's homemade wooden clocks and thermometers were the biggest hit in the Fine Arts Hall.

"It was considered wonderful that a boy on a farm had been able to invent and make such things, and almost every spectator foretold good fortune," he recalled. "But I had been lectured by my father above all things to avoid praise . . ."

His budding mechanical genius welcomed by the administration, Muir enrolled at Wisconsin's state university in 1860, where he lived on a dollar a week, studied geology, and read deeply and thirstily, including the works of Emerson, Wordsworth, and Thoreau, who, back in Concord, would soon die of consumption at age forty-four. Muir happened to attend the university at a particularly heady moment in the field of natural history. Darwin's startling and new *Origin of Species* had been published only the year before, in 1859, exploding the notion that life on Earth was created in one stroke by the hand of God for the benefit of Man. Soon after Darwin, George Perkins Marsh, in his *Man and Nature,* systematically proved how human civilization, rather than living in "harmony" with the earth, had thoroughly degraded, deforested, and altered the landscapes of the Mediterranean basin.

Muir's personal awakening in botany arrived in a kind of Bartramian flash when, as he stood on the stone steps of North Hall, a fellow student named Griswold reached up and plucked a blossom from an overhanging locust tree and handed it to Muir.

" 'Muir,' he said, 'do you know what family this tree belongs to?'

" 'No,' I said, 'I don't know anything about botany.'

" 'Well, no matter,' said he, 'what is it like?'

" 'It's like a pea flower,' I replied.

" 'That's right. You're right,' he said, 'it belongs to the Pea Family.'

" 'But how can that be,' I objected, 'when the pea is a weak, clinging, straggling herb, and the locust a big, thorny hardwood tree?' "

Griswold pointed out the blossom's similarities in petals, stamen, and pistil, the locust tree's dangling seed pods like pea pods, and had Muir taste the locust tree's leaves. To Muir's surprise, they tasted like pea leaves.

"Now, surely you cannot imagine that all these similar characters are mere coincidences," said Griswold. "Do they not rather go to show that the Creator in making the pea vine and the locust tree had the same idea in mind, and that plants are not classified arbitrarily? Man has nothing to do with their classification. Nature has attended to all that, giving essential unity with boundless variety, so that the botanist has only to examine plants to learn the harmony of their relations."

"This fine lesson," wrote Muir in his autobiography, "charmed me and sent me flying to the woods and meadows in wild enthusiasm. Like everybody else I was always fond of flowers, attracted by their external beauty and purity. Now my eyes were opened to their inner beauty, all alike revealing glorious traces of the thoughts of God, and leading on and on into the infinite cosmos."

Highway 205 ran along the base of a long, bald slice of rimrock that protruded from the sagebrush flats, the Catlow Rim. Around a bend of the rim, a distant, yellow-green patch of willows and cottonwoods slid into view, and underneath the trees a large cluster of ranch buildings, surrounded by green pastures. Something tubelike and bright metallic-white shone on a pasture nearby, like a space capsule descended onto this green and sere landscape, this looming rock rim and these broad sagebrush flats.

It was a Citation jet.

"Roaring Springs Ranch," announced a sign beside the highway. A creek gushed forth from the rimrock, giving the ranch its name.

A few men and boys in windbreakers and caps fished in a marshy pond along the road. I pulled over. The wind blew hard as I walked to the fencing that stood between us.

"Can I help you?" one of the men said politely.

It turned out to be Rob Sanders himself, a businessman from the West Coast who, with other family members, purchased the ranch in the early 1990s.

I told him I was interested in the history of the ranch.

"If you really want to know its history," he said, "you should talk to the foreman, Stacy Davies."

"Where do I find him?"

"They're all out branding in the desert."

"Can I drive there from here?"

"You can, but it'll take a while. And it's pretty rough in spots. What kind of vehicle do you have?"

He glanced over at my rusting Isuzu Trooper—an early, scrawny-looking version of an SUV.

"You should be okay in that. You have good clearance. Just be sure you have plenty of fuel, and a spare tire."

"I have a spare, and I have lots of extra water, and enough food to last for days."

"As long as you have all that good stuff, you should be all right."

Like Mandy's at the hotel, the directions Sanders gave me were exceedingly simple in this big country—go straight down the highway for another twenty or thirty miles until the place where the highway bends, then bear right on a dirt road out into the desert for a long ways. He wasn't sure exactly how far.

"Just keep heading south," he said. "If you keep heading south and stay on that main dirt road you'll run right into them. They've been out in the desert branding for the last two or three days."

An hour or so later, I was "walking" the car—driving at a crawl—up a steep, narrow canyon. The rubber tires twanged as I jounced over big chunks of rock and the car bucked forward and back, side to side. I hadn't seen a single person nor structure since I'd left Rob Sanders. After thumping off the highway onto the crude dirt road, I'd driven through a long series of sagebrush flats, through dusty valleys, through barren, sun-scorched hills, with a pocket compass lying on the console to ensure I was always heading south.

Halfway up the rocky canyon, I came to a small flat spot and got out to relieve myself. The wind blew hard but the sun shone pleasantly. Just for reassurance, among all these big, tire-puncturing rocks, I double-checked that I had air in my spare tire, mounted to the rear of the Trooper. I pounded the tire with my fist. It felt nice and firm.

But then I noticed . . . there was a *padlock* on the spare. In all the years I'd owned the car, I'd never used the spare. And I'd never noticed that it was padlocked to the rear door to prevent theft. And I didn't re-member ever seeing a key for the heavy-duty padlock.

"Oh, shit!" I said.

I tugged on the lock. It was thick . . . and solid. I looked at the rocks lying scattered about. If I had to, could I smash the padlock with a rock? I doubted it would break. I remembered seeing a metal stake a ways down the canyon. I might be able to use that to pry it off if I had to.

I climbed back into the car. I checked the odometer. I'd driven ten or twelve miles since turning off the highway. If I had a flat tire now, I could walk that distance to get back to civilization—or at least a road. But I didn't want to turn back. I wanted to get to the branding.

I wouldn't perish out here—I had plenty of water and food. I had a cell phone with me but hadn't received a signal since about sixty miles up the road, back near Burns. How much inconvenience was I willing to risk to experience a blank spot? I'd been down this same road, so to speak, many times before on various travels, and occasionally I'd had to make the equivalent of an unwelcome fifteen-mile hike back to the highway. But there is a certain time in one's life when that starts seeming less like a wild adventure and more like . . . what?

More like a whole lot of effort.

I decided to keep going . . . at least a few more miles. I checked my pocket compass. I was still heading south. Lumbering upward in first gear, the car slowly climbed farther up the canyon. I wished I had my family with me. They'd be getting a big kick out of this. To Molly and Skyler, it would all look like adventure and not like difficulty.

As I emerged from the canyon, the rocky hills on each side drew back. I crested a rise, overlooking yet another wide sagebrush valley. I paused, scanning across it, tracing with my eye the sinuous line of the two dusty tire ruts until they disappeared in the far distance. Nothing. Not a building, not a fence, not a truck, not a horse, not a cow. Nothing but sage and rock and wind.

JOHN MUIR FOUND THE WILDERNESS LONELY, too—at first.

His first epic adventure was a draft dodge. In late 1863, after two years at Wisconsin's state university, Muir planned to enter medical school at Michigan, when President Abraham Lincoln called up another half million men to send into the bloody, raging battles of the Civil War. Muir's brother Dan had already fled to Canada. Considering himself more a Scotsman than an American obligated to fight in American wars, John also fled for Canada.

It's not clear exactly what his plan was, or if he had one. For six months, he largely kept out of touch, wandering through the swamps and forests in the wilderness north of Lake Huron. Alone, homesick, sleeping at farmhouses when he could find one, he spent much of his time collecting botanical samples. It was here he had a central epiphany of his life.

One day in June 1864, Muir struggled across a great tamarack swamp where he'd been collecting plants. Following a rough compass course to reach the far side, he found himself still in the swamp as dusk fell, hungry and tired and worrying whether he could find a house on dry ground to spend the night, or would have to weave himself a nest of branches in which to sleep above the soggy ground. Despairing in the gloom, he ventured beside a stream, and happened to spot two beautiful white flowers sprouting from a bed of yellow moss. These were *Calypso borealis*—"Hider of the North"—a rare orchid. The distraught Muir instantly identified with the flowers as his soul mates.

> They were alone. I never before saw a plant so full of life; so perfectly spiritual, it seemed pure enough for the throne of its Creator. I felt as if I were in the presence of superior beings who loved me and beckoned me to come. I sat down beside them and wept for joy.

Not unlike William Bartram and Henry David Thoreau, Muir discovered in plants and in the wilds a kind of universal love and acceptance . . . a love and acceptance, one could conjecture, that hadn't been forthcoming from his stern father and the harsh life of clearing a farm. In the complex and paradoxical equation of familial emotion, John Muir discovered love's embrace in the very place—in the wilds, among the delicate, crushable plants—that his father, in his single-minded drive to homestead in the virgin forest, had long attempted to destroy.

After his wilderness sojourn north of Lake Huron, Muir joined up with his brother and hired on as a mechanic in an Ontario woodworking factory, staying over a year. When the Civil War ended and the factory burned—and with it his precious botanical collections—Muir wandered back to the United States, taking a job at a steam-powered wagon-parts factory in Indianapolis. He had a bright future as mechanic and inventor because the U.S. economy, spurred by the Civil War and the munitions manufacturing and rail transport it demanded, was quickly transforming from agrarian to factory-based.

One day at the wagon factory Muir was using a metal file to pry apart a splice in a power belt and accidentally jammed the file's sharp end into his right eye. As he stood at a window, the aqueous humor that filled the eye dripped out into his palm, and with it, his sight disappeared in that eye. A few days later, due to nerve shock, his other eye went blind, too.

For days, he lay in a sickbed in a darkened room, the pain spreading through his body, tortured by the thought of being blind for the rest of his life. But after a month's slow recovery, the sight returned to both eyes. During this ordeal Muir resolved that he would return to the natural world he so loved, and that loved him, as embodied by those rare and delicate "Hiders of the North" orchids. He pledged that he would go on an epic wilderness romp—what became a "grand sabbath day three years long." His plan was to walk south to the Gulf of Mexico. From there he would voyage to the Amazon, and strike into its deep jungles, following in the footsteps of his childhood hero, the explorer Alexander von Humboldt.

AT TWENTY MILES OFF THE HIGHWAY, according to the Isuzu's odometer, I began to have doubts. The dirt track still wound through the sagebrush valleys and barren hills, and I still hadn't seen a structure nor living thing. Was this the right track I'd chosen? I checked the compass. It showed that I still headed south, as Rob Sanders had instructed. But if I got a flat tire, which seemed quite likely on the track's rocky sections, twenty miles would prove a very long walk.

At mile twenty-one, I crested another rise. Again, I scanned across another broad sagebrush valley bounded by low, dry mountains, looking for something, anything, that indicated a human presence. At first nothing . . . then, scanning again, I spotted what appeared at first like a faint plume of smoke, blowing away on the cold wind. It was maybe four miles away at the base of a dry, tawny mountain. I looked closer. Some faint dark lines lay there. No buildings. But a corral? The wind whisked up another white plume, glimmeringly backlit by the afternoon sun. Dust? Some living creature had to be kicking up that dust.

I drove steadily toward it on the two dirt ruts winding across the valley. Drawing closer, I saw that it was, in fact, a wooden corral. A few boxy pickup trucks and a horse trailer sat near it. With mounting excitement, I jounced up the track that led to it, and stopped the car. A herd of several hundred bellowing cattle milled between the wooden fences, kicking up plumes of dust blown away on the wind. Riders circled on horseback among the dusty herd, swinging lariats.

Yes! I thought. *I've just arrived in the Old West.*

SOMEONE SHOULD—okay, maybe I will, someday—write the story of the women who influenced the thinking of the "great men" who shaped our notions of Wild Nature. Rousseau had Madame de Warens, the aristocratic Deist and herbalist with the Savoy country estate who, supposedly converting the runaway teenager to Catholicism, educated him in the arts of love and literature, and as a nature worshipper who questioned "civilized" man. Thanks in good part to Madame de Warens, Rousseau would go on to change the Western world's thinking about Wild Nature and Savage Man.

Billy Bartram left home in Philadelphia for his uncle's plantation at Cape Fear. There, amid the semitropical lushness of the Carolinas, he secretly fell in love with his first cousin, Mary Bartram. Their love forbidden, Billy Bartram cherished the memories of his and Mary's cavortings in the "eternal spring" as he wandered alone for four years, as if in exile, in the Southeast wilderness. The book that resulted, Bartram's *Travels,* would broadly influence the European Romantic movement and transform the American wilderness—or, rather, the image of it—from a place of forbidding and evil to one of soulful and "sublime" experiences.

Thoreau found muses in two proper young New England women. He apparently went so far as to propose to Ellen Sewall, who shared his love of the outdoors, but whose father strictly forbade her to marry this Concord weirdo and demanded she cut off all relations. Thoreau also apparently fell in love with another young Massachusetts woman of good family, Mary Russell, who also rejected him. Thwarted twice in love with young women, Thoreau took to the woods, where, by his own only partly tongue-in-cheek admission, he "found a match at last" during one winter afternoon's walk. Its dead leaves and branches poking above the snow and whispering wintry thoughts to him, reports Thoreau, "I fell in love with a shrub oak."

All were odd men, standing off from social conventions of their times—often vehemently opposed to them. Each was infused with his own idiosyncratic passion that ultimately expressed itself in love for wild places. Through their writings, they became famous for it. But only "great men" of the era were recognized to write "great books," and history itself followed their biographies. At least until contemporary times, few women appear in the written record of our changing ideas and feelings toward wild places. If you read between the lines, however, you can detect the profound influence of women who encouraged these "great men" of the wilds, sometimes loved them, and almost always gave them the gift of much deeper insight into the value of Nature.

Such was the case with John Muir and Jeanne Carr. The two met through her husband, Ezra, one of Muir's professors of geology and chemistry at the University of Wisconsin. Having moved to the Midwest from New England, the Carrs personally knew Ralph Waldo Emerson and his circle, and knew the writings of Thoreau, whose *Walden* had recently been published, in 1854. Introducing him to Emerson's writings, Professor Carr deeply impressed on Muir "the harmony, the oneness, of all the world's life"—a view that Jeanne shared.

Daughter of a freethinking Vermont doctor and a mother of old New England stock, Jeanne Carr's Puritan ancestors, like Emerson's, had arrived in New England seven generations earlier, convinced that Satan inhabited the North American wilds and the devil possessed the heathen Indian. Like Emerson and others in the Concord circle, Jeanne Carr broke dramatically with that dark, hoary view of Wild Nature.

With her curious and progressive mind, she found herself frustrated by the constricted female role in mid-1800s America of homemaker and housewife and helper to her husband's career. She chafed for ways to reach out intellectually, to transcend this narrow life, having at various points enrolled in a seminary, worked as a schoolteacher, and pursued amateur botany. When John Muir, working at the sawmill in Canada to escape the draft and feeling lonely and homesick, wrote a letter to Professor Carr, Jeanne quickly replied to Muir. She remembered him as standing out from other students for "your power of insight into Nature, and the simplicity of your love for her." Jeanne proposed to John Muir, via letter, that they begin an exchange of ideas:

> [I am] a woman whose life seems always to be used up in little trifling things, never labelled "done" and laid away as a man's may be. Then as a woman I have often to consider not the lilies only, in their perfection, but the humble honest wayside grasses and weeds, sturdily filling their places through such repeated discouragements.

Thus began an intimate, ten-year correspondence between the two. She exposed Muir to her wide-ranging intellectual interests—from painting to feminism, to landscape gardening, to poetry, to psychic phenomena, to Asian philosophies. He was twenty-seven years old and an odd-mannered farmboy draft dodger, and she forty and a polished New England lady. She served as both his muse and his guide, a mother figure and sister, and offered him a kind of universal love as she loved the "humble honest wayside grasses and weeds." It was as if Nature itself provided the lush medium through which their feelings for each other flowed.

At the time, psychic readings were much in vogue across the United States. While John Muir lay in bed recovering his sight after poking his eye with a file, and deciding to follow the explorer Humboldt's steps to South America, Jeanne Carr wrote him to say that a friend of hers, a psychic, predicted he would end up in the western United States and the Yosemite Valley.

Muir read the prediction with skepticism.

"My faith concerning its complete fulfillment is weak," he wrote to Mrs. Carr.

THEY'D SEEN ME COMING—my tiny Trooper in the distance kicking up a plume of dust far across the sagebrush valley. As I neared, bumping up through the sage, one of the riders sidled his horse to the edge of the corral. As I got out of the car, he dismounted and walked over to the fence, leading his horse by the reins, while eyeing me carefully. It wasn't as if someone would just *stumble* across this place; you'd have to be way *beyond* lost. I'd be suspicious, too.

I gave him a jaunty little wave, hoping to look friendly, hoping to look *unarmed.* I approached closely enough so he could hear me above the bellowing, churning, dust-shrouded mass of animals behind him.

"Hey," I said in greeting, as warmly as I could.

He watched me steadily with cool blue eyes from under his cowboy hat.

"Can I help you?" he replied evenly.

"Rob Sanders sent me," I said, figuring that invoking the boss's name might put him at ease. "Are you Stacy Davies?"

He said he was. I hurriedly explained what I was up to—my quest for the blankest, emptiest places in America. He listened carefully while his horse stood patiently beside him. A long lariat was looped over the saddlehorn. He wore dusty leather chaps on his legs, battered cowboy boots, an old tan coat.

I noticed the other riders, working their horses through the "pairs"—each consisting of a mother cow and calf—swinging lariats and throwing them down to rope the calves. It looked like a Western. They were *dressed* like in a Western: heavy leather chaps; dusty worn boots; cowboy hats; bandannas knotted around their necks. They hadn't dressed up for me, or for anyone else. They just were. I thought the American cowboy was dead. But here he was—cowboys and cowgirls—*vaqueros,* the old Spanish called them in California, or *buckaroos* as they were known here, a bastardization of the Spanish noun. There was a pretty *vaquera,* too, with tight jeans and leather chaps and white hat and knotted black bandanna around her slender neck, wearing silver earrings, and working near the fire. It blazed bright orange at the far end of the corral. Branding irons poked from it. I'd walked onto a damned movie set! It felt more surreal than a movie set, less explicable, because we were way, way, *way* out here in the desert . . . as if in the many intervening miles since I'd last seen another human and through that long sequence of empty sagebrush valleys I'd slipped through a rent in the fabric of time and emerged in the 1880s.

Davies pointed to a hole in the fence to crawl through, so I could stand in the dusty corral and talk more easily.

"So what do you want to know?" he asked.

Still the cows bellowed and dust flew and wind blew and the riders roped.

"Well, I want to know how a ranch like this works, and what it's like to live here in such empty country, and how *big* it is."

"This allotment we're standing on is 640,000 acres," he said, with some pride in its sheer scale. "One pasture is 427,000 acres. The whole ranch is one million acres. From here it's forty-five miles back to ranch headquarters. It's twenty miles to pavement. It's eighteen miles to the Nevada border."

A boy of maybe eleven walked up, wearing a sweatshirt with shoved-up sleeves. Dried blood, caked over with white dust, smeared his hands, forearms, face. Wind and dust matted his hair, like some Huck Finn of the High Desert, and in one hand he gripped a short, el-egantly curved and very sharp knife, and in the other, a whetstone, on which he worked the knife blade back and forth, honing it.

He asked Stacy a question about what he wanted done next with some pairs.

"This is my boy," Stacy said to me. "He's been doing the cutting. Do you have kids?"

"I do," I said. "A girl thirteen and a boy ten."

"Good," he said. "I have three boys working here now, and my wife. That couple over there, they're getting married in a month. This is a place where families can work together."

The Davies family, Stacy and Elaine and their sons, lived back at ranch headquarters, forty-five miles away, where I'd encountered Rob Sanders and the Citation jet in the pasture. Stacy said the boys went to elementary school in Frenchglen, about fifteen miles from headquarters. For high school, they'd go to Crane Union High School, a boarding high school in Crane, about seventy-five miles away.

"So exactly how big is a million acres in total?"

"The ranch is seventy miles north to south," he replied. "It's forty-five miles across at the widest point."

He nodded the brim of his hat—nodding it across the broad valley floor, nodding it toward distant bluish hills, nodding it toward the utter, absolute absence of a dwelling or any sign of human life.

"This is the heart of the big empty, as you can see. I don't know anyplace that's farther from a highway."

I had to smile. Wherever exactly the center of that "Long Way to a Latte" map lay, I was pretty sure I was standing on it.

I N SEPTEMBER 1867, at age twenty-nine, Muir walked out of Louisville, Kentucky, pausing at the town's outskirts to spread out a map and trace the wildest way to the Gulf of Mexico. From there, his plan was to follow Humboldt into the Amazon.

Across Kentucky and Tennessee and into Georgia he traipsed—into William Bartram's old territory—through forests and along country roads, staying at sharecroppers' shacks and trappers' cabins. He slept several nights in one memorably peaceful and enchanting graveyard and gained a visceral understanding of how the human body is recycled into the natural world. Ending only two years earlier, the Civil War had left much of the countryside in ruins. Gangs of long-haired highwaymen on horseback prowled the roads. They found nothing in Muir's meager sack—a plant press, botanical samples, crackers, a copy of Milton's *Paradise Lost*, Muir's own journal, inscribed "*John Muir, Earth-Planet, Universe*"—worth stealing. One highwayman, after rummaging through it, thrust the bag back to him in disgust.

These encounters may have encouraged Muir to side with the wild animals and heathen Indians—also victims of ruffians and "honest" citizens alike. The alligators of the Florida swamps were fierce and cruel in the eyes of man, Muir noted, but no doubt they were happy and beautiful in the eyes of God. "Lord Man" felt free to kill a bear or a savage heathen Indian, but if bear or Indian killed Christian man, no matter how worthless that individual, "oh! that is horribly unorthodox, and on the part of the Indians atrocious murder! . . . if a war of races should occur between the wild beasts and Lord Man, I would be tempted to sympathize with the bears."

Reaching Savannah, he boarded a coastal packet for a short passage past Georgia's seaboard swamps, disembarking on the Atlantic coast of northern Florida. Sticking to the only dry ground he could find— a railroad line—he hiked across the entirety of Florida, reaching the Gulf of Mexico at Cedar Key. While waiting two weeks for a lumber boat to take him to Galveston, Texas, from which he hoped to sail to South America, Muir went to work temporarily at a Cedar Key lumber mill. After three days at the mill, a fever came over him "like a storm" and he collapsed into a deep coma.

"I awoke at a strange hour," he wrote later, "on a strange day."

He could hear the mill owner, Hodgson, standing over him and asking if Muir had spoken yet. Someone replied that he hadn't.

"Well, keep pouring in the quinine. That's all we can do."

Somewhere in the swamps of Florida, Muir, unknown to him, had been bitten by an anopheles mosquito carrying the malaria parasite, which then surged through his blood and reproduced in stupendous quantities; it would be decades before researchers discovered that malaria is a parasitical, mosquito-borne disease. One wonders how this knowledge might have changed—if it would have changed at all— Muir's harmonious perception of the natural world, for it was during this "Thousand-Mile Walk to the Gulf of Mexico" and during his days in Florida, amid fever dreams and spectacular sunsets, that Muir underwent a religious conversion about the relation of God and Man and Nature.

He rejected his father's severe Campbellite Christianity—that the world, and the human soul in particular, served as a battleground between God and the Devil, and that the victory of the former demanded intense and constant vigilance. Muir now asserted that God did not make the world for Man alone. Those who claimed to know God's precise intentions were charlatans and the God that they presumed to know was a puppet of their own imaginations.

> The world, we are told, was made specially for man—a presumption not supported by all the facts. A numerous class of men . . . have precise dogmatic insight of the intentions of the Creator, and it is hardly possible to be guilty of irreverence in speaking of *their* God any more than of heathen idols. He is . . . as purely a manufactured article as any puppet of a half-penny stage.

Like John and William Bartram before him, Muir rejected conventional Christianity and speculated about a spiritual force in plants and minerals—beliefs held by many indigenous peoples including Native Americans. On he went in his journal, as he recovered from his malarial dreams in Cedar Key:

> Nature's object in making animals and plants might possibly be first of all the happiness of each one of them, not the creation of all for the happiness of the one. Why ought man to value himself as more than an infinitely small composing unit of the one great unit of creation? . . . The universe would be incomplete without man; but it would also be incomplete without the smallest transmicroscopic creature that dwells beyond our conceitful eyes and knowledge.

This, as Stephen Fox and other Muir biographers have noted, was the central insight of John Muir's life. "Creation," as Fox puts it, "belonged not to a manlike Christian God, but to the impartial force of Nature," and Man, in Muir's words, was only one "infinitely small" part of that Creation.

Muir's was a revolutionary thought in mid-1800s America, as forests were chopped and prairies plowed and lands "gobbled, gobbled" up because God, in the conventional Christian thinking, had put Nature on Earth for the benefit of Man.

From Cedar Key, Muir took a schooner south to Cuba. Still feeling too weak to explore Cuba's inland mountains—much less South America—he then decided to turn north to colder climates until his strength returned. He hopped aboard an orange boat bound for New York, landed there briefly in winter's refreshing cold, but felt overwhelmed by "the vast throngs of people, the noise of the streets, and the immense size of the buildings." On not much more than a whim, a young man at loose ends looking for some sort of a destiny, Muir booked passage to San Francisco. It was this whim that first brought him west. It would be home for the rest of his life, and the heart of his endless explorations—throughout the California mountains, to Nevada, to Oregon, Washington, and Alaska.

Three weeks in March 1868 took him by steamship from New York to Panama, by rail across the jungly isthmus, then via another steamer north to San Francisco's harbor, surrounded by its steep hills. On their arrival in port, Muir was walking up Market Street with a Cockney shipmate when he asked a carpenter the best way out of town.

"Where do you wish to go?" asked the carpenter, in an exchange that has since become legend.

"Anywhere that's wild," Muir said.

In fact, he knew he wanted to go to Yosemite, as in the late 1860s it was already gaining attention for its powerful scenery, sheer cliffs, and groves of giant sequoias and had recently been named a state park. The carpenter directed Muir to the Oakland ferry as the way to start toward Yosemite.

If his thousand-mile walk to the Gulf and fever dreams in Florida served as a religious conversion for Muir, this walk to Yosemite was a kind of rebirth into a newly created world. To Jeanne Carr he wrote a detailed account. The air itself felt new. He and his companion were "new creatures, born again; and truly not until this time were we fairly conscious born at all."

He first gazed on the Sierra Nevada Mountains from the top of Pacheco Pass. This young man from the rolling hills and small lakes of Wisconsin had never seen true mountains before nor vistas of such enormous breadth. He was stunned. One hundred miles away, across the airy space of the San Joaquin Valley, he could scan along an entire three-hundred-mile stretch of the snowcapped Sierras. Descending into the San Joaquin, Muir found himself wading in a thigh-deep sea of yellow and purple flowers. When he reached the Yosemite Valley itself, he felt himself somehow unworthy of such grandeur with its vast rock walls, arcing waterfalls, and nearby groves of "noble" sequoia trees.

After his first brief, weeklong stay in Yosemite, Muir picked up a series of odd jobs down in the California lowlands, harvesting grain, running a ferry, sheepshearing, but still entertained the notion of going to

South America. He was thirty years old. He confessed to his sister Annie in a letter that he was always a little lonely and maybe the time had come "to put away childish things."

"What shall I do?" he wrote in his journal.

"Where shall I go?"

He took work that winter as a sheep herder near Snelling, where the Sierras spilled down in foothills to the San Joaquin. He spent it in a smoky, leaky hut, learning to bake his own bread in the coals. In spring, the valley's acres of flowers bloomed and he counted hundreds of mosses on a tiny patch of rock. He got news from Jeanne Carr. She and her family were moving to Oakland, where her husband had taken a new teaching job at the nearby University of California. Muir was still thinking about going to South America, he wrote his brother Dan, and maybe to Europe. He didn't think he could ever really settle down into a normal working life except maybe to "preach Nature like an apostle," although, if actually at a pulpit, he worried about being accused of blasphemy.

"I fear I should be preaching much that was unsanctified & unorthodox."

You sense, through these letters and journals of Muir's, just how strongly he was searching for his own chosen role in Creation.

In June, he helped an Irishman named Delaney move his herd of sheep from the dry lowlands on the eastern, desertlike side of the Sierras up into the rich, moist pastures of the mountains. With Delaney, who had attended college and studied for the priesthood before joining the Gold Rush and becoming a sheep rancher, Muir found intellectual companionship. This rugged, outdoorsy, priest-educated Irishman taught Muir the rolling cadences of preaching spiritual experience. As they followed the band of sheep, emerging from the crackling dry foothills into green alpine terrain, Muir suddenly knew he was home. He wrote with a sustained religious ecstasy in a journal of the trip, later to become *My First Summer in the Sierra*:

> We are now in the mountains and they are in us, kindling enthusiasm, making every nerve quiver, filling every pore and cell of us. Our flesh-and-bone tabernacle seems transparent as glass to the beauty about us, as if truly an inseparable part of it, thrilling with the air and trees, streams and rocks, in the waves of the sun,—a part of all nature, neither old nor young, sick nor well, but immortal. Just now I

can hardly conceive of any bodily condition dependent on food or breath any more than the ground or the sky. . . . In this newness of life we seem to have been so always.

John Muir, this first summer in the Sierras, in the great West, had discovered what he would do with his life.

He would become a "mountaineer."

STACY DAVIES REMOUNTED HIS HORSE and eased into the bellowing herd of cow and calf pairs. I was free to walk around anywhere in the corral, he'd told me. I stuck to the rail fence at first, apprehensive to stray into the maelstrom of those tens of thousands of pounds of bellowing animal muscle and swirling dust. But, notebook and camera in hand, soon I slipped through the edge of the swirl, stepping across the pulverized dust to the branding fire at the far end.

From my post near the fire, I studied the dance that unfolded between horse and rider, cow and calf, branders and cutters. It was a ballet—delicate and precisely timed—yet heavy and muscular and dusty, an improvisation between animal and human that shifted from upright and poised *en point* and quickly dropped to thudding, sprawled floor work and moments later sprang back upright again.

Stacy joined the three or four other riders moving through the herd of mothers and their unbranded calves, born only this spring. Each guiding his horse at a walk, swinging their lariats in their free hands, they each tried to separate a calf from its mother and the rest of the herd. The pairs constantly shuffled or trotted away in an attempt to avoid the riders, giving the herd its swirling, flowing quality.

But here a calf separated a bit, and sidled out into an open space in the dusty corral. Swinging his lariat, Stacy threw down a loop on the ground in front of it. The calf stepped into the loop, and with a quick, precise bit of timing, Stacy tugged on the rope. The lariat loop closed around the calf's hind legs, binding them together.

All in a matter of a few seconds, Stacy looped his end of the lariat around the saddlehorn of his horse, urged his horse forward, and the rope pulled tauter. The calf, its rear legs bound in the lariat loop, flopped to the ground, and Stacy's horse dragged it through the dust out of the herd toward the branding fire about fifty or sixty feet away.

The fire flared bright orange whenever clouds scudded over the sun and the cold gusts of wind blew, kicking up swirls of dust. Long branding irons protruded from the coals, their wrought, curvilinear ends heating, their handles projecting into the air.

Stacy dragged the calf within twenty feet of the fire, and the *vaqueros* pounced so quickly I hardly followed the sequence. The pretty *vaquera* held him down, the young boy, Jeff, with a few deft strokes of his curved, scalpel-sharp knife castrated the calf, another of Stacy and Elaine's sons injected a hypodermic of vaccine into its neck, and someone removed its horn stubs.

While all this was transacting in a few seconds, the third of Stacy and Elaine's boys applied the hot branding iron to the calf's thick hide. A plume of smoke and the smell of singed hair mingled with the cold, windblown blasts of dust.

I watched, fascinated.

A curtain of hail swept over the scene. Dust streamed from the shuffling hooves of the grunting herd, and out through the corral's wooden fencing, out into the empty sagebrush. It looked like a sepia-toned photograph of the Old West. This is what excited me about "blank spots"—the sense of discovery—that far beyond the homogeneous nodes and exit ramps and strip malls, lay this other life in America, one tied closely to our national identity and history and destiny, that sense of America as a collection of self-possessed individuals, creating an individual destiny, in a vast land, with vast bounty, that has become swallowed up in the anonymity of the interstate exchange and frontage road, among the abstract transactions of hedge funds and mutual funds, among the ephemeral landscapes of cyberspace, the fantasized dramas of television, so that we forget about it, and we lose strength by not seeing it and touching it in its genuine incarnation—in the flesh. But it still blew on the wind, out here, in the flying dust and open sage.

The calf hopped to its feet and trotted away, looking for its mother. The new, raw brand was emblazoned on the hair on its flank. "FG," it read, for "Frenchglen."

IN APRIL OF 1871, two years after he'd decided to become a mountaineer, John Muir, the Wild Man of Yosemite, then in his early thirties, received the startling news that the venerable and aging Sage of Concord himself, Ralph Waldo Emerson, would soon visit Muir's spectacular valley.

"I was excited," Muir later recalled, "as I had never been excited before."

In his time at Yosemite, Muir had worked seasonally running a small sawmill. In his spare time and off-seasons he hiked and climbed Sierra peaks with his homemade gear, developing theories that glacial action had cut the sheer walls of the Yosemite Valley, collecting plant specimens, writing, and indulging in almost orgiastic couplings with Nature, reporting them in detail by letter to Jeanne Carr. On the full moon of April 3 that year he spent the night on a cliff ledge beside the torrent of Yosemite Falls and at midnight, as the moon cast a rainbow through the cascade, Muir inched along the ledge until he'd crept behind the veil of moonlit water, suspended over a drop of hundreds of feet. A wind-driven quiver of the waterfall knocked torrents onto his head and back, nearly knocking him from the ledge, but he managed to escape and built a fire to dry himself on his ledge.

He recounted these details to Jeanne, who was living in Oakland with her husband and children. She replied with the news of Emerson's imminent visit, in the company of a party of Bostonians touring the West.

Emerson called on Jeanne and Ezra Carr in Oakland, his old friends from Boston, and then with his party headed toward Yosemite, arriving on horseback at the crude hotel called Leidig's. Muir hung around the premises, too shy or awed at first to introduce himself. When he heard that Emerson was staying only for a few days, and visiting only the well-traveled places of the valley, he personally slipped him a note with an impassioned invitation:

> Do not thus drift away with the mob, while the spirits of these rocks and waters hail you after long waiting as their kinsman. . . . I invite you to join me in a month's worship with Nature in the high temples of the great Sierra Crown beyond our holy Yosemite. . . . in the name of all the spirit creatures of these rocks and of this whole spiritual atmosphere Do not leave us *now*. With most cordial regards I am yours in Nature, John Muir.

While Emerson seemed open to the idea of a camping ramble into the high backcountry, his Bostonian companions decidedly were not.

They refused to entertain the notion of letting their literary eminence spend even a single night in the Mariposa Grove of Giant Sequoias with Muir.

"No, it would never do to lie in the night air," replied one of them. "Mr. Emerson might catch cold."

And thus the Bostonians—"full of indoor philosophy," Muir ruefully said—nixed Muir's ecstatic plan to introduce the author of the seminal essays "Nature" and "Self-Reliance" to true wilderness, where he'd never been. Emerson, nevertheless, was intrigued enough by Muir—Jeanne Carr had mentioned the Nature-besotted young man to him—that the old philosopher visited the peculiar sawmill and climbed a rickety ladder to Muir's nestlike bedroom suspended over the creek. On repeated visits to the sawmill over the next few days, Emerson asked questions as Muir showed him his botanical collections and sketches, explained his theories of Nature and of the glaciation that he speculated had shaped the Yosemite Valley.

"Muir is more wonderful than Thoreau," Emerson remarked later. "[He is] the right man in the right place—in [his] mountain tabernacle."

And so the connection was made between the Sage of Concord and the Wild Man of Yosemite. If there were a passing of the torch, the handoff occurred obliquely. Muir sent Emerson, then back in Concord, a series of long letters furthering their Yosemite discussions of Nature. Emerson finally replied, inviting Muir to join his circle of thinkers and edit the works of Thoreau, who had died a few years earlier at age forty-four of tuberculosis.

Jeanne Carr, too, had been urging Muir to come out of the wilderness and live with her family in Oakland. For his part, Muir had been wrestling for several years with the decision of what to do with his life. He argued to himself in his journals that of the eight children in his family, seven were "useful members of society"—doctor, schoolteacher, merchant, farmer's wife. As for the eighth:

"Surely, then . . . one may be spared for so fine an experiment," he resolved. "As long as I live, I'll hear waterfalls and birds and winds sing. I'll interpret the rocks, learn the language of flood, storm, and the avalanche. I'll acquaint myself with the glaciers and wild gardens, and get as near the heart of the world as I can."

He declined both Jeanne Carr and Emerson. His immediate passion was glaciers. He embarked on a grand detective investigation over broad swaths of the Sierra spine to confirm his theory that glaciers were born in shaded spots, and had carved the cliff walls of the Yosemite Valley. A scientist from the Smithsonian Institution, Dr. C. L. Merriam, visiting Yosemite, heard Muir's theories and urged him—as did Jeanne Carr—to write them down for publication. Muir, at first, resisted.

"What I have nobody wants," he said. "Why should I take the trouble to coin my gold? . . . There is no market for it."

His obsessive detective search came to focus on a single "Lost Glacier." On his Sundays free from work at the small sawmill, he traced the glacier's scratchings on rock and its piles of moraine rubble from high in the mountains down to the Yosemite Valley. While he was fluent and ecstatically descriptive in letters and journals, the idea of writing for formal publication intimidated him. Instead, he wrote his discoveries in a series of letters to Dr. Merriam. Then the ever-practical Muir simply melded his letters into an article, "The Death of a Glacier," mailed it off to the *New York Tribune,* and was deeply surprised when the newspaper offered him two hundred dollars for its publication, with a request for more articles.

Muir's writing career had launched. Although constantly tugged back into the mountains, he did move down to San Francisco, taking up residence in a rented third-floor room at the bustling Swett household, whose patriarch, John Swett, was a progressively minded educator. Here he became friends with another Swett protégé, Henry George, who wrote as passionately against business monopolies claiming the West's lands as Muir did about his personal experiences with Nature.

> The earth as our common mother should belong to all the people of the planet. Land with the inherent raw resources, is the source of all wealth. Poverty, ignorance, sickness, and crime stem from Land Monopoly. "Man is a land animal," and, dispossessed of land, is reduced to serfdom. "Each for all and all for each," is the Law of the Universe. But man has revised that to read: "All for a few."

Henry George's railing against the land monopoly profoundly influenced Muir's thinking, and, as a result, ours. It was an era—the 1870s—when business interests laid claim to large chunks of the West and monopolies began to dominate the economy, the beginning of the age of the robber barons. The railroads had been granted huge landholdings to build their lines to the Pacific. Especially in resource-rich California, timber barons took great tracts of Sierra forest lands, water companies claimed river flows for irrigation, and agricultural companies swept up large chunks of the rich interior valleys. It's no coincidence that this was the time, the early 1870s, when Dr. Glenn sent Pete French north with the herd of shorthorns to establish a vast ranch in southeast Oregon.

The threat struck Muir viscerally when, in the summer of 1875, he guided two companions to the Mount Whitney and Kings River area. In the South Fork—new territory for Muir—he found a spectacular valley that in parts rivaled his precious Yosemite. But the threesome also found an ominous sign nailed to a pine tree:

> We the undersigned claim this valley for
> the purpose of raising stock, etc.
> MR. THOMAS
> MR. RICHARD
> MR. HARVEY & CO.

Muir, from his days as a sheep herder, was intimately familiar with the damage that overgrazing by sheep—"hooved locusts," he called them—and cattle could do to the pristine flowered mountain landscapes that he loved. The sense of loss—this valley, its wildness about to be destroyed forever—galvanized him to action. He published pleas to nature lovers to visit the spectacular valley before it became a hog and sheep pasture, like the Tuolumne Valley, or, as in the case of the Merced Valley, "has all its wild gardens trampled by cows and horses . . . and all the destructible beauty of this remote Yosemite is doomed to perish like that of its neighbor . . ."

STACY DAVIES CAME to Roaring Springs Ranch in part to repair the kind of damage from cattle that Muir had feared.

The day's branding done, Davies and I climbed into my Isuzu, where we were sheltered from the wind while we talked, as the bawling pairs and branded calves were shooed from the corral out into the sagebrush and the cowhands returned to their camp.

"The Roaring Springs is what's left of the Pete French empire," Davies said as cold gusts of wind rocked the car on its frame. "The heart of his empire was the Blitzen Valley, because it's wetter. After Pete French was killed, that northern half of the ranch was sold off and became a part of the wildlife refuge. The ranch headquarters was moved to Roaring Springs, and the government bought the Frenchglen section, because it was a company town.

"The Roaring Springs changed hands a number of times, and the Sanderses bought it in 1992. Since then, they've doubled the size of the ranch—from one hundred and forty thousand deeded acres, to two hundred and fifty thousand deeded acres. The ranch also leases over 600,000 acres from the Bureau of Land Management.

"I've been here ten years," Davies continued. "The reason I came leads into the conservation angle."

The Roaring Springs had been run hard, over those earlier decades, to try to keep it profitable. Cattle had trampled stream banks and grazed them nearly bare of their covering grasses. The streams—once narrow, clear, and cold—had spread out. They filled with mud washing in from the bare banks. As the streams became shallower and slower, the water temperatures warmed up in the heat of the sun, and the native species of trout could no longer survive.

"The main fish in these streams is the redband trout," Davies explained. "It was endangered."

A subspecies of the rainbow trout, the Northern Great Basin redband, or *Oncorhynchus mykiss newberrii,* lives only in the mountain-and-desert basins of southeast Oregon and a few nearby parts of California and Nevada. During the Ice Age, when watercourses and glacial lakes connected much more of the West than today, fish species moved freely over wide ranges. The redband has been isolated, on its own, in these desert basins since the retreat of the Ice Age glaciers. Here it has evolved its own special characteristics, including the ability to withstand large swings in water temperature due to the cold winters and hot desert summers.

Never a widespread species to start, the Great Basin redband's numbers and range were shrinking fast from overgrazing, logging, road-building, irrigation—to the alarm of fisheries biologists, environmentalists, and sport fly fishers, for whom the redband is a prized species.

"The U.S. Fish and Wildlife Service knew a petition was coming to have the fish listed as an endangered species," Davies explained.

A look at a map of the Northern Great Basin redband's range reveals that the Catlow Valley, where Roaring Springs Ranch is located, sits close to ground zero for the fish. The Fish and Wildlife Service, in so many words, told ranchers and leaseholders such as Roaring Springs, "Either do something, or the fish will be listed as endangered and you'll *have* to do something."

Enter Stacy Davies.

"I learned years and years ago," Davies explained to me, "that if you want to improve a watershed, you start at the top of the mountain and work down. We took the cattle completely off Steens Mountain for five years, to allow the willows to grow back.

"The simplest thing you have to do," Davies said, "is leave enough grasses and sedges along the stream bank to catch sedimentation and graze the willows lightly enough so they can grow.

"This stabilizes the stream banks and gives shade. If you have shade, the water doesn't heat up. The fish need narrow, deep channels, deep pools, and shallow riffles. We allowed the streams to narrow and heal."

Davies and his crews moved ranch roads away from the streams. They reintroduced fire, a natural agent in the landscape, to the Roaring Springs rangelands. They took other measures to improve habitat.

What's surprising—or maybe *not* so surprising—is that by doing all this habitat work for the redband trout, Roaring Springs Ranch also happened to dramatically improve its forage for *cattle*.

As we sat in the Isuzu, Davies's eyes shone intensely blue as he talked enthusiastically about these changes he'd helped bring to Roaring Springs Ranch. Warm patches of sun flipped over the grass-and-sage mountains and flew across the broad valley that spread out before us, punctuated by chilly cloud shadows and blasts of cold wind that shook the car.

Davies came to his larger point.

"The environment and economy are codependent," he said. "If you manage for the health of both, both prosper. If you don't have a prosperous economy, the environment suffers. And if you don't have a prosperous environment, the economy suffers.

"Basically, our mission is to be sustainable—environmentally, economically, and socially sustainable," Davies said. "Our brand is Country Natural Beef. It's a group of over one hundred producers now. We were one of the first fifteen. The beef is carried by the Whole Foods stores."

STACY DAVIES HAD GIVEN ME a lot to think about as I bounced the twenty-five miles across the empty sagebrush valleys, over the dry hills, down the rocky canyons, through the dusty flats.

I loved the notion that the cattle here at Roaring Springs Ranch ended up as beef sold at Whole Foods. Was that the "New West"? "The New Economy"? By restoring the habitat for trout, Roaring Springs had, at the same time, improved its productivity for cows. By helping restore the environment, it had helped to make itself profitable.

I'd heard a phrase for that being kicked around in Montana, where large mining waste sites were being reclaimed, and forests that had been trashed by heavy cutting were being restored: "The Restoration Economy."

Roaring Springs, which supported six thousand mother cows, looked like a prime example of it.

"The simplest way to say it," Davies had told me, in describing the Roaring Springs grazing strategy for going light on the land, "is that we want to bite each grass plant once each year."

He described how the cows and calves make a grand, seasonal circuit around the ranch. "These calves will walk nearly two hundred miles this summer, in a big circle."

The cows and their calves, Davies emphasized, are raised naturally, without hormones, without antibiotics in the feed, on open range, in a healthy environment, and the animals are "humanely handled." The ranch's staff, likewise, is treated well.

"The consumer who buys our product wants to know that our employees are happy and healthy, and the whole operation is sustainable—that's the bottom line."

There have always been ranchers who are very careful stewards of the land—and others who have not been. To me, Roaring Springs Ranch looked like the future of the West by making that stewardship—or "sustainability," or whatever you want to call creating a business enterprise that adheres to a vision of ecological integrity—its overt mission.

Davies clearly loved his work and relished the huge emptiness of

Roaring Springs Ranch. Interestingly, it's easier for very large ranches to be sustainable because small ranches—say, a three-hundred-cow operation—"have to eat every blade of grass every year."

"The corporate ranch gets a big black eye," Davies had told me, "but I maintain that without them, you wouldn't get the big empty spaces."

He listed five or six of the big ranches in southeast Oregon—among them Roaring Springs, Rock Creek, Alvord . . .

"Between us, we control seven million acres of deeded and leased land. We have the important pieces—we have all the water. If we're gone as grazers, you'll see a hunting cabin on every one of those pieces. The private land would be sold in small parcels. It would be fenced off. The roads would be blocked."

Essentially, Davies said, the big empty—all this enormous space around me—would be filled.

AFTER WATCHING THE BRANDING and speaking with Davies, I drove the twenty-five miles of dirt and turned right—southeast—on Highway 205. I twisted up and over a low pass in the grass-sagebrush-rock Pueblo Mountains, and descended into the biggest valley yet. Far off on the valley floor lay its single settlement—the tiny, *tiny* village of Fields.

Like Frenchglen, it had that oasis look to it—a distant, yellow-green island of cottonwood trees on a huge brownish valley rimmed by dry mountains. The highway turned and slowed on the approach. I rumbled into town. Fields, for the most part, consisted of a small general store. It offered everything you needed—from canned goods to maps to liquor—with a small café attached, along with a couple of motel rooms, and a gas pump, plus a post office. The outdoor phone booth struck me as emblematic of Fields. It sat by itself near the edge of the great empty plain, without a door, without a phone book, without lettering or numbering whatsoever on the phone console except for the engraved numbered buttons. Its dark blue plastic casing had bleached and faded to a milky blue by years of exposure to winter blizzards and beating summer sun and dust-blowing gales. I'd never seen such a weather-beaten telephone.

It still hummed pleasantly with a dial tone. My cell phone hadn't picked up a signal since back in Burns, one hundred miles north. I called home to check in.

They were friendly as could be in the general store—"The Fields Station"—and the staff was drinking an after-work beer when I walked in at closing at 6:00 p.m. They rented me a room—it was an entire bunkhouse, really—and I bought a can of clam chowder to heat up for dinner in its little kitchen. The wind shook the cottonwoods and creaked the bunkhouse. I turned on the gas heater in the sitting room, spread out on its table with my clam chowder, and plunged into my reading.

"I WANT YOU TO KNOW my John Muir," wrote Jeanne Carr to Louie Wanda Strentzel, then in her mid-twenties, daughter of a highly educated Polish émigré doctor who had become a prominent California fruit grower. "I wish I could give him to some noble young woman 'for keeps' and so take him out of the wilderness and into the society of his peers."

After several failed attempts to bring the two together—Muir always made himself scarce—the two finally met briefly in 1874 at the Carr house. Trained as a concert pianist and a graduate of what today is Mills College, quiet, intelligent Louie preferred the home life and helped manage her family's prosperous fruit business. It took three years of wandering in the wilderness and writing articles about it before Muir, at age forty and feeling the need for human love, finally took up the Strentzel family's invitation to visit their home.

"Solitude is a sublime mistress," Emerson had warned him, "but intolerable wife."

For his part, Muir wondered if he would end like Ulysses, "always roaming with a hungry heart."

Louie Strentzel and John Muir married in April 1880 on the Strentzel family ranch in the Alhambra Valley. For the next decade, Muir ran the orchards and vineyards, expanding them, growing prized grapes and other fruits, while he and Louie raised two daughters. Each year, from the time the bulk of the planting and tending was done in July, until the harvest in October, Muir—by agreement with Louie—would embark on a wilderness sojourn.

He visited the basin-and-range country of Nevada, about two hundred miles south of Fields Station, seeking evidence of glacial sculpting. During their engagement he had traveled through Oregon, Washington, and Puget Sound, and up to Alaska by commercial ship, then explored Glacier Bay by canoe paddled by Indians.

The "Ice Chief," they called him.

He loved to hear their stories and legends. He felt a deep kindred spirituality when they explained that their deities inhabited natural features such as mountains, rivers, and waterfalls. "Instinct with deity," he called it.

But mostly he worked on the ranch as a hardheaded businessman and talented grower who threw himself into the tasks and made considerable money for his family in doing so. The business life wore on him, though. Formerly wiry and fit, with a lightness to his step as he climbed the Sierras, Muir now suffered digestive and other health problems. He spoke of the "grind, grind, grind" of running the business.

In 1888, while on his annual summer wilderness jaunt, he climbed Washington's massive volcano, Mount Rainier. The climb infused him with some of his old "mountaineering" spirit. Louie, at the same time, had thought about John's future and his flagging health and spirits.

"A ranch that needs and takes the sacrifice of a noble life, or work," she wrote to him in a letter, "ought to be flung away beyond all reach and power for harm . . . The Alaska book and the Yosemite book, dear John, need to be written, and you need to be your own self, well and strong, to make them worthy of you."

On his return, he started the shift away from the ranch toward full-time writing. The following summer, 1889, Robert Underwood Johnson, an editor of *Century* magazine, traveled from New York to San Francisco in search of writers and material. He and Muir visited Yosemite together. Muir was appalled at the condition of the Yosemite Valley he found, now run by a state commission in conjunction with the commercial tourist hotels. In 1864, to preserve its grandeur, the federal government had given some of the Yosemite lands to California for a public state park. But now trees had been cut and meadows plowed for hayfields for cattle to support the hotels and in the Tuolumne Meadows they found great charred stumps and a forest floor eaten as "bare as the streets of San Francisco."

Johnson proposed that they start a campaign to make Yosemite a national park—Yellowstone had been established as the first national park seventeen years earlier, in 1872. At first Muir resisted—earlier attempts at national park status for Yosemite and Kings Canyon had failed, and he felt Californians were obsessed with making money over preservation of wildlands. Johnson finally convinced Muir to write two articles for *Century* describing Yosemite's splendors in his poetic language and proposing a park. Once word was out, Johnson and Muir would spur officials to introduce legislation to protect it.

When Muir's *Century* articles appeared the following summer, they were picked up by newspapers around the country and inspired citizens to write Congress to preserve Yosemite as a national park. On October 1, 1890, only a year after Underwood and Muir began the campaign, a law championed by President Harrison and passed by Congress awarded Yosemite national park status. Soon, a contingent of cavalry was en route to protect it from squatters and timber poachers.

This was the first of Muir's major battles to preserve wildlands as national parks and monuments. Starting from his old base in Yosemite, the fight spread outward to Sequoia National Park, Kings Canyon, the Grand Canyon, and beyond.

B͟Y͟ ͟T͟H͟E͟ ͟T͟I͟M͟E͟ ͟I͟ ͟L͟E͟F͟T͟ southeast Oregon, I'd seen Steens Mountain from many angles. I'd made two full circuits of the sixty-mile-long escarpment by car. I'd talked to ranchers who grazed their cattle on it, and outfitters who packed tourists on horses up it. One night, I'd tried camping below its clifflike eastern face where it dropped to the dry, dusty Alvord Desert. I hoped to gaze up that night at the intense desert stars, but it was not to be. A powerful spring storm swept over the mountain's brow and tumbled down five thousand vertical feet onto the desert like a breaking wave of wind and spray. Even the white pelicans on pondlike Mann Lake huddled in tight clusters along the shore where I camped, heads down, as downbursts of wind splayed and frothed over the lake's surface.

I hurriedly pitched my little mountain tent on the gumbo mud, struggling with the yellow fabric against the gusts, and climbed inside to read, sure that the storm would subside. Three hours later I was still damming the rivulets of water that the roaring downdrafts off the escarpment forced under the rain fly and up through the aging tent seams. I sat there on my shrinking island of dry sleeping bag, pondering what to do. I pictured a long, wind-roaring night in a cold, soaked bag. I'd never been daunted by leaky tents before. I'd been to so many remote and wild places in my life—the mountains of Tibet and the ice fields of Greenland, the forests of Manchuria and the rivers of Mozambique, the highlands of New Guinea and the lowlands of Sumatra. They were always worth—more than worth—the difficulty and discomfort. Why did this prospect look so unpleasant? Why was this different?

Sometimes turning back was more difficult logistically (and sometimes emotionally) than going on, and once you retreated, there was no second chance. Not this time, I realized. The car sat fifty feet away, although its tires had begun to sink into the softening desert ooze. Burns, and a warm, dry motel room, lay a hundred miles up the road. I was by myself and accountable to no one, not part of a team or trying to impress anyone, not passing on to my children the example of the need to persist. They and Amy weren't with me, which gave this empty spot a different kind of emptiness.

I'd learned, over the years, that to be truly there in these wild places, in these blank spots, you had to earn it. Guided tours could get you into the wilds—I'd been on some of those, too, and they could be very rewarding—but, to my mind, they didn't fully get you there. They didn't take you to that totally on-your-own psychic place. A blank spot—a wild place—is as much a state of mind as a geographical reality. In a truly wild place you have no one to rely on but your own little party or yourself. You, personally, carry the weighty uncertainties—route, weather, unknown hazards—unlike traveling with a guide who may have visited this place dozens of times before. Uncertainty—a quality of unknowing, the "unknown"—gives wildness or blankness its special feel.

But I wasn't there. Part of my mind was not in this place at all, but with my family. So many of the explorers over the centuries who truly threw themselves into blank spots on the map were young men, unattached, whose focus was single-mindedly forward and deeper into uncertainty. I could see little uncertainty here, only the certainty of discomfort and the knowledge that I had a simple option to escape. The car was within easy reach, the dirt road leading out of this place ran just around the lake, and two hours' drive, partly on gravel and partly on pavement, and I'd be eating a steak dinner somewhere warm and dry.

So what was the point of lying all night in a wet bag in a leaky tent?

There wasn't one. Or at least there wasn't one at this point in my life.

I pulled up stakes, literally, spread my arms wide to gather up the mud-soaked tent like a flapping bedsheet on a clothesline during a gale, balled it up in a tangle of fabric and cords, stuffed it into the back of the Isuzu along with my sopping sleeping bag, and retreated to Burns.

THE NEXT MORNING, sun flitting in and out between wet clouds, I again, as I had several days earlier on my way to the Frenchglen Hotel, drove past the swampy arms of Malheur Lake and through the Malheur National Wildlife Refuge. A clump of birders in khaki vests stood along the narrow highway, binoculars shoved to eyes, watching a lone white Ross's goose and a flock of darker coots feeding in the green flooded marsh.

In a roundabout way, John Muir had helped with the preservation of the Malheur Refuge. In May 1903, he hosted Teddy Roosevelt, who was much more game for sleeping under the stars than Emerson and his fellow Bostonians, for four days of camping in Yosemite. Roosevelt, who had pledged during his campaign to fight the huge monied monopolies, hoped to get Muir's opinion on conservation issues, in particular what to do with Yosemite Park and millions of acres of national "forest preserves" that had been designated—in considerable part due to Muir's efforts—in the 1890s.

"It was clear weather," Roosevelt later recollected, "and we lay in the open, the enormous cinnamon-colored trunks rising about us like the columns of a vaster and more beautiful cathedral than was ever conceived by human architect."

As they lay side by side on their fern beds, Muir spoke of the natural world, of its trees and plants, of the way glaciers carved the mountains, of the lumber barons and sheep ranchers who were destroying the pristine places of the West, of the great, unifying spirit of nature.

Roosevelt, though a great talker himself, mostly listened, absorbing Muir's point about the need to preserve forests and other lands before it was too late.

"John Muir," he later remarked, "talked even better than he wrote."

It was President Roosevelt who, in 1908, designated Malheur Lake as a bird refuge—only one small part of an enormous amount of federal land he set aside for conservation.

MY FIRST ATTEMPT AT CAMPING had washed out at the base of the eastern escarpment of the mountain, so, a day later, I pitched my tent on the second attempt partway up the gentle western slope of Steens in a juniper grove with a little brook trickling by. On the open hillsides below I'd seen wild horses—"painted pintos"—grazing. In the morning, I rose early, packed my tent, and drove farther up the graveled Bureau of Land Management road that loops fifty-two miles up to the 9,725-foot crest of Steens where the summit looks far down onto the Alvord Desert. That's where I'd attempted to camp before.

It had rained again during the night. I guessed it had fallen as fresh snow up above. As my Isuzu climbed the steep section above camp, it slithered and spun in four-wheel drive through gumbo mud and lurched over boulders. At the top of the steep, the road swung around a hairpin bend to a northern slope. Here fresh snow from last night and the night before suddenly blocked my way—at first, only three or four inches deep. I stopped the car, slipped on my backpack, and started hiking up the snow-covered road toward the Steens summit, another seven miles away up a long, gentle ridge.

After a while I turned to look the way I'd come. I could now see forty or fifty miles across the valley to the west. There was not a sign of human habitation in all that country, except—maybe, *maybe*—a single tiny white spot, which may have been some kind of distant ranch building.

As I hiked, I felt the altitude in my shortness of breath. Soon I came to deeper, firmer drifts—winter's old snow. The sky whipped over my head in a patchwork of sun and cloud. I sweated in the sun patches and shivered a bit in the cold. The ridge opened up, the junipers giving way to alpine terrain. Looking back, toward the northwest, I estimated I could see one hundred miles out across the sagebrush flats and rolling hills. Way out there, on that high desert, the Lost Wagon Trains got lost.

After two hours' hiking, I stopped for lunch. Clambering over the deep snow of the ridgetop, I made my way to the edge of a cliff overlooking a deep gorge. I sat on a chunk of bare, jagged rock at the lip. Two thousand feet below me the Donner und Blitzen River tumbled, sounding like the distant rush of wind, fading and strengthening, as if ululating. Heavy snow cornices hung off the cliffs like thick, white eyebrows, and avalanche tracks spilled down toward the river. Here worked the dynamic forces of the earth. I could plainly see that ancient glaciers had carved this U-shaped canyon. John Muir helped us all to understand that. He would have loved this spot.

He, too, grew less intrepid with age. After his years as the wild man of Yosemite, and amusements like clinging to the slender whipsawing top of a pine tree during a blizzard (describing the ride in detail to Mrs. Carr), Muir had settled down to start a family, manage his in-laws' fruit ranch, and, in his fifties, throw himself into writing and lobbying for the wilds. Likewise, Henry Thoreau. Except for his two years in the woods at nearby Walden Pond and his brief sojourns to Maine, he spent virtually his whole life in his peaceful village of Concord, mostly employed at the Thoreau pencil factory.

Billy Bartram showed a similar arc. After his four-year exploration through the wilds of the Southeast, he returned in his forties to the family gardens outside Philadelphia, and for the rest of his life pottered away in the soil and wrote. In his sixties, he declined invitations from Thomas Jefferson to accompany various exploring parties to the West, including perhaps the Lewis and Clark expedition. Bartram died quietly at home in 1823 at age eighty-four.

They all found—as did I—that the intensity of the truly wild experience is harder to sustain as one grows older. But that makes it no less valuable for having had those experiences, and to keep pursuing them, insofar as you're willing. I'd heard aging Montanans hobbling around with canes say about wilderness, "I can't go there anymore, but I feel better knowing it's out there."

Muir fought for the cause of wilderness to his very end, when he was too frail to experience it directly. He died of pneumonia on Christmas Eve, 1914, at age seventy-six, soon after a final climactic battle to save the Sierra's Hetch Hetchy Valley from being dammed for San Francisco's water supply. Although the battle was lost, it proved a galvanizing moment for the future of wilderness preservation. "[T]he conscience of the whole country has been aroused from sleep," wrote Muir.

Clouds swirled off the rock-and-snow peak of Steens. A quick patch of sun was followed by a blast of cold wind and the hard splatter of graupel—hail-like pellets of snow.

I pulled on my hat and gloves. I zipped up my hood. The graupel pelted hard off the hood, like a rainstorm driving against a roof. It was still several miles' hike to the summit up the broad, gentle ridge. I knew I wasn't going to make it today.

PART IV

THE HIGH,
HAUNTED DESERT OF
NEW MEXICO

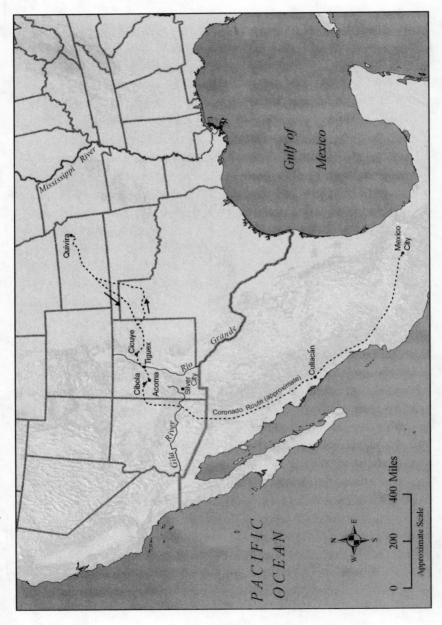

Coronado's route in 1540–42 from Mexico City in search of the Seven Cities of Gold, through present-day Arizona, New Mexico, Texas, Oklahoma, to Kansas.

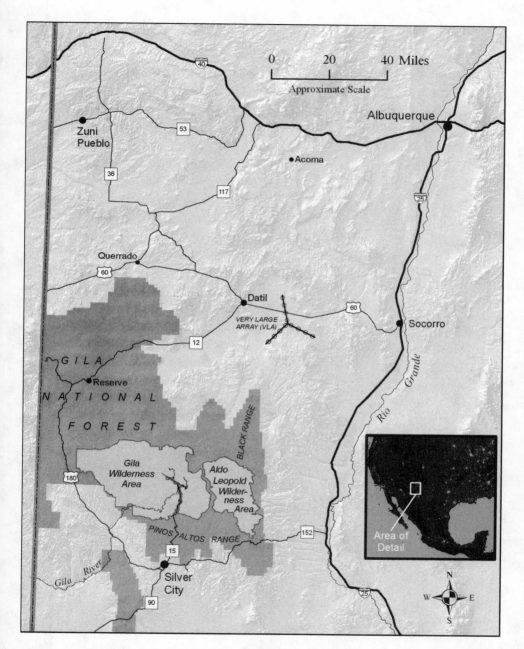

Western New Mexico showing area of hike into Gila Wilderness Area. The Very Large Array (VLA) at center. Inset shows lights of region at night.

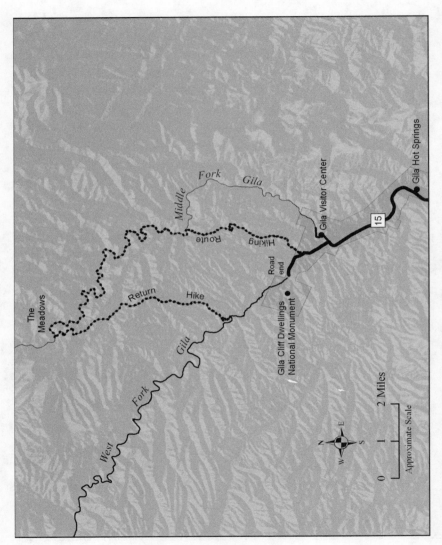

Detail of hike through Gila River canyons in New Mexico's Gila Wilderness Area.

*F*lying into Phoenix at night felt like descending into a video game. Out the window to the west, a beaded, golden grid of lights extended as far as one could see, a great, flat circuit board of lights, millions of lights in long, bright perpendicular rows, and other smaller lights moving along the glowing grid as if carrying messages from one sector to another, telling the sprawling mechanism what to do, telling it how to suck in more electrons from far-off dammed desert rivers and giant furnaces of burning coal, telling it how to feed itself.

Out the airplane window to the east—nothing. Blackness—utter, total blackness.

We four—our little family: Amy, Molly, Skyler, myself—jammed our backpacks into the trunk of a rental car amid the pools of light and shadow in the Mesa airport parking lot where palm trees stood and the air felt balmy. Then we drove east, a lone light-bead arching across empty overpasses and circling along empty ramps and swinging through empty cloverleafs in the total blackness east of Phoenix and Mesa, where it was said a half million more houses were planned but didn't yet exist.

"Where are we?" we said to one another. "This is very strange."

An island of white light hove out of the darkness. It was a mall, standing alone, waiting for the houses that hadn't yet come to nestle warmly around it . . . waiting for the houses that now might never come, lit bravely, hopefully, like a lone Christmas tree on a cold, rainy night. But this was desert and there was no rain and sadness to repel, only the infinite blackness.

We found a motel near the brave mall and rose early, driving east again, into the bright desert sun. Saguaro cacti reached their arms up from arid hills. Dry, rocky mesas glistened before us. Here and there sat a small patch of houses along the road, and then there were none. We drove a long loop southeast, on Interstate 10, to skirt southward around the millions and millions of acres of high, rugged, empty country that lies along the border between Arizona and New Mexico. On the Earth-at-night satellite photo image, three southwestern cities form a triangle defined by three nodes of light: Albuquerque to the north, Phoenix to the west, and El Paso to the east. They lie about three hundred to four hundred miles apart. In the center of this triangle, however, is a vast, shapeless, inky sprawl—one of the largest and most distinct blank spots of the Lower 48 states.

"If you start walking east from Phoenix," I'd heard from a forester I'd met a year or two earlier who was based in Arizona, "you can travel all the way to the middle of New Mexico and cross only three paved roads."

I'd also sat beside a white-haired grandfather at our children's school music recital in Montana, where his grandchildren also went to school. He told me he lived just east of Phoenix.

"Behind our house sits a single row of condos. After the row of condos the Superstition Mountains begin. After that there's nothing—just nothing—for a long, *long* way. I can't tell you how far because I've never been back there. I don't know anyone who has."

Amy drove, while Molly and Skyler, ages fourteen and ten, crammed between camping gear in the backseat of our rental car, read their books. I fell asleep. When I woke we'd swung so far south that we were only fifty miles from the Mexican border. We crossed from Arizona into New Mexico, and left the Interstate, swinging north on a smaller highway, New Mexico 90, toward the heart of that sprawling region—the center of the triangle that had shown so blank on the Earth-at-night photo.

The open desert rose in long rolls, waves of balding ridges topped by scrubby piñon pine and juniper forests. A sign on the crest of one rounded ridge marked the Continental Divide, the spine of North America, where rivers to the east flow to the Atlantic and those to the west to the Pacific. We coasted downward through the Little Burro Mountains, past a large open-pit mine and long heaps of tailings, a former Phelps Dodge mine now owned by Freeport McMoRan, a global giant producing gold and copper, operating huge mines on the island of New Guinea, in the Congo Basin, and in South America. Long before Freeport, or Phelps Dodge, or its predecessors, however, Indians mined copper at this same ore deposit and shaped the soft, golden metal into spear points and ornaments.

Was it rumor—or knowledge—of this very metal deposit that prompted Cabeza de Vaca to give his stunning report in the summer of 1536 to Viceroy Mendoza of Mexico City? After wandering for years in the unknown lands north of Mexico—what's now the southwestern United States—he had finally found his way back to Spanish civilization, or civilization in a manner of speaking. Only fifteen years earlier Mexico City had still been Tenochtitlán, capital of the Aztec empire, until conquered by Cortés. Other Spaniards had conquered lands toward the south of Mexico City, in Guatemala and Honduras and the Yucatán peninsula. But they had little idea what lay to the north. No European did—no explorer had yet penetrated to the interior of the North American continent. Cabeza de Vaca, quite unintentionally, was the first.

Yes, Cabeza de Vaca reported when he reached Mexico City, there could be valuable metals. Yes, perhaps copper . . . gold . . . silver . . . in the unknown lands to the north where he wandered. And, yes, he'd heard of cities there, too—cities built of stone, many stories high.

It was all the news of Mexico City in the summer of 1536, this arrival of Cabeza de Vaca's, and the rumors he brought of gold and cities to the north. He had long ago been given up for dead. But in April of that year a column of mounted Spanish soldiers headed out from the northernmost villages of Mexico to capture Indians to work as slaves on the Spanish plantations. One day the slaving party—having taken few captives because the Indians had fled and hidden—came upon a stranger whose bizarre appearance and words left them literally speechless. He stood before them nearly naked and barefoot, dressed in a few tanned hides and holding a gourd rattle. He addressed them in formal Andalusian Spanish.

He'd been shipwrecked eight years ago, he told the soldiers in the slaving party. He and three others were the only survivors of the great Narváez expedition of three hundred men sent out nine years earlier from Spain by the king himself to claim mainland Florida for the crown. While anchored off the Florida coast, a hurricane had blown away their ships, leaving only bits of planking in the treetops. They didn't give up. They carried on inland, on horses, following rumors of gold. It was said by the Indians to lie to the west—always to the west, they were told. So they kept west. They fought Indians, and they befriended Indians. They ran out of food and stole from Indians. Many men died from illness. Still they kept west, following the curve of the unknown coast. They were stopped by a great swampy delta choked with fallen logs. Starving, they killed their horses, devoured the flesh, and fashioned boats from the stretched horsehides. Still westward they traveled, now by horsehide boat, along the curving coast. After many leagues' sailing, strong currents and powerful storms caught them, sweeping Governor Narváez's boat out to sea, never to be seen again. Another boat overturned. Many died in the water. Others crawled through the surf to shore, naked, in November. Friendly Indians found them, built fires to warm them, and fed them. Still, many died of sickness.

Finally only the four of them remained, three Spaniards and the black Moorish slave. They were separated but got back together, living with the Indians. The Indians asked the strangers to cure their sicknesses. They obliged, using their crosses and their breath, and the sacred Indian rattles and amulets. They became medicine men and traders. The slave, the Moor, Esteben, was a prized medicine man. He could communicate fluently with the Indians by signs, and in their many tongues. For these eight years they lived among the Indians. Gradually, they worked their way west, toward the great ocean that lay there, and toward Mexico—Nueva España—where they knew they'd find the Spanish and Mexico City itself.

So there he stood before the mounted Spaniards of the slaving party, dressed in his tanned skins, mostly naked in their eyes, without sword or armor or lance, nothing whatsoever to reveal his rank, other than the sacred medicine rattle, surrounded by ten Indian companions, and led by the Moorish slave, addressing them formally in Spanish— Alvar Nuñez Cabeza de Vaca, born in Jeréz, Spain, and serving as treasurer of the great expedition that came to so much ruin.

The soldiers stared, dumbfounded.

Could he be taken to their chief? asked Cabeza de Vaca of the soldiers.

They were led half a league to the camp of the captain, who was both desperate for food and desperate to capture some Indian slaves to show something for his mission. The Indian friends of Cabeza de Vaca, out of their own generosity, brought clay pots containing maize to the hungry Spaniards. But after receiving the gifts the Spanish captain wanted to take his friends as slaves. Cabeza de Vaca argued bitterly against it.

Many weeks later they reached Mexico City, where they were received joyously by Viceroy Mendoza and by Cortés himself. They wanted to know—everyone in Mexico City wanted to know—if he'd seen any signs of gold in his eight years of wandering. It seems Cabeza de Vaca suggested there could be gold, at least the possibility of it. He'd also heard from the Indians—and perhaps seen them with his own eyes—of seven cities existing in these unknown lands to the north.

The Mexico City authorities asked Cabeza de Vaca if he would be willing to lead an expedition back to the north to find the gold and the cities—or the Seven Cities of Gold, as they quickly became known amid the spreading rumors.

Cabeza de Vaca declined, wishing to return home to Spain, but suggested that maybe one of the other three survivors, such as the Moor, Esteban, could guide a party there.

And with that began the official Spanish exploration of this great unknown blank spot to the north of Mexico. Much of it is now part of the southwestern United States. Some of it—the part toward which we aimed our rental car stuffed with camping gear—remains blank today.

By late afternoon, we'd arrived in Silver City, New Mexico, an old mining town of about ten thousand surrounded by high desert. To the north, toward the very heart of that big blank spot, rose the mountains of the Pinos Altos range, and beyond them the Diablo range, the Mogollon range, and many more. These were encompassed by the Gila Wilderness Area and the Gila National Forest. At 3.3 million acres, it is the largest national forest in the contiguous United States.

We drove into the small downtown—the historic district—and parked. Billy the Kid's childhood log cabin perched beside the creek that rushed through town and that, during an 1895 flash flood, had washed out Silver City's Main Street and torn a fifty-five-foot-deep arroyo in its place—a gully that still bisects the middle of downtown. Late-nineteenth-century brick buildings lined the narrow side streets, the shady side of the street chilly at six thousand feet, and the sunny side warm in the clear, desertlike October light. The contrast felt like a black-and-white photo from the old mining days, except above arched that deep, deep blue sky that darkens with high altitude and desert dryness, the sky that makes you sense that the infinity of space begins just beyond this thin envelope of air.

"This place feels a little bit creepy," said Molly, looking around.

We walked to the Palace Hotel, a funky, mostly renovated old pile, built as a bank in 1882 and made a hotel in 1900. We entered its eclectic old lobby and took a small two-room suite. Just around the corner was a great coffeehouse that Amy immediately homed in to—the Javelina—and two doors from the Javelina stood a famous biker bar, the Buffalo. Small art galleries and knick-knack shops lined the streets. Silver City had become something of a magnet for artists and bohemians, a kind of tiny, scruffy Santa Fe. As we walked along checking the tempting restaurants for that evening's dinner possibilities, I swear I smelled patchouli oil drifting in the late afternoon sun.

Back at the Palace Hotel, I sprawled out on our bed and studied the maps I'd bought at the headquarters of the Gila National Forest and more at the Gila Hike & Bike shop. One of the dilemmas of exploring "blank spots," I'd found, is to figure out just where to go amid all that blankness. Selecting a route into the wilderness is a choice like certain others in life that can sometimes feel arbitrary and capricious, yet, in the end, lead to all sorts of tribulation . . . or wonder.

Later, over dinner at Diane's—seared pork medallions for me, Thai curry for Amy at this, our last supper before the wilderness—I presented to our little family the options, as I saw them. They all centered on the Gila Wilderness:

1. Hike straight into the highest part of the Mogollon Mountains and return by the same route.

2. Hike up a river canyon to a hot springs, then follow another river canyon to the ancient cliff dwellings.

3. Hike straight north across the entire Gila Wilderness and Forest, which was likely to involve some very long days on the trail, until we emerged on the far side at the VLA—the Very Large Array—a huge pattern of satellite dishes spread across the high desert that listen to signals from outer space.

They all listened intently to the options. Skyler was savoring his New York steak—always his first choice if it appeared on the menu—

and Molly her filet mignon. I wondered how we'd brought up our children so their palates always gravitated to the most expensive dishes on the menu. The dim, high-ceilinged old room was nearly full. Amy had observed that not all of the customers looked like hippie artists. Rather, there were some slim, elegantly dressed older couples amid the mix of black clothes and body piercings. Clearly, some lifestyle money had already found Silver City.

I pointed out that each of the three routes had its advantages and disadvantages, and listed some of them, like scenery—or lack of it— and distance, and weather, and cultural interest.

"What do you want to do, Dad?" Molly said.

"Yes, what works best for you?" said Amy.

"Dad, what feels best for you?" echoed Skyler.

I was quite touched to receive all this consideration from my family. I wondered if Amy had prompted the children ahead of time, or they were being that thoughtful on their own. Often—not always, but often, especially on the important things—they showed a true thoughtfulness toward others. Filet mignon and thoughtfulness.

I sipped my beer, trying to sort my own priorities.

"I want to do first of all what's possible for all of us to do," I said, envisioning ten-year-old, seventy-five-pound Skyler trying to hike twenty-five miles per day under the load of a backpack in order to cross the entire Gila Wilderness.

"And second, I want to take a route that gets us into a wild place. And third, a route that's beautiful and fun. And fourth, a route that has an interesting cultural story."

"What's possible for us all to do is certainly important, too," said Amy. "But we want you to get out of it what you need."

"Okay," I said, "let's vote."

Option 1—One vote, for the high mountains, from Skyler. What appealed to him was that the approach required walking on a mile-long catwalk suspended over a river gorge.

Option 2—Two votes, from Molly and Amy, for the hot springs and cliff dwellings.

Option 3—Zero votes for the hike across the entire Gila.

I said I'd vote for either Option 1 or 2. So, without any argument, we decided on Option 2, the hot springs and cliff dwellings and river canyons, with the promise to Skyler that, after our wilderness hike, we'd seek out the suspended catwalk and walk it.

We then ordered up several large, thick, chocolaty desserts, knowing they would be our last for some time.

MY ORIGINAL PLAN, in this quest for blank spots, was to avoid national parks or "designated" wilderness areas, as they were too well known and defined. But the Gila Wilderness was the exception. It was very large, to begin with, and geographically fascinating with its high-desert mountains, its deep, winding river canyons, and its ancient cliff dwellings. Most important, it was the nation's—in fact, the world's—first land preserved as actual wilderness (as opposed to, say, a national park or game preserve). This occurred largely through the efforts of Aldo Leopold. An early twentieth-century ecologist, Leopold formulated a philosophy of wilderness and a famous dictum, "The Land Ethic," which still guides much of today's thinking about the moral value of wildlands. You could argue, convincingly, that Aldo Leopold was the first modern "green"—the first modern "environmental philosopher."

I felt some personal bond with Leopold, too. Born in Iowa, he'd started his career as a forest ranger in the Southwest, then spent much of his adult life in Wisconsin as a professor, writer, and philosopher, and owner of a run-down farm. I'd grown up in Wisconsin. John Muir had, too. So I had several good reasons to visit the Gila. I wanted to understand what, as a young man, Aldo Leopold had seen there that caused him to devote his life to writing and thinking about wildlands. And I wanted to understand what, in my native Wisconsin, helped bring Leopold's ideas to fruition.

The next morning found me rummaging through the racks of women's discount shoes at Silver City's Wal-Mart. I tossed into my cart a pair of size 7 and size 8 of low, white, rubber-soled shoes of the type formerly worn by firm, strong-armed women softly treading infirmary floors. "Nurse's shoes," we would call them. They were for Molly and Amy. My research had turned up the need for a spare set of shoes or protective footgear while wading the river canyons of the Gila Wilderness. I'd heard from someone in Silver City that cheap tennis shoes work as well as anything.

For Skyler it was a pair of Chinese-made runners with rocket-booster heels, and for me a set of boatlike, Velcro-strapped sneakers that looked like a whole lot of shoe for only ten dollars. While I shopped for the shoes, Amy and Molly and Skyler roamed a Silver City supermarket loading up on food and snacks—*lightweight* food, I'd cautioned them repeatedly, as, before eating it, we were going to be *carrying it on our backs.*

We then rendezvoused back at our hotel. It was past checkout and, with a new guest imminent, the maid was cleaning our suite. We hauled our gear from our room and spread all our belongings out on the floor of the hotel lobby as people came and went through the rubble—tents, sleeping bags, pads, clothing sacks, nurse's shoes, water bottles, gas bottles, lightweight stove, headlamps, packages of batteries, lighters, emergency kits, cooking pots, cups, knives, plus many bags of ramen, oatmeal, cheese, trail mix. Sorting through it, mixing up ziplock bags of trail mix and granola, we began to load it into our packs.

By two o'clock—the usual two hours late and with a quick stop at the Javelina—we were in the small rental car, packed cheek-to-jowl with our new shoes and food and gear, heading north on a narrow, twisting road that climbed over the Pinos Altos mountains toward the Gila Cliff Dwellings and our jumping-off point.

THE SPANISH IN MEXICO CITY headed north, too, toward this same region, carried along by the rumors from the shipwreck survivor Cabeza de Vaca, and convinced that there to the north lay the Seven Cities of Gold.

One can understand how a vague rumor from Cabeza de Vaca transformed into seven glittering cities. Cortés had conquered the wealthy Aztec empire only fifteen years earlier, in 1521, and only four years before Cabeza de Vaca's report from the unknown lands, the conquistador Francisco Pizarro in 1532 had captured the Inca king, Atahualpa, and ransomed him for an entire roomful of Inca gold. The Spanish had already found astounding quantities of gold in the Americas. So it didn't take much imagination for Cabeza de Vaca's sketchy reports of metal deposits and tall stone cities in the unknown lands to the north to race through Mexico City and transform quickly via word of mouth into the glittering Seven Cities of Gold.

The legend was well known in Spain at the time, although it actually dated back hundreds of years, to 1150, when, in the eighth century, the Moors of North Africa invaded what's now Spain and held it for centuries thereafter. It was said that seven Christian bishops escaped from the Moorish conquest, sailed westward into the Atlantic Ocean, and disappeared to a far-off and unknown land, founding fabulously wealthy cities of gold. There were seven cities—one for each bishop. Thus the legend of the Seven Cities of Gold.

Viceroy Mendoza, head of New Spain, wanted to send a party north to investigate the rumors of the Seven Cities of Gold, and hoped one of the shipwreck survivors would guide it, but none accepted. Cabeza de Vaca yearned to return to his native Spain as quickly as he could. Finally, the viceroy offered to purchase the Moorish slave, Esteban, who'd been one of the castaways, from his owner, Dorantes, also one of the four survivors, for five hundred pesos on a silver platter. Dorantes refused the money but agreed to lend the Moor to the expedition in return for a share of any riches that Esteban discovered. Perhaps he also felt a much deeper bond with Esteban beyond ownership after their little party of four had wandered so long in the North American wilds. Meanwhile, Esteban, dressed in his preferred bright clothing and quite a charming celebrity in Mexico City, was apparently enjoying the settlement's gambling and women.

For an expedition leader, Viceroy Mendoza consulted the Franciscan order of monks, which had sent missionaries into some of the nearer lands north of Mexico City. On the advice of Franciscan officials, the viceroy chose Fray Marcos de Niza, a French native who had been to Peru, "was endowed with all virtues," and knew, in addition to his Bible, how to navigate by the stars. To this small, lightweight expedition—Esteban as guide, Fray Marcos as leader, and Spanish-speaking Indians as messengers and aides-de-camp—the viceroy gave a weighty mission, written out carefully.

First, the expedition should promise the Indians to the north that the Spanish would no longer capture them as slaves. They would be well treated on behalf of His Majesty, the king of Spain, as long as the Indians remained at peace with the Spanish. If not, however, "they will be punished and will receive no mercy." Furthermore, Fray Marcos and

Esteban were to note the fertility of the soils and the abundance of rivers, and whether a gulf or waterway crossed the continent. Finally— and this was a key instruction—they were to observe the rocks "and the metals that it contains" and, if possible, bring or send back these ore samples "so that His Majesty may be fully informed."

Paralleling the Pacific Coast northward, Fray Marcos showed the samples of gold he carried to the Indian tribes that the little expedition encountered. Several said they knew of such a yellowish material, used by interior tribes and fashioned into bowls and ornaments for the nose and ears, and some "made little scoops of the same metal with which they scraped away the sweat to rid themselves of it." Fray Marcos dispatched Esteban ahead some 150 miles to scout, with the instructions to send back a prearranged sign if he found a "rich and sizable" country. The sign was to be a white cross one hand high if the country was of ordinary size, a white cross two hands high if the country was larger, and a larger cross still if the country was larger than New Spain itself.

Only four days later Indian messengers returned from Esteban to Fray Marcos's comfortable and well-provisioned camp. The runners bore a cross the size of a man and a message from Esteban that he had found people who told him they knew of the largest country of the world. One of the Indian runners Esteban sent back to Fray Marcos had been to that country himself. Through interpreters and signs, he reported to Fray Marcos:

> . . . that it was thirty days' travel from the place where Estevan was to the first city of the country called Cíbola. . . . there are seven very large cities all of which belong to one ruler. Large houses of stone and lime are to be found there . . . there are some of two and three stories. That of the ruler has four, very well laid out. At the doors of the main houses many turquoise ornaments are to be found, which stones are very common in the area. The inhabitants of these cities are very well dressed.

Fray Marcos broke camp and hurried north in Esteban's footsteps, expecting to catch up with him, but Esteban kept moving northward himself, leaving crosses behind to mark every good camping spot for the friar. The friar received warm welcomes at Indian villages whose inhabitants had traded with the distant country called Cíbola, and even worked in Cíbola, in exchange for the abundant bison hides and turquoise jewelry the friar spotted adorning the village inhabitants. In addition to Cíbola, he heard, there were three other kingdoms. The people in those regions, he heard, wore clothing woven of cotton—considered a luxury in the early 1500s.

One senses Fray Marcos's excitement as he hustled north, with Esteban just ahead of him. (One wonders, with all this haste, if Esteban was following instructions from his owner, Dorantes, to reach the Seven Cities first and lay Dorantes's claim to the finder's share of the riches.) On May 9, 1539, having traveled two months, and still in the footsteps of Esteban, Fray Marcos crossed what was probably the Gila River. He now heard that the largest of the seven cities of Cíbola was called Ahacus. From the Gila River, in another twelve days' travel, he neared this largest of the seven. It was then, at the end of the twelfth day, that an Indian messenger suddenly appeared in Fray Marcos's camp along the desert trail, his body covered with sweat and his face contorted with sorrow.

He told Fray Marcos that Esteban had approached within a day's travel of Cíbola. Just outside the city, Esteban had sent a messenger carrying his healer's rattle, adorned with feathers and bells, into the city to announce his arrival. This was always his practice when reaching an unfamiliar settlement. Taking the rattle, the chief of the city grew enraged, threw it to the ground, and told the messengers to leave. He said the rattle wasn't of their own style. The chief said he knew these people and would kill them if they entered the city. But the charming Esteban, outside the city and hearing this account from his returning messengers, reassured the messengers that those chiefs who initially received him coolly always warmed up on meeting him. He went unabashedly onward to the city entrance with a contingent of more than three hundred Indians who had joined him during his travels.

The residents blocked his way. They then shut Esteban into a large house outside the city, stripping him of all his trade goods. The next morning, Esteban's Indian messenger left the house to get a drink from the river, and returning toward the city, spotted Esteban and his Indian followers fleeing, pursued by a band of warriors. The Indian messenger had escaped slaughter by hiding near the river.

So went the messenger's account to Fray Marcos. The next day, a few other survivors stumbled into Fray Marcos's camp smeared with blood, pierced by arrow wounds, and wailing over their losses. Once the friar quieted them enough to hear what had happened, he learned that they had survived only because they'd been buried alive beneath the carcasses of their fleeing companions. Esteban had been killed, also.

"... I confess I was at a loss what to do," wrote Fray Marcos to his superiors. "I told them that Our Lord would chastise Cíbola and that when the Emperor knew what had happened he would send many Christians to punish its people."

This didn't satisfy the grieving Indians. No one could withstand Cíbola's power, they said to the friar. Fray Marcos struggled with the situation, justifiably. Alone, hundreds and hundreds of miles from the nearest Spanish outpost, he had become the trigger of hostilities between two formerly peaceable groups of Indians whom—by orders from his superiors—he was supposed to pacify while searching for their gold. He finally walked off a stone's throw to compose himself, to pray to God, and to try to figure out what to do next.

When he returned an hour and a half later, the grief of the Indian followers had turned to anger. They were ready to kill Fray Marcos. They blamed him not only for the deaths of their three hundred fathers, sons, and brothers, but were convinced that he would be the cause of their deaths, too.

At this point, he changed tactics. He gave away all his trade goods to them. He said that they could go ahead and kill him, but it would do him no harm, as he would go to heaven, while those killing him would suffer, as Christians would come looking for Fray Marcos and kill all those who killed him.

"With this and many other words I pacified them somewhat, although there was still high feeling on account of the people killed."

Thus Fray Marcos escaped death by vengeance for the three hundred dead. But he still desperately wanted to see Cíbola and also learn any news of Esteban. No one was willing to accompany him, and so Fray Marcos said that he would go himself. Finally two chiefs agreed to go along. Traveling quietly, they neared a settlement on about June 5, 1539. Climbing a hill, they spied the city, which sat on a neighboring hill protruding from a plain. Fray Marcos wrote:

> ... it looks very pretty; it is the largest city I have seen in these parts. Having climbed onto a rise from whence I could observe it, I saw that the houses were built as the Indians had told me: all of stone,

with several floors, and surmounted by terraces. This city is more extensive than that of [Mexico City] . . . Having told the chiefs who accompanied me that I found this city very beautiful, they assured me that it was the smallest of the seven cities . . .

The chiefs told him that the city of Tontonteac was far larger—"there is no end to it." And so, Fray Marcos, calling the land "the new kingdom of St. Francis," built a large cairn of stones with the help of the Indians, and stuck onto it a small cross, not having enough wood handy on this barren hillside to fashion a larger one. In the name of Viceroy Mendoza of New Spain and the emperor of Spain himself, King Charles, Fray Marcos claimed from this hillside all seven cities as well as the kingdoms of Tontonteac, Acus, and Marata, admitting, however, "I did not go into them, in order that I might return to give an account of what I had done and seen."

On his return, the word of his discoveries spread wildly among the Spanish inhabitants of Mexico City. Viceroy Mendoza declared that he would send a major military expedition to Cíbola and its Seven Cities, which matched the old legend perfectly and convinced the Spanish that here shimmered the next great gold bonanza of the New World. Pleading with King Charles to be leader of the Seven Cities expedition were both Cortés, conqueror of the Aztecs, and Hernando de Soto, future explorer of the Mississippi. But instead of these two illustrious explorers and would-be conquistadors, Viceroy Mendoza chose his friend to head it, Francisco Vásquez de Coronado.

Wrote one inhabitant of Mexico City of that time:

The [city] was so stirred by the news which the friar had brought from the Seven Cities that nothing else was thought about. Everybody wanted to go so much that they traded for the licenses which permitted them to go as soldiers, and people sold these as a favor, and whoever obtained one thought it was as good as a title of nobility at least.

Barely nine months after Fray Marcos had first stood on that barren hillside and surveyed the city of Cíbola, fashioning his little wooden cross and reciting his words to the air, a full-scale military expedition under Coronado headed north to seize the riches of the Seven Cities of Gold. Fray Marcos's hillside, and the Indian pueblo he saw in the distance that seemingly confirmed the rumors of the Cities of Gold, lay just on the northern edge of a great blank spot—blank then, too— now known as the Gila Forest and Wilderness. Just on the southern edge of the wilderness lies Silver City and its copper deposits, which may be the same metal deposits that triggered Cabeza de Vaca's rumors of gold in the late 1530s that started the madness.

WE FOLLOWED HIGHWAY 15 north out of Silver City—significantly not named "Gold City"—as it rolled gently upward toward that blank spot. We drove past tasteful, adobe second-home haciendas scattered on the tawny juniper hillsides just out of town, then climbed through the weathered old hamlet of Pinos Altos, as the road started its serious climb into the pine-covered mountains—twisting upward through dozens and dozens of switchbacks, downward through dozens and dozens more, and then upward again. There were no houses now. A single power line skipped through the forest from switchback to switchback. The state highway dwindled to a single lane of corkscrewing asphalt. A sign warned, "No Center Line Next 18 Miles."

"It's only forty-two miles," someone in Silver City had cautioned me about the road north from Silver City to the cliff dwellings and our departure point, "but expect it to take a long time."

We played road bingo with Molly and Skyler. The items we each had to spot were a bird, a green sign, a yellow flower, a dead tree. No one even bothered to suggest anything typically domestic, like "mailbox" or "flagpole" or "lawn ornament" or—laughably—"stoplight," because the chances of seeing one here were nil. Dead trees, however, were easy. Birds, surprisingly, were not.

The road crested a tall ridgetop and we stepped out of the car at a turnout and looked around. The westering sun backlit one of those landscapes that shone so enormously and silently and lucidly that it reminded me of a museum diorama of, say, the Mesozoic Era. There was a dead, windless silence except for the occasional primordial caw of a crow and the crunch of gravel under our shoes. From our feet the mountainside fell away into a deep chasm of luminous bluish air, then, maybe five miles off, the bottom crumpled up into still more layered, bluish ranges of mountains whose faces were split and contorted by canyons, cliffs, and escarpments of naked, tannish rock, and beyond them rose still more bluish ranges. Creatures from a different era existed out there . . . spirits from a different time.

WE ALL WOKE AT FOUR A.M., shivering. Molly and Skyler were sleeping in cocoon bags in our small winter-weight tent, and Amy and I in our summer-weight one, pitched side by side beneath piñon pines in a deserted campground at road's end. We heard their rustlings.

"Mom, I'm cold," said soft voices muffled still softer by layers of pile clothing, sleeping bag hoods, and tent fabric.

When Amy switched on her headlamp, the LED beams glistened like hundreds of tiny stars on the ice crystals that coated the ceiling of our tent. Outside, the night was a deep black. Icy, intense stars of the heavens glistened through the pine boughs. In these high, dry mountains in late October, the daily temperature swung enormously: from up around 70 degrees during the sunny, blue day, to far below freezing at night.

Amy unzipped their tent, wrapped the children in more clothes, and stuffed them deeper into their sleeping bags. She and I both added layers. Then we nestled in our own bags, pressed back to back, our warmth radiating to each other.

We didn't stir until the sun hit the tents, warming them. Climbing out, we discovered the water in our water bottles and in the pots on the campsite's picnic table had frozen solid. As we chipped ice out of the breakfast pots, the palm trees at the Mesa airport two days before seemed very far away.

It took us most of the day to get our act together to step beyond this point: a leisurely breakfast; reading in the warm sun; a quick walk up the hill behind camp to survey this cozy river valley where we'd camped—the West Fork of the Gila; drive a mile back down the road to the Gila Visitor Center to buy more maps, a wildlife guide, and to leave word of our route, so they'd know where to look in case we didn't return.

As I was going over maps at the Visitor Center's counter, one of the clerk ladies, an indoor-looking type, glanced skeptically over at Skyler and Molly as they checked out the racks of gifts and guidebooks.

"Do you know it was nineteen degrees last night?" she said to me.

"Yes . . . we were camping."

"Have you ever done anything like this before?" she asked.

"Well, we went backpacking last summer for one night in Montana," I said, then added, "These children are both soccer players. Skyler just ran a ten-K race. They're in very good shape. I *know* they can do this hike physically. Whether they'll *want* to do it mentally is another question."

This seemed to satisfy her, now that I'd framed our well-being as a matter of parental discipline.

Think of the map as a box within a box within a box. The innermost box, almost like a miniature national park, is the Gila Cliff Dwellings National Monument. Located up a side canyon of this innermost box are the cliff dwellings themselves. This national monument box is surrounded by another box, the 760,000-acre Gila Wilderness Area and Aldo Leopold Wilderness Area—named after their founder—which are themselves set within the sprawling, 3.3-million-acre Gila National Forest, a tract that measures roughly seventy by seventy miles, and even larger than that if you include adjoining national forests.

Our plan was to start hiking at the innermost box—the national monument—leaving from a trailhead near our campground. We'd loop out into the Gila Wilderness Area for several days, trekking through its river canyons and exploring its hot springs. We'd then return by a different route so that we ended up not far from where we started. At the very end of the hike, on the last day, we'd go up the side canyon and explore the Cliff Dwellings themselves.

It was 1:37 p.m. when we locked the white rental car, leaving it under the shade of a scrawny tree, hefted our backpack straps over our shoulders, cinched our pack belts around our waists, and walked across the trailhead parking lot known as TJ Corral—a surface of mangled sagebrush, dust, and dried horseshit. Where the parking lot ended a steep, rocky, sun-baked hillside began, dotted with juniper trees, and the beginning of a trail. With that particular sense of finality—the knowledge that with this footstep you've just severed all recourse to the comforts and requisites of civilization except those carried on your back and in your head—we began.

WITHIN FIVE MINUTES we were dripping sweat. After the morning's hat-and-glove cold and frozen water pots, we paused to strip down to shorts and T-shirts. The sky shone so deep blue and serene above the hillside that I didn't mind the heavy pack pushing down on shoulders and hips. *Clunkity-clunk* went our hiking boots up the rocky trail. It wound up the sparse grass cover of the hillside, dipped across little brushy gullies, swung onto the grassy open again, threaded between clumps of juniper trees, and, always, kept climbing. This wasn't, as it had appeared, simply a small hillside at the edge of the TJ Corral parking lot. It was a long, gradual mountain ridge that we had to climb up and over, in order to descend into the river canyon that lay beyond.

I led. Amy was lingering in the back, taking photos. Skyler and Molly hiked right behind me.

"Dad," Skyler said after about ten minutes. "How far do you think we've gone?"

"Maybe a third of a mile," I replied, turning my head back.

"How far is it to the top of this mountain?" he asked.

"Maybe about two miles."

"Then we have a mile and two thirds left to go," he calculated, liking to do numbers in his head. "So how long will that take?"

"Maybe an hour and a half," I said. "It depends on how fast we hike. Why don't you lead the way and set the pace."

"Okay."

He squeezed past me on the trail, his small blue mountaineer's pack bulging with his sleeping bag and pad, his clothing and his water bottle, and—his share of the communal family burden—all our lunch food. Small as he was, he strode upward at a decent pace.

In a moment, he began to sing.

"One hundred bottles of beer on the wall, one hundred bottles of beer, take one down, pass it around, ninety-nine bottles of beer on the wall.

"Ninety-nine bottles of beer on the wall, ninety-nine bottles of beer . . ."

At first I thought, "This is going to drive me nuts if he runs through the whole song." But then I realized that if the song kept him occupied, it was one way we could travel a lot farther than we might otherwise.

Molly and I, just behind Skyler, joined in singing. With Skyler's personal set of metrics to gauge our progress—miles, hours, and bottles of beer on the wall—we hiked past the little sign marking the bound-

ary of the National Monument and the beginning of the 760,000 acres
of the Gila and Leopold Wilderness.

In today's terms, the launch of the Coronado expedition in February 1540 was the equivalent of, say, sending a manned spacecraft to Mars. Surely it was dispatched with as much—if not more—formality and fanfare. Not since Europeans arrived in the New World had there been an undertaking of such opulence and brazenness—"the most brilliant company ever assembled in the Indies," wrote its chronicler, Pedro de Castañeda, "to go in search of new lands."

Gathering in Compostela, a Spanish outpost near Mexico's Pacific Coast, the army underwent three days of formalities demanded by the departure of so grand a venture—first a High Mass by the Father Commissary of New Spain, followed by Viceroy Mendoza's review of the entire column as it marched past his stand, and the viceroy's short, eloquent speech exhorting the spiritual and financial rewards that lay ahead for every man—providing he kept loyal to his leader—then a precise inventory of every man and his mounts, his armor, and his weaponry.

Finally each soldier placed his hand on a cross and swore to "uphold the service of God and his Majesty [and] to be obedient to the said Francisco Vásquez de Coronado . . . as a gentleman should do . . ."

Imagine the clouds of dust roiling around the column as it moved out of the mountain town of Compostela on February 23, 1540, bound for the unknown lands of the north and their Seven Cities of Gold. At its head, wearing a suit of gilded armor and a feathery plume in his helmet, rode the thirty-year-old Coronado himself, born of a landed Salamanca family but whose brother had inherited the family estate. Coronado, looking for grander possibilities than being a landless aristocrat in Spain, had come to the New World at age twenty-five with his friend Mendoza, who soon rose to viceroy. Behind the gilded and plumed Coronado were 336 Spaniards, most of them on horseback and trailing extra mounts, upwards of a thousand Indians, three soldiers' wives, four Franciscan priests, including the "discoverer" of the Seven Cities of Gold, Fray Marcos himself, and hundreds of pigs and sheep driven along to feed the men. In addition, two ships were to sail up the Pacific Coast bearing extra baggage.

The three hundred were not ordinary professional Spanish soldiers, however, but men of aristocratic bloodlines. Their family connections had given them first shot at joining the great expedition that was expected to add "another Mexico" to Spain's New World empire, as well as bestow unspeakable wealth on its participants, and, along the way, convert the lost, heathen Indians to Christianity. "Get Rich While Doing Good"—it was a concept that proved as irresistible then as it is now.

But you also sense an aura of amateurism that beset the expedition, precisely *because* the soldiers were aristocrats rather than professionals. Wearing assorted bits of armor they'd scrounged, mixed with native dress, they toted along every odd piece of weaponry they could carry, from muzzle-loading harquebuses to Aztec war clubs to giant two-handed swords. Of course, they also packed their finest robes and linens in order to be properly attired for their grand entrance into the golden cities. Likewise, Castañeda implied that the leadership was shaky. He backhandedly remarked that Captain General Coronado should have worried more about leading his men and less about his wife and his estates, which were actually his wife's, back home. Castañeda humorously describes how the aristocratic "soldiers" didn't even know how to load their own horses, so their belongings were constantly falling off in the beginning.

"In the end necessity, which is all powerful, made them skillful, so that one could see many gentlemen become carriers . . ."

And so they headed out of Compostela toward the north, toward that blank spot—a blank spot far larger than any of the armored Spaniards could comprehend, the blank spot that was in actuality the whole interior of North America, and, more specifically, toward the region that held the even blanker spot that's now the Gila Wilderness in New Mexico.

The first bad news arrived at Chiametla, a tiny Spanish outpost two hundred miles north up the coast from Compostela. Earlier, Coronado had sent ahead a scouting party of "a dozen good men" under Melchior Diaz to learn more about the Seven Cities. The scouts had traveled nearly a thousand miles north until they came to the edge of a great wilderness where no one lived, " . . . and there they turned back, not finding anything important." Four hundred years later, it would be left to Aldo Leopold to find the importance of the great empty places like this one that thwarted Coronado's scouting party.

Returning south, the scouting party met the cumbersome main expedition—pigs and sheep trailing, the gear falling off—at Chiametla and presented their reports to Captain General Coronado. He and the officers attempted to keep the disappointing news a secret, that there was only wilderness to the north, but word leaked out through the men. Fray Marcos, addressing the grumblings and rumors among the ranks, "cleared away these clouds, promising that what they would see should be good, and that he would place the army in a country where their hands would be filled, and in this way he quieted them so that they appeared well satisfied."

Onward they marched, reaching the last Spanish settlement, Culiacán, at Easter, where, in a bit of ceremony provided by the Spanish inhabitants, the army was greeted with a mock battle of resistance and finally allowed to "win" the town, although one of Coronado's artillerymen lost his hand by giving the order to fire the cannon before he'd drawn out the ramrod. Here at Culiacán the gentlemen soldiers gave away their finery to anyone who asked for it, weary of the hassle of packing it on their horses. From Culiacán, Coronado himself marched ahead from the main army, moving quickly and lightly northward, with fifty horsemen, the Franciscan friars, and hundreds of Indian allies. After traversing modern-day northern Mexico, populated by Indian villages, they crossed the Gila River and spent fifteen days trekking over the great stretch of desert and mountain wilderness in that region east of today's Phoenix, still largely empty of people nearly five hundred years later, and where the Gila Forest and Wilderness is located.

BEYOND THE WILDERNESS they came to the "Red River"—the Zuñi River—where Coronado and company encountered the first Indians from the Seven Cities, who ran and spread the news of the strangely mounted Spanish approaching. The Indians were unfamiliar with the sight of horses, and of men riding on their backs. The next night, as Coronado's party camped within five or six miles of the first city, a group of Indians yelled out from a hiding place in the darkness. This so excited Coronado's gentlemen soldiers into action that some saddled their horses backward, but the veterans among them managed to chase the Indians away. Castañeda reported what happened next:

> The following day they entered the settled land in good order. When they saw the first *pueblo,* which was Cibola, such were the curses that some of them hurled at Fray Marcos that may God not allow them to reach [his ears]. It is a small pueblo, crowded together and spilling down a cliff. In Nueva España there are *estancias* [farm buildings] which from a distance have a better appearance.

After five months and more than a thousand miles, it came as a crashing, angry disappointment to discover that this first of these celebrated Seven Cities of Gold consisted of an adobe village of two hundred warriors rather than a metropolis shimmering with towers of precious metals. Yet it still had to be conquered. Coronado's men assembled outside its walls, while "defiant" villagers—Zuñi Indians in a settlement near today's Zuni Pueblo south of Gallup, New Mexico—came out to meet them. Coronado and his men attacked the Zuñi Indians and pushed into Cíbola's narrow, twisting entrance. The Indians hurled stones from the roof terraces and shot arrows. A large stone caught Coronado in the head as he was trying to climb a ladder to the roof terraces, knocking him to the ground, where he lay in his gilded armor and plumed helmet, unconscious. Coronado would have been killed on the spot if two of his officers hadn't thrown themselves on him, taking the blows of more hurled stones, and dragged their commander to safety.

After an hour's battle, and with the help of hundreds of their Indian allies who had accompanied them from Mexico, the Spanish took the village and fell eagerly on the food in its storerooms. The Zuñi quietly escaped down the back walls and fled to their other villages. Jars of cornmeal weren't exactly bags of gold but provided nourishment, after all, for the near-starved men. Of some consolation, too, was that they heard from the subdued inhabitants of Cíbola that bigger and wealthier Indian towns lay ahead.

THE PROMISE OF OUR SEARCH for the hidden canyons and hot springs of the Gila Wilderness spurred us forward. As we crossed the crest of the ridge above Little Bear Canyon about 3:30 p.m., the warm sun still shone in the blue sky but we could sense it lowering—a spear's length above the horizon, as the old accounts put it—and anticipate the layers of cold that, beyond sundown, would settle over this high, dry country. We paused and looked north, our direction of travel, where the country fell away into a broken maze of cliffs and rims, forests and mountains. Somewhere down there twisted the Middle Fork of the Gila River, our immediate destination. Centuries earlier, Coronado's army skirted this mountain-and-canyon wilderness of the Gila River headwaters, passing north and west of us by one hundred miles.

Down we dropped into Little Bear Canyon. The trail wound through shady, cool pine forest and padded over the sandy, dried-up creek bed. Then the canyon narrowed and steepened and we squeezed through rock slots, and jumped down rock ledges that had been smoothed by flash floods. The cliff walls loomed higher as we descended. Molly and Skyler shouted to hear their voices echo and dodged off the trail to explore the smooth, cavelike alcoves under the overhanging rocks. One of these, we learned later, contained cave paintings.

By four thirty we'd descended to the mouth, where Little Bear opened up like a doorway to the canyon of the Gila's Middle Fork. We entered a sun-dappled little clearing at the confluence. The sun hung on the canyon rim and its last rays jumped over the dark, cliffy shadows and filtered through a grove of yellow-leafed cottonwood trees and feathery pines, painting the scene in warm golds and chilled greens. The Middle Fork spilled a swift, clear green between tannish cliffs. During this dry season, the river itself wasn't that big—maybe fifty feet wide and knee-to-thigh deep—and ran smoothly over rounded rocks.

"What do you want to do?" I asked. "We can camp here, in this really nice spot, or go on and try to find the hot springs."

"Let's go on," Molly and Skyler immediately replied.

"It'll probably be almost dark when we get there," I warned. "And we might not even get there tonight. And we're going to have to wade across the river."

"Let's keep going to the hot springs," they repeated.

"Okay, if you're sure you're up for it. We can have a quick lunch and then everyone put on their water shoes."

Amy pulled the lunch items from Skyler's backpack. As she sliced with her Swiss Army knife, the four of us devoured most of a block of sheep's-milk cheese she'd found in Silver City that came from Ronda, which we'd once visited in Spain, and we knocked off a dried salami, as we'd eaten nothing since our breakfast of mush but a few handfuls of trail mix.

"Dad!" Skyler said, eating his salami thoughtfully while sitting on a driftwood log in the sunlight. "Remember how mad you got when the sausage rolled off the cooler into the river on our canoe trip in Maine?"

"Yeah, Dad, remember that?" Amy teased.

"Yeah, Dad," Molly said. "You were so *mad*!"

"No!" I responded. "I'd like to correct that statement! The salami didn't just 'roll off the cooler into the river' by itself. It rolled off because Skyler was jumping from one canoe to another, pretending he was boarding a pirate ship while I was getting out lunch, and he rocked the canoe and the salami rolled off the cooler and sank. *That's* why I was mad. I'd been looking forward to that salami for days! I really, *really* wanted that salami and it ended up somewhere on the bottom of the river!"

They laughed. In the psychological arc of wilderness trips, morsels of food assume increasing symbolic significance as days pass and supplies dwindle. So do words, and gestures, and repeated annoying patterns of behavior. In an urban setting these things would be diluted or absorbed by thousands of other words, gestures, acts, bits of food. But here in wilderness it's just you—or the four of you—and whatever you carry on your back and in your heads. Whatever distraction you find derives solely from memory or from nature. In dozens of different ways, over the course of his lifetime, Aldo Leopold, who would eventually found the Gila Wilderness, would make this point, expand it, constantly reach for wilderness's importance. His concept started simply:

> Wilderness areas are first of all a series of sanctuaries for the primitive arts of wilderness travel, especially canoeing and packing. I suppose some will wish to debate whether it is important to keep these primitive arts alive. I shall not debate it. Either you know it in your bones, or you are very, very old.

"We've got to keep moving or we're not going to make it to the hot springs by dark," I said.

We packed away the lunch things—Skyler's backpack now lighter by two pounds—and pulled off our hiking boots. We tied them by their shoestrings to the backs of our packs, and put on our water shoes. In their white shoes and backpacks, Molly and Amy looked hilariously incongruent—prim nurses from the waist down, pack animals from the waist up.

"Okay, ready?" I said.

I took the first step into the Middle Fork of the Gila River. Cold water splashed up to my calves, then above my knees, as I shuffled across the slippery, rounded rocks of the bottom, arms outspread for balance. I looked back. The other three were shuffling after me, Skyler pulling up his shorts because the water went well up his thighs.

"It's not bad," I called back. "Just a little deep in the middle."

I reached the far shore where the trail notched into the bank, and splashed out, my big shoes trailing streams of water like a wet dog's legs, while the others splashed out behind me.

"That's one down," Skyler called out. "Only fourteen more to go."

According to the hiking guidebook to the Gila Wilderness, there were fifteen river crossings along this trail to reach the hot springs. We'd torn out the pages and stuffed them in the top pocket of my pack.

The canyon walls twisted, shoving the river from side to side. A chilly shade enveloped the bottom. The sun had vanished until morning. Our shoes squished. The trail cut through dim patches of forest—gambel oak, ponderosa pine—that filled the elbows of the river bends. We emerged from a copse onto the riverbank again. Down we scrambled, splashed in, and waded across, clambered out dripping from the cold water to the shady forest. That was two out of fifteen. This, I started to think, could be a cold, grim haul. We needed something to keep our minds off it. I remembered Skyler's beer-bottle song. I amended it, starting to sing, "Fifteen river crossings . . ."

Molly immediately picked it up, then Skyler, then Amy. As a family, we hashed out the lyrics as we hiked along.

> *Fifteen river crossings in the canyon,*
> *fifteen crossings to go.*
> *Wade through one,*
> *pull yourself out,*
> *fourteen crossings to go.*
> *Fourteen river crossings in the canyon,*
> *fourteen crossings to go.*

Wade through two,
pull yourself out,
Thirteen crossings to go.

An hour later, we were on the eighth crossing. I began to doubt that we'd make it to the hot springs this night. It was getting really dim. Everyone was chilled, bare legs against cold water. Amy and I had some tense words about whether we'd make it, which then made Skyler upset. We all got past it.

"Seven river crossings in the canyon . . . seven crossings to go, wade through nine, pull yourself out, six crossings to go."

It took concentration to do the math, sing, and balance across the river at the same time. Down to five . . . four . . . three . . . It was now almost dark. We came to a small opening in the forest. I told everyone to remember the spot, as we might have to come back and camp here if we couldn't find the hot springs.

At the fourteenth crossing, I smelled a whiff of sulfur in the air. Climbing up the bank from the fifteenth crossing, we entered a dark grove of trees. A small rivulet ran across the trail. I put my hand in it.

"Feel this," I said to Molly.

She dipped her hand.

"It's warm!" she exclaimed.

Nearby lay a clearing under the trees and a circle of stones someone had shaped into a fire ring. We threw down our packs. We had a race to put up the tents—Amy and I versus Molly and Skyler—before it was too dark to see at all.

"Now that we've helped with the tents," Molly asked, "can we go swimming while you make dinner?"

They scrambled up a short trail leading up the hillside above camp, slanting up toward the canyon walls. By headlamp, I collected dead wood and made a fire, got a pot of river water simmering on our little campstove, while Amy laid out sleeping bags and pads in the tents.

It was dark by the time I climbed up the hillside to check on the children. There was a large boulder overhanging the pool. They'd strewn their clothes and hiking shoes atop it, and dropped their head-lamps on the boulder, too, so they shone down into the pool. The beams illuminated the rock basin of slightly steaming water, with its bluish gravelly bottom. Molly's and Skyler's white shapes glided contentedly about in the clear water, like goldfish. An arched bower of leaves overhung the pool and from a cavern under massive tree roots a torrent of warm water gushed forth, replenishing the rock pool. On the pool's far end, it spilled out over a small waterfall into a series of smaller, lower pools, and then streamed down the hillside toward the river below.

They were the most beautiful natural hot springs I'd ever seen.

IT WAS ABOUT 125 MILES north of these hot springs that Coronado had attacked and taken the Zuñi Indian village where he was almost killed by flung stones. The Zuñi knew the place as Hawikku, one of a group of seven close-knit villages. This was the origin of the "seven cities" of Cíbola (Cíbola was a southern tribe's name for the group of seven Zuñi cities) that Fray Marcos had reported to the authorities in Mexico City after his first visit and rumors of which Cabeza de Vaca may have heard.

Angry and disappointed, Coronado and his army had still not found anything remotely resembling the Seven Cities of Gold, but they didn't entirely abandon hope in this arid, goldless landscape. That summer of 1540, based at the village he'd conquered and renamed—dreams of grandiosity still alive—Granada, Coronado sent messengers back to Mexico City to report the bad news to Viceroy Mendoza. He also sent Fray Marcos back to Mexico with the courier party in order to put the friar out of reach of the angry soldiers in Coronado's army.

"Fray Marcos has not told the truth in a single thing that he said," Coronado wrote to the viceroy, "except the name of the cities and the large stone houses . . . God knows that I wish I had better news to write your Lordship . . . Be assured that if all the riches and treasures of the world had been here, I could not have done more than I have done."

He added a note, clearly intended to generate some sympathy for his hardships and deprivations, that the expedition no longer had any raisins to eat, nor sugar, nor oil, nor wine, "except barely half a quart."

Coronado also dispatched three smaller exploring parties in three different directions. One bore southwest toward the coast to find the support ships that had sailed up from Mexico. But the ships had left only a packet of messages buried under a tree, pointed out by the Indi-ans, which contained the explanation that they'd waited a long time for the army to appear and now were heading home because worms were eating the wooden hulls. A second exploring party tracked northwest from Cíbola, and, in today's northeastern Arizona, encountered the first Hopi villages. After a brief skirmish, the Spanish subdued these "very intelligent people"—as Castañeda described them—and began friendly trading for turquoises and for the cotton cloth woven by the Hopi.

The Hopi told the Spanish about a large river that lay beyond a desert country. With Hopi guides, the party traveled twenty days across the wilderness and reached a canyon rim. Seen from the rim, the river below appeared only about six feet wide and the canyon not deep, although the Indians reported that the river was actually far wider than it seemed. The skeptical Spanish sent their three lightest, most agile men scrambling down, and, after an entire day, they reemerged on the rim saying the canyon was far steeper and deeper than it looked. They hadn't made it even one third of the way down. The rocks in the canyon that looked from the rim only as tall as a man were, in fact, taller than the Giralda bell tower of the great Cathedral of Seville—which was 275 feet high—and the river was indeed very wide.

These humbled Spaniards were the first Europeans to see, and hike into, what's now called the Grand Canyon of the Colorado River. Still a third exploring party went east from Cíbola. They'd been invited in that direction by a tall, strong young Indian they nicknamed "Bigote"—"Whiskers" in Spanish, because he wore a long mustache—who came from the east. Bigote had brought the Spaniards gifts—strange woolly hides that looked like very heavy cowhides but weren't, and sturdy leather shields and helmets crafted from the same material. Bigote said his country was full of these large animals.

Coronado sent one of his captains, Hernando de Alvarado, and twenty men guided by Bigote to check out the country of the strange cows. Heading east from Cíbola, in a few days' travel they reached the "Sky City"—Acoma—sitting atop an inaccessible, 357-foot-high rock mesa . . . "so high," wrote Castañeda, "that it was a very good musket that could throw a ball as high." The village could be approached only via a dizzying series of handholds. The Spaniards, not having much recourse to conquer it, made peace with Acoma. Today it is still a thriving adobe village atop its prominent rock—the oldest continuously inhabited settlement in the United States—about sixty miles west of Albuquerque.

Still farther east, they came to a very strong village, Cicuye, of four-story buildings where they met a slave of the Indians whose original home lay still farther east, toward Florida. They nicknamed the slave "The Turk," because, writes Castañeda, "he looked like one."

"[The Turk] told them so many and such great things about the wealth of gold and silver in his country that they did not care about looking for cows, but returned after they had seen some few, to report the rich news to the general."

Among other things, the Turk reported a river six miles across (likely the Mississippi) where giant canoes were paddled by forty Indians each, the prow adorned with an eagle made of gold. The chief took his naps under a large tree hung with gold bells that tinkled melodically in the wind. The people of this land used golden jugs and bowls, the Turk told the Spaniards.

The Coronado expedition had been largely peaceful to this point. They were under both orders from Viceroy Mendoza and edicts from the king and queen of Spain to treat the natives humanely. But that suddenly changed. Gold was at stake. The frustration mounted among the Spanish as they wandered around the pueblo villages of the Southwest, month after month, squeezing the native inhabitants ever more tightly with the question, "Where's the gold??!!"

The fighting started over a few bracelets that probably never existed. The Turk claimed to have owned several gold bracelets that were taken from him by the people of Cicuye when he was captured as a slave. Captain Alvarado went to Cicuye—a pueblo village just east of today's Santa Fe, now called Pecos—and demanded the gold bracelets from Cicuye's leaders. They said they knew nothing about gold bracelets, that this slave, the Turk, was lying. Captain Alvarado didn't believe them. He threw both Cicuye's chieftain and Bigote, who was also a leader of Cicuye, into chains. He transported them to the Indian village of Tiguex, where Coronado had set up his winter camp among a cluster of pueblo villages on the Rio Grande. Here Captain General Coronado kept the twosome captive. It was from this point forward that the Indians didn't trust Coronado and his army, according to Castañeda.

"This began the want of confidence in the word of the Spaniards," he wrote.

It was now snowing and cold in the high desert and the Rio Grande was frozen solid. The Spaniards took over all the pueblo houses in the village of Tiguex, forcing its inhabitants to move in with relatives in neighboring villages. Coronado also demanded from Tiguex's chieftain three hundred pieces of clothing for his freezing men, these warm-blooded Spaniards from Mexico. When the chieftain replied that the request had to be sent to each village separately, Coronado's men simply went into the other villages and took the robes off people's backs.

The tension escalated when one of the Spaniards apparently sexually assaulted an Indian woman. The Spaniards did not bring forth the culprit, so the Indians responded by driving off the Spaniards' horses, which they feared ate people. The Spaniards retaliated by besieging the village where the assault occurred. Both sides eventually agreed to a peace and the Indians surrendered on the understanding they wouldn't be harmed, but Coronado had sent instructions to make an example of the rebel village and not to take prisoners. His commanding officer at the scene, Don García, interpreted that to mean he should roast his two hundred Indian captives at the stake, which he proceeded to do.

All trust vanished. Fighting broke out. The Indians retreated to two villages where the Spaniards besieged them—for fifty days in one case. The Indians suffered from lack of water. In one village they dug a well, but the well collapsed, killing a number of them. The Spaniards offered asylum to the women and children but the Indians didn't trust them or their promises. Finally, one night, the Indians tried to escape the siege. They were run down by the cavalry, died while swimming across the icy Rio Grande, or captured and made into slaves of the Spaniards. This ended the siege, noted Castañeda, on March 31, 1541. Several weeks later, in early May, with the Pueblo country "pacified," Coronado's army started marching northeastward toward the Plains in search of the Turk's golden land of Quivira.

IN OUR CAMP NEAR THE HOT SPRINGS we could have used some buffalo robes, too. The temperature plunged with the falling of darkness. Wearing our pile jackets, our hats, our long underwear, we sat on the forest floor around the fire and spooned up our bowls of beans and rice mixed with chunks of canned chicken, then nibbled on chocolate. Molly curled up in the warmth of Amy's lap, and Skyler in mine, staying off the cold ground, their backs warmed against our bodies, their fronts warmed by the jumping flames. It was a sweet moment, these fast-growing children on our laps around the fire, a moment that I wanted to remember when they were grown and I was old.

"I'm getting cold," Molly said.

They'd climbed wet out of the hot springs in the cold air and had been chilled since then.

"Why don't you go to your tent and crawl into your sleeping bags and I'll come in and read to you aloud," Amy proposed.

Headlamps flashed and nylon rustled as they disappeared in their yellow tent, lit from within by flashlights as if it were a large, soft Japanese lantern. I rinsed out the bowls, put away the pots, hung the food in a backpack on a tree branch out of the reach of animals. Then I snapped off my headlamp and stood by myself in the blackness next to the dying orange coals of the fire, sipping a bit of dark rum from my camp cup, savoring the peaceful moment.

I listened. Several different layers of sound lulled through the black night of the canyon bottom.

Amy's quiet murmuring, reading in the glowing tent.

The soft susurration of the Middle Fork of the Gila, a hundred feet away through the dark grove of trees.

The chirp of crickets and buzz of insects, oddly vibrant in the cold desert night in late October. How could it be? I then realized the insect sounds emanated from a hot springs seep on the hillside above camp, where tall, wide-bladed grasses grew with a jungly lushness. Here, powered by the interior heat of the earth, lay a little patch of the tropics amid the arid, cold mountains.

A coal popped in the fire, sending up a spark.

I looked up to the night sky.

The stars looked so hard, and bright, and sharp, little diamond chips spangled through the treetops, so many, many stars—the milky bands of stars, the swirls of stars, the clusters, the constellations.

It occurred to me, standing there, that I gazed up at the inverse image of my "blank spots" satellite photo. From one of the earth's dark patches, I peered up to where the lights of the heavens shone brightest. There were no human-made lights for miles around. The desert air was dry. The altitude was high. I was at the bottom of a deep canyon.

I'd found my perfect blank spot . . . a kind of black hole.

I let my mind roam over the surface of the earth. I could see scores of sprawling cities and their beaded strings of lights. But so much of the earth, I saw, remained lightless. So much actually remained or became a blank spot. I thought of all the oceans, and the deserts, and the high mountain ranges, and the deep forests, and the icy poles. They all remained lightless in the satellite image in my mind. They all remained places where the stars shone as intensely on the earth's surface as they did right here.

But so rarely did we venture to these places. They were difficult to reach. They lay far beyond the convenience of our airports and our cars, beyond that web of wires and buildings and roads that bind the accessible parts of the earth. It was easy to become convinced they didn't exist anymore. We think blanks spots are gone because we, as individuals and as a species, almost always follow the crowds.

But the stars are out there, with effort, for us to see.

ALDO LEOPOLD KNEW THIS. As a young man, he developed a crude formulation for what constituted a true "wilderness," distance from "civilization" being of primary importance. A wilderness was, he wrote, a wild area "big enough to absorb a two-weeks' pack trip."

When he first arrived here in the Southwest in July 1909, as a twenty-two-year-old U.S. forester, his crew hated him. Overeducated and stiff in their eyes, a graduate of Yale and its new Forestry School, Leopold quickly demonstrated he was incompetent, too.

He'd grown up in a big house on a bluff overlooking the Mississippi River in Burlington, Iowa, in a family with a passion for the outdoors. His businessman grandfather, German-born and educated, loved to spend his leisure time landscaping gardens and parks. His father, owner of a Burlington desk-manufacturing company, loved to hunt ducks— a passion that young Aldo quickly adopted. His mother provided a literary and artistic influence. A lover of poetry who had an Eastern boarding-school education, she nudged Aldo to boarding school— Lawrenceville, in New Jersey—in order to prepare him for undergraduate work at Yale, which he followed with a master's at the Forestry School.

Dandified up in his newly purchased cowboy outfit (including the pistols), and riding his stallion Jiminy Hicks, young Forest Assistant Leopold, with the East Coast ivy still clinging to his ears, brought to his job "the fervor of a sawdust evangelist"—as his boss later phrased it—mated with a greenhorn's lack of experience.

His first big assignment came a few weeks after his arrival when his boss put him in charge of a crew mapping the Apache Forest's remote eastern edge—not far from where we hiked in the adjoining Gila Forest—and appraising its timber value. Never strong in math, Leopold couldn't make the maps he drew match up one to the next. He refused help from more experienced mapmakers. He repeatedly left off the mapping job to track poachers and predators of deer and elk. The crew fell so far behind schedule that the survey dragged far into the autumn and early mountain snows became a threat. At one point, he abandoned his crew of five—two lumberjacks and three foresters—to go looking for a promising location to place a game refuge.

The camp ran short of food. Leopold returned to find his crew in a state of rebellion. He'd never been in charge of anything before, and, at least in this situation, sympathy wasn't his strong suit.

"Why damn their whining souls," Leopold wrote to his sister that October 4, "wait 'til it begins to snow. That will take the conceit out of them. . . . It looks like it [will] take all the tact and patience I can raise to hold the party together until I finish the job."

Tact and patience is what he didn't have, not then. There would be a Forest Service investigation afterward into why the mission had gone so badly.

"In my opinion," one crew member would testify, "Mr. Leopold considered the Apache reconnaissance a picnic party instead of a serious matter."

But the ultimate significance of the Apache reconnaissance didn't lie in Leopold's beginner's incompetence (the investigation concluded he was simply inexperienced and would be given another chance) nor in the mapping work it did. Rather, it lay in one seemingly inconsequential incident on one afternoon in a river canyon not unlike the one where we had camped.

Aldo Leopold and another crew member or two were eating lunch on a rimrock overlooking a whitewater river, and, down below, spotted what they thought was a deer swimming across the river toward them. As the creature climbed onto the shore and shook its tail, they realized it was a wolf. Her pups joyfully jumped out of the willow bushes to greet their mother, tails wagging, jumping over one another playfully, on a bit of open ground along the shore. Years later, in one of his most famous essays, "Thinking Like a Mountain," Leopold described what happened next with the frolicking wolf pack that autumn afternoon:

> In those days we had never heard of passing up a chance to kill a wolf. In a second we were pumping lead into the pack, but with more excitement than accuracy . . . When our rifles were empty, the old wolf was down, and a pup was dragging a leg into impassable slide-rocks.
>
> We reached the old wolf in time to watch a fierce green fire dying in her eyes. I realized then, and have known ever since, that there was something new to me in those eyes—something known only to her and to the mountain. I was young then, and full of trigger-itch; I thought that because fewer wolves mean more deer, that no wolves would mean hunters' paradise. But after seeing the green fire die, I sensed that neither the wolf nor the mountain agreed with such a view.

MOLLY WOKE UP at four a.m. in our hot springs camp as she had the night before. But this time it wasn't the cold.

"I'm having really bad growing pains in my legs," she called out to us from the neighboring tent.

"It's not growing pains," I murmured to Amy. "It's all the hiking she did with a heavy pack."

"I'll come massage them, sweetie," Amy called back.

She switched on a headlamp. The inside of our the tent was coated with frost, but it was not quite as cold as the previous night.

Grateful for Amy's offer, I hunkered deeper into my warm sleeping bag. Sleeping seldom felt so delicious. A small tent stuffed with fluffy bags made me feel like a hibernating animal curled up in a dry, grass-lined burrow. During storms, I'd found it remarkable how long one could sleep in a tent. Once, during a storm on an island off Greenland, Amy and I slept for most of two straight days until wakened by our Inuit guide, who told us the sea ice was breaking up in the storm and we'd better get our asses on his dogsled and back to the mainland before it did.

That was before children. We now scaled our adventures to what we hoped they could handle. Oddly, it was still no less adventurous. Children threw into the mix another set of uncertainties entirely, which at times could be just as adventurous—challenging, hair-raising, satisfying to overcome—as whether, for instance, the sea ice was about to go out from your island.

We woke again at eight, lingering another half hour before dragging ourselves out of the warm bags into the shady cold of the canyon bottom. The sun was striking the cliffs high above, illuminating them gold against the canyon rim higher up still—dark green, pine-draped—and that seamless, deep blue sky. It felt like standing in the bottom of a deep, beautifully painted pottery bowl.

We started a fire for warmth and slurped up big, steaming bowls of ramen noodles and camp cups of hot chocolate and tea for breakfast. By the time we finished, the sunbeams had tilted down far enough to illuminate the cottonwoods along the river, and a few minutes later filtered through our leafy grove into camp.

Molly helped pack the tents while Skyler scrambled up a huge, slanting Arizona sycamore. With their smooth, thick trunks and heavy limbs, their flaky bark and star-shaped leaves, these look very much like the big plane trees you see lining the streets in Paris. They also make great climbing trees. He sat up there like a monkey, throwing down bits of debris and surveying the canyon, entirely content.

Amy and I used this moment to hike up to the hot springs, strip down, and slip in. The water felt evenly smooth on my skin, like a perfectly tempered bath. I felt the clean pebbles of the bottom massaging the sore soles of my feet. We wallowed, up to our necks. The pool rippled as we moved, spilling over the waterfall, the pool's water blue-tinted from the stones of the bottom. Tendrils of steam rose from the surface and curled up into the morning sun. The bower of branches arched over the pool and the gusher of warm water poured in from the cavern under the tree roots.

It was one of those moments in marriage—in life—of perfect poise. The distractions of our daily scramble back home now lay so far away they didn't even enter our consciousness. We'd finally reached that geopsychic region where there is only the present.

"This feels delicious," said Amy.

That zone seemed harder and harder to reach. It made me wonder about the cell-phone-texting generation, Molly's generation, and whether they'll ever be able to reach it. There was no cell-phone reception out here. But sometime in the not-too-distant future cell phones will link into satellite reception and it will be perfectly possible to sit in this hot springs pool in the midst of the wilderness and text with your friends back home.

CORONADO HAD NO SUCH close connection with his base, which lay more than a thousand miles away back in Mexico City. Warmer weather arriving and the ice gone from the Rio Grande, the plumed and gilded Coronado marched eastward in spring of 1541 from the Pueblo villages where he'd wintered. Out there, somewhere, lay the Seven Cities of Gold. He was convinced of it. He knew well the old Spanish stories of the seven bishops who, carrying the Christian riches, escaped the Moorish conquest and fled to the west. He'd heard the reports of Cabeza de Vaca, and of Fray Marcos, who, while discredited and sent back to Mexico City in shame for his false reportings of Cíbola, surely had encountered *something* to bolster the suspicion of the golden cities. The Indians would have very good reason to hide the true location of the golden cities. They sensed the fierceness of the Spaniards' hunger for gold. Yes, this was why they were so difficult to find. It was because the Indians were not forthcoming.

But there was the slave, the Turk, who promised that the gold was that way . . . toward the rising sun. And so winter gone and spring arriving, toward the rising sun they marched. The whole Coronado expedition now hinged on the Turk's guidance.

Nine days' march eastward from the last Pueblo village, Coronado's army descended from the mountains onto the Plains. Here they arrived at their first encampment of Plains Indians—the Querechos, or Eastern Apaches—whose nomadic life amazed the Spaniards.

Reported members of the expedition:

These people sustain themselves entirely from the cattle [buffalo] . . . With the skins they build their houses; with the skins they clothe and shoe themselves; from the skins they make rope and also obtain wool. With the sinews they make thread, with which they sew their clothes and also their tents . . . These people have dogs. They load these dogs like beasts of burden and make light pack saddles for them like our pack saddles, cinching them with leather straps. When the Indians go hunting they load them with provisions. When these Indians move—for they have no permanent residence anywhere, since they follow the cattle to find food—these dogs carry their homes for them. In addition to what they carry on their backs, they carry the poles for the tents, dragging them fastened to their saddles.

They were very intelligent people, added Castañeda, and could speak fluently to other tribes without interpreters by using sign language. They were moving their encampment eastward, and so they traveled alongside Coronado's army for two days. The marching army now saw so many buffalo on the Plains that it "seemed something incredible." Trying to kill some of the buffalo, the advance guard of Coronado's army triggered a stampede, and the charging buffalo tumbled into a ravine. It filled with their writhing bodies, so that other buffalo ran right over the top of them, and three Spanish horses, equipped with saddles and bridles, fell into the furry maelstrom and completely disappeared.

Following the Turk's instructions, Coronado's army veered southeast, into the territory of the Teyas Indians—later to give their name to Texas. The Turk told the Spaniards he was leading them to a nearby settlement, Haxa, and then on to Quivira, where golden bells dangling from trees tinkled in the breeze. Another Indian with the expedition, Ysopete, a native of Quivira, claimed that the Turk was lying but no one believed Ysopete. Coronado sent out an advance party to find the settlement of Haxa, which the Turk promised lay near.

"Nothing but cows and sky," they came back to report.

Another four days' march brought them all to a large Indian settlement in a deep valley. The shipwrecked Cabeza de Vaca and the Moorish medicine man Esteben had passed through this same settlement several years earlier on their wanderings across the Southwest, believed to be the Blanco Canyon area near Lubbock, Texas. Upon Coronado's arrival, the Indians piled up hundreds of buffalo robes and teepees for him to bless, in the manner that Esteben worked his medicine, but— and here is a key difference between the two parties—Coronado wanted to divide up the pile of robes as spoils. His soldiers, each clamoring for first choice of robes, suddenly rushed at the pile, and, in less than a quarter of an hour, reported Castañeda, "nothing was left but empty ground."

You wonder if America would be different today—a gentler, more integrated land—if later European explorers had traveled as attuned to their cultural surroundings as Esteban and Cabeza de Vaca did, rather than with Coronado's and his army's obliviousness. But then, their objectives were very different, as were the objectives of all who came after. Coronado and his men wanted gold. Esteban and Cabeza de Vaca wanted to survive.

For several more days, Coronado's army followed the Teyas settlements through the fertile river valley where walnuts and grapes grew and fowl thrived. One day a storm pummeled them with hailstones so large that they dented the Spanish armor and broke their crockery. From these Teyas Indians in the valley, they learned that Quivira was, in fact, to the north—*far* to the north. Nor was there a good trail to get there from here. The Turk's reputation began to sink, rapidly. Ysopete's stock rose.

In its search for Quivira, the army had already marched thirty-seven days from the Pueblo villages—two hundred and fifty leagues, or about five hundred miles, as measured by one Spaniard whose job it was, all day, to count his steps. With another long journey ahead, now to the north, Coronado, wishing to travel quickly, sent the cumbersome main body of the army back to the Pueblo settlements. After resting for two weeks, killing five hundred buffalo and drying the meat into jerky, Coronado swung due north toward Quivira with only his best horses, his ablest men, and a few Teyas Indian guides. The Turk was with them—now shackled in chains.

You can imagine what the Spanish soldiers said to the Turk, after his guidance had brought them in the wrong direction five hundred miles out onto the Plains. Castañeda, who wrote the account of the expedition, apparently wasn't fast enough for the final Quivira run and returned with the main army to the Pueblo villages in the mountains, so from him we have only the barest details of the final push to Quivira.

Due north they marched, hard and fast, across the Plains. After thirty days they reached the River of Quivira. We call it the Arkansas River. They crossed it near today's Dodge City, Kansas. For another week's riding, they hugged it downstream, toward the northeast. It was then they finally arrived at the first settlements of the golden-belled, promised land—Quivira.

They were not built of stone, or of wood, or even of mud. The houses were built of straw. They were not cities. They were small settlements. There were no golden bowls or golden bells dangling from the trees. The only metal the Spaniards saw was a single copper plate hanging around a chieftain's neck.

Again, a guide had led astray Coronado and his army of aristocrats in their quest for the Seven Cities of Gold. Fray Marcos had gotten off easy. The Turk not so. The Spaniards garroted him.

"IT SMELLS LIKE MINT," Molly said as we were making the day's first crossing of the Middle Fork of the Gila.

It was nearly noon by the time we left camp near the hot springs, slipped into our wet wading shoes, and, not a hundred feet from camp, scrambled down the bank for the slosh across. I could smell the sweet, minty fragrance, too.

"It's probably growing along the bank where it's wet and shady," I said, wading to the far side.

Then I abruptly turned around and waded back across the Gila to pluck leafy bunches of the sweet mint and stash them in my backpack. I had a feeling we could use the mint come evening.

We'd given Molly and Skyler the option of choosing the day's route. Should we stay at the hot springs, and eventually hike out the way we'd hiked in? Or should we continue on up the Middle Fork canyon, until we reached a place where it opened up, called the Meadows, and camp there?

They chose the latter. Before we'd left camp, they'd sat down together with our detailed topographical map and tried to count how many times the faint, dotted line of the trail might cross the snaking course of the Middle Fork between here and the Meadows.

"It's hard to see," Molly reported, "but I think about fifteen."

Skyler did a double-check of her count.

"Maybe eighteen."

In the chilly shade of canyon cliffs, the trail wound through piney glens, where our feet padded on fallen needles, and through copses of thick, gnarled, golden-leafed oaks.

Straight above us, over a thousand feet up from the canyon bottom, a jagged crack of intense blue sky split the sunlit canyon rims, which cast their diffuse reflected light to the forest floor. With little underbrush, it was the archetypal forest—a fairy-tale forest.

"Elf forests," we called them.

In other places we strode through patches of horsetails, up to Skyler's chest.

"These look like the trees in Maine," he said of the trees along the river with horizontally striated bark whose branches sparkled in the sun.

"You're right," I said, proud of his observation. "These are birch trees like the ones we saw in Maine. But these are called water birches."

The river crossings chilled us, cold water splashing high up our bare legs, as we shuffled carefully over the slippery rocks and through rushing water, hiking up our shorts even higher. We'd hop up gratefully on dry land. Swinging through another sharp bend, the canyon would change its direction and, ahead, we'd spot a golden patch among the dark green where the sunlight penetrated to the canyon floor. You could feel it coming as you walked through the needle-carpeted glens, a soft warmth of air mixing with the shady cold under the cliffs, and then you'd break out into the sunlight and feel suffused with the warmth and peacefulness thrown down by that big burning star. It was easy to understand how the native peoples in these black and white, shade and sun, cool and hot climates—the Aztecs in Mexico, for instance—would have their sun gods.

In April 1913, Aldo Leopold, four years out of Yale Forestry School and supervisor of New Mexico's Carson National Forest, was riding a hired horse alone through the Jicarilla Mountains when a major spring storm drenched him with sleet, hail, rain, and snow. For two days he grew increasingly wet and chilled. When the storm finally let up, he headed eastward out of the mountains aimed for the warmth of his new cabin and the embrace of his bride, Estella Bergere, a quiet, dark-haired beauty from an old New Mexican family.

Trying to reach a rail line in this empty quadrant, Leopold got lost. He and his horse stumbled onto the household of an Apache Indian, who gave him a warm place to sleep and a fire to dry his clothing and bedroll. The following day, as he rode farther east, his legs and knees began to swell. Soon they'd grown so large he had to slice open his boots.

When he finally staggered into Chama, the town doctor diagnosed the swelling as a bad case of rheumatism. He headed back home to his and Estella's cabin at Tres Piedras, although she, now pregnant with their first child, was visiting her family in Santa Fe, so she didn't see the ailing Leopold arrive. At his office, Leopold's forest assistant took one look at his bloated face and immediately sent him to Santa Fe for treatment. He was diagnosed with Bright's disease, a form of kidney failure, and immediately sent to bed. For six weeks he remained there, hovering between life and death.

With his recuperation dragging out many months, he took a long leave from the Forest Service and, at his family's urging, he and Estella returned to his family home in Burlington, Iowa. All that summer of 1913, Leopold sat on the front porch of his parents' home on the bluff overlooking the Mississippi River and reflected on the larger issues that lay before him. In the meantime, Estella was about to give birth to the first of their five children, Starker.

From this high vantage point over the Mississippi and with a newborn nearby, Leopold saw clearly that the life of a U.S. forest ranger was so cluttered with reports, grazing permits, timber harvesting, and special cases to consider, that it was easy, quite literally, to lose sight of the forest for the trees.

"We ride," he wrote to his forest rangers, "but are we getting anywhere?"

Rather than get too caught up in these items, he urged them to think about how to protect the entirety of "the Forest"—"timber, water, forage, farm, recreative, game, fish, and 'scenic' resources." All decisions should be made with this *entirety* in mind.

"[T]he sole measure of our success," he wrote them, "is the effect on *the Forest*."

The "final specific truth," he emphasized again, is "THE EFFECT ON THE FOREST."

What's interesting here is how Leopold was pushed toward this holistic way of thinking about the natural world. Where Rousseau's view of nature was shaped by his lover Madame de Warens, a Deist nature worshipper, and William Bartram's view shaped by his father and the

British poets, and Thoreau's view of nature by Emerson's philosophy, Aldo Leopold's philosophy was shaped in part by his work as a government bureaucrat.

Or, to be fair, he shaped his philosophy in *reaction* to his work as a government bureaucrat, combined with his scientific training and solid literary background. His desk work as a forest administrator shoved his nose into the minute details of grazing management, timber harvesting, water flows, erosion, game species numbers. He had to crunch the numbers, he had to write the reports, his desk work tempered by long rides through the forest. It didn't make sense to him at first, all these bits of the mosaic. The decisions felt random. Only when he began to fit the bits of the puzzle together—to look at the entirety of the forest, to think holistically—did they begin to form a pattern that would shape his guiding philosophy.

AFTER FOURTEEN CROSSINGS in two hours of the Middle Fork of the Gila River we were thoroughly chilled and wondering how much farther to the Meadows, where we planned to camp. Molly and Skyler had calculated fifteen crossings total to the Meadows. That was beginning to seem like a considerable underestimate.

We hugged a cliff on the left bank through a long stretch of shady forest.

"At the next patch of sun," I suggested, "let's stop for lunch."

Yes! Yes! Yes! Let's stop! Everyone agreed.

We spotted a golden luminance ahead where the river canyon carved hard to the left. Suddenly we broke from the deep cliff shadow into warm sunlight and a sunny crossing. We waded to the far shore, pulled off our shoes, and sat on a big driftwood log that sun and water had bleached to a smooth white.

We pried open a can of smoked oysters. We dug from Skyler's pack peanut butter, hard cheese, a little more dry sausage. These all tasted wonderful piled up on one piece of tortilla. We lay sprawled on the warm log, absorbing the sun, passing along morsels of food, flicking them into our mouths like a languorous lizard would snag a fly on its tongue. Amy pulled out a bag of gummi worms. Those vanished—the sweet succulent, red, orange, green worms.

We suddenly heard voices. We sat up. We hadn't heard voices other than our own in a day and a half.

They emerged from the forest, striding down the trail toward us, a young couple, moving quickly, swinging their arms, using ski poles for balance, each draped with a sun hat.

"Well, look at this!" I remarked. "People! Information!"

"Hi," we called out.

"How far is it to the Meadows?" Amy asked before they'd even reached our log.

He was in the lead. I noticed that he'd duct-taped two water bottles to the front straps of his backpack, so he didn't have to stop hiking to take a swig of water, but only bend down his head. They both looked sun-crisp, and slightly smudged, and their limbs ropy with exercise.

"Twenty-six crossings," he replied.

The guy wore big snow gaiters zipped over his soaking-wet hiking shoes, reaching up to his knees. He had a stubble on his chin that looked at least a couple of weeks old. Her lips were smeared with white cream against the sun. Their packs looked small and light and compressed compared to ours.

"How far back?" I asked, thinking that twenty-six more crossings was going to be a long, long day.

"We left there about eleven-thirty," he said.

"Did you camp there?" I asked.

"No, we camped at the head of Indian Creek and came down Indian Creek this morning," he replied. "We've been hiking the Continental Divide Trail."

I was impressed.

"We started in Glacier National Park, Montana, on the Canadian border on June fifteenth," he continued. "Now we only have the last two hundred miles to go to Mexico."

"That's, like, *five straight months of hiking*!" I marveled.

"So you started hiking at one foreign country," Skyler asked with amazement, "and now you're hiking all the way to another foreign country?"

"Yes, that's right."

"How far do you go in a day?" I asked.

"Twenty to twenty-five miles," he replied. "Now it's a little farther because sometimes the trail follows roads. Even at that pace, you can barely make the length of the Continental Divide Trail in one season. You can't start any earlier than June fifteenth because of the snow up in Montana. And then you have to keep moving south to stay ahead of winter. We got out of Colorado just in time. It was starting to snow in the high country."

He started making a move toward the creek, as if eager to keep moving. Amy was chatting with the woman about the equipment they carried and the high-tech, lightweight, accordionlike sleeping pads strapped to their packs.

"It's a little thin," she confessed to Amy.

The man made another move toward the creek. They were trying to get to the hot springs for a soak this afternoon, and then camp farther down the canyon where Little Bear Creek joined it. This meant that they'd be hiking in the next *four hours* what it took us *two days* to cover, plus squeeze in a quick soak in the hot springs. Yes, they were moving *fast*. The entire Continental Divide Trail covers 3,100 miles. The trail's existence was, in many ways, due to Aldo Leopold and his efforts on behalf of wilderness preservation. This couple would, in a single day, hike across most of the Gila Wilderness. It felt like they were in a race. I wondered whether the raw need to make mileage had obliterated the psychic rewards of wilderness.

"You have fifteen crossings to the hot springs," I told the man, "and another fifteen to Little Bear Creek."

They looked chilled already, after the twenty-six crossings they'd already done today. That would total fifty-six in one day. There wasn't any insulating fat on their sinewy bodies. Now I understood why the man wore the knee-high snow gaiters—for warmth in the chilly water. Clearly impatient to get going, he waded onward into the creek. She followed.

"Goodbye," we called out. "Good luck."

We watched them splash across, quickly mount the stone-cobbled far bank with ski poles clicking, and disappear into the shady forest under the cliff wall. There was something obsessive about it. You either had to be obsessive to start, or certainly had to be obsessive to finish, a hike so long, so quickly.

"I wonder if they'll still be together at the end of this hike," Amy mused as they vanished down the canyon.

CORONADO'S OBSESSIVENESS propelled him forward, too—toward a psychological breaking point. He returned to the Pueblo villages along the Rio Grande to spend the winter of 1541–42. In the spring, he planned to head eastward again, to chase down stories of rich cities even farther off and reports from the Indians of a broad river plied by huge canoes.

These rumors weren't entirely false. Archaeologists have noted that ancient peoples occupied large settlements along the Mississippi River. The Cahokia Mounds site in southern Illinois, which, at its peak around A.D. 1250 was larger than London at the time, covered six square miles and housed a population of 10,000 to 20,000 people. The settlement included monumental earthworks and giant sun calendars. On the Mississippi River, as the rumors reaching Coronado had suggested, the Indians traveled in huge canoes powered by dozens of paddlers.

But it wasn't to be. It was a tough winter for the Spaniards. They had missed the comforts of New Spain for almost two years. It was cold in the Pueblo village they'd appropriated along the Rio Grande, about 120 miles northeast of where we were hiking. They lacked warm clothing. They pulled apart the adobe houses and used their wooden posts and beams for firewood, and dug up the buried Indian containers of corn. The Pueblo Indians were hostile toward them, if not quite outright at war. Coronado received a letter, delivered by reinforcements coming up from Mexico, from his wife, whom he missed deeply or, as some may have speculated, suspected of having affairs in his absence. Another letter arrived addressed to one of Coronado's closest officers, Don García López de Cárdenas, informing him that his brother had died and he was now heir to the family estates back in Spain. Coronado granted him permission to go home, especially in light of his broken arm, which wouldn't heal.

That winter, too, during a feast day, Coronado was out racing his powerful horse, which he liked to do for his amusement, against Don Rodrigo Maldonado, when the girth broke. Captain General Coronado tumbled to the ground between the two horses and was run over by Maldonado's horse. Its hoof struck him in the head.

"[This] laid him at the point of death," wrote Castañeda, who was in the encampment that winter, "and his recovery was slow and painful."

When Coronado finally was well enough to get up from his bed, he discovered that his close officer López de Cárdenas had returned. He bore the terrible news that the way back to Mexico was blocked. He had reached the Spaniards' supply base at Suya, near today's southern Arizona border. He found it in ruins, smoldering and deserted, and the Indians in the whole region in rebellion against the Spanish. He retreated back to Coronado's winter camp. Turning up months later, Spanish survivors described how their leader at the outpost, a man named Alcaraz, forced sex with Indian women and stole Indian provisions. One night the Indians crept silently into the Spanish pueblo and attacked with their poison-tipped arrows, killing between thirty and sixty Spaniards and many of their fearsome horses.

Coronado heard the news in his winter camp and took to his bed again.

You can imagine him, lying there, in the adobe room of a Pueblo village along the frozen Rio Grande. The winter wind blows. There is little wood to burn for warmth. Everyone is beset by fleas. His army is scattered about the Tierra Nueva—the New Land. His supply base, he has just learned, has been burned and its soldiers killed. With all the fanfare that had attended the expedition's departure from Mexico, he has nothing to show for two years of hard effort at attaining glory and wealth and the Seven Cities of Gold to add to the empire of the king of Spain but loss and humiliation and a few stolen buffalo robes, his quest dashed by a small collection of straw huts five hundred miles out on the Plains.

It's no wonder he took to bed. Where could he possibly go from here but toward deeper humiliation?

There was still talk of returning to Quivira and the rumored settlements and broad river farther east. But then, reports Castañeda, perhaps with a bit of cattiness and contempt, Captain General Coronado, lying in his bedchamber in the adobe pueblo, recalled a prophecy given to him by an astrologer friend back in Salamanca.

" . . . that he would become a powerful lord in distant lands, and that he would have a fall from which he would never be able to recover."

This plunged Coronado deeper into depression. If he were to die, which it appeared he might, he wanted to be with his wife and children when it happened, writes Castañeda.

Some of Coronado's officers and soldiers, however, hungered to carry on the search for the rumored gold and the fabulous cities. Coronado undermined them through subterfuge, according to Castañeda. Using his gossipy physician as intermediary, he reached out to several of the expedition's "gentlemen" who agreed with him about returning to Mexico, and had these gentlemen talk in small groups among the soldiers, who then signed petitions, which were also signed by officers, to Coronado requesting that the army head back. The main argument for returning was that they had found neither gold nor settlements large enough to provide Indians as forced laborers for all the members of the expedition. Signatures obtained, Coronado immediately announced the expedition would return home. Many of the men recanted, and wanted to stay and keep the search alive with a core group of sixty. They broke into Coronado's bedchamber and stole his locked chest to get the signed papers back, but Coronado, reports Castañeda, had stuffed the documents into his mattress for hiding.

"He guarded them so that he did not leave one room, pretending that his ailment was much worse and posting guards over himself and the room, and at night on the roofs where he was sleeping."

Coronado's army turned south toward Mexico, leaving behind a few of the friars, who weren't under his command and who hoped to convert the Indians to Christianity or be martyred (they were soon murdered). The captain general was happy, although respect for his authority sank on the homeward journey, and the army had to work its way through rebellious Indian regions. Horses died. At times during the journey home, two or three men perished each day by either sickness or poisoning—no one really knew why. When they finally reached the first outposts of New Spain—Mexico—the men began to drop out. The captain general's authority was all but disregarded. He took to his bed again, pretending to be sick, according to Castañeda, so he could hold conversations in secret and try to convince his officers and gentlemen to stay with the expedition until it reached Mexico City. He was carried part of the way on a litter.

Captain General Coronado arrived in Mexico City in the summer of 1542. Less than one hundred men from the original grand expedition still accompanied him. It was an ignominious return. Viceroy Mendoza met the captain general—not graciously, reports Castañeda, but he nevertheless gave him an honorable discharge.

"From then on," states Castañeda flatly, "he lost his reputation."

Viceroy Mendoza, who had been Coronado's friend and ally, must have tried to move delicately. The viceroy eventually took over for himself the governorship of Nueva Galicia, the northwest part of Mexico, which Coronado had held. Coronado went bankrupt from debts he'd run up mounting the expedition. In its aftermath, he was subject to an investigation into whether he mistreated the Indians. He was cleared and abuses against the Indians—of which there were clearly many, in direct violation of edicts from the king and queen of Spain—were blamed on Coronado's soldiers, not the captain general.

Coronado did retain a seat on the Mexico City council, thanks to his friendship with Viceroy Mendoza. There he remained, in Mexico City, a gentlemen still, until his death in 1554. You can imagine him, an aging council member, who led a once-great expedition into the Tierra Nueva—the Unknown Lands of the North. Parents must have pointed him out on the street to their children. They must have told the story. He went away in a great parade of hundreds of eager gentlemen soldiers and powerful horses and wearing a suit of golden armor with a feathery plume en route to discover the Seven Cities of Gold, went away on a mission from the king himself, and he returned, two years later, exhausted, trailed by only a few stragglers who didn't really obey him anyway, having found not heaps of gold and fabulous cities in the Unknown Lands but a place where nothing exists but grass and sky, having found . . . Kansas.

There was a lesson to be learned.

WHILE SITTING ON THE SUMMERY PORCH of his parents' home overlooking the Mississippi River recuperating in 1913, Aldo Leopold read the just-published *Our Vanishing Wildlife* by William Temple Hornaday. Director of the New York Zoological Society, Hornaday sounded the alarm about the rapid depletion of U.S. wildlife. Deer, ducks, elk, and other species prized by hunters were being wiped out by market gunners. The 60 million or so buffalo that had grazed the Great Plains in Coronado's day had shrunk, by 1913 when Leopold was reading Hornaday's book, to a few hundred scattered animals. The following year, the last known passenger pigeon of hundreds of millions would die at the Cincinnati Zoo.

"For educated, civilized Man to exterminate a valuable wild species of living things is a crime," wrote Hornaday. "It is a crime against his own children, and posterity."

Firing up to the cause, Leopold resolved to take on the mission to save southwestern game species, melding with a growing national concern about game protection, and his own deep passion for hunting.

During his seventeen-month recuperation in Iowa, he crafted a plan to establish game reserves on national forest lands. A Washington bureaucrat shot it down. Back in New Mexico, his sympathetic boss, Arthur Ringland, created a position for Leopold as a public-relations officer to promote the new activity of "tourism" and "recreation" on National Forest lands that had formerly been used mainly for commercial timber harvest and grazing. Leopold ran with the job, organizing game-protection groups in New Mexico, giving talks, writing for the Forest Service its first *Game and Fish Handbook.*

Wrote Teddy Roosevelt in a letter to Leopold, with characteristic gusto, "I think your platform simply capital. It seems your association in New Mexico is setting an example to the whole country."

Nor did his energy and eloquence go unnoticed among Forest Service higher-ups in Washington, who offered him a job in public relations in the nation's capital. Leopold declined it.

"I do not know whether I have twenty days or twenty years ahead of me," he wrote to Arthur Ringland. "Whatever time I have, I wish to accomplish something definite . . . This 'one thing' for me is obviously game protection."

The coming of the Great War, with its need for timber and beef for the troops, severely strained the cause of game protection on the national forest lands. After a brief stint at the Albuquerque chamber of commerce—where he came to descry "boosterism"—Leopold rejoined the Forest Service after the war as second-in-command for all 20 million acres of National Forests in the Southwest.

He was shocked by what he saw. When he personally toured the forests, he observed how overgrazing and destructive logging had triggered massive erosion. Roughly ten years earlier, when he'd first arrived in the Southwest, he had ridden through the Blue River country of the Apache Forest. A mere decade later 90 percent of the arable soil along the Blue had washed away or blown away because of overgrazing of the grasses and overcutting of timber.

"One day," he wrote to his mother back in Iowa, as he did regularly throughout her life, "we came home with cakes of mud a quarter of an inch thick surrounding our eyes—stuff that had blown into our eyes and 'teared' out so you had to pull off the lumps every few minutes."

Leopold's focus began to shift—from single-minded game protection and the elimination of game-killing predators like wolves, it broadened to include the condition of the soil, and thus of the land itself. He wrote passionately about the soil, and how earlier peoples of the Southwest had managed to use it for centuries without destroying it, until the settlers of the last few decades:

> Destruction of the soil is the most fundamental kind of economic loss which the human race can suffer. With enough time and money, a neglected farm can be put back on its feet—if the soil is there. By expensive replanting and with a generation or two of waiting, a ruined forest can again be made productive—if the soil is there. . . . But if the soil is gone, the loss is absolute and irrevocable.

WHEN WE GOT BACK on the trail after the lizardlike lunch on the sun-warmed log, Molly and Skyler marveled at the number of crossings ahead for us to reach the Meadows—twenty-six, the couple had reported.

"The map said it was, like, fifteen," said Skyler, "and today we'll cross the river forty-one times."

But the crossings came quickly. It was pleasant hiking in the sunny canyon and shady forest. I'd chosen walking sticks for Molly and Skyler from a pile of driftwood branches near our lunch log. Skyler used his with great determination, swinging it along the trail, going out front to measure the depth of the river crossings with it, and giving us a report. If it was deep, he hurled his walking stick like a spear to the far bank so he could free both hands to hike up his shorts to his hips.

We sang the beer-bottle song—once, which was enough. I realized why the infantry sings as it marches—to occupy the mind, to bond the marchers in rhythm, and thus in a single body. A corps.

We chatted amiably, the four of us, about the sycamores and oaks. In the deepest, most twisty bends of the canyon, we admired the forests of the Elf-Kings that we crept through.

Finally, an hour before dusk, as the crack of clear blue sky deepened toward a shade of purple, the canyon's high rock walls meandered apart from each other. Between the tawny cliffs lay a wide meadow, through which the river ran. Open groves of Ponderosa pines studded the meadow, rising like giant columns.

It was a perfect camping spot.

Then, under the perfect grove, we spotted two tents, sitting side by side.

Shit! I thought.

I knew Amy was thinking the same.

There's a palpable tension—almost a ritual—to finding a camping spot in the wilderness, one that I feel quite intensely and have since my first wilderness trips as a child. I've wondered if this tension is genetically coded, recalling our hundreds of thousands of years as a species of nomadic hunter-gatherers. The right—or wrong—choice of a camping site could mean security, or encounters with predators or enemies, it could bring abundant food or starvation, water or thirst, warmth or debilitating cold. The two tents sitting off there in the perfect grove could signify friends or rivals. In any case, we felt they were crowding "our" space in the wilderness—and they probably felt the same to see us coming down the trail.

"Look! More humans!" a woman's voice called out.

It was a surprise, for all parties, to see anyone after the silence of the canyons.

A middle-aged man bearing a droopy, graying handlebar mustache rose from where he was stooping over, staking down one of the tents. Near him stood a middle-aged woman, dark-haired and fit-looking, and a blond teenage girl lingered off in the grove, perhaps gathering firewood. I noted instantly that the couple wore the same style of high-tech synthetic clothing we did—pile jackets, breathable waterproof fabrics—as if this signified they belonged to our own tribe.

A subtle unspoken dance began about what distance we'd maintain between our two parties and our campsites.

"Hike! . . . Hike! . . . Hike!" the woman sang, cheering on Molly and Skyler in their strides as we came down the trail past their camp.

We paused for a moment. We asked if they knew where the trail forked ahead. They hadn't been there.

"But another fellow told us there's another nice campsite a little ways on, under a big dead snag," said the man. "You can't miss it."

"If you can't find a spot to camp," the woman added, "you can come back here."

We thanked her, and kept hiking. It was a generous gesture on her part, a family willing to give up the solitude they'd presumably come for, in order to give us a space should we need it. We belonged to the same tribe—distantly related.

A half-mile on or less, we looked across a meadow of tall grass and spotted the big dead ponderosa. Beyond it the Gila wove between willowy banks, and the cliff wall of the canyon rose beyond that. Four or five towering ponderosas created a vaulted cathedral ceiling of pine and beneath it lay an old fire ring assembled of char-blackened stones. It was a beautiful place to camp. What's odd is how there is a kind of universal agreement on what constitutes a beautiful campsite, which makes me think it is indeed a genetic impulse. I felt tucked in, secure in this spot—the meadow afforded a view, visibility for anyone approaching, the ponderosas gave shelter and wood, the cliff wall a kind of security at our backs, and the Gila coursing past offered a source of water, and, if I wished, a place to gather fish.

Soon we were sitting on logs and on the pine-needle-matted ground around a popping fire of fragrant pine logs, the children sipping hot mint tea and Amy and I mojitos made with a squeeze of lemon, rum, sugar, and the crushed bunch of mint I had plucked from the bank when we left our morning's camp.

IN THE LATE SUMMER of 1919, Aldo Leopold took a Sunday off and went trout fishing. For his outing, he chose an area at the headwaters of the Gila River. He had a family connection here. Estella's mother, a member of an old New Mexico family, had inherited a large sheep outfit, the N-Bar Ranch, whose grazing lands included parts of the Gila National Forest and its Gila River headwaters.

While fishing, Leopold admired the lack of telephone poles and automobile roads in the area. It got him thinking: Was there a way to preserve the pristine quality of the Gila River canyons before the inevitable roads and human structures invaded them?

The timing was crucial. The automobile had become a practical means of transportation in the decade since he'd first come to the

Southwest from Yale. The year before he'd arrived, in 1908, Henry Ford had introduced the first affordable and mass-produced automobile, the Model T—"the car that put America on wheels." What had recently been "horse country"—accessible only on foot or by horse—was just a decade later opening up to the average citizen's automobile. The federal government, meanwhile, was encouraging the settlement of unused lands in the West. Leopold had witnessed how a few years of heavy grazing and logging had wiped out the Blue River bottomlands, reducing its once-rich grasses, soils, and pine groves to a wide bed of stony cobbles washed by flash floods.

One option was to designate pristine wild areas on federal lands as national parks, such as Yellowstone or Yosemite. But Leopold had observed firsthand what national-park status brought to the South Rim of the Grand Canyon—glaring electric signs, ticky-tacky hotels, hawkers of tourist geegaws, rotting piles of garbage, and rivulets of raw sewage.

"To cherish we must see and fondle," he later wrote about the mass tourism encouraged by national parks with their roads and hotels, "and when enough have seen and fondled, there is no wilderness left to cherish."

About three months after that wonderful Sunday of trout fishing in the roadless, telephone-poleless solitude of the Gila headwaters, Leopold attended a meeting of foresters in Salt Lake City. It was here he first heard about an oddball young forester in Colorado whom colleagues called the "Beauty Engineer." His real name was Arthur Carhart—the first landscape architect hired by the U.S. Forest Service. He had recently made the blasphemous proposal that a pristine wild lake, Trapper Lake in Colorado's White River National Forest, be preserved just as it is, without roads, cottages, or other "improvements."

Leopold went out of his way to meet Carhart in Colorado, where, in their enthusiastic talk, each inspired the other to the wildlands cause and took their case to Forest Service higher-ups, Carhart arguing for the natural beauty of these pristine areas, and Leopold for their usefulness as recreation. The great boulder that lay in their path was the "wise use" dictum set down by the original head of the Forest Service, Gifford Pinchot. (This was the man whom John Muir, twenty years before, had told off in a Seattle hotel lobby over the issue of sheep-grazing on federal lands, with the rebuke, "I don't want anything more to do with you.") Under the Pinchot philosophy, the National Forests were being managed for the "highest use" and "wise use," which meant, first of all, a steady supply of harvested timber and grazing lands.

Leopold's first shove at removing that boulder came in a 1921 article in the *Journal of Forestry,* in which he argued that preservation of their wilderness qualities ranked as the "highest use" for certain pristine national forest lands. Instead of invoking John Muir's lofty temples of the spirit, Leopold cast his argument for the wilderness in hard, practical, even economic, terms: It provided a certain type of recreation unavailable anywhere else, and in ever-shorter supply, especially since the arrival of the Model T and mass tourism.

"Sporting magazines are groping toward some logical reconciliation between getting back to nature and preserving a little nature to get back to," he wrote. "Lamentations over this or that favorite vacation ground being 'spoiled by tourists' are becoming more and more frequent."

He argued for a large expanse of pristine wildland in order to pursue certain types of recreation, like hunting and fishing. Here he laid out his original definition of wilderness: "[A] continuous stretch of country preserved in its natural state, open to lawful hunting and fishing, big enough to absorb a two weeks' pack trip, and kept devoid of roads, artificial trails, cottages, or other works of man."

Leopold now proposed the first wilderness area: nearly a million acres among the canyons at the headwaters of the Gila River in New Mexico.

"It will be much easier and cheaper to preserve, by forethought," he wrote, "than to create it after it is gone."

"STOP LAUGHING, you're waking me up," called Skyler sleepily from the next tent.

It was 6:30 a.m. It was still dark, and the temperature hovering around twenty degrees. Amy and I were lying inside our warm sleeping bags, joking laconically about the difficulty—the glaring lack of immediate reward—of getting out of bed. Awaiting us was an early-morning wade across the frigid river. This would be followed by a hard nine miles of hiking.

"That's what we're trying to do," I called back to Skyler, as we laughed even harder, "wake you up!"

We aimed to hike to the Gila Cliff Dwellings this day. This would entail climbing out of the Gila River's Middle Fork canyon, hiking over a mountain ridge, dropping into the Gila's West Fork canyon, and following it downstream until we reached the Cliff Dwellings, at the wilderness edge. We'd have to arrive by four p.m., when they officially closed the site for the day. This meant an early start and an all-day, fast pace.

By seven o'clock I'd managed to drag myself out of the tent. Amy remained inside and stuffed our bags and rolled our pads. I fired up the stove, brewed hot chocolate and tea, and distributed them to the tents, along with a frozen granola bar for everyone to gnaw on. Molly eventually crawled out, began packing her backpack. She picked up one of her nurse's shoes from where we'd set them near the fire to dry the previous night.

"Look at this! It's frozen solid!"

The fake white leather and foam insole had, spongelike, absorbed so much water during the previous day's river crossings that the entire shoe had literally frozen to a block of white ice. The shoelaces sprung out rigidly in all directions like pieces of frozen white spaghetti.

Amy's shoes and laces were just as frozen, as were Skyler's. With my Velcro straps and porous fabric, my uppers were slightly more flexible, but the insoles were as stiff as iced oak boards. The heavy, hard nurse's shoes fascinated Skyler, who started throwing them around like rocks. He hurled one of the nurse's shoes at a ponderosa tree where he and Molly had propped their walking sticks. The nurse's shoe hit Molly's stick, shattering it into multiple pieces.

"Did you see *that!?*" he marveled.

The previous evening around the campfire, Molly had very conscientiously calculated that we needed to leave camp by 8:30 a.m. to make the Cliff Dwellings before 4:00 p.m. This was after she'd figured out that, so far in our hike through the canyon, we'd averaged about 0.75 miles per hour. We left at nine. Just beyond camp, we came to a trail junction and took the branch that led southward out of the canyon. We'd hiked only a hundred yards or so before the trail came to a crossing of the Gila.

This crossing looked no different from the last fifty-odd crossings we'd already made, except for the fact that, after the frigid night, the water was way, way colder and our river shoes frozen solid.

Amy and Skyler opted to wade barefoot across the slippery, rounded stones of the bottom.

"Will someone please give me a piggyback across?" Molly asked sweetly.

I thought about it for a moment and looked across. I had the better shoes. She wasn't *that* heavy, and it wasn't *that* far.

I removed my hiking boots and dry socks, strapped them to my pack, and—as my river socks were frozen solid—jammed my bare feet into my cheap, frozen river shoes. It was excruciating. It felt like standing barefoot on a frozen lake, and then having knobbly, frozen washcloths duct-taped around the upper part of my feet. It was then I realized I'd have to make *five* crossings of the river—the first one carrying my pack, going back to lug Molly piggyback, and then going back for *her* pack.

I plunged in with my pack on, grunting at the cold and effort, scrambled across, dumped my pack, splashed back for Molly.

"Get on! Get on!" I shouted.

I sensed the nerves numbing in my feet, so they felt like they were two more frozen stones grinding over the frozen stones of the bottom. I began stumbling.

She leaped on my back. She had experience as a ballet dancer and knew how to hold herself in a partner's lift. Her 125 pounds on my back didn't seem any more burdensome, and felt even more balanced, than my own pack.

I dumped her on the far bank, scrambled back for her pack, stumbled back across, now tripping over the stones on the bottom. Reaching the dry bank, I threw myself to the ground and ripped off the Chinese ice shoes. There Skyler and Amy and I sat, among the white-frosted bushes on the frosted-grass riverbank in a little patch of sunlight that had finally slipped over the high canyon rim, rubbing our feet as the vapor rose from our wet, white skin into the chill canyon air.

I hadn't felt this intensity of physical discomfort for quite a long time. It had also been quite a while since Amy and I'd had such a good laugh while lazing in bed.

This, surely, was exactly what Aldo Leopold had in mind when he talked about the recreational benefits of wilderness.

Y OU WONDER IF A DEAL was struck. Leopold's highest boss, U.S. Forest Service chief William Greeley, wanted Leopold elsewhere—not the Southwest. In particular, he wanted him to move to Madison, Wisconsin, to head the Forest Products Laboratory. Leopold didn't want to go. He loved the Southwest, and his wife, Estella, was deeply committed to her family and its long history in New Mexico.

It wasn't the first time he'd been asked to move. There had been complaints, at least at the beginning, of his work as second-in-command of the southwestern forests—that he was too sure of himself, untactful with his staff, and not grounded enough in management details. His immediate boss, Frank Pooler, head of the Southwest Region, had proposed a transfer of Leopold to the Northern Region. Leopold wouldn't go.

"There is an extraordinary amount of ability and originality stored up in this man," Frank Pooler reported back to headquarters in Washington, D.C. "The FS can hardly afford to lose it. It will be my business to try to draw it out and get it properly applied."

Leopold hung on, managing the southwestern forests under Frank Pooler. At the same time, he spent five years observing, detailing, taking minute note of the natural processes—forest fire history, soil erosion, grazing impacts, shifting game populations—at work in these forests. The erosion problem especially puzzled him—what caused it, and caused it so profoundly? And he thought hard about how to save the wilderness qualities that remained.

When he finally agreed to the Madison job up north, one wonders if some quid pro quo had been reached between Leopold and his Forest Service higher-ups. A mere five days after leaving his southwestern post, in May 1924, his former boss, Frank Pooler, finally approved Leopold's plan for 755,000 acres to be preserved as a special category, "wilderness," on the Gila National Forest in the Gila headwater canyons. There hadn't been anything like it before. This was the nation's first designated wilderness on Forest Service land.

Beyond his bureaucratic maneuvering, Leopold stretched intellectually in these early years of the 1920s, making his first attempt at melding his tight scientific observations about the forest with an ethical, and even spiritual, foundation. He read the work of the Russian philosopher, mathematician, and mystic P. D. Ouspensky, a disciple of Gurdjieff, who postulated that the entire earth constituted a single living organism. Wrote Leopold in a 1923 essay, circulated among his colleagues but never published during his lifetime:

> Possibly in our intuitive perceptions, which, may be truer than our science and less impeded by words than our philosophies, we realize the indivisibility of the earth—its soil, mountains, rivers, forests, climate, plants, and animals, and respond to it collectively not only as a useful servant but as a living being.

And, in this same probing though unpublished essay titled "Some Fundamentals of Conservation in the Southwest," he touched implicitly on the Old Testament belief that God gave to man dominion over the earth and its creatures. Leopold asked whether, in turn, humans had a moral obligation to care for the land.

> If there be, indeed, a special nobility inherent in the human race—a special cosmic value, distinctive from and superior to all other life— by what token shall it be manifest? By a society decently respectful of its own and all other life, capable of inhabiting the earth without defiling it? Or by a society like that of John Burroughs' potato bug, which exterminated the potato, and thereby exterminated itself?

It was fortunate that, by sheer happenstance, much of Leopold's work occurred in the Southwest—one of North America's baldest landscapes. Drought never lay far away. Soils were fragile and vegetation cover thin. Unlike wetter climates with richer soils, say, around Walden Pond, it took little to disrupt this landscape, and once disrupted, a long time to repair it. It was very hard to ignore the damage when an entire rich bottomland washed away into an expanse of stony rubble, such as happened along the Blue River.

The question plagued Leopold. Why were these landscapes eroding? Exactly what caused it all of a sudden and so dramatically?

His Forest Service colleagues largely dismissed erosion as the natural process of mountains wearing down. But Leopold began to suspect a far more complex interaction, one that turned on naturally occurring forest fires and grass fires—or lack of them—and overgrazing by cattle, and vegetation changes.

Leopold targeted the erosion at Sapillo Creek in the Gila Forest, about twenty miles south of where we started our hike.

"A century of fires without grazing did not spoil the Sapello, but a decade of grazing without fires ruined it."

His theory, in simple terms, ran like this. Leopold studied old tree trunks and saw char marks in the still living trees from many decades ago. He realized that, over the centuries, fires—set by either lightning or native hunters—regularly burned these southwestern grasslands and forestlands, clearing out the forests but letting many trees survive. When European settlers moved cattle onto the grasslands, and the Forest Service took over management of the forests around 1900, they stamped out all the fires they could, believing that fires destroyed valuable resources—timber and grass. In fact, Leopold theorized, fires had done just the opposite. They had exerted a beneficial effect on the landscape by keeping them clear of dense brush. But now brush had taken over. In the heavy downpours it couldn't hold soil as well as grass. The invasion of brush, combined with overgrazing of grass by the settlers' cattle, triggered the massive erosion trenches and swept-away bottomlands that he'd witnessed. Likewise, the lack of regular, low-intensity fires allowed dense thickets of yellow pine to spring up on mountainsides that before had supported trees more widely spaced. When these pine thickets finally did catch fire, they roared into major conflagrations that couldn't be stopped.

The erosion problem in the Southwest represented to Aldo Leopold, in some ways, what the Galápagos Islands did to Darwin— a baseline for an understanding of the natural world. He'd observed it closely over years. He understood its complexity. It allowed him to draw conclusions about the larger natural world at a pivotal moment when scientists were reconceptualizing the larger natural world.

The term *ecology* had been coined back in 1860 by the German zoologist Ernst Haeckel, from *oikos*—Greek for "home"—and *logos,* or knowledge, referring to the interrelationship between an animal species and its home range, or "home knowledge." In the 1920s the study of these relationships blossomed. In 1920 a German freshwater biologist, August Thienemann, realized that, in lakes, food energy passes up through various "levels" of plant species, then up to levels of animal species.

A year later, in 1921, a young Oxford undergraduate in zoology,

Charles Elton, tagged along on Julian Huxley's expedition to the Arctic archipelago of Spitsbergen and studied its animal populations over the next several years. As the Southwest did for Leopold, the baldness of the Arctic landscape threw into dramatic relief the interaction among species, their environment, and their food sources. In 1927, at the age of only twenty-seven, Elton published his landmark work, *Animal Ecology*, in which he developed the concept of "food chains," "ecological niches," and "pyramids of numbers." Three years later he postulated, provocatively, that all natural systems, instead of being static and fixed, were dynamic and ever-changing.

"The balance of nature," Elton wrote, "does not exist and perhaps never has existed."

You might compare this new perspective brought by Elton and others to looking at a painting—a Rembrandt, say. Instead of seeing only the power and beauty of the Rembrandt itself, you understand why Rembrandt chose that particular subject, how his style was shaped by several centuries of Western painters before him and by all that was going on around him in the Amsterdam of 1650—his patrons, his religion, his society, his health, his bankruptcy—and how his painting in turn shaped other painters, and even influenced the social climate of his time.

In 1935, another British scientist, Arthur Tansley, put a name to any given sphere where all this mingling occurred—this interrelationship of various species of plants and animals, soil and climate, food energy and ecological niches.

He called it an "ecosystem." Today, the study of ecosystems is what we know as "ecology."

Aldo Leopold absorbed these ideas introduced by Elton (whom he befriended in 1931 at a biological conference) and Tansley and other ecologists. The difference was, Leopold continually struggled to reach beyond ecological science's moral neutrality. What Aldo Leopold sought was an *ethical* dimension to ecology. He strived for some kind of moral guidance to direct the human relationship with the land.

AFTER THE FRIGID, early-morning river crossing, we put on our dry socks and hiking boots in the little patch of frosty sunlight, hefted our backpacks, and started up from the canyon bottom to its rim—1,140 vertical feet overhead. The trail switchbacked up through a notch in the canyon wall, up steep slopes of open ponderosa pines. I noticed that, sometime in the last few years, a forest fire had rushed up these steep slopes in a V starting from the Meadows below. It had cleared out the underbrush, opened the forest, charred to black the thick bark of the ponderosas, which are adapted to withstand these kinds of low-intensity fires. I wondered what had ignited it. A runaway campfire? A "prescribed" burning? Lightning? It looked healthier than the cluttered, overly thick unburned forest.

"My feet are finally warm," Amy said after half a mile of climbing through the shady forest.

We stripped off a layer of clothing, hats, and gloves, and kept going.

After an hour, the river looked very small and winding, and the Meadows a small open patch way down among the maze of cliffs. In an hour and a quarter we topped out, on a broad ridgetop in sun-and-shade glades of piñon pine and juniper. We dropped our packs, wolfed down trail mix, and sucked water from our bottles. After five minutes' rest, we kept going. We were determined to reach the Gila Cliff Dwellings before they closed.

The trail ran along the broad ridgetop, up and down through small draws and sandy washes in the sun-striped forest where we saw the tracks of deer. We sang the beer song—once—led by Skyler. It lasted us for about a third of a mile of entertainment. We calculated that, starting at a thousand bottles on the wall, we'd taken the inventory down to six hundred in the course of our hike.

"I'm kind of sick of 'Bottles of Beer on the Wall,' " Skyler said.

We kept going. By 12:30, still hiking along the ridgetop, we were hot and tired.

"When can we stop?" asked Skyler.

"Let's go a little farther," I replied. "Let's get to where the trail starts to drop down into the West Fork canyon."

By 1:15, I could see he was losing it, and the trail still wasn't dropping.

"I'm really hungry," he complained, for the first time on the trip.

"Okay, the next good place you see to stop, let's stop."

He walked about fifty yards.

"Here," he said, and dropped his pack and walking stick in the shade of a little grove of junipers.

It always felt as if I were training a dog, dangling out some little reward, some immediate goal, some distraction or entertainment, to keep
everybody—and especially a ten-year-old boy—moving down the trail.
For twenty minutes we sprawled on the soft, dry ground under the
shade of the junipers and ate, hungrily, spicy tuna and peanut butter on
tortillas. We poured down water. Our canteens were almost empty, although we'd started the morning with them full, and our food bags
limp, our packs noticeably lighter.

"We'd better go," I said.

Like a hard-run dog after a half-hour's rest, Skyler bounced back.

"I was hurting there for a while," he said. "But I'm fine now."

And so we hefted our packs, and kept going.

STARTING IN THE EARLY 1930S, Leopold pointed out big choices
facing American consumer culture. His favorite metaphor for con-
sumerism was "the Ford"—and by implication the roads it created into
the few remaining wild places.

"But what is the good life? . . . Man cannot live by bread, or Fords,
alone."

So he asked in the introduction to his 1933 book, *Game Management.* He concluded the volume on an even stronger note:

> In short, twenty centuries of "progress" have brought the average cit-
> izen a vote, a national anthem, a Ford, a bank account, and a high
> opinion of himself, but not the capacity to live in high density with-
> out befouling and denuding his environment, nor a conviction that
> such capacity . . . is the true test of whether he is civilized.

Frustrated with the administrative work, he'd by then quit his job
at the Forest Products Lab. He struck out on his own as a forestry con-
sultant, conducting game surveys for hunters' groups, writing his book,
and barely scraping by during the Depression with a wife and five children to support, his income supplemented by dividends from the
Leopold Desk Co.

Still a classic in the field today, *Game Management* was far more
practical than philosophical.

"[G]ame can be restored," he wrote, "by the creative use of the same tools which have heretofore destroyed it—axe, plow, cow, fire, and gun."

It helped convince the University of Wisconsin to establish a professorship in game management—the first of its kind anywhere—and to choose Aldo Leopold to fill it.

The new job as a professor, which he began in 1933 right after the book's publication, allowed Leopold the intellectual freedom to roam in ways as never before under the bureaucracies where he'd spent the first half of his career. The advances in ecology by scientists such as Elton and Tansley had enlarged his perspective. Then three personal events in the mid-1930s conspired to change how he viewed intensive human management of the natural world—which is what he had strongly advocated thus far.

He toured the forests of Germany and—with deep dismay—observed how heavily managed they were. While they produced a good yield of spruce wood and deer, in other respects they were nearly biological deserts—essentially tree farms swept clean of their once-rich variety of flora and fauna. After the German experience, the idea of pure management of the forest for maximum yield of game animals and timber looked a lot less appealing. Leopold began to rethink his former advocacy of killing predators to increase game. Meanwhile, reports had filtered back to him of the Gila Forest and certain other areas of the Southwest where predators had been killed. They had now become utterly overrun by deer.

He addressed the issue after his return from Germany:

> We, Americans, have not yet experienced a bearless, wolfless, eagleless, catless woods. We yearn for more deer and more pines, and we shall probably get them. But do we realize that to get them, as the Germans have, at the expense of their wild environment and their wild enemies, is to get very little indeed?

That same year, the drought year of 1935, while Dust Bowl storms blew away Oklahoma's prairie soil, Leopold and family purchased an abandoned farm along the sandy Wisconsin River bottomlands outside Madison, not far from where John Muir had grown up at Fountain Lake. With its forest cut and soil exhausted, all that remained, besides blowing sand and ruts, was an old chicken coop that the Leopolds happily fixed up and dubbed "The Shack." On their weekend treks to the Shack, Aldo Leopold laid down a Thoreau-like dictum to the family, that they could take along only the "absolute essentials."

He aimed to restore the barren, abused land to its native condition. He soon discovered, however, the difficulties and intricacies of the task. The family planted thousands of trees. Many of them died. They had to decide what species to plant. They had to decide where to plant them. There were constant choices to be made that would have long-term consequences. The choices that the previous owners had made were painfully obvious in the results. The experience brought home to Leopold the profound necessity for an "ethic" to guide how humans treated the land.

But the truly life-changing experience for Leopold during the mid-1930s was a hunting trip in the fall of 1936 to the Rio Gavilan in the Sierra Madre of Mexico. Its pristine, wild quality amazed and delighted him. The river's waters ran clear between uneroded, mossy banks and under overhanging trees, periodic fires had worked healthily through the landscape, and predators like wolves and mountains lions lived—and preyed on—thriving deer herds.

"It was here that I first clearly realized that land is an organism, that all my life I had only seen sick land, whereas here was a biota still in perfect aboriginal health."

THE TRAIL STILL DIDN'T DROP. It had climbed steeply from our camp at the Meadows out of the Gila's Middle Fork canyon. Now we followed it along the high, wooded ridgetop separating the Middle Fork canyon from the canyon of the West Fork. We expected the trail to sheer off the ridge at any moment and drop down into the West Fork, but it stubbornly clung to the heights.

I checked the map. I checked my watch. This would be the only day we could see the Gila Cliff Dwellings, which were in the West Fork canyon, and we needed to arrive by 4:00 p.m. I hated schedules and I hated deadlines, and I especially hated them when in the wilderness—these artificial, iron-claw constraints reaching out from a distant, alien world of cityscapes to grab you. It was hot now, and we were tired, and we'd been going hard since 9:00 a.m. and all needed distraction.

"Let's come up with a new verse about our hike for 'My Favorite Things,' " Amy suggested.

It was her old standby song to lull Molly and Skyler to sleep at night. She'd added extra verses over the years, reciting our family's favorite things. As we traipsed along the ridge's spine, waiting for it to start dropping into the West Fork canyon, we started to call out lines and rhymes to one another.

"What rhymes with *city*?"

"How about *mitty*?"

"What rhymes with *river*?"

"Quiver!"

We worked the composition as we strode along the trail, until we pieced it all together.

> *Art coffeehouses in old Silver City,*
> *Freezing cold mornings, with fingers in mittys,*
> *Climbing tall pine trees, as if I had wings,*
> *These are a few of my favorite things.*
>
> *Hiking gold mountains, with heavy backpacks,*
> *Dropping down canyons, with sore, aching backs,*
> *Happy to find clear, candle-lit springs,*
> *These are a few of my favorite things.*
>
> *Fifty-six crossings of the Gila River,*
> *Cold toes in nurse's shoes, that shiver and quiver,*
> *Yellow oak forests with magic Elf Kings,*
> *These are a few of my favorite things.*
>
> *When the snake bites,*
> *When the cactus stings,*
> *When I'm feeling cold,*
> *I simply remember my favorite things,*
> *And then I don't feel . . . so old!*

As we finished, the trail dipped downward—first gently, then steeply. It switchbacked across a stony, open face that permitted a view.

Yes, there was a canyon below, with shady cliffs opposite. We spotted the yellowy-green tops of cottonwood trees in the cleft below us, in contrast to the darker-green shades of juniper and pine higher up the cliffs. Yes, cottonwoods meant water, which meant the West Fork of the Gila lay directly beneath us.

Soon we bottomed out in the canyon, walked through a patch of cottonwood shade, and out onto a sunny, stony bar, with the river lying just beyond. Here our trail dropping from the rim intersected the larger trail that ran along the West Fork. At the junction, it was odd to see standing there a fit-looking, middle-aged couple, with their day packs and sun hats and hiking shoes, holding a map between them and studying it intently. They looked so . . . touristy. So . . . clean.

By now it was nearly 2:30. An hour and a half left. A carved wooden sign pointed the way downstream. "Gila Cliff Dwellings— 1¾."

We waded the West Fork, this time barefoot, because the water had warmed under the afternoon sun and our feet were hot and sore and no one wanted to take the time to switch to river shoes. Down the trail we hustled. It was going to be close. We talked. We strode silently. We stumbled. We looked ahead for indications of anything that resembled cliff dwellings

After an hour, and another few river crossings, the bottom of the canyon widened into grassy meadows ringed by lower cliffs. Plants that resembled squash grew from the meadow along the trail. I wondered, was this where, centuries ago, the cliff-dwelling peoples might have planted their corn and squash? Were these wild-looking squash plants the modern descendants?

I tried to imagine this enclosed valley seven hundred years ago—its own world, self-contained and secure, surrounded by the tawny cliffs, watered by the clear river full of trout, sustained by the meadow soils that sprouted corn and squash and beans, by the fat mule deer that roamed the forests, by the rabbits, by the delicious, fatty nuts of the piñon pine. It felt like a perfect place to live, seven centuries ago.

It was now 3:45. Fifteen minutes. We splashed across the West Fork one last time, followed the widening trail as it cut through a kind of wall of underbrush, and suddenly emerged . . . in a parking lot.

A small administrative building stood there, surrounded by a shady wooden porch. On the porch stood a tall plastic water cooler and cups, and nearby, a man in a ranger's outfit. I braced myself to be thwarted—the Gila Cliff Dwellings National Monument closed. Government overtime regulations, you know.

I was panting and sweating from the last sprint down the trail. Molly was with me, Amy and Skyler farther back

"Are the cliff dwellings still open?" I breathlessly asked the man in the uniform. "We've been hiking since nine this morning to get here by four."

"Plenty of time, plenty of time," he replied soothingly. "Help yourself to some cool water."

WHAT I REMEMBER MOST distinctly are the corncobs. They were tiny little cobs, dried and brownish, missing their kernels. I knew that the corn plant had first been domesticated in Mexico eight or nine thousand years ago, but I'd never seen examples of that ancient genetic lineage, its cobs much smaller than today's forearm-sized hybrids. Here they lay—scattered about the earthen floor of an ancient room under the cliff, just where the little cobs had been dropped, seven hundred years ago.

I remember the wonderful soft light, too. The opening of the cliff dwelling faced south. The late afternoon sun bounced upward off the rock floor at the entrance and illuminated deep into the entire cavern and its many stone structures. It was shaded from the direct sunlight, and the temperature inside the great hollow of rock held at a perfect coolness. In the midst of winter, we heard, the sun, then lower, entered the cavern directly and warmed it.

From the parking lot—an asphalt island at wilderness's edge connected with faraway Silver City by that twisting, single-lane road—we'd hiked half a mile up a narrow canyon to these high cliff openings.

The Mogollon people had lived here, or rather used it as both a living and ceremonial center. No one knows why they came here, and then why they suddenly disappeared. To the north—where the ancient Anasazi people lived—the population had suddenly soared in the decades after A.D. 1050. Those were the big pueblo villages around Zuñi—what Coronado five centuries later called the Seven Cities or Cíbola. This Gila Canyon, however, was a very remote spot. It was sparsely populated or uninhabited. But suddenly people moved in here in much greater numbers. They built these cliff dwellings, their stone walls still standing, between 1270 and 1290, based on tree-ring dates from the roof timbers. They crafted beautiful pottery with striking black-and-white geometric designs. They ground their corn into meal in still-visible hollows in these boulders at the caverns' mouths. They followed the lunar year with calendars carved beside the grinding hollows—a circle of thirteen cups carved in the rock. Then, just as suddenly, a few decades later, they abandoned the spot, never to live here again.

Had warfare and enemies driven them here, to this remote sanctuary of a valley?

Or had they come to escape drought and overpopulation elsewhere? Much of the Southwest suffered a major drought during those same decades in the late 1200s. Those many large villages to the north simply couldn't sustain themselves—too little water, too little soil, too little food?

People came here and found what they needed. Here they always had the Gila, flowing cold and clear from the high mountains through its deep canyons. Here they had the protected, secluded valley to guard them from enemies. They built irrigation canals and headgates—little dams to control the flow into the canals—to water their fields of corn, bean, squash. When the first known white—a prospector named H. B. Ailman—stumbled across this remote valley in 1878, the headgates were still visible, six hundred years after they'd been built.

What drove these people here, and what drove them away? Why would they abandon this perfect place?

No one—at least no modern researcher—knows with certainty. But the tiny, dried corncobs scattered about the earthen floor under the arching cavern roof seemed a symbol of the answer.

I wondered if they had learned, seven hundred years ago, what we're still learning today. I wondered if they had learned—so very long ago, in this fragile, arid environment, so easily depleted by too many people or too many animals using it too hard—what Aldo Leopold had learned here, too. That the natural world is so intimately interconnected. That you can't change, or exploit, or deplete, or destroy one part of it without affecting the whole.

Not far from this spot, as a young man "full of trigger-itch," Leopold shot wildly into the wolf pack and hit the mother, approaching her in time to see the "fierce green fire" die in her eyes. He described, years later in the essay "Thinking Like a Mountain," just what he'd come to understand since that moment.

> Since then I have lived to see state after state extirpate its wolves. I have watched the face of many a newly wolfless mountain, and seen the south-facing slopes wrinkle with a maze of new deer trails. I have seen every edible bush and seedling browsed, first to anemic desuetude, and then to death. . . .
>
> I now suspect that just as a deer herd lives in mortal fear of its wolves, so does a mountain live in mortal fear of its deer . . .
>
> So also with cows. The cowman who cleans his range of wolves does not realize that he is taking over the wolf's job of trimming the herd to fit the range. He has not learned to think like a mountain. Hence we have dustbowls, and rivers washing the future into the sea.
>
> We all strive for safety, prosperity, comfort, long life, and dullness. The deer strives with his supple legs, the cowman with trap and poison, the statesman with pen, the most of us with machines, votes, and dollars, but it all comes to the same thing: peace in our time. A measure of success in this is all well enough, and perhaps is a requisite to objective thinking, but too much safety seems to yield only danger in the long run. Perhaps this is behind Thoreau's dictum: In wildness is the salvation of the world. Perhaps this is the hidden meaning in the howl of the wolf, long known among mountains, but seldom perceived among men.

No one that I know of, before or since, has expressed so vividly and so gracefully and so succinctly as Leopold does in this passage the complex interrelatedness of the natural world and the all-too-common human ignorance of it. Here, in this passage, lay the seeds for Leopold's final and most powerful rationale to explain the importance of wild places.

EPILOGUE

The Mogollon had carved thirteen moons at the cliff dwellings' entrance. Seventy-five miles due north of this ancient Mogollon lunar calendar sat another kind of celestial observatory: the VLA. Twenty-seven radio telescope dishes, each weighing 230 tons, or about the weight of ten fully loaded semitrailers, were arrayed in a "Y" pattern on the Plains of San Agostin just north of the Gila Wilderness. The "Y" itself was twenty-six miles long, which is how it got the initials VLA—Very Large Array. It listens to the very farthest reaches of the universe.

It took us most of the day to drive there. Starting from Silver City, where we'd supped the night before on an exquisite posthike dinner at a restaurant called Shevek & Co. (Kobe tips, calamari piccata, veal scaloppine, lamb tagine), we looped far to the west and north on deserted Highway 180 to skirt the great roadless heart of the Gila Wilderness and Forest. Big, big empty country greeted us the whole way, rolling grasslands and dry hills, and in the distance on both sides, sometimes near, sometimes far, rose empty, bluish mountains. We were in Catron County—the largest and least populated in New Mexico.

I felt that sense of discovery again—that far beyond the homogeneous nodes and exit ramps and strip malls, lay this other life in America, one tied closely to our national identity, of America as a collection of self-possessed individuals creating an individual destiny in this vast land.

We had a late Sunday lunch at a roadside café in the tiny (population 387) county seat of Reserve, where the green chili stew sprang sweat from my forehead and sent tears rolling down my cheeks. The women at the family table next to ours were dark-haired and wore elegant Sunday dresses. They carried themselves almost aristocratically, as if of old Spanish descent. Their men wore huge silver belt buckles.

Eventually the smaller highway joined U.S. 60 and we swung east, over the top of the big emptiness. A few cars and pickups passed us now. Suddenly the highway spilled out of low hills onto the Plains of San Agostin.

"There it is!" someone said.

The brownish high desert of the plain spread before us about twenty-five miles across. In the distance it finally washed against a breaking wave of scrambled mountains. But strung across that huge flat expanse was a perfectly symmetrical row of what looked like perfect half eggshells, spaced about a mile apart, each one in the row appearing smaller in the distance until they were so tiny and far away they disappeared, as if over the horizon. They pointed expectantly up to the northeast quadrant of the late-afternoon blue sky, all in precisely the same direction with a kind of surreal symmetry, as if they were some kind of alien beings taking orders from somewhere far beyond this world.

We drove a spur road a few miles to a cluster of hangars and headquarters buildings. The place felt deserted. *Twilight Zone* territory. A tame antelope stood passively beside the empty parking lot of the little visitors' center. Inside, we gave ourselves the self-guided tour—a video, the exhibit room. It explained that the VLA, built in the late 1970s by the National Science Foundation and a consortium of universities, is far more powerful than normal optical telescopes because it listens to the broader spectrum of radio waves emitted from distant objects. With the dishes spread out as far as they are across the Plains of San Agostin, it is the equivalent of one giant dish twenty miles across. Here before us stood one of the most powerful listening tools on Earth.

We exited through the rear door and walked down a graveled path several hundred yards to the nearest dish itself. It was beautiful, in its own way, standing there in the last of the low, golden sunlight, this giant, cream-colored, perfect eggshell—as large as a baseball diamond, the exhibit inside had noted—propped high up on its spidery white scaffolding. A soft whirring emitted from electronic components suspended beneath the dish, where supercooled fluids kept their temperature at minus 427 degrees Fahrenheit. Faint radio waves emitted by objects in distant outer space hit the dish's curve and bounced up to the listening device suspended on a kind of tripod projecting from the center of the dish. They were amplified, and then processed in banks of computers in a two-story building a few hundred yards away. It had a balcony and large blank windows that overlooked the site. It looked deserted, too.

They'd chosen this spot on the Plains of San Agostin, a sign explained, because it was so distant from cities and sheltered by mountains from man-made electrical signals. It occurred to me that this was another definition of a blank spot.

Suddenly there was a low hum, startling us.

"Look!" Amy called, pointing up. "It's moving!"

The giant dish was, in fact, shifting, slowly upward and to the right. It moved a few inches, and then it stopped.

We watched it for a minute or two. Then the low hum began again and the dish shifted a few more inches.

I began to figure out what was happening. The dish—all twenty-seven of them across the plain were no doubt moving in unison—was shifting position slightly every few minutes to compensate for the rotation of the earth and the earth's movement around the sun. The dish's movement kept it fixed on whatever distant spot in the universe that particular experiment was exploring.

On the wall of the visitors' center auditorium, I'd seen a poster trumpeting one of the VLA's achievements: "Astronomers Find Enormous Hole in the Universe."

Discovered by scientists at the University of Minnesota using the twenty-seven dishes of the VLA, the hole in the universe measures nearly 1 billion light-years across.

"[It is] empty of normal matter such as stars, galaxies, and gas, and the mysterious, unseen 'dark matter.' "

They'd stumbled on a blank spot, too.

It all made sense, in a strange way. Seventy miles to the south, across the Gila Wilderness, at the Cliff Dwellings cavern, we'd run our fingers over the rock-inscribed thirteen moons of the lunar cycle. Nothing had changed, really. The power and the mystery still lay there—out, out, in the heavens.

It lay here, too, in the big empty spaces. It lay on the great, silent plain, as the last rays of the sun illuminated the line of dishes extending to the mountains on the horizon, all pointing silently upward. It lay in the silence of the wilderness, or in the rush of the river in the canyon, or in the howl of the wolf.

Leopold fought hard to preserve the wilderness. Over the years his stated rationale shifted, or became deeper and more complex. He knew, all along, that there were very good reasons—or rather deep needs—for it. Finally he argued in favor of wilderness on the basis of what we now call biodiversity: that ecosystems are so rich, and so complex, we can't possibly understand them entirely, or presume to manage them, without the danger of losing some of their precious complexity. Some had to remain intact. Otherwise, how would we ever know what these ecosystems were?

In the end, not long before he died in 1948 at the age of sixty-one while fighting a brush fire near the Shack, Leopold had arrived at a simple formulation, an "ethic" that he had strived for his whole life. He managed to phrase it in two short sentences. The concept still guides us today. It is found near the end of his essay "The Land Ethic":

> A thing is right when it tends to preserve the integrity, stability, and beauty of the biotic community. It is wrong when it tends otherwise.

What wilderness does—these blank spots, these empty places—is help us grasp the point that Leopold tried to make his whole life. It tells us to listen, and to observe, and to be patient. It hints at the depth of complexity of the natural world . . . far more complexity and richness than we can know, or even guess.

Most profoundly, it points up our own place within that complexity. Man has long been under the impression he has dominion over the earth. It says so in the Old Testament. For a short time, in a particular place, perhaps he does. But in the long run, and over the entire planet, and certainly beyond it, he doesn't. Not even close.

When you are standing alone in a blank spot you know this intuitively, as in no other place. Whether you are a young Mogollon man on a vision quest, fasting for four days on a lonely mesa top, or in the middle of the Gila Wilderness at the bottom of a canyon listening to the river flow, you know that you don't have dominion. Maybe Coronado learned it out here, too, in the Unknown Lands, and that's what finally caused him to abandon his quest for gold and empire, and turn back, chastened by the endless grass and sky that revealed the sheer vanity of the human enterprise.

Thoreau learned his place well while on Maine's Mount Katahdin amid the cold, blowing clouds and the barren, ghostly cliffs, where, to his considerable surprise, his ego was blithely repelled—flicked away—by the mountain's power: " . . . inhuman Nature has got him at a disadvantage, caught him alone, and pilfers him of some of his divine faculty." John and William Bartram glimpsed a spirit in all living things while roaming the forests of Pennsylvania and the wilderness of the Southeast, bending down to examine curious petal-closing species like the tipitiwitchet. "I have queried," wrote the senior Bartram, "whether there is not a portion of universal intellect diffused in all life." A century and a half later, John Muir saw the entire forest as a way to connect with the divine—"The clearest way into the Universe is through a forest wilderness"—while Aldo Leopold, nearly another century after Muir, and a scientist by training, was humbled as he began to fathom the incredible complexity of entire wild ecosystems and made it his life's work to articulate their intangible value.

The thinking about the wilds had evolved so far since the first European arrivals in the New World that it had almost inverted. Wilderness had transformed from a dark, Satanic stronghold that had to be subdued—crushed—to less of an actual place than a medium through which to grasp the complexity of life and touch something that approached the divine.

I hoped that, during these travels to the wilds of Maine, New Mexico, and beyond, Molly and Skyler had picked up some of the lessons that wilderness imparts. Almost surely they would live most of their lives—as I had, as almost all of us do—in some sort of urban or semirural setting where "nature" has been gentrified and we are sustained and connected to one another by fossil fuels extracted from beneath the earth's surface and delivered via a vast network of pipes, wires, and electromagnetic waves.

You don't learn the lesson standing in the big-shouldered Loop of Chicago, or in the man-made canyons of Manhattan, or in the sinuous sprawl of LA, or in the long corridors of the Pentagon. You don't learn it with a cell phone in your hand standing in line at the ATM or supermarket checkout. You do learn it in the middle of a wilderness during a blizzard, or on foot in a desert, or alone on a mountaintop. The astrophysicist on the Plains of San Agostin surely knows. If you're peering up with a giant radiotelescope from a high-desert plain seeking the ends of the universe, finding energy sources countless times more powerful than our own staggeringly powerful sun and discovering blank spots a billion light-years across . . . the truth is clear.

Creation is enormous and infinitely complex. Man is only the tiniest, tiniest, tiniest part of all Creation. And you—yes, *you*—are even tinier than that.

That's what blank spots tell us.

ACKNOWLEDGMENTS

In the Prologue, I've told the story of how I came to love the wild, empty places of the world, the blank spots on the map. There are many people who made this book possible, but in a deeper, familial sense, my first debt goes to my grandfather, who papered the walls of his upstairs hallways with maps from all over the world, and whose fire-lit library shelves groaned under the weight of bound leather volumes of *National Geographic;* and also to my late father, William F. Stark, who had a passion for the early history of the North American continent and wrote local history books on the settlement of Wisconsin.

This book had its most immediate inception during an editorial meeting with Nancy Miller, then editor in chief of Ballantine Books, as I described my fascination with wild, empty places.

"My son and I like to study maps together and search out the blankest spots," she remarked.

"Blank spots!" I replied. "I love blank spots!"

And so this book was born.

Right at the outset, I contacted my friend Alex Philp, a historical geographer and partner in GCS Research in Missoula, Montana, which produces sophisticated map-based data systems. Philp, as I recount in the Prologue, showed me the way to find the blankest of the blank spots and different ways to think about them.

Philp's partner at GCS, Michael Beltz, spent many hours designing the engrossing maps that appear in this book. It amazed me with what ease—and geniality—he could include whatever I wanted in the maps, change it in countless different ways, add or subtract "layers" of data to accentuate the information that we wished to highlight as effectively as possible.

In each of the "empty places" I visited—despite, or perhaps because of, their lack of population—I found people who were very hospitable and willing to help bring this project along.

These include several "blank spots" I investigated in person but, for one reason or another, don't appear in this book. In the East Dismal Swamp of North Carolina, Fred Willard of the Lost Colony Center for Science and Research graciously invited me on an archaeological excavation searching for traces of the "lost colony" of Roanoke Island. The colony disappeared in the late 1580s, and its settlers—including Virginia Dare, the first known British child born in North America—may have retreated to the fastness of the swamp. Phil McMullan Jr. also helped me with background during the excavation.

In the Upper Peninsula of Michigan, Neal and Ruth Beaver of Grand Marais told me vivid anecdotes of life on this remote stretch of the Lake Superior shoreline, known as the "Shipwreck Coast."

Our canoe trip down the St. John River of Northern Maine was greatly helped by Betsy and Galen Hale, who not only supplied us with canoes and shuttling from their outfitting business, Nicatou Outfitters, but whose ancestral roots in the northern Maine area are fascinating and deep and connect to Henry David Thoreau's visits there. David Shipper, as shuttle driver with the Hales, provided us good company on the road and an endless supply of local information. At Camden on Maine's Penobscot Bay, Capt. Al Philbrick, who took us out on his lobster boat, was a useful source of information about coastal life and anecdotes of the Acadian migrations.

In Pennsylvania, Kim Mattern, amateur archaeologist and lifetime resident of the Penns Creek area, is an authority on the Le Roy Massacre. He personally guided me to the places where significant events occurred, shared his artifact collection, and provided me with a paper he has produced from his research on the Le Roy Massacre. Likewise, Bill Mattern provided information about the area. In Renovo and Tamarack, Richard Kugel, assistant district forester at the Sproul State Forest, and Doug D'Amore, district forester, took time out to speak with me about the forest and early land-use history. Eric and Peggy Lucas of Tamarack provided a great deal of local history, much of it compiled by Peggy's late mother, Dorothy M. Bailey, a respected historian of the area. Nancy and David Swanson helped sketch out the history of the Warren area, and their son, Carl, a friend of mine in Missoula, gave me an overview of Pennsylvania geography (especially advice on choice fly-fishing spots). Les McComber and Dennis Lytel showed me their hospitality on the Seneca Reservation and told me about the history of the Seneca people.

The huge empty spaces of Oregon proved to be populated, however thinly, with most welcoming people. At the enormous Roaring Springs Ranch, owner Rob Sanders graciously pointed the way to manager Stacy Davies, out in the desert at a branding, who, when I finally found him, was a fount of information and enthusiasm on ranch life and restoration of the rangelands and watersheds. His wife, Elaine, and sons, Erik, Jeff, and Scott, along with the other hands, all welcomed me at the branding and gave me a little hands-on experience, too. René Villagrana, at ranch headquarters, provided more background about seasonal ranch life.

Both the Frenchglen Hotel, and its manager, John Ross, and the Fields Station, and Sandy Downs and sister Gail, were hospitable, helpful and informative. At the Harney County Library, Karen Nitz of the Claire McGill Luce Western History Room extracted from various file drawers exactly the manuscripts and articles I needed to learn about the Lost Wagon Trains. The folks at the Alvord Ranch took time out from a busy day to talk to me, and John Wetzel, of Steens Mountain Outfitter and the Wildhorse Ranch, laid out the economics of ranching for me and, as an expert outfitter on the mountain, pointed the way to the summit of Steens Mountain. Gary Miller of the sprawling Rock Creek Ranch showed me a place that was still run in the old family way, while his young son rode by on horseback in the background, helping to round up bulls.

As Gary put it succinctly, which applies to so much of this arid region, "My grandfather witched for water and hit a well thirty-six-feet deep, and that's the only reason the Millers survived, because we had water."

In New Mexico and for help with our Gila Wilderness hike, thanks to Jay Hemphill at Gila Hike and Bike in Silver City for his route suggestions, Marcine Page for looking out for us, and to Matt Gardiner of the VLA (Very Large Array) for showing us around. Displayed in the hallway leading into the operators' room was a poster that proclaimed in large letters "VLA—Center of the Known Universe." It felt that way. We stood surrounded by computers and looked out from the observation windows at sunset over the desert array of massive satellite dishes as they peered up through the twilight into deepest space.

While the Bibliography and Endnotes cite the many invaluable sources I used in my research for this book, I feel a particular debt to certain works that comprehensively made sense of difficult-to-follow periods of early North American history. These are especially *Crucible of War: The Seven Years' War and the Fate of Empire in British North America* by Fred Anderson, and *A Great and Noble Scheme: The Tragic Story of the Expulsion of the French Acadians from Their American Homeland* by John Mack Farragher. Without them, I would have spent a long time floundering in the complicated historical thickets of the French and Indian War, the web of European diplomatic alliances of the mid-eighteenth century, and the many threads of the Acadian settlement and expulsion from Nova Scotia.

Christopher Preston, associate professor of philosophy at the University of Montana, and William Bevis, retired professor of English at the University of Montana, read the manuscript and brought to it their own very substantial knowledge of the literature—and the actuality—of wild places.

It's been nothing but pure pleasure to work with the editors at Random House and Ballantine who made this book possible and nurtured it to fruition. I can't express enough gratitude to Jennifer Hershey, editorial director at Random House, and Courtney Moran, assistant editor, who worked together on the manuscript and whose editorial suggestions invariably were graceful, thoughtful, and wise. Allison Dickens, formerly of Ballantine Books, originally commissioned the book and played an instrumental role in its conception and overall shape. John McGhee copyedited the manuscript in meticulous detail and, with a firsthand knowledge of Nova Scotia, clarified some blurry geography. I owe a huge debt to my agent, Stuart Krichevsky, for so many things both literary and business that I don't even know where to begin except to express my deep gratitude for his tremendous knowledge, judgment, and support.

Finally, my gratitude and love to Amy, Molly, and Skyler, who accompanied me every paddle stroke and footstep of the way, even when I was alone.

NOTES

PROLOGUE

ix   **John Rudberg, one of the first Swedes to immigrate to Wisconsin Territory**   William F. Stark, *Pine Lake,* p. 88.

xii   **"For many years," wrote Thoreau, "I was self-appointed inspector of rainstorms and snowstorms . . ."**   From Thoreau's *Journals.*

xii   **Emerson, his friend and mentor, bought forty acres along the pond to save it from being logged**   Walter Harding, *The Days of Henry Thoreau,* p. 179.

PART I. WHERE THE ACADIANS DISAPPEARED IN NORTHERN MAINE

4   **All men and "lads"**   John Mack Faragher, *A Great and Noble Scheme,* p. 343.

9   **"They can do no harm at Baccalaos"**   Francis Parkman, *Pioneers of France in the New World,* p. 223.

9   **Baccalaos was the Spanish and Portuguese name**   Ibid., pp. 191–92.

10   **Cartier was put out to pasture**   Ibid., p. 226.

10   **the region known to the French as "L'Acadie"**(and origins of the name Acadia).   Faragher, *A Great and Noble Scheme,* p. 6. Several different theories account for the name Acadia. It may have been given by the Italian seafarer Verrazano, who, exploring the North American coast in 1524 in the service of France, called the lush shorelines "Arcadia," after the mythical pastoral region of ancient Greece, and the "r" was later dropped from maps and references. On the other hand, the name possibly derives from a Micmac Indian word meaning "place of abundance," *akadie.* Or "Acadia" may have been a blending of these two words. Originally the French used it to refer to a huge part of North America but later the term "New France" came into more common use for the greater holdings and Acadia more specifi-

cally defined the coastal and inland regions around present-day Maine, Nova Scotia, and the other Maritime provinces. (See the Acadian Genealogy Homepage for more theories of the origin of the word *Acadia* at http://acadian.org/acadian.html.)

10   **L'Acadie or La Cadie took in everything**   Parkman, *Pioneers of France in the New World,* p. 247.

10   **King Henri IV had granted**   Marc Lescarbot, *The History of New France,* vol. II, pp. 211–16.

10   **"From the Spanish settlements northward"**   Parkman, *Pioneers of France in the New World,* p. 256.

11   **"fly from a corrupt world"**   Ibid., p. 263.

11   **" . . . there came from the land odors"**   Ibid., p. 266. (Translation differs slightly in Lescarbot, vol. II, p. 309.)

12   **St. John River**   The St. John River, according to Marc Lescarbot, the Parisian lawyer who accompanied the earliest settlers, was so named because during their coastal explorations of Acadia, the French arrived at the mouth of this unknown river on June 24, the day of the Feast of Saint John the Baptist, naming it in his honor. (See Lescarbot, *History of New France,* vol. II, p. 239.)

15   **"as if we sucked at the very teats"**   Henry David Thoreau, "Ktaadn," in *The Maine Woods,* p. 35.

15   **"I do not recognize your authority"**   Harding, *The Days of Henry Thoreau,* p. 41, quoting original Harvard report.

16   **Harvard's new president, Josiah Quincy**   Ibid., p. 33.

16   **The Romantic spirit was channeled**   Max Oelschlaeger, *The Idea of Wilderness,* p. 116.

17   **"American Scholar" address**   quoted from "The American Scholar" address given by Ralph Waldo Emerson at the Phi Beta Kappa Society, Cambridge, Massachusetts, August 31, 1837, as it appears at www.emersoncentral.com/amscholar.htm.

17   **"his grave Indian stride"**   Harding, *The Days of Henry Thoreau,* p. 40, quoting John Weiss, "Thoreau" in *Christian Examiner* LXXIX (1865), p. 98.

20   **" . . . it was a wondrous sight"**   Lescarbot, *The History of New France,* vol. II, p. 312.

27   **"Land of the Porcupine"**   *History of Madawaska,* reprinted on Acadian website at http://acadian.org/Indians.html.

27   **"the Beautiful River"**   C. Gagnon, "Native Peoples in the Upper St. John River Valley," at www.upperstjohn.com/history/natives.htm.

28   **hunting in the forest with the Micmac**   Lescarbot, *The History of New France,* vol. II, p. 344.

28   **"Our sons will marry your daughters"**   Faragher, *A Great and Noble Scheme,* p. 47.

30 "The Nature Conservancy" from oral interview 11.13.06 with Bruce Kidman of the Nature Conservancy staff and written history of St. John purchase, "The Defining Moment for Maine Conservation," at www.nature .org/wherewework/northamerica/states/maine/about/art22181.html.

31 **Deacon Ball, of the school committee** Harding, *The Days of Henry Thoreau*, pp. 52–53.

31 " 'What are you doing now?' " Ibid., p. 70.

32 "To the Maiden in the East": Ibid., p. 107.

32 "*short, explicit* and *cold* manner" Ibid., p. 102.

33 "a wild, irregular, Indian-like sort of character" Ibid., p. 140.

34 "traveling, trucking, and marrying with the savages" Faragher, *A Great and Noble Scheme*, p. 41, quoting Richard Guthry, "A Relation of the Voyage and Plantation of the Scotts Colony in New Scotland under the conduct of Sir William Alexander the Younger" (1629).

35 "Get thee behind me, Satan!" Lescarbot, *History of New France*, vol. II, p. 67.

36 **soft, luxurious coats of marten and otter** M. A. MacDonald, *Fortune & La Tour*, p. 12.

36 **The young Frenchmen learned** Faragher, *A Great and Noble Scheme*, p. 36.

36 "wives, children, dogs, kettles, hatchets, matachias" Lescarbot, *History of New France*, vol. III, p. 192.

37 **the supreme spirit was Manitou** MacDonald, *Fortune & La Tour*, p. 14.

37 "strange hissings" Faragher, *A Great and Noble Scheme*, p. 36, quoting Champlain's memoirs.

37 " . . . [V]igorous and tough" Intendant Jean Bochart de Champigny; the Marquis de Denonville; and a French officer, in W. J. Eccles, *The Canadian Frontier* (New York, 1969), pp. 90, 92, as quoted in MacDonald, *Fortune & La Tour*, p. 12.

38 *[A] waste and howling wilderness* Roderick Frazier Nash, *Wilderness and the American Mind*, p. 36.

41 **Helen Leidy was the eldest of six children** Helen Hamlin, *Nine Mile Bridge*, p. x.

42 "The ice is going out!" Ibid., pp. 229–31.

44 **Thoreau traveled by steamship** Thoreau, *The Maine Woods*, p. 1.

45 **marked with the king's sign** interview with Galen Hale, 6.18.06.

46 **a great knob of granite** from Maine Geologic Survey website at www.maine.gov/doc/nrimc/mgs/explore/bedrock/katahdin/glacial.htm.

47 "most childlike, unconscious and unblushing egotist" Harding, *The Days of Henry Thoreau*, p. 150, quoting Perry, *The Thought and Character of William James*, p 49.

49 "I have had no help or relief" MacDonald, *Fortune & La Tour*, p. 18, quoting La Tour's letter to the king, "Charles de la Tour au Roi, July 25, 1627."

50 Claude had risen from modest beginnings Ibid., pp. 19–23.

50 his ex-tutor William Alexander Faragher, *A Great and Noble Scheme*, p. 39.

52 "This answer," writes Nicolas Denys Nicolas Denys, *The Description and Natural History of the Coasts of North America (Acadia)*, pp. 133–36.

53 richest source of furs in this entire region MacDonald, *Fortune & La Tour*, pp. 38–39.

53 "good sense, discretion, fidelity, experience and great industry" Ibid., p. 39.

57 On the morning of September 7, 1846 Thoreau, *The Maine Woods*, p. 59.

60 ". . . inhuman Nature has got him at a disadvantage" Ibid., p. 85.

62 "It is difficult to conceive of a region uninhabited by man" Ibid., p. 94.

65 *A quart of* arbor-*vitae* Ibid., p. 55.

67 La Tour agreed, in 1633, to split the fur-trade profits in half MacDonald, *Fortune & La Tour*, p. 51.

68 After the formal marriage ceremony Ibid., p. 77.

69 a paltry four hundred or so in New France's Ibid., p. 91.

71 Françoise Jacquelin fell ill and died Ibid., pp. 170–71.

73 He died, probably at Port Royal Ibid., p. 180.

78 The Acadian population had soared Faragher, *A Great and Noble Scheme*, p. 65.

78 "They Lavish, Eat, Drink, and Play" Ibid., p. 72.

79 Six days later, on September 11, 1755 Ibid., p. 353.

79 Le Grand Dérangement from "Encyclopedia of Cajun Culture," at www.cajunculture.com.

80 probably escaped detection by the fledgling United States "Deane and Kavanaugh's Survey of the Madawaska Settlements, July–August 1831," posted on www.upperstjohn.com/aroostook/dkobservations.htm.

PART II. THE WILD LANDS OF WESTERN PENNSYLVANIA

84 Early on October 16, 1755 Marie Le Roy and Barbara Leininger, "The Narrative of Marie Le Roy and Barbara Leininger," p. 429.

84 Karondinhah, as the Indians knew it Paul A. W. Wallace, *Indian Paths of Pennsylvania*, p. 126.

84 They either shot or tomahawked him Kim Adair Mattern, "The Leroy Incident, and Observations."

85 "We are Allegheny Indians, and your enemies!" Le Roy and Leininger, "Narrative," p. 429.

86 Far more than the Revolutionary War Fred Anderson, *Crucible of War*, p. xvi. Anderson here addresses the significance of the Seven Years' War on a continental and global scale.

88   In the autumn of 1753   Ibid., p. 43.

88   reached Fort Le Boeuf, near Lake Erie, on December 11, 1753   George Washington, *The Diaries of George Washington,* vol. I, pp. 148–52.

88   "The lands upon the River Ohio"   Anderson, *Crucible of War,* p. 44.

90   what the Iroquois believed was only the Shenandoah Valley   Ibid., p. 23.

90   "place of the setting of the sun"   Solon J. Buck and Elizabeth Hawthorn Buck, *The Planting of Civilization in Western Pennsylvania,* p. 56.

90   The Ohio Company then gave stock to Lieutenant Governor Dinwiddie   Anderson, *Crucible of War,* p. 30.

93   While an older and more confident commander might have considered his options   Ibid., p. 51.

93   "amounted to an invitation to start a war"   Ibid.

94   written by a young officer covering up his lack of control of the situation   Ibid., p. 53. Washington's account of the event is as follows: "We were advanced pretty near to them, as we thought, when they discovered us; whereupon I ordered my company to fire; mine was supported by that of Mr. *Wag[gonn]er's,* and my Company and his received the whole of Fire of the *French,* during the greatest Part of the Action, which only lasted a Quarter of an Hour, before the Enemy was routed.

    "We killed Mr. *de Jumonville,* the commander of that Party, as also nine others; we wounded one, and made Twenty-one Prisoners, among whom were M. *la Force,* M. *Drouillon,* and two Cadets. The *Indians* scalped the Dead, and took away the most Part of their Arms . . ." (From Anderson, p. 53, quoting Jackson, *The Diaries of George Washington,* vol. I, p. 195.)

94   But a careful reconstruction based on several other eyewitness accounts   Anderson, in *Crucible of War* (pp. 53–59), carefully weighs accounts by a French Canadian named Monceau who slipped off into the woods at the first fighting and watched it; from a young Irishman in Washington's regiment who, while not actually present, heard corroborating accounts of the battle from several survivors and gave a sworn statement; and, most significantly, from Denis Kaninguen, apparently an Iroquois Indian, who had been part of the Washington camp during the Jumonville fight. Kaninguen directly witnessed Jumonville's death and heard Tanaghrisson's remarks. Within a few weeks, he had deserted to the French side and gave his report of the battle to Captain Contrecoeur at the Forks.

94   shrewdly calculated political move on his part   Ibid., pp. 56–57.

95   "All North America will be lost"   Ibid., pp. 68–70.

96   Franklin wasn't so sure   Winthrop Sargent (ed.), *The History of an Expedition Against Fort Du Quesne in 1755.*

96   Braddock replied, "The English should inhabit"   Anderson, *Crucible of War,* p. 95.

98   a contingent of camp women   Ibid., p. 97.

99   "Whenever he saw a man skulking behind a tree"   Sargent, *History of an Expedition Against Fort Du Quesne*, p. 230.

99   a story persisted that Braddock had been shot by one of his own troops   Ibid., p. 246.

100 "Who would have thought it?"   Ibid., p. 237.

100 "He looked upon us as dogs"   Ibid., p. 173.

101 "Nothing is more calculated to disgust the people of those Colonies"   Anderson, *Crucible of War*, p. 151.

103 taking extensive notes on *The Morals of Confucius*   Thomas P. Slaughter, *The Natures of John and William Bartram*, p. 16.

103 *Slave to no sect*   Ernest Earnest, *John and William Bartram*, p. 147.

104 "It is through the telescope"   Ibid., p. 140.

107 led the girls to the top of a nearby high hill   Le Roy and Leininger, "Narrative," p. 430.

108 "what is commonly called a gentleman"   Earnest, *John and William Bartram*, p. 92.

109 "[T]hee need not hinder half an hour's time"   Slaughter, *The Natures of John and William Bartram*, pp. 129–30.

110 "[N]o colouring," he wrote, "can do justice"   Ibid., p. 160.

112 "Go to Renovo"   Conversation with Andy Warga, forester, November 2005, Santa Fe, New Mexico. Warga especially recommended the tiny town of Orviston, Pennsylvania.

115 political shock waves roiled out around the entire globe   See Anderson, *Crucible of War*, pp. 170–78, on Britain and France going to war and European treaties unraveling. The complicated web of European treaties is explained on pp. 124–32.

116 didn't think it right that the regular farmers should pay a tax   Ibid., p. 161.

117 The horrified Quakers at this point withdrew   Ibid., p. 162.

118 "[T]he Leg and Thigh of an Indian"   Ibid., p. 163.

119 The ridgetops were the ancient folds   see Wikipedia under "Appalachian orogeny."

122 " . . . the first sight of him startled me"   William Bartram, *Travels Through North & South Carolina*, p. 21. Available online at http://docsouth.unc.edu/nc/bartram/bartram.html.

123 "the man who tells the truth"   Earnest, *John and William Bartram*, p. 90.

124 misread a compass in order to cheat the Indians   Bartram, *Travels*, p. 40.

126 to stage a major attack on Fort Duquesne   Anderson, *Crucible of War*, p. 248.

126 "It is plain that you white people are the cause of this war"   Ibid., pp. 270–71, quoting Christian Frederick Post's "Journal."

127 **brief biography of Simeon Pfoutz** Nancy C. Werts Sporny, a pamphlet on the Pfoutz family (unpublished).

131 **may have been the source of the name Acadia** see above, note to p. 9.

132 **"I ASCENDED this beautiful river"** Bartram, *Travels*, pp. 48–49.

132 **Bartram was one of the first—if not the first—to apply this concept** Nash, *Wilderness and the American Mind*, p. 54.

133 **Lying under a shade tree to rest and read a newspaper** Jean-Jacques Rousseau, *The Confessions of Jean-Jacques Rousseau*, p. 540.

134 **captured a new passion between Man and Nature** For more on the deep influence exerted by Rousseau in shaping a new way to view nature, see Roland N. Stromberg, *An Intellectual History of Modern Europe*, p. 149; Richard Bevis, *The Road to Egdon Heath*, pp. 80–81; Oelschlaeger, *The Idea of Wilderness*, p. 111; and Nash, *Wilderness and the American Mind*, p. 49.

135 **"Meditations there take on an indescribably grand and sublime character"** Jean-Jacques Rousseau, *Julie, Or the New Heloise*, p. 64.

136 **"[We] enjoyed a most enchanting view"** Bartram, *Travels*, pp. 356–57. (Quoted passage also appears in Slaughter, *The Natures of John and William Bartram*.)

137 **As the British advanced in the Ohio Valley** Anderson, *Crucible of War*, p. 258.

138 ***O bring us safely across the river!*** Le Roy and Leininger, "Narrative," p. 434.

141 **Samuel Taylor Coleridge was deeply smitten by Bartram's *Travels*** For more on how Bartram's imagery (and the African explorer James Bruce's) appears in Coleridge's "Kubla Khan" see *The Road to Xanadu: A Study in the Ways of the Imagination* by John Livingston Lowes (Boston: Houghton Mifflin, 1927), p. 8 and pp. 364–65.

143 **"the idea of Nature for the idea of God"** Earnest, *John and William Bartram*, p. 34, quoting Harper.

PART III. THE LOST COUNTRY OF SOUTHEAST OREGON

154 **He was found in mid-October 1853** Leah Collins Menefee and Lowell Tiller, "Cutoff Fever—Part V," in *Oregon Historical Quarterly* (Dec. 1977), p. 304.

158 **John Day was a forty-year-old Virginian and crack rifle shot** Washington Irving, *Astoria*, pp. 138, 351–53. Available online at http://quod.lib.umich.edu.

160 **"[B]ut his constitution . . . was completely broken"** Ibid., p. 361.

162 **A former mountain man by the name of Stephen Meek** For Meek's own account of his life see Stephen Hall Meek, *The Autobiography of a Mountain*

Man, 1805–1889. For an account of the rebellion in Meek's wagon train and journal entries from its members, see Karen Bassett, Jim Renner, and Joyce White (eds.), "Meek Cutoff 1845."

162 **Their pilot, one Elijah Elliot, had been paid five hundred dollars** Menefee and Tiller, "Cut-Off Fever—Part IV," p. 247.

162 **It's hard to exaggerate just how much water these wagon trains needed daily** For example, one settler in the Meek party remarked that "198 wagons, 2299 head of cattle, 811 head of oxen, 1051 souls all consume a heap of water." See Bassett et al., "Meek Cutoff 1845," quoting Solomon Tetherow.

163 **"Mc[lure]. was Sick. & discouraged"** Menefee and Tiller, "Cut-Off Fever—Part IV," p. 233.

163 **"Bright and early next morning we struck out"** Ibid., pp. 244–45.

165 **"Oh what visions of Bred butter pies Cakes"** Menefee and Tiller, "Cut-Off Fever—Part V," p. 300.

166 **"I think I was never so glad to see any human"** Ibid., p. 311.

168 **"[While it was] still in a state of pristine wildness"** Nash, *Wilderness and the American Mind,* pp. 72–73, quoting a letter to Irving's brother.

169 **"We send our youth abroad to grow luxurious and effeminate in Europe"** Andrew Burstein, *The Original Knickerbocker,* quoting *A Tour on the Prairies.*

169 **The nervous, hyperintellectual Parkman** Francis Parkman, *The Oregon Trail* (Wisconsin), p. 29a.

171 **In the spring of 1872, Dr. Glenn financed Pete French** George Francis Brimlow, *Harney County, Oregon, and Its Rangeland,* p. 58.

171 **"I'll fight any man"** Ibid., p. 215.

172 **Titled "Long Drive for a Latte"** map produced by InfoGraphics lab at Department of Geography, University of Oregon, *Oregon Quarterly* (Autumn 2007), p. 13.

174 **The Donner und Blitzen River** Origin of name from website of Oregon Natural Desert Association at www.onda.org/.

175 **"This sudden plash into pure wildness"** John Muir, *The Story of My Boyhood and Youth,* p. 63.

176 **"Come! Come, mother!" shouted Father Muir** Ibid., pp. 205–6.

177 **Soon after Darwin, George Perkins Marsh** Oelschlaeger, *The Idea of Wilderness,* pp. 106–8.

177 **"I don't know anything about botany"** Muir, *The Story of My Boyhood and Youth,* pp. 282–83.

180 **His first epic adventure was a draft dodge** Stephen Fox, *John Muir and His Legacy,* pp. 42–43.

181 **"They were alone"** Ibid., p. 43, quoting Muir's account in *Boston Recorder,* Dec. 21, 1866.

184 "the harmony, the oneness, of all the world's life"   Ibid., p. 38, quoting Muir's autobiographical papers housed at the University of the Pacific.

184 "[I am] a woman whose life seems always to be used up"   Ibid., p. 47.

187 *"John Muir, Earth-Planet, Universe"*   Linnie Marsh Wolfe, *Son of the Wilderness,* p. 110.

188 "oh! that is horribly unorthodox"   Fox, *John Muir and His Legacy,* p. 52, quoting Muir's journals.

188 "Well, keep pouring in the quinine"   Thurman Wilkins, *John Muir: Apostle of Nature,* p. 54.

189 "The world, we are told, was made specially for man"   Wolfe, *Son of the Wilderness,* p. 115.

189 "Nature's object in making animals and plants"   Fox, *John Muir and His Legacy,* p. 53.

189 "Creation," as Fox puts it, "belonged"   Ibid.

190 "Where do you wish to go?"   Wilkins, *John Muir: Apostle of Nature,* p. 57.

190 He first gazed on the Sierra Nevada Mountains   Frederick Turner, *Rediscovering America,* p. 164.

190 somehow unworthy of such grandeur   Ibid., p. 165.

191 "preach Nature like an apostle"   Ibid., p. 170.

191 "We are now in the mountains"   Ibid., pp. 172–73.

194 On the full moon of April 3   Wilkins, *John Muir: Apostle of Nature,* pp. 76–77.

194 "Do not thus drift away with the mob"   Fox, *John Muir and His Legacy,* p. 5.

195 "No, it would never do to lie in the night air"   Wilkins, *John Muir: Apostle of Nature,* p. 78.

195 "full of indoor philosophy"   Fox, *John Muir and His Legacy,* p. 5, quoting Muir writing in *Our National Parks* (Boston: Houghton Mifflin, 1901).

195 "Surely, then . . . one may be spared for"   Wolfe, *Son of the Wilderness,* p. 144, quoting Muir's autobiographical notebooks.

196 "What I have nobody wants"   Ibid., p. 153, quoting the autobiographical notebooks.

196 "The earth as our common mother should belong to all the people"   Ibid., p. 182, quoting Henry George's 1871 pamphlet, *Our Land and Land Policy.*

197 "We the undersigned claim this valley"   Ibid., p. 184.

200 "The Restoration Economy"   This is also the title of a book by Storm Cunningham, *The Restoration Economy: The Greatest New Growth Frontier* (San Francisco: Barrett-Koehler Publishers, 2002).

202 "I want you to know my John Muir"   Wolfe, *Son of the Wilderness,* p. 174.

202 "Solitude is a sublime mistress"   Ibid., p. 199.

203 "Instinct with deity"   Ibid., p. 209, quoting Muir's notes.

203 **"A ranch that needs and takes the sacrifice"** Ibid., pp. 243–44.

203 **Muir was appalled** Ibid., p. 245, citing Robert Underwood Johnson's memoir, *Remembered Yesterdays*.

206 **"It was clear weather"** Wilkins, *John Muir: Apostle of Nature*, pp. 215–17, quoting Roosevelt's article "John Muir: An Appreciation," in *Outlook* magazine, vol. 109 (Jan. 6, 1915).

PART IV. THE HIGH, HAUNTED DESERT OF NEW MEXICO

215 **there could be valuable metals** Franklin Jameson (gen. ed.), Frederick W. Hodge and Theodore H. Lewis (eds.) *Spanish Explorers in the Southern United States, 1528–1543,* p. 111. Cabeza de Vaca reports rumors of gold in other places in his *Narrative* and findings of turquoise and arrowheads of emerald (see ibid., p. 106). Also for Cabeza de Vaca's rumored cities and gold to the north see George P. Hammond, *Coronado's Seven Cities,* p. 4.

216 **Could he be taken to their chief? asked Cabeza de Vaca** Jameson et al., *Spanish Explorers,* p. 112. For added details on Cabeza de Vaca's meeting with the Spanish, see Rolena Adorno and Patrick Charles Pautz, *Álvar Nuñez Cabeza de Vaca,* vol. II, pp. 365–66. Also for a detailed treatment of Esteban and his role in the shipwrecked expedition and further explorations see Robert Goodwin, *Crossing the Continent 1527–1540.*

222 **The legend was well known in Spain at the time** For more on the legend of the Seven Cities, see Goodwin, *Crossing the Continent,* p. 297.

222 **the viceroy offered to purchase the Moorish slave** Ibid., pp. 300–301. Goodwin quotes a Spanish chronicler, Baltasar Obregón, on the offer to purchase Esteban and Dorantes's refusal.

222 **"was endowed with all virtues"** Adolph F. Bandelier, *The Discovery of New Mexico by the Franciscan Monk, Friar Marcos de Niza in 1539,* p. 69.

222 **"they will be punished and will receive no mercy"** Ibid., pp 70–71.

223 **" . . . that it was thirty days' travel"** Ibid., p. 75.

224 **The chief said he knew these people and would kill them** Ibid., pp. 86–89. Bandelier quotes the account Fray Marcos de Niza gives in his original "Relación." Adorno (vol. 2, p. 422) cites other evidence and accounts disputing that Fray Marcos had made it as far north as "Cíbola," as he claimed, and that Esteban was killed well south of the pueblo of Zuni.

224 **Esteban's Indian messenger left the house to get a drink** Account of the massacre from Bandelier, p. 87, and from Fray Marcos de Niza, "A Relation of the Reverend Father Fray" from "Marcos de Niza, Touching His Discovery of the Kingdom of Ceulo or Cíbola . . ." (originally written in 1539 and published in English in *Principall Navigations, Voiages and Discoveries of the English Nation,* ed. Richard Hakluyt (London: 1598–1600, 3rd vol., final

edition). (Partial text available online at http://etext.lib.virginia.edu/subjects/eaw/essays/nizatext.html.)

225 **"With this and many other words I pacified them"** Fray Marcos de Niza, "Relation."

226 **"The [city] was so stirred by the news"** Hammond, *Coronado's Seven Cities,* p. 9.

231 **"the most brilliant company ever assembled in the Indies"** quote from Castañeda in ibid., pp. 17–19. For many details of the Coronado expedition as recorded in documents of the time, see Richard Flint and Shirley Cushing Flint, *Documents of the Coronado Expedition, 1539–1542.* Among many other documents, this includes a "Muster Roll of the Expedition" that lists each member, and exactly what armaments and horses they brought with them. For example, "Juan Gallego [is taking] a [chain mail] vest, [chain mail] breeches, an elk hide jacket, a crossbow, other native and Castilian arms and armor, and seven horses" (p. 139).

232 **born of a landed Salamanca family** Hammond, *Coronado's Seven Cities,* pp. 9–10.

232 **"In the end necessity, which is all powerful, made them skillful"** Castañeda's "Narrative" in Jameson et al., *Spanish Explorers in the Southern United States,* p. 295.

232 **" . . . and there they turned back, not finding anything important"** Ibid., p. 296.

234 **"The following day they entered the settled land"** Castañeda's "Narrative" in Flint and Flint, *Documents,* p. 393. I use the Flint and Flint version of Castañeda's "Narrative" here instead of the Jameson version because of the former's precise translation of a very key passage.

234 **while "defiant" villagers** Castañeda's "Narrative" in Jameson et al., *Spanish Explorers in the Southern United States,* p. 300.

234 **Zuñi Indians in a settlement near today's Zuni Pueblo** For a fascinating account of life in Zuni at the time of Coronado's arrival, see "Zuni on the Day the Men in Metal Arrived" by Edmund J. Ladd in Richard Flint and Shirley Cushing Flint (eds.), *The Coronado Expedition to Tierra Nueva,* pp. 225–33. A map of sixteenth-century Zuni appears on p. 230. The village that Coronado is believed to have entered was known as Hawikuh, also spelled "Hawikku." See also Richard Flint, *No Settlement, No Conquest,* p. 97.

234 **dragged their commander to safety** See Castañeda's "Narrative."

236 **"Wilderness areas are first of all a series of sanctuaries"** Aldo Leopold, "Wilderness," in *A Sand County Almanac,* pp. 270–71.

239 **This was the origin of the "seven cities" of Cíbola** Flint, *No Settlement, No Conquest,* p. 97.

239   **"Fray Marcos has not told the truth"**   Hammond, *Coronado's Seven Cities,*
p. 35. Another translation of Coronado's letter to Viceroy Mendoza appears
in Flint and Flint, *Documents,* pp. 254–62.

240   **the Giralda bell tower of the great Cathedral of Seville**   Castañeda in
Jameson et al., *Spanish Explorers,* p. 309.

240   **"throw a ball as high"**   Castañeda in ibid., p. 311.

241   **"[The Turk] told them so many and such great things"**   Castañeda in
ibid., p. 313.

242   **"This began the want of confidence in the word of the
Spaniards"**   Castañeda in ibid., p. 315.

242   **interpreted that to mean he should roast his two hundred Indian captives**   Castañeda in ibid., pp. 319–20.

244   **"big enough to absorb a two-weeks' pack trip"**   Marybeth Lorbiecki, *Aldo
Leopold: A Fierce Green Fire,* p. 90, quoting Leopold's 1921 article in the
Journal of Forestry.

245   **Dandified up in his newly purchased cowboy outfit**   Ibid., p. 40. A photo
appears in this edition of Lorbiecki's book showing Leopold in all his cowboy gear as a newly arrived forester in Arizona.

245   **"the fervor of a sawdust evangelist"**   Ibid., p. 39, quoting a characterization of Leopold by Leopold's boss, Arthur Ringland.

245   **"Why damn their whining souls"**   Ibid., pp. 42–43, quoting a letter from
Leopold to his sister.

246   **"In those days we had never heard of passing up a chance to kill a
wolf"**   Aldo Leopold, "Thinking Like a Mountain," in *A Sand County Almanac,* pp. 138–39.

248   **"These people sustain themselves entirely from the cattle [buffalo] . . . "**   Hammond, *Coronado's Seven Cities,* pp. 62–63. This passage is
originally from "La Relación Postrera de Cíbola," written in the 1540s by
Fray Toribio de Benavente, who apparently recorded other Spaniards' eyewitness accounts of the customs of the Plains Indians. It is not clear just
who these informants were. (A translation of his entire "Relacíon" appears
in Flint and Flint, *Documents,* pp. 296–300.)

249   **They were very intelligent people**   Castañeda in Jameson et al., *Spanish
Explorers,* p. 330.

249   **believed to be the Blanco Canyon area near Lubbock, Texas**   Possible locations of this Indian settlement visited by Coronado's expedition are discussed in an essay by Joseph P. Sánchez, "A Historiography of the Route of
the Expedition of Francisco Vásquez de Coronado: Río de Cicúye to
Quivira," in Richard Flint and Shirley Cushing Flint (eds.), *The Coronado
Expedition to Tierra Nueva.* Also see, in the same volume, "Una Barranca
Grande: Recent Archaeological Evidence and a Discussion of Its Place in
the Coronado Route" by Donald J. Blakeslee, Richard Flint, and Jack T.

Hughes. The latter essay cites "two pieces of chain mail" that were discovered in Blanco Canyon by ranchers in the 1950s and 1960s, as well as later discoveries of crossbow bolt heads (pp. 371–72).

249 **Coronado wanted to divide up the pile of robes as spoils** Castañeda in Jameson et al., *Spanish Explorers,* p. 332.

250 **We call it the Arkansas River** See Sánchez, "A Historiography of the Route," in Flint and Flint, *The Coronado Expedition to Tierra Nueva,* pp. 296–97.

257 **"[This] laid him at the point of death"** Castañeda in Jameson et al., *Spanish Explorers,* p. 368.

258 **He bore the terrible news** Flint, *No Settlement, No Conquest,* p. 187.

258 **". . . that he would become a powerful lord in distant lands"** Castañeda in Jameson et al., *Spanish Explorers,* p. 369.

259 **He was carried part of the way on a litter** Hammond, *Coronado's Seven Cities,* p. 70.

260 **"From then on," states Castañeda flatly, "he lost his reputation"** Castañeda as translated in Flint and Flint, *Documents,* p. 430.

260 **Aldo Leopold read the just-published *Our Vanishing Wildlife*** Lorbiecki, *Aldo Leopold,* p. 59.

261 **Wrote Teddy Roosevelt in a letter to Leopold** Ibid., p. 74.

261 **"I do not know whether I have twenty days or twenty years"** Ibid., pp. 73–74.

262 **"Destruction of the soil is the most fundamental kind of economic loss"** Ibid., p. 88, quoting a speech Leopold gave at the University of Arizona, 1921.

264 **While fishing, Leopold admired the lack of telephone poles and automobile roads** Ibid., pp. 83–84.

265 **heavy grazing and logging had wiped out the Blue River bottomlands** for more detail on the dramatic transformation of the Blue River bottomlands by erosion, see Julianne Lutz Newton, *Aldo Leopold's Odyssey,* pp. 55–57.

265 **"To cherish we must see and fondle"** Lorbiecki, *Aldo Leopold,* p. 85, quoting "Marshland Elegy" in *A Sand County Almanac.*

265 **Leopold went out of his way to meet Carhart** Ibid., pp. 84–86.

266 **"Sporting magazines are groping toward some logical reconciliation"** Curt Meine and Richard L. Knight, *The Essential Aldo Leopold,* p. 36, quoting "The Wilderness and Its Place in Forest Recreational Policy" in *Journal of Forestry* (Nov. 1921).

274 **"[G]ame can be restored"** Lorbiecki, *Aldo Leopold,* p. 117, quoting the Preface to *Game Management.*

275 **"We, Americans, have not yet experienced a bearless, wolfless, eagleless"** Ibid., p. 134.

276 **The river's waters ran clear between uneroded, mossy banks** Susan Flader essay, "Aldo Leopold and the Evolution of a Land Ethic," in Thomas Tanner (ed.), *Aldo Leopold: The Man and His Legacy,* p. 16.

279 **the population had suddenly soared in the decades after A.D.1050** Stephen Plog, *Ancient Peoples of the American Southwest,* p. 93.

280 **the first known white—a prospector named H. B. Ailman** Laurence Parent, *Gila Cliff Dwellings National Monument,* p. 11.

EPILOGUE

286 **"A thing is right when it tends to preserve the integrity"** Leopold's essay "The Land Ethic" in *A Sand County Almanac,* p. 262.

287 **"The clearest way into the Universe is through a forest wilderness"** from John Muir's "Journals," available online at http://library.pacific.edu/ha/ digital/muirjournals/muirjournals.asp. Muir's biographer Linnie Marsh Wolfe also published a collection of these previously unpublished journals under the title *John of the Mountains: The Unpublished Journals of John Muir,* ed. Linnie Marsh Wolfe (Madison: University of Wisconsin Press, 1979).

BIBLIOGRAPHY

GENERAL AND PROLOGUE

Bevis, Richard. *The Road to Egdon Heath: The Aesthetics of the Great in Nature* (Montreal: McGill-Queen's University Press, 1999).

Callicott, J. Baird, and Michael P. Nelson (eds.). *The Great New Wilderness Debate: An Expansive Collection of Writings Defining Wilderness from John Muir to Gary Snyder* (Athens: University of Georgia Press, 1998).

Nash, Roderick Frazier. *Wilderness and the American Mind* (New Haven: Yale University Press, 1967; 4th ed., 2001).

Newby, Eric. *The World Atlas of Exploration* (New York: Crescent Books, 1985).

Oelschlaeger, Max. *The Idea of Wilderness: From Prehistory to the Age of Ecology* (New Haven: Yale University Press, 1991).

Royal Geographical Society. *Oxford Atlas of Exploration* (New York: Oxford University Press, 1997).

Stark, William F. *Pine Lake* (Sheboygan, Wis.: Zimmerman Press, 1984).

Stromberg, Roland N. *An Intellectual History of Modern Europe* (Englewood Cliffs, N.J.: Prentice-Hall, 1975).

Turner, Jack. *The Abstract Wild* (Tucson: University of Arizona Press, 1996).

PART I. WHERE THE ACADIANS DISAPPEARED IN NORTHERN MAINE

Bible, George P. *An Historical Sketch of the Acadians, Their Deportation and Wanderings Together with a Consideration of the Historical Basis for Longfellow's Poem Evangeline* (Gretna, La.: Pelican Publishing Co., 1998; reprinted from an earlier edition).

Denys, Nicolas. *The Description and Natural History of the Coasts of North America (Acadia)*, trans. Willam F. Ganong (Toronto: Champlain Society, 1908), pp. 133–36.

Faragher, John Mack. *A Great and Noble Scheme: The Tragic Story of the Expulsion of the French Acadians from Their American Homeland* (New York: W. W. Norton & Co., 2005).

Hamlin, Helen. *Nine Mile Bridge: Three Years in the Maine Woods* (New York: W. W. Norton & Co., 1945; published with additional materials Yarmouth, Me: Islandport Press, 2005).

Harding, Walter. *The Days of Henry Thoreau* (New York: Alfred A. Knopf, 1966).

Lescarbot, Marc. *The History of New France,* trans. W. L. Grant, 3 vols. (1609; Toronto: Champlain Society, 1911).

MacDonald, M. A. *Fortune & La Tour: The Civil War in Acadia* (Halifax: Nimbus Publishing, 2000).

Parkman, Francis. *Pioneers of France in the New World: France and England in North America* (1865; Williamsport, Mass.: Corner House Publishers, 1970).

Sanborn, F. B. *The Life of Henry David Thoreau, Including Many Essays Hitherto Unpublished and Some Account of his Family and Friends* (Boston: Houghton Mifflin Co., 1917).

Thoreau, Henry David. "Ktaadn," in *The Maine Woods* (Boston: Houghton Mifflin Co., 1892). ("Ktaadn" was originally published as an essay, "Ktaadn and the Maine Woods," in *The Union Magazine,* 1848.)

Violette, Lawrence A. *How the Acadians Came to Maine* (Madawaska, Me: Madawaska Historical Society, 1979).

PART II. THE WILD LANDS OF WESTERN PENNSYLVANIA

Anderson, Fred. *Crucible of War: The Seven Years' War and the Fate of Empire in British North America* (New York: Alfred A. Knopf, 2000).

Bartram, William. *Travels Through North & South Carolina, Georgia, East & West Florida, the Cherokee Country, the Extensive Territories of the Muscogulges, or Creek Confederacy, and the Country Containing the Chactaws (etc.)* (Philadelphia: James & Johnson, 1791). Available online at http://docsouth.unc.edu/nc/bartram/bartram.html.

Borneman, Walter. *The French and Indian War: Deciding the Fate of North America* (New York: HarperCollins, 2006).

Buck, Solon J., and Elizabeth Hawthorn Buck. *The Planting of Civilization in Western Pennsylvania* (Pittsburgh: University of Pittsburgh Press, 1939).

Crevecoeur, Michel-Guillaume Jean de. *Eighteenth-Century Travels in Pennsylvania and New York,* trans. Percy G. Adams (University of Kentucky Press, 1961).

Earnest, Ernest. *John and William Bartram: Botanists and Explorers, 1699–1777, 1739–1823* (Philadelphia: University of Pennsylvania Press, 1940).

Le Roy, Marie, and Barbara Leininger. "The Narrative of Marie Le Roy and Barbara Leininger," in *Papers Relating to the Provincial Affairs of Pennsylvania, 1682–1750, 2nd series, v. 7* (Harrisburg, Penn.: 1891).

Mattern, Kim Adair. "The Leroy Incident, and Observations" (unpublished paper, 2007).

Merrell, James H. *Into the American Woods: Negotiators on the Pennsylvania Frontier* (New York: W. W. Norton and Co., 1999).

Rousseau, Jean-Jacques. *Julie, Or the New Heloise: Letters of Two Lovers Who Live in a Small Town at the Foot of the Alps,* trans. Philip Steward and Jean Vaché (Hanover, N.H.: University Press of New England, 1997).

———. *The Confessions of Jean-Jacques Rousseau,* trans. W. Conyngham Mallory (New York: Tudor Publishing Company, 1928).

Sargent, Winthrop (ed.). *The History of an Expedition Against Fort Du Quesne in 1755 Under Major-General Edward Braddock, Edited from the Original Manuscripts* (Philadelphia: Historical Society of Pennsylvania, 1855).

Slaughter, Thomas P. *The Natures of John and William Bartram* (New York: Alfred A. Knopf, 1996).

Wallace, Paul A. W. *Indian Paths of Pennsylvania* (Harrisburg: Commonwealth of Pennsylvania, Pennsylvania Historical and Museum Commission, 2005).

Washington, George. *The Diaries of George Washington* (vol. I), Donald Jackson, ed.; Dorothy Twohig, assoc. ed. The Papers of George Washington. (Charlottesville: University Press of Virginia, 1976).

PART III. THE LOST COUNTRY OF SOUTHEAST OREGON

Bassett, Karen, Jim Renner, and Joyce White (eds.). "Meek Cutoff 1845" (published by Oregon Trails Coordinating Committee). Available online at endoftheoregontrail.org/oregontrails/meek.html.

Brayman, Pauline, and Vickie Britton (eds.). *A Lively Little History of Harney County: A Centennial Souvenir Album, 1889–1989* (Burns, Ore.: Harney County Centennial Publications Committee, 1989).

Brimlow, George Francis. *Harney County, Oregon, and Its Rangeland* (Burns, Ore.: Harney County Historical Society, 1980).

Brooks, Van Wyck. *The World of Washington Irving* (Cleveland: World Publishing Co., 1944).

Burstein, Andrew. *The Original Knickerbocker: The Life of Washington Irving* (New York: Basic Books, 2007).

Davis, Leilani M. *The Shadow of the Steens* (Bend, Ore.: East Steens Mountain Press, 2004).

Fleck, Richard F. *Henry Thoreau and John Muir Among the Indians* (Hamden, Conn.: Archon Books, 1985).

Fox, Stephen. *John Muir and His Legacy: The American Conservation Movement* (Boston: Little, Brown and Co., 1981).

Irving, Washington. *Astoria; or, Anecdotes of an Enterprise Beyond the Rocky Mountains* (New York: G. P. Putnam, 1861).

————. *The Adventures of Captain Bonneville, U.S.A., in the Rocky Mountains and the Far West (digested from his journal by Washington Irving)*, edited by Edgeley W. Todd (Norman: University of Oklahoma Press, 1961).

Larrison, Earl J. *Owyhee: The Life of a Northern Desert* (Caldwell, Idaho: Caxton Printers, 1957).

McNary, Lawrence A. "Route of the Meek Cut-Off," in *Oregon Historical Quarterly* (vol. XXXV, no. 1, March 1934).

Meek, Stephen Hall. *The Autobiography of a Mountain Man, 1805–1889*, ed. Arthur Woodward (Pasadena, Calif.: Glen Dawson, 1948; originally published 1885 as "A Sketch of the Life of the First Pioneer").

Menefee, Leah Collins, and Lowell Tiller. "Cutoff Fever" Parts IV–V, in *Oregon Historical Quarterly* (Sept. and Dec. 1977).

Miller, Sally M. (ed.). *John Muir in Historical Perspective* (New York: Peter Lang, 1999).

Muir, John. *The Story of My Boyhood and Youth* (Boston: Houghton Mifflin Co., 1913).

Nash, Wallis. *Oregon: There and Back in 1877* (Corvallis: Oregon State University Press, 1976; originally published 1878).

Olsen, Jack. *Give a Boy a Gun: A True Story of Law and Disorder in the American West* (New York: Delacorte, 1985).

Parkman, Francis. *The Oregon Trail*, edited by E. N. Feltskog (Madison: University of Wisconsin Press, 1969).

————. *The Oregon Trail: Sketches of Prairie and Rocky-Mountain Life* (Williamstown, Mass.: Corner House Publishers, 1980, 4th ed.; originally published 1872).

Turner, Frederick. *Rediscovering America: John Muir in His Time and Ours* (San Francisco: Sierra Club Books, 1985).

Wilkins, Thurman. *John Muir: Apostle of Nature* (Norman: University of Oklahoma Press, 1995).

Williams, Stanley T. *The Life of Washington Irving* (2 vols.) (New York: Oxford University Press, 1935).

Wolfe, Linnie Marsh. *Son of the Wilderness: The Life of John Muir* (Madison: University of Wisconsin Press, 1978; originally published 1945).

PART IV. THE HIGH, HAUNTED DESERT OF NEW MEXICO

Adorno, Rolena, and Patrick Charles Pautz. *Álvar Nuñez Cabeza de Vaca: His Account, His Life, and the Expedition of Pánfilo de Narváez* (3 vols.) (Lincoln: University of Nebraska Press, 1999).

Bandelier, Adolph F. *The Discovery of New Mexico by the Franciscan Monk, Friar Marcos de Niza in 1539*, trans. Madeleine Turrell Rodack (Tucson: University of Arizona Press, 1981).

Beck, Warren A. *New Mexico: A History of Four Centuries* (Norman: University of Oklahoma Press, 1962).

Cunningham, Bill, and Polly Burke. *Hiking New Mexico's Aldo Leopold Wilderness* (Guilford, Conn.: Globe Pequot Press, 2002).

———. *Hiking New Mexico's Gila Wilderness* (Guilford, Conn.: Globe Pequot Press, 1999).

Flader, Susan L. *Thinking Like a Mountain: Aldo Leopold and the Evolution of an Ecological Attitude Toward Deer, Wolves, and Forests* (Columbia: University of Missouri Press, 1974).

Flint, Richard. *No Settlement, No Conquest: A History of the Coronado Entrada* (Albuquerque: University of New Mexico Press, 2008).

Flint, Richard, and Shirley Cushing Flint. *The Coronado Expedition, from the Distance of 460 Years* (Albuquerque: University of New Mexico Press, 2003).

———. *Documents of the Coronado Expedition, 1539–1542* (Dallas: Southern Methodist University Press, 2005).

Flint, Richard, and Shirley Cushing Flint (eds.). *The Coronado Expedition to Tierra Nueva: The 1540–1542 Route Across the Southwest* (Niwot: University Press of Colorado, 1997).

Goodwin, Robert. *Crossing the Continent 1527–1540: The Story of the First African-American Explorer of the American South* (New York: Harper, 2008).

Hammond, George P. *Coronado's Seven Cities* (Albuquerque: United States Coronado Exposition Committee, 1940).

Harris, Richard K. *Off the Beaten Path: New Mexico* (Guilford, Conn.: Globe Pequot Press, 2005).

Jameson, Franklin (gen. ed.), Frederick W. Hodge and Theodore H. Lewis (eds.). *Spanish Explorers in the Southern United States, 1528–1543: The Narrative of Alvar Nuñez Cabeça de Vaca; The Narrative of the Expedition of Hernando de Soto by the Gentleman of Elvas; The Narrative of the Expedition of Coronado, by Pedro de Castañeda* (New York: Charles Scribner's Sons, 1907).

Kessell, John L. *Kiva, Cross & Crown: The Pecos Indians and New Mexico, 1540–1840* (Tucson: Southwest Parks and Monuments Association, 1986).

Leopold, Aldo. *A Sand County Almanac, with Essays on Conservation from Round River* (New York: Ballantine, 1970).

Lorbiecki, Marybeth. *Aldo Leopold: A Fierce Green Fire* (Guilford, Conn.: Globe Pequot Press, 2005; 1996).

Meine, Curt, and Richard L. Knight. *The Essential Aldo Leopold: Quotations and Commentaries* (Madison: University of Wisconsin Press, 1999).

Minge, Ward Allen. *Ácoma: Pueblo in the Sky* (Albuquerque: University of New Mexico Press, 1991).

Newton, Julianne Lutz. *Aldo Leopold's Odyssey* (Washington, D.C.: Island Press, 2006).

Niza, Marcos de. "A Relation of the Reverend Father Fray" from "Marcos de Niza,

Touching His Discovery of the Kingdom of Ceulo or Cíbola . . ." (originally written in 1539 and published in English in *Principall Navigations, Voiages and Discoveries of the English Nation,* ed. Richard Hakluyt (London: 1598–1600). (Partial text available online at http://etext.lib.virginia.edu/subjects/eaw/essays/nizatext.html.)

Parent, Laurence. *Gila Cliff Dwellings National Monument* (pamphlet) (Western National Parks Association).

Plog, Stephen. *Ancient Peoples of the American Southwest* (London: Thames & Hudson, 1997, 2008).

Reséndez, Andrés. *A Land So Strange: The Epic Journey of Cabeza de Vaca* (New York: Basic Books, 2007).

Tanner, Thomas (ed.). *Aldo Leopold: The Man and His Legacy* (Ankeny, Iowa: Soil Conservation Society of America, 1987).

INDEX

ABOUT THE AUTHOR

PETER STARK has written about "blank spots"—the remote and wild places of the world—for many years. A correspondent for *Outside,* Stark has undertaken travels and assignments to Tibet, Manchuria, Greenland, Antarctica, Afghanistan, Iceland, Irian Jaya, the Sahara Desert, and by kayak down the unexplored Lugenda River of Mozambique, a country where he and his young family later lived for a year. His articles have appeared in *Smithsonian* and *The New Yorker* and have been anthologized in *The Best American Science and Nature Writing.* His books include *At the Mercy of the River: An Exploration of the Last African Wilderness* and *Last Breath: The Limits of Adventure,* as well as a collection of essays, *Driving to Greenland.* He is also the editor of an anthology of writings about the Arctic, *Ring of Ice.* He lives in Missoula, Montana, with his wife and their two children.

ABOUT THE TYPE

This book was set in Garamond, a typeface originally designed by the Parisian type cutter Claude Garamond (1480–1561). This version of Garamond was modeled on a 1592 specimen sheet from the Egenolff-Berner foundry, which was produced from types assumed to have been brought to Frankfurt by the punch cutter Jacques Sabon (d. 1580).

Claude Garamond's distinguished romans and italics first appeared in *Opera Ciceronis* in 1543–44. The Garamond types are clear, open, and elegant.